Gender at Work in Economic Life

SOCIETY FOR ECONOMIC ANTHROPOLOGY
(SEA) MONOGRAPHS

Deborah Winslow, University of New Hampshire
General Editor, Society for Economic Anthropology

Monographs for the Society for Economic Anthropology contain original essays that explore the connections between economics and social life. Each year's volume focuses on a different theme in economic anthropology. Earlier volumes were published with the University Press of America, Inc. (#1–15, 17), Rowman & Littlefield, Inc. (#16). The monographs are now published jointly by AltaMira Press and the Society for Economic Anthropology (http://nautarch.tamu.edu/anth/sea/).

Current Volumes in the Series:

Vol. 1   Sutti Ortiz, ed., *Economic Anthropology: Topics and Theories.*

Vol. 2   Sidney M. Greenfield and Arnold Strickon, eds., *Entrepreneurship and Social Change.*

Vol. 3   Morgan D. Maclachlan, ed., *Household Economies and their Transformation.*

Vol. 4   Stuart Plattner, ed., *Market and Marketing.*

Vol. 5   John W. Bennett and John R. Brown, eds., *Production and Autonomy: Anthropological Studies and Critiques of Development.*

Vol. 6   Henry J. Rutz and Benjamin S. Orlove, eds., *The Social Economy of Consumption.*

Vol. 7   Christina Gladwin and Kathleen Truman, eds., *Food and Farm: Current Debates and Policies.*

Vol. 8   M. Estellie Smith, ed., *Perspectives on the Informal Economy.*

Vol. 9   Hill Gates and Alice Littlefield, eds., *Marxist Trends in Economic Anthropology.*

Vol. 10   Sutti Ortiz and Susan Lees, eds., *Understanding Economic Process.*

Vol. 11   Elizabeth M. Brumfiel, ed., *The Economic Anthropology of the State.*

Vol. 12   James M. Acheson, ed., *Anthropology and Institutional Economics.*

Vol. 13   Richard E. Blanton, Peter N. Peregrine, Deborah Winslow and Thomas D. Hall, eds., *Economic Analysis Beyond the Local System.*

Vol. 14   Robert C. Hunt and Antonio Gilman, eds., *Property in Economic Context.*

Vol. 15   David B. Small and Nicola Tannenbaum, eds., *At the Interface: The Household and Beyond.*

Vol. 16   Angelique Haugerud, M. Priscilla Stone, and Peter D. Little, eds., *Commodities and Globalization: Anthropological Perspectives.*

Vol. 17   Martha W. Rees & Josephine Smart, eds., *Plural Globalities in Multiple Localities: New World Border.*

Vol. 18   Jean Ensminger, ed., *Theory in Economic Anthropology.*

Vol. 19   Jeffrey H. Cohen and Norbert Dannhaeuser, eds., *Economic Development: An Anthropological Approach.*

Vol. 20   Gracia Clark, ed. *Gender at Work in Economic Life.*

Gender at Work in Economic Life

EDITED BY
GRACIA CLARK

Published in cooperation with the
Society for Economic Anthropology

ALTAMIRA
PRESS

A Division of
ROWMAN & LITTLEFIELD PUBLISHERS, INC.
Walnut Creek • Lanham • New York • Oxford

AltaMira Press
A Division of Rowman & Littlefield Publishers, Inc.
1630 North Main Street, #367
Walnut Creek, CA 94596
www.altamirapress.com

Rowman & Littlefield Publishers, Inc.
A division of The Rowman & Littlefield Publishing Group
4501 Forbes Boulevard, Suite 200
Lanham, MD 20706

PO Box 317
Oxford
OX2 9RU, UK

British Library Cataloguing in Publication Information Available

Library of Congress Cataloging-in-Publication Data

Gender at work in economic life / edited by Gracia Clark.
    p. cm.—(Society for Economic Anthropology (SEA) monographs; v. 20)
    Includes bibliographical references and index.
    ISBN 0-7591-0245-7 (hardcover: alk. paper)—ISBN 0-7591-0246-5 (pbk.: alk.
paper)
    1. Sexual division of labor—History. 2. Women—Employment—History. I. Clark,
Gracia. II. Series: Society for Economic Anthropology monographs; v. 20.

HD6053.G4625 2003
306.3'615–dc21   2002013473

Printed in the United States of America

⊗™ The paper used in this publication meets the minimum requirements of American
National Standard for Information Sciences—Permanence of Paper for Printed Library
Materials, ANSI/NISO Z39.48-1992.

Contents

Acknowledgments

These chapters were originally submitted for the Society for Economic Anthropology Conference on Gender and Economic Life, held April 21–23, 2000, at Indiana University, Bloomington, in conjunction with the meetings of the Central States Anthropological Association. Financial assistance from the College of Arts and Sciences and the Office of the Vice President for Academic Affairs is appreciated. The IU Department of Anthropology provided welcome financial and clerical assistance and volunteers for the conference, and clerical assistance for the preparation of the manuscripts.

Deborah Winslow, the SEA general editor, was generous with her encouragement and practical help. Florence Babb and another anonymous reviewer provided valuable comments that helped pull the chapters together. The contributors were blessedly cooperative from their far flung homes and field homes. The editorial team, Rosalie Robertson and Lori Pierelli, worked hard to coordinate the last stages of preparation. The patience and commitment they have all shown was essential to seeing this volume come out amid our several transitions and competing demands.

Introduction: How Gender Works, in the Practice of Theory and Other Social Processes

Gracia Clark

Greater awareness of the role gender plays in economic processes, alongside and within the dynamics of class, race, ethnicity, nationality, age, and individual strategizing, has significantly deepened and sharpened scholarly understanding of the broadest possible range of economic activity. As a strict conceptual boundary becomes ever less credible between economic and other human endeavors, discussions within economic anthropology become more relevant than ever to important debates over social theory and public policy. Work that interrogates the role of gender in economic life has the capacity to transform our understanding of general social processes as well as to clarify our understanding of men's and women's participation in them.

The chapters in this book follow the thread of gender through every level of anthropological analysis, from evolutionary models of human history through the regional comparison of work patterns to buying a new blender. These authors address cultural concepts and social contexts that are of interest to anthropologists of every persuasion and to scholars from adjacent disciplines. They apply a broad range of analytic approaches to a wide variety of qualitative and quantitative materials. They all start by taking a hard look at the evidence, whether ethnographic, archaeological, historical, or statistical. This rigor enables them to convincingly identify interpretive assumptions still current in their fields of expertise, assumptions that are based more on contemporary cultural norms than contemporary research standards. Research founded on such assumptions only reproduces knowledge that confirms them. As a result, these studies provide not only a vital challenge to insufficiently grounded past work, but a firmer basis and inspiration for future research and analysis.

These authors present critical new appraisals of how gendered material relations and ideological assumptions about gender are mutually constitutive of key social institutions and analytic concepts. Concrete gender relations may reinforce or contradict such ideological assumptions, but both material and symbolic gender relations are important building blocks of the social institutions through which economic systems maintain, reproduce, and transform themselves in their multifaceted historical specificity. Rather than forming a separate element in such cultural constructions, gender seems to work most effectively by permeating the various social arenas that support production, reproduction, and stratification. Like the proportion of sand to cement in concrete, strong social formations rest on a carefully balanced fusion of gender with other conceptual systems like property, honor, responsibility, and freedom. Significant historical change involves renegotiating the entire interlocking framework of concepts and material relationships. Consequently, in evaluating structural economic change we always need to consider the role of gender, whether in historical analysis or for planned intervention (Berry 1993; Guyer 1997).

THEORETICAL TRAJECTORIES

Renegotiations of gender issues should and do take place as continually within scholarly ranks as in the rest of cultural life. Anthropologists of gender in general have taken up questions of gender with the perspectives and concerns of their subfields and theoretical backgrounds more or less intact (di Leonardo 1991). This has not only guaranteed a rich diversity of contradiction within gender studies, but has also meant that investigations of gender have addressed the central issues of each branch of anthropology, however one divided it, as these concerns continued to unfold over time.

Early feminist anthropologists in the "anthropology of women" line began by describing women's activities and relationships, which had often been unreported or undervalued (Weiner 1976). As pioneering social constructionists, they established that gender was not a biological and/or a historical fact, but was always inflected by each specificity of space, time, and hierarchical location (MacCormack and Strathern 1980). Practice theory provided a conceptual framework reconciling the empowerment of individual actors and the force of cultural structures that was enthusiastically received by feminist and many other anthropologists (Bourdieu 1997; Ortner 1996). As social actors, women (and men) continually strategize to defend and improve their own positions in relation to gender and other power hierarchies, by choosing from among the options currently available to them. Postcolonial writers took the dynamic aspects of gender expression to a new level by examining their implication in relations of power and domination, not excepting the academy (Mohanty et al. 1991). Multiple crosscutting identities also found their expression in the family and other workplaces, providing leverage for both resistance and superexploitation.

The growing scholarship on gender and the economy incorporated these changing interests as it expanded. Excellent gender-aware analyses (including those in this volume) can be linked to every theoretical stripe of economic anthropology, from neo-Classicist to neo-Marxist to new institutionalist. Early cohorts of feminist anthropologists gave considerable attention to topics and concepts also dear to the pioneers of economic anthropology, including the division of labor, systems of exchange, the gift, commercialization, entrepreneurship, and household production. As in kinship studies, this initial effort provided the critical information needed to move on and reevaluate fundamental interpretations and conclusions not bounded by women's roles or experiences.

Like other gender analysts, those among the economic anthropologists both reacted to theoretical trends in their subdiscipline and, in some cases, instigated them. For example, studies of household production and informal trade were once thoroughly embroiled in the substantivist/formalist debate were now hopefully laid to rest (Polanyi 1957; Bohannon and Dalton 1962; Chayanov 1966; Sahlins 1972; Schneider 1974). (Formalists insisted that rational choice models of maximization applied equally well to all human economic activity. Substantivists insisted with equal vehemence on substantial differences over time and space, often endorsing evolutionary models. Few authors on either side paid serious attention to gender, age, and other inequalities, or to the dynamics of interhousehold and intrahousehold relations.)

While documenting gender disparities and contestations in household labor and income allocation, feminist ethnographers opened up the whole arena of intrahousehold and interhousehold dynamics (Young, Wolkowitz, and McCullagh 1981; Dwyer and Bruce 1988). Although it may seem unthinkable now to analyze these activities without any direct consideration of gender, economic anthropologists, among others, did manage to do so for a number of decades (Babb 1990). Some authors continue today to blank out relations of power based on age, ethnicity, class, and other social categories as well as those based on gender, reverting to the "black box model" of the unitary household with mysterious "preferences" (Albeida 1997; Wilk and Netting 1984; Wooley 1996). The black box model of the household (so named for leaving any internal dynamics in the dark) assumes that each household acts as a single unit on the basis of joint preferences, generated by cultural processes that mysteriously reconcile the interests of its diverse members. Although convincingly critiqued both on theoretical and evidentiary grounds, this model has remained in surprisingly frequent use, due perhaps to its comfort and convenience for Western academics.

Marxist and neo-Marxist analyses replicated this pattern of theoretical development. Some classical Marxists, following Engels, show full awareness of women as historical participants in class processes, but even when talking about women they analyze changes in gender relations as by-products of class relations (Engels 1972; Etienne and Leacock 1980). Nor do Marxists entirely escape the sexualized fantasies that contaminate so much European writing about "primitive" women (Meillasoux 1975). The neo-Marxists centered on the domestic mode of production and other articulated modes of production, giving them new interest in the small-scale and subsistence-oriented work many women do (Rey 1979; Bromley and Gerry 1979). Still, old circular assumptions can still bleed through; subsistence farming was too often production when men did it and reproduction when women did it. Childbirth, childcare, sex, and other work of motherhood were generally classed as biological rather than economic activities. At about the same time, a distinct stream of feminist materialists began to analyze production and reproduction as integrated processes, recognizing the same historical dialectic within gender relations that means they are actively negotiated by both men and women (Edholm, Harris, and Young 1977). These authors contributed especially substantially to household analysis, and their influence extends well into the ranks of political economy, more broadly defined (Guyer 1981; Dwyer and Bruce 1988; Hansen 1997).

Current gender analysis emphasizes the concept of gender performance, which grafts more scope for individual creative improvisation and audience response onto the more structured strategizing proposed in practice theory (Visweswaran 1997). So far, much analysis of gender performance has centered mainly on the arena of sexuality, defined to include bodily practices, object preference, and self-presentation (Morris 1995). Sexuality is a significant aspect of gender, to be sure, but also one that western scholars have been accused of overemphasizing (Davis 1989). Men and women also perform their gendered economic roles: the joke goes, "I feel like a woman every time I look at my paycheck." Since enactions of economic genders are always inflected by class, ethnicity, and the like, they show just as much historical and cross-cultural variability as sexuality does. These economic performances also retain all the dimensions of negotiation, transgression, and unthinkability that apply to sexual performances, so some of the same theoretical apparatus should be extensible to them.

THE FOUR SECTIONS

Although any single volume can present only a tantalizing sample of the existing variation, the twelve chapters here give an excellent taste of the wide range of kinds of fruitful analysis that can be expected to continue producing substantial new insights. They clearly demonstrate that many concepts widely accepted and used in anthropological analysis carry a hidden burden of gender assumptions, but they also move beyond that essential stage. Reevaluating and redefining these basic concepts and reconfiguring their conceptual frameworks to take advantage of those changed building blocks has enabled these authors to perceive new data more accurately and to reinterpret already-available data. Improvisation and continual renegotiation emerge more clearly, both at the societal and individual levels, uncovering exciting new vistas highly suggestive of future research directions.

Part I focuses on the process of reevaluating the fundamental concepts that organize how contemporary analysts think about social stratification, inequality, and social hierarchy in general. As Pyburn makes so clear in chapter 1, these concepts often draw on unspoken assumptions from the social context of the theoreticians who originated or popularized them, and so reveal more about the social organization of academic intellectual life than about the social organization of the societies explicitly analyzed. Opening these "conclusions" to scrutiny, even on the basis of already published excavation findings, uncovers surprisingly shaky foundations to many time-honored classificatory schemes and evolutionary scenarios.

It then becomes particularly valuable to consider the case of Pare, Tanzania, as a comparative exercise in the interpretation of more recent prehistoric evidence. Håkansson does this in chapter 2 and also presents a contrasting Pare ideology of economic process, in which the gendered nature of the analytic framework was extremely explicit. Far from encoding unspoken gender hierarchies and dichotomies within supposedly gender-blind concepts, the Pare use gender concepts to encode a complex framework of geographical, climatological, and economic relationships. The gender division of labor is an integral, even central part of the Pare cosmological framework, and Håkansson shows how it both reflects and initiates historical and ecological change. The sacralization of gender does not prevent historical development and individual or community-level renegotiation of concrete gender practices and their meanings.

Blackwood, in chapter 3, then shows the same tenacity in examining ethnographic materials in order to question the basic concepts used to trace changes in household patterns over time, one of the major frontiers of gender research. She shows how the presumption that a marital couple is the core of the normal household has significantly distorted understandings of the internal dynamics of households, whether they do or do not contain such a couple. Her own revealing material from Minangkabau matrilineal households is skillfully related to cases from other matrilineal cultures and to the "problem" of female-headed households in the Caribbean and the United States. She attacks assumptions about control of income for investment and consumption and about patterns of stability and conflict that have survived several rounds of critique to remain very influential in debates over public policy as well as social theory, giving this chapter a broader significance outside academia.

Concepts of entrepreneurship (discussed in Part II) also have a long history in economic anthropology, continued or revived recently in relation to the applied sphere of international economic development (Firth 1975; Hill 1963; Dewey 1962). Browne's chapter here about entrepreneurs from three Caribbean countries thus builds on these classic ethnographic works about farmers, fisherfolk, and traders. For the past several decades, the Bretton Woods institutions (the International Monetary Fund and the World Bank) have presided over a revival of neoclassical or neoliberal theories particularly supportive of their free market policies. They drew on early modernization theory to glorify innovation and risk-taking among entrepreneurs to compensate for demand-side austerity measures. Browne demonstrates that self-employment may be considered more or less deviant than waged work for women in each country, creating specific gender risks and strategies that mitigate them.

Milgram (chapter 5) and Werner (chapter 6), like Browne, historicize the state policy climates that set the stage for entrepreneurial opportunities and constraints. Privatization and globalization, alongside other current policy buzzwords, incorporate implicit gender frameworks that both reinforce and contradict preexisting patterns of domination. These contradictions give leverage for improvising new organizing relations of production and trade, but they also raise the risks of exploitation and backlash. The Philippine craftswomen in Milgram's case literally recombine male and female gendered crafts as well as economic roles. In Werner's Kazakhstan example, contestations over Islamic and Soviet gender ideals complicate the equation. This section moves well beyond reporting whether women can and do participate effectively in the steamroller of capitalism, to show how new and old ideologies are enacted by families and states struggling for a new sustainable balance amidst the tidal waves of a global economy.

For women still deeply implicated in the cultural values and material resources tied to respectable family life, innovation and autonomy can come at a high price. The three contributions by Rankin, Basu, and Bautista-Vistro in Part III show how concepts like love and honor can be explicitly counterposed to selfish "economic" interests yet still constitute a fundamental aspect of the economic system. Dowry transfers are subject to historical redefinition in Rankin's piece, away from the "traditional" gold jewelry women were encouraged to lend personally. The more "modern" dowries of consumer goods consolidate the household's reputation and standard of life, and so represent a shift away from commercialization. Basu explains ideologies of property and entitlement that induce women to forgo their inheritance rights for the more reliable and valuable moral position of self-sacrifice. Next, Bautista-Vistro explains in detail the tactful allocation of wages from Philippine factory workers through purchases of food and small housewares and pocket money for gender-appropriate activities.

Migration (Part IV) is another classic topic in economic anthropology that is of enormous contemporary interest. Again, gender-sensitive approaches reveal important structuring features. Cliggett follows the subtle interweaving of guilt and self-interest with concepts of loyalty to mothers and fathers in Zambia. Her careful attention to gender and wealth factors within the arguments and principles that generate care and support for elders adds a new chapter to the long ethnographic saga of the resettlement and sequential migration of the Plateau Tonga, already an early model of gender sensitivity. Holtzman then traces out the ideals of young manhood among Kenya's Samburu *moran*, an ethnographic archetype of maleness, which now find expression through labor migration more often than in the cattle camp. Self-denial, extrafamilial residence, and even sexuality have been renegotiated with new content for old concepts, retaining the illusion of stability, or perhaps its essence. Siquiera, McCracken, Brondizio, and Moran examine another classic situation, the frontier, which the United States' common thinking often associates with more autonomy for "pioneer women." In Amazonian Brazil, Siquiera et al. track shifts in ecological, labor, and decision-making processes across newer settlements that turn out to limit women's work roles more sharply, and older settlements from which women leave for town.

CONCLUSION

The solid contributions collected here constitute a justification for continuing in their footsteps to analyze gender as an integral part of economic life and vice versa. For the many people concerned with survival and accumulation during their lifetimes, some of the most significant aspects of gender identity concern control of income (their own and other people's), married women's property rights, and norms of inheritance. Security and enrichment opportunities arise within conventions that are often not considered conscious choices because of their emotional rooting in human experiences of childhood and parenthood. Ideals and concrete social relations of gender and kinship clearly overlap and resonate with each other but cannot usefully be reduced to each other. In the cases analyzed here, the language of emotion and entitlement, of love and loyalty, creates a kind of moving equilibrium of economic practice.

This dynamism must be not only gendered, but historicized as it finds its roots in continual renegotiation and testing. Transnational cultural and economic networks continue to transmit and transform expressions of gender as integral aspects of their power and attraction (Hansen et al. 2000; MacGaffey 2000). The intricacies of ideal, expected, and actual practice very often generate explicit bargaining, but also structure negotiation processes by delimiting areas where bargaining is not legitimate. These limits nonetheless remain highly subject to historical change and optional performance, acted out through cycles of transgression and its consequences. Gender-appropriate aspirations and forms of activity, the meanings of particular consumption items, and the fallback positions considered acceptable or viable can be reforged historically and even individually, as transgressions are tolerated and safety nets left unmended.

Contestations over gender have repeatedly shown their potential to spark theoretical innovation and accelerate the production of new knowledge of the history of economic change and economic processes of all kinds. These studies confirm that when academic gender assumptions are subject to clear-headed verification, research quickly begins to suggest surprising new features. Much remains to be said even about relations of authority and entitlement between and within households, a topic that incorporated gender relatively early. Attention to gender is not a corrective measure that can be applied once and for all, but a mother lode that continues to yield substantial returns as work on these issues continues to mature.

REFERENCES

Albeida, Randy. 1997. *Economics and Feminism.* New York: Twayne.

Babb, Florence. 1990. "Women's Work: Engendering Economic Anthropology." *Urban Anthropology* 19: 277–301.

Berry, Sara. 1985. *Fathers Work for Their Sons.* Berkeley: University of California Press.

———. 1993. *No Condition Is Permanent.* Madison: University of Wisconsin Press.

Bohannon, Paul, and George Dalton. 1962. *Markets in Africa.* Evanston, Ill.: Northwestern University Press.

Bourdieu, Pierre, 1977. *Outline of a Theory of Practice.* Cambridge, U.K.: Cambridge University Press.

Brodkin, Karen. 1997. "Race and Gender in the Construction of Class." *Science and Society* 60: 471–77.

Bromley, Ray, and Chris Gerry, eds. 1979. *Casual Work and Poverty.* New York: John Wiley.

Chayanov, A. V. 1966. *The Theory of Peasant Economy.* Homewood, Ill.: Irwin.

Davis, Angela. 1989. *Women, Culture, and Politics.* New York: Random House.

Dewey, Alice. 1962. *Peasant Marketing in Java.* New York: Free Press of Glencoe.

di Leonardo, Michaela. 1991. *Gender at the Crossroads of Knowledge.* Berkeley: University of California Press.

Dwyer, Daisy, and Judith Bruce, eds. 1988. *A Home Divided.* Stanford, Calif.: Stanford University Press.

Edholm, Felicity, Olivia Harris, and Kate Young. 1977. "Conceptualizing Women." *Critique of Anthropology* 3: 101–30.

Engels, Friedrich. 1942. *The Origin of the Family, Private Property, and the State,* ed. by Eleanor Leacock. Reprint, New York: International Publishers, 1972.

Etienne, Mona, and Eleanor Leacock, eds. 1980. *Women and Colonization.* New York: Praeger.

Firth, Raymond. 1975. *Primitive Polynesian Economy.* New York: Norton.

Guyer, Jane. 1997. *An African Niche Economy: Farming to Feed Ibadan.* Edinburgh, U.K.: Edinburgh University Press/IAI.

———. 1981. "Household and Community in African Studies." *African Studies Review* 24: 87–137.

Hansen, Karen Tranberg. 1997. *Keeping House in Lusaka.* New York: Columbia University Press.

————. 2000. *Salaula*. Chicago: University of Chicago Press.

Hill, Polly. 1963. *Migrant Cocoa Farmers of Southern Ghana*. Cambridge, U.K.: Cambridge University Press.

MacCormack, Carol, and Marilyn Strathern, eds. 1980. *Nature, Culture, and Gender*. Cambridge, U.K.: Cambridge University Press.

MacGaffey, Janet et al. 2000. *Congo/Paris*. Bloomington, Ind.: Indiana University Press.

Meillasoux, Claude. 1975. *Femmes, Greniers, Capitaux*. Paris: Maspero.

Mohanty, Chandra et al., eds. 1991. *Third World Women and the Politics of Feminism*. Bloomington, Ind.: Indiana University Press.

Morris, Rosalind. 1995. "All Made Up: Performance Theory and the New Anthropology of Sex and Gender." *Annual Review of Anthropology* 24: 567–92.

Ortner, Sheryl. 1996. *Making Gender*. Boston: Beacon Press.

Polanyi, Karl. "The Economy as Instituted Process." In *Trade and Markets in the Early Empires*, ed. by Karl Polanyi, Conrad Arensberg, and H. Pearson. New York: Aldine, 1957.

Rey, Pierre Philippe. 1979. "Class Contradiction in Lineage Societies." *Critique of Anthropology* 13–14: 16.

Sahlins, Marshall. 1972. *Stone Age Economics*. Chicago: Aldine-Atherton.

Schneider, Harold. 1974. *Economic Man*. New York: Free Press.

Visweswaran, Kamala. 1997. "Histories of Feminist Anthropology." *Annual Review of Anthropology* 26: 591–621.

Weiner, Annette. 1976. *Women of Value, Men of Renown*. Austin, Tex.: University of Texas Press.

Wilk, Richard, and Robert Netting. 1984. "Households: Changing Forms and Functions." In *Households*, ed. by Robert Netting, Richard Wilk, and Eric Arnould. Berkeley: University of California Press.

Wooley, Frances. 1996. "Getting the Better of Becker." *Feminist Economics* 2: 114–19.

Young, Kate, C. Wolkowitz, and R. McCullagh, eds. 1981. *Of Marriage and the Market*. London: CSE Books.

I

CONCEPTS OF GENDER WITHIN ECONOMIC CHANGE

Archaeology and the Gender without History

K. Anne Pyburn

Richard Wilk is an ethnographer who did his first fieldwork among the Kekchi Maya of southern Belize (Wilk 1991). He tells the story of an interview that he once carried out with a village elder. The interviewee was an old man who was well respected and of high status. His equally elderly wife was ostensibly excluded from this discussion between men by staying behind the walls of her house in her "private space," while the men conferred out front in the open. As the ethnographer began to ask the old man questions, however, the old woman made her presence known.

"How long have you been married?" Rick asked.

"Forty-five years," said the old man, but an irritated voice from inside the house said, "Forty-seven."

Without blinking, the old man said, "Forty-seven."

"How many grandchildren do you have?" asked Rick.

"Nineteen," said the old man. "Twenty-one, you idiot," said the voice from the house.

"Uh, twenty-one," corrected the old man.

"Gee," said Rick, beginning to feel uncomfortable, "how long have you lived in this village?"

The old man hesitated in silence for a moment until "Since 1942," said the voice behind the wall.

"Since 1942," said the old man, as though he had just come up with it himself.

In effect, the voice behind the wall controlled this entire interview, although the visible old man behaved as if only he could hear the voice. The Kekchi have been identified as patriarchal, and when I first heard this story I thought the old woman was amazing to stand up to her husband after years of domination, or that perhaps this was an indication of the latitude allowed post-menopausal women, but now I have changed my mind. If the man had been behind the wall, and the woman out front having her every word challenged and contradicted, I would have taken this as an indication of male domination. If the woman had been behind the wall, I would have seen the wall as an indication of male dominance. If the woman had been in front of the wall, I would have seen the voice as an indication of male dominance. I realized that there were no conditions under which I would be able to see a woman not dominated. This is a perceptual problem I seem to share with many anthropologists and especially with my fellow archaeologists.

This experience got me wondering: "What if we couldn't assume that the relationship between women and men in ancient civilizations was any more obvious than the significance of the wall in front of the Kekchi woman?" What if the political and economic subordination of women wasn't a given for prehistoric or precontact societies; what if things really *were* different before the world system? What if, in fact, the inferior role of women in complex political economies is really a result of integration into the world system? Would we know? *How* would we know?

I have been thinking about this set of questions for almost three years. I set a group of students to work on figuring out what exactly we do know about ancient women, and we came up with some surprising results. Together we investigated two questions in the context of nine cultures (Pyburn, forthcoming).

The first question we asked was framed by Eric Wolf. In *Europe and the People without History* (1982), Wolf argues that Western ideas about cultural purity and the discreteness of tradition blossomed within anthropology. He then shows how the model of cultural isolates allowed ethnographers to see cross-cultural similarities as the result of human nature rather than the result of contacts and interrelations. The result was a naïve, inaccurate, and often inherently racist construction of cultural difference, promoted inadvertently by scholars who were actually trying to be open-minded.

We asked: "What if Eric Wolf's critique was applied to the anthropology of women instead of to whole cultures?" What if the role of women has always been seen by merchants, missionaries, anthropologists, and other social scientists through the lens of a sexist capitalist system, and manipulated accordingly, so that both the ethnohistoric and ethnographic records of cross-cultural similarity in gender roles are the result of recorder bias and historical contact? What if, instead of having their great quantity and variety cancel out the random bias of particular observers, the vast majority of the records compiled in the huge cross-cultural database of the Human Relations Area Files (HRAF) are biased in exactly the same way? This problem is less obvious than it seems, and it is not easy to correct, as can be shown by looking at Wolf's own arguments.

Wolf does not address gender directly, although he discusses how relations between men and women were affected by the economic changes that were encouraged and spread by European capitalism. When Wolf does discuss changes in the division of labor, his treatment is particularly instructive. For example, in discussing the economic relations that developed between Portuguese traders and the people of the Kongo, Wolf explains that Kongolese organization was matrilineal and that a system of bridewealth and gifts initiated by royal lineages and redistributed to lower-ranking lineages was the economic backbone of lineage power. He argues that participation in the slave trade with the Portuguese fundamentally changed this system. This new source of revenue made wealth and status objects available directly to lower-ranking lineages, allowing them to compete for power with higher-ranking groups and undermining the power held by ranked matrilineages. Wolf argues that matrilineality gave way to patrilineal clusters because participation in slave trade required more manpower for slave hunting which, in turn, resulted in men laying claim to their own children produced by their own slaves.

Wolf's argument rescues Kongolese men from essentialism by showing how their system was made more "standard" through historical contact with the Portuguese. But his explanation still leaves women without history. This happens in two ways. First, although Wolf rejects characterization of "peripheral" cultures as timeless and traditional, he accepts the existence of timeless matrilineality, a system "discovered" and recorded by European male anthropologists that allows women a visible position in social structure but still places control of most resources in the hands of men: uncles and brothers rather than fathers and husbands. Whether this might have been a biased interpretation of Kongolese culture is not discussed. Second, and more importantly, when Wolf describes the change from matrilineality to patrilineality, he attributes it to the need for more men to participate in the taking of slaves. This to him is implicitly a natural outcome of an emphasis on a violent mercantile economy. The possibility that women might have participated in warfare and raiding—either directly or through continuing to lay claim to the male offspring of their slaves—and in maintenance of economic control does not get consideration.

Here is a classic situation that lends itself to critical questioning. A preexisting system in which women received some sort of recognition, pigeonholed by anthropologists accustomed to an essentialized view of culture as "matrilineal," becomes patrilineal as a result of interaction with Western capitalism, in this case from Portugal. The cause is said to be economic change that favored male strategies over female strategies as though the two were inherently different. This construction goes unquestioned because the lack of participation by women in the new system is implicitly attributed to the nature of womanhood, not to the nature of the European influence. But really, wouldn't the patriarchal view of the world and the essentialist European perspective of the Portuguese toward women have influenced the nature of change in lineage power? Would Portuguese sailors have looked for women to help them catch slaves or negotiate trade agreements? Implicit assumptions about gender shape historical constructions without ever becoming a topic of discussion.

The process through which modern capitalism fosters hegemony over local economies typically occurs in part through the naturalization of Western gender distinctions within the local system. In fact, establishing the political and economic subordination of women within local systems regardless of their previous situation is one of the primary modes of capitalist expansion. Recent research on beauty pageants provides an important example of how this process works and explains how by essentializing gender, local groups become complicit in their own exploitation (Wilk 1996). The question for us regarding early civilizations is whether gender subordination can be a strategy of any expansionist state, or whether it is a special feature of Western capitalism. Marx (1965) was clearly correct in his assertion that capitalism would necessarily have a profound impact on gender roles, but Engels's (1884) position was slightly different. He proposed that the rise of class-based society and state hierarchies, which moved away from kinship as a source of status and power, must therefore necessarily undermine the status of women. Women's social value, he reasoned, must come from the family. Clearly Engels had an essentialized view of women; he also had no data from the time periods about which he speculated.

Which leads to a second question, one not asked by Wolf: What if Engels was wrong and class stratification per se does not cause gender subordination? What if kin-based systems are not necessarily the source of female power and authority? What if there really were early civilizations in which gender was not the determining factor we believe it must be; where men and women competed on the same field or even in which women controlled the political economy? How would we know? What if there were once other possibilities for cultures before the modern world system—Engels didn't have any data about such societies, because such data would almost have to be archaeological.

In each of the nine cultures our group examined, we attempted to separate out the assumptions about ancient gender roles from the actual bits of relevant data. All investigators were wary of ethnographic analogy and questioned traditional ethnographic categories. We tried to focus on a particular ancient culture at the point of its transition to complexity, to statehood, to civilization. This led to problems, as this transition is hard to identify in most cases (and controversial) and partakes of the very same evolutionary assumptions that plague gender studies. Was Zimbabwe or Cahokia or Viking Denmark really a complex society? A state? Are we seeking objective characteristics, or are we measuring the Moche against Greece or the Harappans against Washington, D.C.? In the end, we simply looked at a variety of relatively unrelated groups during the period when each group began to show evidence of social status distinctions based on economic differences. This seemed like the closest we could come to testing Engels's original proposition against non-European or pre-European societies.

Almost every case study resulted in a debate not only about the status of women, but about the status of their culture. And invariably, the stronger the public role of women, the less likely archaeologists are to characterize a culture as a civilization. Were women powerful because state organization had not developed or because the state that had developed did not subjugate them? Ultimately we were able to show that *in only one culture* did the rise of social classes with economic and political reality and a decisive signature in the archaeological record pretty clearly correspond to the subjugation of women as a subordinate class at the onset of rising status distinctions, and that culture is one in which the subjugation of women may have existed already. All our investigations consistently demonstrated that cultural evolutionism involves so much misunderstanding and essentializing of the division of labor and the significance of gender, that it is clear we need a new framework for organizing our data.

Another problem we faced was the obvious historical interrelatedness of several of the civilizations investigated. Although it would be ridiculous to claim cultural continuity between Mesopotamia or Greece and Viking Scandinavia, it would be equally foolish to ignore the history of Scandinavian or Zimbabwean economic and political interaction with earlier or contemporary expansionist states, even before the transformational impacts of Christianity and Islam. Having made a case for the impact of capitalism through the world system on the role (and the perceived role) of women, yet I am not willing to assume that only industrialized capitalism can or has used this mechanism of dispersal and control. Another way to characterize the phenomenon might be the "underdevelopment of women."

Our findings are reported at length elsewhere (Pyburn, forthcoming), but here I will just give a brief overview to make some general points about the archaeological reconstruction of women's roles in complex societies. Instances in which a lack of clear male dominance seemed to have affected archaeologist's opinions about whether the culture in question had achieved a state level of organizational complexity include investigations of Moundville, Harappa, and the Vikings. In cases in which organizational complexity is not much at issue, even the flimsiest evidence of gender difference becomes evidence of subordination, as with the Moche, the early Aegeans, and surprisingly—Harappa! In cases in which gender differences seem more obvious, as with the Maya and the Sumerians, little attempt has been made to use data to interrogate assumptions or test hypotheses, and negative evidence is gendered. If women are underrepresented in a sample, this is considered normal; if men are, further investigation is undertaken. And when things get really desperate, powerful women can always be designated "priestesses" to get them out of the economy, or as mother of the king to get them out of politics. Invariably, in every culture area, the direct historic approach is used to construct and reinforce models of ancient gender hierarchies with data from colonial periods.

The problem with the processual approach that arose in American archaeology in the 1960s and still influences data collection and analysis is that it unintentionally oversimplified human behavior and history into a small set of categories more related to Western thought than to a full range of possibilities. Convinced they were doing science, researchers could only see data as relevant if they fit into preconceived categories of human organization and behavior. According to the paradigm, groups would not evolve from a tribe to a chiefdom without changes in material cultural correlates of social rank, which begs the question of other sorts of cultural change involving increased complexity that this model doesn't recognize. For the study of gender, the problem is the same: science can only recognize women archeologically if they behaved like women—that is, if their activities correspond to what archaeologists expect women to do; we can only see evidence of female behavior that fits our preexisting definition of female behavior. Women who left traces of hunting, ruling, making stone tools, raiding, or controlling economic institutions are likely to be either misidentified as men or interpreted as exceptional, without much data on what constituted the cultural background to the exception. The exception they provide is really to the model of cultural evolution, which is basically a cleaned-up folk model Western intellectuals have employed for a couple of centuries to describe the superior development of Western culture by measuring everybody else against themselves. Exceptions to this model are exceptions to our way of conceiving society. By this mechanism, what is essentially ethnocentric (and androcentric) rhetoric ends up looking to the investigator like empirical truth.

Ethnographers have long known that by abstracting selected details from an unlimited number of cultures it is possible to support almost any argument. Determining the categories in advance determines which data will be acknowledged and which ignored, and holds out little possibility that something new will be recognized. When cultural evolutionism is the basis of the comparison the resulting analysis is likely to be both ethnocentric (as Eric Wolf so aptly demonstrated) and oversimplified to the point of inaccuracy.

The chapter on households in a recent book entitled *Women in Ancient America* (Bruhns and Stothert 1999) provides a useful example of the application of a processual model to ancient gender systems. The authors treat archaeological data on houses as though they were equivalent to ethnographic data on households (which they are not; cf. Wilk and Ashmore 1988), so the degree of oversimplification is already profound. Then, comparing the simplistic picture of the household organization of the Maya (living and dead) to Teotihuacan, Grasshopper, Valdivia, and the Navajo, without any critique of the accuracy of the recording or inquiry into the subtle variation between such institutions as Teotihuacano patriarchy and Maya patriarchy, it is not surprising that the authors conclude that the nuclear family was "the main unit of production, reproduction and consumption" and "women have more control within the household," and even less surprising that "women are responsible for childbearing." Beginning with the premise that objective truths can be elicited by archaeological research through the application of the scientific method via accepted models of cultural evolution, the authors verify everything we already knew before we started. Despite continual recognition of exceptions by the authors, they show repeatedly that women in ancient America had more control in the family than in politics, that women had more visibility in religion than in the military, that women cared for children but men didn't, and that women sometimes shared power but men usually didn't.

Without straying too far from traditional models of how cultures evolve complexity, let's take the example of the role of warfare. Traditional constructions of cultural evolution suggest that warfare results in a loss of status for women and an increase in organizational sophistication allied with defensive and aggressive institutions that are necessarily the province of men. "The fact that women did not customarily participate in warfare in the later kingdoms of Peru must have made it difficult for them to achieve status and gain authority" (Bruhns and Stothert 1999, 260). This interpretation is based on androcentric logic and ethnographic analogy derived from examples occurring after the rise of the modern world system. A logical alternative might be that, as has been demonstrated by a number of ethnographies, also from after the rise of the modern world system, the absence of men, both temporary and permanent, leaves rulership and production in the hands of women, thereby greatly increasing their political and economic power. The fact that men are waging war (even if we assume that only men do this) increases organizational requirements placed on the "home front" and decreases the number of men available to achieve them. A number of historians have pointed out that the division of labor in the United States became much more gendered after World War II in order to get women out of the workforce when men returned. The rhetoric of sexual difference used to promulgate this economic change is still with us. An equally logical construction of the rise of complex society based similarly on select ethnographic analogy might propose that complex society arises in some cases when participation in warfare undermines male domination, allowing state-level organization based on economic rather than kin and gender differences to arise.

Although many archaeologists have begun to situate the civilizations they study in a historical framework, gender roles are still not treated as variable or influenced by historic contacts. Tracy Luedke (in press) looked at data from Great Zimbabwe and found that archaeologists still regard women a priori as "keepers of tradition" and as such not only outside of, but resistant to, historical processes. To date, study of the remains of Great Zimbabwe has added absolutely nothing to our knowledge of women; all that has occurred is that preexisting knowledge and beliefs about women have been extended into the past, on behalf of Great Zimbabwe. In recent years archaeologists have become interested in documenting the indigenous development of states in Africa to supplant the colonial perspective that African states were actually the result of transplanted populations and ideas. Predictably, the possibility that these indigenous states were structurally different from European complex societies is equated with the idea that they were not "real" states and is downplayed. The idea that women may have had a more prominent role in public life before world system domination of African states has not to my knowledge received consideration by archaeologists. This is unfortunate, because the African context would seem to be an excellent place to begin with the premise that many styles of complex society existed before the world system, and evidence for a non-Western attitude toward women would underscore the originality of the African achievement.

Laura Pate (in press) found that gender distinctions are not clear from archaeological data on the Moundbuilders, but gendered assumptions prevail. In a classic example, one study reports the carved shell spoons buried with women as "domestic implements," but the ochre buried with men is described as a ceremonial pigment signifying membership in a male society. If the depositional pattern had been reversed, no doubt the spoons would have been "ceremonial wands" and the ochre interpreted as lipstick. More common even than these ethnocentric interpretations is total avoidance of the subject of gender, especially by archaeologists wishing to argue that Cahokia may have been an early state.

Lena Mortensen (in press) found that despite the powerful mythology of the masculine Viking, women clearly participated as full members of Viking political economy. The famous ship burial of a Viking Age (ca. 850 A.D., Arwill-Nordbladh 1991) queen and her assistant at Oseberg in Norway has not shaken this image of male domination in Viking society, despite the fact that the ship contains one of the richest Viking hoards ever found. This would seem to suggest a possible example of the rise of organizational complexity, including increased social stratification, economic integration, and political hegemony (beyond raiding) resulting from the structural pressures of warfare and raiding. The absence of men either because they were perpetually away on raids or because they had a disproportionately high mortality rate would seem to emphasize the political and economic acumen of women, who were home and who lived longer. In fact, the emphasis on male dominance displayed on monuments erected by women (usually to husbands lost at sea) and in epic sagas may be seen as an attempt at reconciliation rather than a reflection of reality. Of course, the Vikings are not usually characterized as having a state, and there is no sense in which gender roles in ancient Scandinavia could be considered independently invented or unaffected by the rise of the European economic world system. This is clearly a case in which traditional models of cultural evolution fail to capture the nature of organizational complexity.

Early Sumer has been one of the most popular loci for the instanciation of Marxist theory. Layla Al-Zubaidi's (in press) examination of Sumerian women showed that their contribution to their state was almost exactly the same as that of men, though men are distinguished by degree of wealth and power rather than by absolute differences of opportunity or dominance. As with many early states, the visibility of women in public contexts is described as ritual or ceremonial rather than as evidence of genuine authority, economic control, or political autonomy.

Wright (1996) has recently offered an important critique of current knowledge about the role of women in Mesopotamia. She argues convincingly that weaving was a feminine technology, that weaving was the most tightly state-controlled industry, and that weavers, predominantly female, had the lowest status and least autonomy of any craftspeople. This situation resulted in reinforcing both gender and class differences at the core of a class hierarchy.

Sumerian women were acculturated into a world system that had as much to do with creation of the modern world system as with isolation from it. In fact, the use of naturalized gender categories in the service of a hegemonic political economy may also be another "first" for the Near East, just like writing, settled agriculture, and cities. Nevertheless, Al-Zubaidi's research opens the tantalizing possibility that even in Mesopotamia, gender subordination may have become the norm sometime shortly *after* the establishment of class distinctions rather than being integral to the inception of class hierarchies. And Wright (1996) and others have also pointed out that an ideology of gender subordination does not amount to the subjugation of all women, but that women at both ends of the hierarchy may well have held positions of economic power and political visibility. Elite women clearly had some control over resources and even, to some extent, the means of production, whereas women from rural contexts or in families involved in craft production (besides weaving) may have had more autonomy and authority than state-sponsored written records are likely to tell us. The real question for our purposes here is not whether women weavers were part of an oppressed and alienated labor force, but whether other women were involved in their oppression and benefited directly from the labor of weavers and other laborers. The answer to this question appears to be yes. Although the relationship between gender and class stratification (chronological, ideological, political, economic) would bear more scrutiny, the evidence is fairly convincing that, in Mesopotamia at least, the two intertwined. Despite the fact that some women retained some degree of control of the means of production, Engel's premise is supported.

Archaeologists interested in South American empires, such as Irene Silverblatt (1987) and more recently Cathy Costin (1996), have come closer to investigating the issues considered here than any other archaeologists. These authors have analyzed the Inca performance of gender, and both have supported the idea that the rise of the social classes is concomitant with the subordination of women. Emphasis on warfare and de-emphasis on kin-based organization and household production are central to both their arguments. Silverblatt's analysis of the impact of the Inca Empire on gender is an application of a Marxist model, rather than a test of either Marx's or Engels's propositions with archaeological data. It is possible that empires have a different effect on gender hierarchies than states, and perhaps empire building is in some ways more akin to capitalist processes than state formation. Although this would be an interesting proposition to consider, it is not what Silverblatt argues. Instead, she proposes that the Inka Empire was categorically different to the systems in play prior to its hegemony, some of which have also been characterized as empires, albeit smaller ones. Though this may be true, the influence of the conquest (which Silverblatt sees as profound) on ethnohistoric records (considering who wrote them, for what purpose, and in what context) as well as on lived experience (where behavior and ideas of correctness changed) must be somewhat responsible for our perception that the Inka were more like capitalists than their predecessors were.

Costin (1996) relies on HRAF data to argue that the gender associated with a particular type of labor or production varies tremendously but that most societies expect men and women to do different things, and that men are more likely to be craft producers (producing products for sale or use outside the household). Her position is that women in pre-Inka societies did most weaving within the household as a part of the household economy; elite households were polygynous and therefore had more weavers participating in a system that she calls "intensified household production." After the Inka conquest incorporated local cultures into the Inka political economy, the cloth tax imposed more labor on women and girls but repaid them nothing, whereas men's labor through conscripted work gangs was regularly recompensed through feasting and other forms of redistribution. Though specialized weavers existed outside the household context, women were attached specialists without families (sequestered virgins), whereas male weavers were full-time or part-time specialists who could marry and have children.

These carefully made arguments follow the standard pattern of processual gender reconstructions. Beginning with a general premise (women and men have different tasks; men produce crafts) that has been verified by cross-cultural comparison, ethnohistoric data are used to construct a picture of the past that confirms the proposition. If instead we attempt to rule out competing hypotheses, the data are immediately less clear. If we ask not "How might cultural patterns have been unaffected by the conquest yet parallel to European behavioral expectations?" but instead, "What evidence is there that Pre-Hispanic culture might have been different before the Spanish Conquest?" other possibilities and lines of inquiry come into view. To some extent, the fact that both men and women were professional weavers in the Inka Empire itself violates the HRAF generalization that men are usually the craft producers cross-culturally. As we have seen even in this brief survey, women in many complex societies act as craft production specialists, but there is a strong tendency to consider craft production as something else if women do it. HRAF data collected with this implicit bias are called upon to support that bias; in this case, if women do it, it is not a craft specialization because it takes place within the household (even if we are not entirely sure that it always did). When women do specialize at craft production outside the household, their production is that of "attached specialists" who have no control over the means of production or the products of their own labor. But if they did, how would we know? Would ethnohistoric documents be reliable? Why would the HRAF files *not* be systematically biased?

My research group attempted to investigate a pre-Inka state to determine if the development of state characteristics resulted in gender subordination, as this is the era comparable to the focus of the other studies. Looking at literature on the Moche of Peru, Cristina Alcalde (in press) found that the same preexisting assumptions guide most interpretations, despite the important position attributed to women in Moche art. Population movements and a lack of identification with the ancient Moche on the part of modern residents of the Moche homeland make cultural continuity doubtful, and the impact of celibate Catholic male missionaries was undoubtedly profound. Yet ethnohistory and recent ethnographies continue to be simplistically applied to support conclusions about gender hierarchies in the Peruvian past.

Gabriel Wrobel (in press) found that the information on Predynastic Egypt is more equivocal than expected. Easy assumptions about subordination are contradicted with the striking amount of legal and economic independence, and even political influence, afforded elite women. Instances of equal treatment of males and females in death results in the usual interpretation: kin organization. Wrobel's observations on the literature of burial data from the Predynastic period showed that although evidence for status distinctions skyrocketed in this era of rising bureaucracy, clear gender distinctions were vague. Many discussions are typified by the situation at the cemetery of Tarkhan, where the discovery that more grave goods appear with female than male interments has been met with the counter that status was indicated by the size of the burial hole. Untangling the rise of complex society in Egypt from the rise of a world system in ancient times that involved interaction with other cultures will require a great deal of analysis.

Candice Lowe (in press) found that data from Harappa on the numerous dressed and bejeweled female figurines in contrast to the few representations of naked men gets the predictable interpretation in the literature. There is no empirical way to be sure that the presence of decorative apparel indicates lower status than nudity; were the situation reversed, the dominance of men would certainly be asserted. More recent analyses of Harappan material considering skeletal evidence and evidence from specialist manufacturing make this picture even more unclear. Physical anthropological analysis of human remains from Harappa have been used to suggest more stress on female children, and the presence of more dental caries among women has been used to support the idea that women had a poorer diet. Of course the simple fact that women's diet was different does not rule out the possibility that it was actually higher-status, or of equal status to that of men. Harappa is generally a very difficult case to work with, as there is a profound lack of data on social organization and the archaeological data offer little evidence of social hierarchy, despite the fact that other earmarks of complex society are present.

The greatest surprise from the societies researched by the group came from recent work in the Aegean. Association with the infamously misogynist Greeks caused us to anticipate a similarly unequal treatment of women by men among their ancestors. Sean Dougherty's (in press) discussion of Minoan culture certainly encountered the Western romance with Classical cultures. Recent work by Rehak (1998) on Bronze Age Aegean iconography indicates that women dominate representational art: women are shown more often than men, and they are shown larger.

When I teach the archaeology of the Maya, I begin my gender lecture with pictures of stelae depicting men and women. I tell the class which are female and which male, and ask them to enumerate the differences between the representations. Without any urging, students immediately point out that women are shown cradling something in their arms while men are shown with more open, assertive body language; that the women have a bowl of something, perhaps food, and the men appear to be holding weapons. The figures associated with the women are more lifelike and less stylized; women are more covered up than men; women are kneeling and men are sitting on elevated platforms, making them look taller. All these automatic distinctions have status implications that clearly come out in class discussions. Students are usually shocked to hear that the cradled bowl contains paper spattered with sacrificial blood and that the "natural" figure below the woman's feet is a bound captive. Furthermore, the woman's position in the lower register may indicate power in the underworld, and, in fact, as the drawing I show is from a lintel and would have been above the head of the viewer, higher and lower would not have been so obvious (Joyce pers. comm.). Of course, when *women* are less clothed, we take this to indicate female subordination to a male gaze. Not only are Maya women likely to be more covered up, they sometimes wear men's clothing, and the males may be depicted wearing women's clothes (Joyce 1996).

In the literature on the Maya, women are invariably constructed as "keepers of tradition" and are especially prone to being seen living in an ahistorical epic past. Evidence from their daily lives is mixed casually with evidence taken from the ethnohistoric documents of Spanish missionaries during the conquest and colonization of Maya lands by Europeans and from present-day women living in modern nation-states. The bias of recorders who were not only altering the Maya system as rapidly as possible, but who had promised their god to eschew the wicked influence of women, is almost never discussed, and modern practices are recorded as authentic only if they correspond to gender stereotypes. As with most investigations into the archaeology of gender, the absence of evidence is the major support for the dominance of men. For example, a recent article on male dominance among the Maya argues that the prevalence of men in Maya art indicates domination of the political order by men (Haviland 1997; note that this has not been the typical interpretation of art that primarily represents women as in Harappa and the Aegean). Similarly, burial treatment that differs between men and women that has no necessary or even obvious status loading is invariably taken to indicate the inferior status of women.

McAnany and Plank (2001) use abstraction of data from ethnohistoric records to interpret epigraphic representations that result predictably in a patrifocal model of ancient Maya courts and households. Noble women weave and ordinary women prepare food in private space, while common men plant corn and noble men run the government in public areas. Besides weaving, craft production is in the hands of men; female weaving is alienated labor but strictly household-level production and therefore not a source of wealth.

In the first truly radical departure from processual analyses of gender, Rosemary Joyce (2000) has developed a completely new vision of Maya gender. By outlining a gendered value system in which the transformation of nature into culture is accomplished through production of children, body modification (dress, tattoo, tooth filing, head deformation), production of dress through weaving, and preparation of food, Joyce effectively stands Lévi-Strauss on his head. Elite men are associated with forest products such as jaguar skins and are often sparsely clothed. If she is correct, Maya women were to culture as men were to nature.

Joyce proposes that most Classic Maya representations are intentionally asexual, as the sexuality of the actor is only relevant under some circumstances. Sex characteristics become prominent on monuments in the post-Classic period as a new political economy, restricting women from public ritual and political action, arises at later sites such as Chichen Itza. Joyce associates these organizational changes as arising from warfare, which required a structural solution to the tension between house-based economic production and more centralized government control. This perspective parallels my own argument that women may lose status they achieved during wartime when men return home from warfare and attempt to address the imbalance of power that arose during their absence. But as Joyce points out concerning Maya monumental inscriptions, "We must consider such media as suggestive hints at the lack of uniformity rather than the reverse" (2000, 200). Ultimately,

Joyce's analysis makes it clear that the rise of class distinctions among the Classic Maya was very incompletely associated with gender until much later in the Terminal and post-Classic periods, when we may be dealing with a political entity (or set of entities) less like an early independent state and more like those inhabiting Peru immediately before the Inka Empire claimed them.

These are really only preliminary studies. Nevertheless, the failure to find ubiquitous and unequivocal support for the patterns of gender distinction long considered to be well established suggests that further investigation would be worthwhile in a broader field. Other scholars have argued that capitalism commodifies women; Wolf argues that capitalism essentializes cultures. Capitalism also essentializes women in order to commodify them, but this is a historical process that situates women outside of history in the same way the world system creates underdeveloped peripheries. Like geographic peripheries, women are characterized as natural, traditional, fertile, uncivilized, dangerous, pacified with trinkets, and in need of government control. But women have used this liminal status outside history as a source of power and a means of survival and resistance, even though as yet no one has been able to reset the terms of the debate to allow for the possibility that women have history. Archaeologists, even many feminist archaeologists, continue to use the inadequate tools of cultural evolutionism to think with. But archaeologists can begin to reevaluate the data; look at prehistory for evidence of other ways of framing gender; and insist that essentialism is as wrong for gender studies as it is for cultural studies. Perhaps in this way archaeologists can begin to ask questions that will give more objective, more interesting, and more useful answers.

REFERENCES

Alcade, Cristina. In press. "Leaders, Healers, Laborers, and Lovers: Re-interpreting Women's Roles in Moche Society." In *Ungendering Civilization*, ed. by K. Anne Pyburn. London: Routledge.

Al-Zubaidi, Layla. In press. "Tracing Women in Early Sumer." In *Ungendering Civilization*, ed. by K. Anne Pyburn. London: Routledge.

Arwill-Nordbladh, Elizabeth. 1991. "The Swedish Image of Viking Age Women: Stereotype, Generalization, and Beyond." In *Social Approaches to Viking Studies*, ed. by R. Samson, 53–64. Glasgow, U.K.: Cruithne Press.

Bruhns, Karen Olsen, and Karen E. Stothert. 1999. *Women in Ancient America*. Norman: University of Oklahoma Press.

Costin, Catherine. 1996. "Exploring the Relationship Between Gender and Craft on Complex Societies: Methodological and Theoretical Issues of Gender Attribution." In *Gender and Archaeology*, ed. by Rita Wright, 111–40. Philadelphia: University of Pennsylvania Press.

Dougherty, Sean. In press. "The Minoan Goddess and Isolation in Exchange: Problems in Minoan Prehistory." In *Ungendering Civilization*, ed. by K. Anne Pyburn. London: Routledge.

Engels, Friedrich. 1884. *The Origin of Family, Private Property, and the State.* New York: International Publishers.

Haviland, William A. 1997. "The Rise and Fall of Sexual Inequality: Death and Gender at Tikal, Guatemala." *Ancient Mesoamerica* 8 (1): 1–12.

Joyce, Rosemary A. 1996. "The Construction of Gender in Classic Maya Monuments." In *Gender and Archaeology*, ed. by Rita Wright, 167–95. Philadelphia: University of Pennsylvania Press.

———. 2000. *Gender and Power in Prehispanic Mesoamerica.* Austin: University of Texas Press.

Lowe, Candice Marie. In press. "All the Harappan Men are Naked, but the Women are Wearing Jewelry. In *Ungendering Civilization*, ed. by K. Anne Pyburn. London: Routledge.

Luedke, Tracy. In press. "'Turning Names into Things' (Wolf, 1982:6): the Gendered Implications of Archaeological Explanations for the Rise of the Zimbabwe State." In *Ungendering Civilization*, ed. by K. Anne Pyburn. London: Routledge.

Marx, Karl. 1965. *Pre-Capitalist Economic Formations.* New York: International Publishers.

McAnany, Patricia A., and Shannon Plank. 2001. "Perspectives on Actors, Gender Roles, and Architecture at Classic Maya Courts and Households." In *Royal Courts of the Maya*, ed. by T. Inomata and S. Houston, 168–94. Boulder, Colo.: Westview Press.

Mortenson, Lena. In press. "The 'Marauding Pagan Warrior' Woman of the Vikings." In *Ungendering Civilization*, ed. by K. Anne Pyburn. London: Routledge.

Pate, Laura. In press. "The Use and Abuse of Ethnographic Analogies in Interpretations of Gender Systems at Cahokia." In *Ungendering Civilization*, ed. by K. Anne Pyburn. London: Routledge.

Pyburn, K. Anne. Forthcoming, 2004. "Ungendering the Maya." In *Ungendering Civilization*, ed. by K. Anne Pyburn. London: Routledge.

———. In press. "Untangling the Sexist Legacy of Cultural Evolutionism." In *Ungendering Civilization*, ed. by K. Anne Pyburn. London: Routledge.

——— (ed.). In press. *Ungendering Civilization.* London: Routledge.

Rehak, Paul. 1998. "The Construction of Gender in Late Bronze Age Aegean Art." In *Redefining Archaeology: Feminist Perspectives*, ed. by Mary Casey, Denise Donlon, Jeanette Hope, and Sharon Wellfare. Canberra, Australia: ANH Publications, RSPAS, Australian National University.

Silverblatt, Irene. 1987. *Moon, Sun, and Witches: Gender Ideologies and Class in Inca and Colonial Peru.* Princeton, N.J.: Princeton University Press.

Wilk, Richard R. 1991. "Household Ecology: Economic Change and Domestic Life among the Kekchi Maya in Belize." *Arizona Studies in Human Ecology.* Tucson: University of Arizona Press.

———. 1996. "Belizean Beauty Queens on the Global Stage." In *Beauty Queens on the Global Stage: Gender, Contests, and Power*, ed. by Colleen Cohen, Richard R. Wilk, and Beverly Stoeltje, 217–32. New York: Routledge.

Wilk, Richard R., and W. Ashmore. 1988. *Household and Community in the Mesoamerican Past.* Albuquerque: University of New Mexico Press.

Wolf, Eric. 1982. *Europe and the People without History.* Berkeley: University of California Press.

Wright, Rita. 1996. "Technology, Gender, and Class: Worlds of Difference in Ur III Mesopotamia." In *Gender and Archaeology*, ed. by Rita Wright, 79–110. Philadelphia: University of Pennsylvania Press.

Wrobel, Gabriel D. G. In press. "New Answers to Old Questions: The Benefits of an Archaeology of Gender for Predynastic Egypt." In *Ungendering Civilization*, ed. by K. Anne Pyburn. London: Routledge.

2

Rain and Cattle: Gendered Structures and Political Economy in Precolonial Pare, Tanzania

N. Thomas Håkansson

INTRODUCTION

In this chapter, I will explore the logic of production and exchange among the Asu of South Pare, Tanzania,[1] as they were informed by gendered principles for the reproduction of social relationships and human prosperity. As social domination in South Pare was achieved through the harnessing of gendered powers through production and exchange, economic activities affected the relationship between men and women both on the level of ritual and cosmology and in the everyday affairs of the family/household. While the skewing of gendered exchanges facilitated male political and economic power, the economic capital that made this power possible derived from intensive cultivation that was largely based on female labor. However, women's involvement in irrigation agriculture also gave them independent access to resources that resulted in a partly separate female sphere of exchange and wealth accumulation.

I will begin by outlining what I call the econo-cosmology of the Asu as it was related to their economic system and will then outline three examples of how the gendered rules of exchange interact through human agency to produce different patterns of gender relationships. First, I will show that while the patrilineal descent system supported male control over economic resources, intensive cultivation and the exchange economy gave women resources through which they were able to maintain some independent control over their production. Second, the same principles that governed the exchange of cattle for wives also made it possible to exploit the labor of young, cattle-poor men. Third, the contemporary increase in unwed mothers is directly related to new uses of these rules of exchange that affect bridewealth and lineage membership.

Before focusing on the specific case of South Pare, I will explore a few general issues in economic anthropology relevant to my later analysis. At the most general level, I follow a large body of work within feminist anthropology that has shown that gender is a universal category of symbolization that organizes thinking about the world and social relationships. Gender enters into every aspect of social interaction and is therefore constitutive of any social process we analyze. To analyze such a broad category, even for a single society, would be an overwhelming task; we must select only a few aspects at a time to usefully conceptualize. I will do so by first sorting out a category of societies that anthropologists have, to name a few terms, called tribal, segmentary, kin-ordered, and chiefdoms. Although gender symbolism is pervasive in our own capitalist state and culture, it does not provide what may be called the structural logic of capitalism. That logic is based on private property and monetary exchange values that allow accumulation of wealth outside social relationships. But if we peruse the literature on kin-ordered societies from Melanesia (Weiner 1992; Strathern 1988; Munn 1986) to Africa (Moore 1986; Clark 1994; Udvardy 1995; Håkansson 1990), it appears that gender is at the very root of their economic systems both as a metaphor and as a central organizing principle for exchange, production, and consumption. That is, in kin-ordered economies, wealth derives from the reproduction of social relationships (cf. Gregory 1982).

As elsewhere, gender relationships provide a central organizing code for the social relationships that underlie the indigenous societies of eastern Africa. Female and male genders are metaphorical expressions of forces that are believed to interact in order to produce generalized fertility. Just as fertility is generated through exchange and the mingling of female and male substances (Jacobson-Widding 2000; Udvardy 1995), so the exchange of material goods is directed by group members toward increasing the growth and wealth of the kin group. On the cosmological level, this model of fertility enhancement in the broadest sense is expressed through ritual exchanges that aim at sustaining and enhancing the generation of human beings, livestock, crops, and generalized well-being through the exchange of material goods in sacrifice. Such models contain transformative schemata that provide a logic for the political-economic processes in a fashion analogous to the function of private property and money in capitalism. In the latter, exchanges and production aim at capital accumulation by individuals, and commodities and money are fetishized as forces acting outside human volition. In kin-ordered societies, exchange aims at increasing the growth of kin groups through the accumulation of people. In this model it is the forces of the respective genders that are believed to lie behind the proliferation of life, and which are harnessed to produce wealth.

In 1986 Stephen Gudeman published a book entitled *Economics as Culture*, in which he argued that the process of gaining a livelihood is culturally constructed in diverse ways and that purportedly universal economic theories such as Marxism and neo-Classical economics are themselves locally derived models that are of little use in understanding other economies. Instead of privileging Western models, he calls for the cross-cultural comparison of local, cultural constructions of economies (Gudeman 1986: viii, 28). His book provides several examples of how gendered cosmologies in kin-ordered societies provide local models for how wealth and prosperity are achieved.

Gudeman's observations are astute, but his examples and analysis do not account for change and rest on notions of bounded and homogenous cultures (Wilk 1996: 128). The notion that cosmologies are the cultural resources upon which societies draw in order to reproduce themselves is useful. In a similar vein, Weiner (1992: 4) suggests that such cosmologies and classificatory schemas are not merely ideologies but play a fundamental role in how production, exchange, and kinship are organized. This, too, is a valuable insight, but in my opinion, it privileges symbolic constructions over material resources and human choice. Indeed, a large literature using a variety of cultural constructionist approaches to economic processes has developed, taking inspiration from Marcel Mauss's *The Gift* (1990). As Wilk (1996: 131) has pointed out, Mauss's work has had a strong impact on the cultural economic perspective in anthropology because it demonstrates that values are produced through human relations and cultural conventions. I agree with Wilk that this approach takes the analysis to radical relativity and obscures a common human rationality that underlies theories of optimization and reflexive monitoring (Giddens 1984; Donham 1990) as well as obviating theorizing about the material circumstances of human existence.

Rather than analyzing exchange and production as parts of cosmological schemata, I would like to use these cultural models to ascertain the rules that, together with resources, constitute structure in Anthony Giddens's (1984: 21) sense. He defines rules as techniques or generalizable procedures applied in the enactment and reproduction of social practices. As usual, Giddens's definitions are somewhat vague. Some further clarification may be sought in his statement that rules are the unstated procedures for action and aspects of praxis. Let me use an example from our own society that I think will be helpful in illuminating the concept. In the United States, in discussions about childcare policies, the praxis or rule seems to be that only women can care for children. Solutions never include men as caregivers and, hence, particular institutional arrangements are built around an unchanging rule. The difference between Giddens's use of rules and Gudeman's cultural models lies in that the latter interprets how people believe wealth and subsistence are generated, and the former allows the analyst to formulate generalizable models of how wealth and subsistence are actually produced and distributed. Rules enter into agency and strategy together with material and institutional resources as parts of the factors that affect people's actions over time. Hence, Giddens's approach[2] allows the analyst to develop cross-culturally valid models of social processes and institutions based on both rules and individual agency through the application of such concepts as optimization and relations of production.

In a similar way we can discover, in the cosmologies of kin-ordered societies, rules that pertain to economic relationships and processes. The logical precondition for the reproduction of patrilineal descent groups in eastern Africa was (and, to a great extent, still is) the ability to exchange some other form of wealth for women's fertility. In order to become a vehicle for male reproduction, women's childbearing capacities had to be moveable and be possible to accumulate. This was possible through exchange in which male-controlled wealth in the form of livestock was transferred as bridewealth, which affiliated a woman's children to her husband's patrilineage. Although in such societies, effective rights in cattle were vested at the household and individual level, they were also a collective resource that reflected the power of the lineage and its potential for reproduction and growth. Hence, any alienation of livestock had to be compensated by an equivalent resource that contributed to the growth of the lineage, and this was usually a wife. Accordingly, female lineage members' fertility could not benefit any other lineage without compensation. One could envisage the logic of this system as a ledger in which the credit column must always at least balance the debit column, not for profit but for the expansion of the descent group. Hence, the exchange rules are based on cattle as symbolic equivalents of people.

The exploration of structures or underlying principles of social organization is, of course, an old practice in anthropology, which often leads into severe epistemological problems, including the construction of ad hoc deep structures and an inability to account for change. Instead, by using Giddens's notion of structuration, albeit vague, it may be possible to relate structure to agency and change over time. To try to expose the rules of exchange in a given culture or region is not a goal in itself but a means of uncovering the parameters within which actors transact over time and how such rules are interpreted and used in social and economic activities.

SOUTH PARE

My discussion centers on nineteenth-century South Pare mountain in northeastern Tanzania. South Pare is part of a broken chain of mountains, which rises from the dry plains at about 800 m above sea level to a little over 2,000 m above sea level. It is about 60 km long and 15 km wide. The eastern side of the plateau receives an average rainfall of approximately 1,000 mm per year (Yoshida 1985). As well as having the highest rainfall, the eastern side of the mountain also has most of the natural drainage. In contrast, the steep and dry western escarpments, which are dominated by grasses, receive only 500–750 mm of rain per year.

The known history of the northern Tanzanian coast begins in a dim past of regional and transoceanic contacts. Although such a wider context is surely relevant to the issues discussed here, I will for the sake of theoretical focus only present a short account of the immediate precolonial interactions that pushed South Pare into the chaos of the ivory and slave trades. For a treatment of the nineteenth-century regional processes I refer the reader to my other works (Håkansson 1995, 1998) and for the contemporary situation to Porter (1997). In the beginning of the past millennium, the Swahili civilization emerged on the coast, the interior plains were occupied by pastoralists and gatherer/hunters, and iron-producing cultivators resided in the mountains (Nurse and Spear 1985; Soper 1967). Trade and population movements between the coast and the interior were frequent during the several periods dating back to at least the 1100s (Allen 1993). In the nineteenth century, the expansion of the ivory and slave trades greatly influenced political and economic processes in the Pare Mountains. Swahili caravans traversed the plains, buying slaves and ivory from local chieftains and hunters and giving cloth, beads, and guns in exchange.

Alongside the caravan trade from the coast, thriving local exchange networks and local markets existed on the mountains and the plains. Different environmental conditions at different altitudes, together with the localized occurrence of raw materials such as iron ore and clay for the manufacture of pottery, encouraged exchange (Kjekshus 1977; Moore 1986). Not only grain, but also livestock and their products, was traded. Furthermore, iron from Pare was famous all the way to the coast and was traded in the whole region, where salt, root crops, meat, honey, and crafts were also produced and exchanged. It was not until the nineteenth century that trade and coastal political ambitions became ubiquitous in the form of large-scale caravans, new political alliances and, finally, German colonial occupation in 1891.

ASU SOCIETY

Asu society was organized into dispersed nonexogamous patriclans. Women retained their natal clan and lineage affiliation throughout life but were dispersed at marriage to their husbands' localized patrilineages. Marriage was established through the transfer of bridewealth which, in the early 1900s, consisted of three to four head of cattle and four goats (Kotz 1922: 87). Clan members maintained connections through the observance of common rituals and the maintenance of religious shrines (Guth 1932; Kotz 1922: 189). Though eastern South Pare was organized into small chiefdoms with extensive irrigation, in the west political order was based on territorial clan associations with an agro-pastoral economy and little irrigation.

The local corporate descent group consisted of a core of adult men descended from a common paternal grandfather, their wives (Guth 1932), as well as matrilateral (through the mother) and affinal kin who, over time, could become incorporated into the clan (Omari 1990: 64f). This group of extended families controlled and defended their land and, in areas where irrigation was practiced, the system of channels built by its members. The immediate control over land use and inheritance was in the hands of the extended family, and several families of one lineage tended to live in one area along a common irrigation channel (Håkansson 1995; Lebulu 1979). Productive agricultural land was the result of high levels of labor investment in channels and dams, manuring, perennial crops in the form of banana groves, bench and stone terracing, and ridging (Dannholz 1989: 30; Lebulu 1979).

Each wife and her children formed a household with its own fields, granaries, and livestock. Such households were in turn set within the matrix of the extended patriarchal family. The oldest brother was the ritual head of the family and executor of the father's estate (Ankermann 1929: 59f; Kotz 1922: 275). He maintained formal control over the cattle and the irrigated land, which he allocated to his sons, younger brothers, and their sons when they were in need. Women were responsible for producing crops to feed the family, and men were responsible for herding, constructing and repairing irrigation channels, and clearing the fields.

The land, irrigation furrows, and most of the livestock ultimately belonged to men, either as family heads or as a corporation. In the patrilineal model of society, women could not permanently inherit land or cattle and were jural minors throughout life. In reality, though, women, especially older women and widows, were able to act independently in economic and political matters. Senior women also assumed roles in the adjudication of intralineage land disputes and other lineage conflicts (Porter 1997). In addition, the possibility for men to exploit women's labor was constrained, and women retained rights in the livestock they obtained through exchange, gifts, and as fees for their daughters' lost virginity.

As elsewhere in East Africa, cattle in Pare fulfilled the role of investment capital, media of exchange, and prestige goods. In the latter capacity, they took on symbolic significance as replacement for people and as representatives of the fertility and growth of the lineage. Cattle were necessary for the building of social relationships of kinship, pawnship (debt bondage), and political clientage. They were also used as blood wealth and for sacrifices to God or the dead. Cultivation of crops for exchange was a common way to obtain livestock for bridewealth payments (Ankermann 1929: 275; Kotz 1922: 146). The possibility of converting crop production into livestock was based on a regular barter trade with the dry, pastoral-oriented regions on the western side of the mountain and on the plains, from which people brought cattle to the eastern side and carried food crops back.

PATRILINEAL COSMOLOGY AND ECONOMY

As is common in eastern African societies, the Asu patrilineal social organization and gender relationships were supported by, and expressed, a cosmological model in which male generative power encompassed female powers. A common metaphorical expression referred to the husband as being like the large tree that, in its shade, protected and "brought up" the banana plants (i.e., the wives and children). Bodily metaphors were used to express the complementary but hierarchical nature of gendered power. The right side was male, strong and active; the left was female, weak and passive. However, the male was also dependent on the female, which was essential for the success of any action upon the world, from ensuring a bountiful harvest to success in warfare. All ritual working entailed the combination of male and female metaphors (Dannholz 1989: 103, 111). In the Asu econo-cosmology, the patrilineage grew through a circular interaction of forces embodied in crops and livestock. The work was directed toward family prosperity in order to create a harmonious and balanced place and cool social relations of unity. Livestock were transferred in exchange for a woman's capacity to bear children and to work on the farm in order to produce food for the nourishment of her husband's descendants. The cattle came from the male effort of bestowing male fertility in the form of water to the crops. Male control over social units and patrilineal organization was based on the primacy of male generative powers, which in turn were visible in ritual and cosmology. Cattle and rain generated fertility, well-being, and peace through an exchange of cattle for women's fertility, which in turn caused the growth of the patrilineage and the patrilineal family.

The maintenance of a state of peace and prosperity necessitated the hierarchical complementarity of male and female. Any act of creation involved metaphorical representations of these gendered forces. For example, the sprinkling of water, symbolic of maleness, during rainmaking ceremonies was done with a brush made from a banana plant, a female fertility symbol (Kotz 1922: 63). The irrigation furrows were a male domain, but the intake was called the mother of the canal. The fetish of the clan was composed of two figurines, a male and a female. Similarly, the lineage was composed of both male and female members, and its daughters were required to assist in all-important rituals. As sisters could not themselves bear children for the lineage, they were obliged to get married to provide the livestock for their brothers' marriages. Women retained membership in their natal lineages for life and therefore had inalienable rights to land through their father and brothers (Porter 1997: 233). Through marriage, women exchanged their capacity for childbearing and work for livestock, which in turn were necessary for the growth and prosperity of their lineage and family. As I will show, this connection with their natal lineage provided a resource that gave women leverage in their relationships with their husbands and their husbands' lineages.

Suprahuman powers were channeled through a hierarchy of social inclusiveness and through persons who were believed to have the ability to affect the impact of these forces on life, such as male and female clan elders, ritual experts of various kinds, and chiefs. Like material resources, ritual knowledge was restricted (Porter 1997: 169) and hierarchically ordered, so that each important level of social relationships was evoked through ritual performances. Women were not allowed to be clan-level ritual specialists but could participate as assistants to men.

On top of the hierarchy was the chief who, with the help of other ritual specialists, performed rainmaking and cooling rituals in a sacred grove where cattle were sacrificed and prayers directed to God (Porter 1997: 95). The clans had initiation forests where the boys, at regular intervals, underwent initiations under the direction of senior male elders. Although many clans were dispersed in areas outside South Pare, their boys had to come to the clan's ancestral forest on the mountain for the ceremony. The forest was regarded as a source of male fertility and power and as being consistent with the model of male encompassment and superiority. Girls were subjected to shorter ceremonies that took place in their homes under the supervision of female elders (Kotz 1922).

The main ritual center for the lineage was the *mpungi*, a sacred grove where the skulls of dead lineage members, *nkoma*, were preserved in a small cave. Sacrifices were performed by the senior male elder to the ancestors and ancestresses, as well as to God, for fertility, health, and rain. Older women were allowed to attend sacrifices to the *nkoma* but were not allowed into the inner parts of the cave (Omari 1990: 202). Finally, each extended family performed libations and sacrifices in their homesteads; these could also be supervised by a senior female elder in addition to old men. The sacrifices of livestock to the dead and other suprahuman powers paralleled exchanges between the living, in which the exchange of goods was coded as gendered complementarities. The transfer of cattle as bridewealth demanded female fertility and, ultimately, children and food in return. Food crops were female and could be exchanged for livestock that represented male generative powers. At the level of political hierarchy the chief cooled the land and made rain for which he obtained crops and livestock in return. Although there is nothing inherently hierarchical in complementary gendered powers, the exchange relationships were skewed to support power inequalities and social and political domination at the level of the family household, between women and men, and at the political level between the powerful and the dominated.

The planting season was initiated by cooling rituals performed by the chief, which entailed a number of gendered exchanges symbolizing both male generative power in general and the chief's capacity to channel male and female forces in a creative act that benefited the whole chiefdom. At the onset of planting, the chief placed maize kernels in a pot with consecrated water. He then went early in the morning to his field and planted the seed, after which all farmers in the chiefdom got some of these kernels and started planting their own fields. The male family heads also received some of the consecrated water and sprinkled it on the fields, livestock, and family members. This water symbolically made the chief the supplier of male fertility to the whole chiefdom. At harvest time, the chief sent messengers to obtain corn ears that were placed at a crossroad where they could be taken by anyone in need. This signaled the beginning of the harvest season and a new season of plenty.

On a certain day, all married women arose in the early morning and extinguished the fires in the homesteads. The fires symbolized the old sun and the disease that was believed to emanate from the sun, which was thereby also extinguished. Each wife brought a calabash with cooked maize and a piece of firewood, both metaphors of female fertility and women's generative powers. Like a woman's fertility, the wood was dormant until kindled by the vitality of male fertility (symbolized by fire that they received in exchange for the female maize porridge). The wood was placed outside the chief's house. Then a ritual specialist led the gathering to a bush on which the women left their shawls. They then retreated without looking back at the chief's homestead. This was called: "to throw out the disease." At the chief's house a ritual specialist started a new fire to symbolize the new sun, and each woman took her piece of ignited wood and brought it back to her own home to start a new fire. For each of four days, men sprinkled the houses, fields, people, and cattle with water (Kotz 1922: 185–86).

Ritual exchanges provided the ingredients for the Asu local economic model that I am sketching here. In contrast to Gudeman (1986), who would focus on interpreting the meaning of such constructs, I regard them only as the beginning of an analysis that, in his perspective, privileges the researcher's cross-culturally valid models. Such local models of how fertility and prosperity were generated were part of agency in resource management, the exchange of goods and services, the unintended consequences of actions on the wider economic system, and the contexts of power relationships. I will attempt to show that the combination of intensive cultivation and cattle-keeping created a particular dynamic that intertwined economic and social processes in the context of gender relationships. These interactions connected the cosmological realm of gendered powers of fertility and generation with political and social transactions and institutions. First, the economic logic of the production and exchange system generated economic inequalities. Second, the preoccupation with rainmaking and cooling was directly linked to the importance of crops, for exchange for cattle that in turn were crucial for the reproduction of social relationships and power. Third, the local community composition and marriage patterns meant that women usually resided close to their natal lineage and thus maintained a support network that was based on the fact that they retained membership in their natal lineages through life. Fourth, the importance of rainmaking produced by the system of exchange coupled with economic inequalities in cattle wealth, maintained political centralization.

Irrigation and Cattle

Irrigated cultivation allowed for considerable surplus production, which could be converted into labor and cattle. Through its last 500 years, South Pare experienced a small but steady increase in population through immigration and natural growth. The increase in areas under cultivation in turn affected herd management and the rate of livestock accumulation. Although agricultural intensification in the short term increased the flow of cattle, the long-term effect was the opposite. Indeed, Östberg (in press) suggests that among the Marakwet of western Kenya, intensification by irrigation was a self-reinforcing process.[3] The production of crops for the purpose of increasing cattle herds had the unintended consequence of depressing the natural growth of the herds. The establishment of stable and dense settlements affects livestock husbandry, especially cattle, by pushing grazing further away from human habitation. This created problems of supervision and led to a shortage of good grazing, resulting in a decline in herd productivity. Labor constraints are at the root of these costs where livestock and cultivation compete for scarce labor. Either cattle must be restricted to easy reach of the farm, or the family labor force must be divided to take cattle elsewhere, which affects agricultural productivity (Mace 1993). The effect of a primarily agricultural economy, as compared to pastoral or agro-pastoral husbandry, on herd growth may be great, with decreases in calving rates of between 40 and 70 percent (Mace 1993; von Rothenan 1966). In addition, cattle accumulation by sedentary, intensive cultivators invited raiding by pastoralists and other sedentary neighbors (cf. Östberg, in press). In South Pare, the increase in herds usually attracted attention from Maasai and Kwavi warriors (Dannholz 1989: 42). Hence, agricultural intensification aimed at increasing cattle holdings produced the contradictory effect of actually depressing herd growth, a condition which in turn put pressure on cultivators to produce more goods for exchange. Once large-scale irrigation had been established, the population became captured by contradictions in economic strategies that created relative and localized scarcities of cattle and economic inequalities (Håkansson 1998).

Thus, access to labor to support the development of durable productive investments like irrigation works and cattle was crucial (Håkansson 1995). Such an economy lends itself to the emergence and maintenance of economic and social differentiation in which wealthy families and individuals could wield political power based on their own production and manipulation of exchanges. Hence, political and social ambitions were directed toward producing a surplus of food that could be exchanged for livestock, which in turn were used to build large families and political power. However, maintaining the intensive cultivation system demanded not only labor but also the influence of suprahuman powers.

Cattle and Rain

The German missionary Dannholz (1989: 20) explained the Asu model of the good and proper state of the community of humans thus:

> People of the same mind move in, the farm grows on account of both birth and arrivals. This is how the farm becomes firm due to *mporere* [peace] and *vuhoo* [coolness], as if trodden down by the feet of many people.

In the Asu world, a cool farm experiences no crop failures and no premature births. The women give birth; the cows calve at the right time, without contracting fever. The rain and the dew from the mountain make the earth rich and cool, and open it up to germination. This generates *vuhoo*, the peaceable and cool disposition of the husband and master of the farm. The master becomes the shade tree that provides coolness to the homestead and banana plantation. However, to achieve this preferred state of existence was a difficult balancing act that involved the continuous ritual engagement of cosmological forces (for other African examples see Jacobson-Widding 2000; Udvardy 1995). Too much coolness would lead to death and lack of vitality, but too much heat would lead to disease, drought, and war. Death, disease, drought, famine, war, conflict, infertility of humans and livestock, and misfortune were the result of punishments from the ancestors, from God, or the effects of witchcraft (Dannholz 1916).

The sun and the moon respectively were the male and female representations of God or the supreme power (Omari 1990: 145). The sun could cause drought, disease, and locust invasions as well as induce fertility of humans and livestock, the preferred state of coolness, and general health and peace. The contrasting qualities of God were symbolized by the sun in the hot, dry steppe, where its harsh light and heat were believed to be connected with dry conditions and the presence of disease. In the high, humid mountain, with its lack of malaria and other diseases found on the steppe, the sun was represented as the mild late afternoon sun, the positive light that kept spirits away, made the crops grow, and provided rain (Dannholz 1989: 19f). Female fertility and generative powers were associated with pools, groves, and caves. Rain symbolized such male generative power as that of semen (Dannholz n.d.). It initiated growth and supplied the essential water, which, together with cattle, made the farm cool (Dannholz 1989). The family grew through marriages, and prosperity was based on exchange of life-giving livestock. This life-giving property of cattle exchanges was paralleled in sacrifices of cattle to the spirits of the dead, who in return allowed the crops to grow and humans and livestock to multiply.

At least a partial representation of the gendered Asu "economic" model can thus be outlined. Fertility and prosperity derives from exchanges between complementary male and female substances and forces, in which the male is represented as active and the female passive. Water is a metaphor for male fertility and semen that ultimately lead to the harmonious, peaceful state of plenty that is reached through cattle (cf. Sheridan 2002). The connection between cattle wealth and agriculture is conceptualized as a series of exchanges in which water as rain or irrigation fertilizes the fields and produces crops, which in turn both nourish the family and are used to obtain cattle, which are capable of attracting people as wives and clients. As in the wedding ceremony, rainmaking also included the sacrifice of large quantities of beer and an ox. Water was sprinkled around, and the rain was called using the same words that the herders used in calling the cattle (Kotz 1922: 188).

The preoccupation with rainmaking and cooling was directly linked to the importance of agricultural production for exchange for cattle, which were crucial for the reproduction of social relationships and power. Hence, I argue, the insecurity of cattle access generated a strong emphasis on male fertility rituals that were concerned not only with the physical rainfall but also with the metaphorical efficacy of falling water, which was believed to cause conception (Dannholz n.d.). This hypothesis is partly supported by the fact that rainmaking was much less important on the agro-pastoral dry, western slopes of the mountain[4] (Kimambo 1969), where cattle were plentiful and cultivation not a significant means to obtain livestock. It may be argued that rainfall is not as important for agro-pastoralists as for cultivators and, consequently, the former would not be expected to be as concerned with rain as the latter. However, the agro-pastoralists were dependent on crops for survival, and a failure of the rain created hardships and the loss of livestock, both through death and through barter for crops. Hence, rainmaking is not simply an attempt to alleviate disaster through supernatural means, but a response to a socially constructed environment.[5] Finally, as I have shown elsewhere (Håkansson 1998), the male fertility rituals of cooling and rainmaking became the foundation of political centralization on the eastern side of South Pare.

Labor and Cattle

Although the econo-cosmological model in itself presents a set of static symbolic associations between forces, the structural principles expressed were in turn part of people's strategies and attempts to harness resources. In addition to the ritual harnessing of suprahuman forces for growth and prosperity, human labor was the other important ingredient in the household economy. Access to labor was the precondition for social reproduction and the establishment of a large and prosperous family and lineage. The scarcity of cattle and the importance of intensive cultivation for social reproduction had important consequences for gender relations and social stratification. There was a constant struggle to use the cosmological forces as well as material resources to create social relationships that benefited individuals and groups. I will use three examples to show how gendered structures were involved in processes of social and economic change in nineteenth-century and contemporary South Pare.

In the first example, I argue that the resources available to women in the nineteenth century enabled them to maintain a degree of independent control of the fruits of their labor within the patriarchal family and lineage organization. Women's access to, and control over, resources in this patrilineal society was linked to their position in two partially conflicting social institutional contexts: as members of their natal patrilineage and as wives and mothers in their husbands' and children's descent groups. As members of their natal lineages, women could accumulate livestock and had use rights to land.[6] At marriage, such livestock had to be left with the women's brothers but could be requested later in life. A woman's father also gave her heavy neck rings of brass or iron, or a goat to buy such rings, which were the daughter's personal property. These rings represented considerable value, were exchangeable for livestock, and were inherited by daughters matrilaterally.

As is common in patrilineal societies, with the exception of these rings, women's access to property was never direct but always connected to their relationships to men. Men remained in the lineage, but its women moved out and thus occupied an intermediate position as absent members of their natal lineage and not "real" members of their husbands' lineages (cf. Udvardy 1995). However, as I will discuss below, women's lineage identity gave them a degree of latitude to exploit and to broaden their independence, while at the same time contributing to the growth of their husbands' lineages. As I have shown above, the gendered exchange rule placed a woman's fertility and labor at the disposal of her husband and his lineage. As a mother, her and her husband's interests were partially overlapping. They both desired many children and grandchildren. Thus, a wife who invested her livestock in her sons' marriages built her own power and influence as well as her husband's. However, there was potential latitude in patrilineal societies in how much control husbands and their agnates could exercise over lineage wives' resources and labor. Elsewhere, I have shown that there is wide variation both cross-culturally and historically (Håkansson 1988, 1989, 1994b) in female–male resource control in patrilineal family/households. At one extreme, husbands appropriate the fruits of their wives' labor for their own ends, such as the use of bridewealth for marriages, and the transfer of livestock to other wives' sons. At the other extreme, wives have virtual control over their own production, provided that resources are not permanently alienated from the lineage. Hence, the gendered exchange rule that cattle alienated from the lineage should be replaced by a resource that furthers the lineage's growth as expressed in the Asu econo-cosmology does not by itself determine institutional form. In order to understand the process of both change and continuity, we have to include the resources available to both

women and men. Such resources are both material, involving the economics of irrigation, and social, in the form of kinship.

The degree of resource control and independent decision making by married women was ambiguous. The missionary accounts reflect a situation in
which one official male view is reported together with what appear to be direct observations of actual behavior. For example, Kotz (1922: 106) writes
that, "The marriage is in the eyes of the natives a purchase through which the
woman becomes the property of the husband. The work performed by the
wife, and her children are regarded as interest on the capital [i.e., the
bridewealth] paid. . . . Everything that she produces belongs to the husband,
because he has also 'bought her hands.'" He also claims that a husband can sell
one of the wife's fields without consulting her but that she will have joint
rights over the cattle received in payment. Another missionary (Ankermann
1929: 275) first gives the same general impression of the husband's total control over his wife's labor but then writes:

> If the mother, as often happened, had her own property, it can be inherited by
> her daughters if neither father nor brothers live. The property of the wives con-
> sists of the cattle that they bought with grain and potatoes, and the natural
> growth of these cattle; the herd deriving from the *misanga* goats, and a goat that
> she gets from her father to buy jewelry.

The latter information is also supported by oral histories that I collected
from older women who remembered that their mothers exchanged crops for
brass rings and goats in the markets, and that such property was theirs to control, rather than their husbands'. Many young men obtained cattle for
bridewealth from their mothers' accumulated livestock, which created ties of
debt and obedience to the mother.

The contemporary sources reveal an official ideology of male control coex-
isting with seemingly contradictory practice. However, if we expand the context we find that all lineage members and wives were interconnected in a
complex web of rights and obligations, with the oldest living man at the top
and unmarried children at the bottom. In a sense, the oldest lineage head
"owned" all the members of his lineage, and old grandmothers with many
children exercised considerable authority themselves by virtue of their "ownership" of a large number of descendants. Hence, actual male or female control over resources was the outcome of both their positions in the social
network and the personal resources that they could harness.

Intensive cultivation affected women's access to, and control over, resources
in two ways. First, a woman's labor was not only essential for the production
of subsistence but also for the continued social existence of the patrilineage
through bridewealth payments. Second, the marriage pattern allowed women
close residential proximity to their natal families, which enabled them to

maintain close ties with brothers, sisters, and parents. A woman's labor was crucial for a family's ability to obtain livestock either for her sons' marriages or for a husband. This seems to have given women a certain amount of leverage in family economic affairs.

Exactly how women and men negotiated their respective control over household resources and women's labor is very difficult to ascertain from the missionary sources or even from contemporary oral traditions. However, I will make some inferences from the sources that at least will give us some indication of the strategies employed by women. One important weapon for married women in patrilineal societies was the threat of leaving the husband. The effectiveness of this type of action depended on both the effects on the husband's social and economic situation and on the ability of the woman to rally support from her natal family. In case of divorce, the latter had to return the bridewealth and was therefore reluctant to support a daughter/sister. However, Asu women could utilize their rights as lineage members in requiring support, and I speculate that the demand for labor was so high that parents may have been content to accept their daughter back to help on the farm until she got remarried. In fact, lineage daughters' position was strong enough for missionaries to observe that uxorilocal marriages occurred, albeit at an unknown frequency (Ankermann 1929: 124).

There is indirect evidence for the use of divorce as leverage by women. Divorce must have been devastating for a man, not only with respect to food production but also to his ability to obtain cattle.[7] There was a marked difference in divorce rates between the eastern agricultural side and the dry, primarily pastoral, western side of the mountain. In the former districts, especially in Gonja (the most densely populated and trade-oriented district), divorce is reported to have been very common. Women usually initiated it, on many general grounds, such as lack of personal attention and too little sexual interest by the man, reasons not acceptable on the western side where divorce was uncommon. In the more pastorally oriented economy, women's labor was not as important for access to cattle because of the higher natural growth rates of the large herds and the protected, spacious pastures. Hence, if women in this patriarchal society could make demands on their husbands' affection and could fairly easily divorce, their ability to wield power in the control over household resources must have been relatively great. One may therefore speculate that this leverage was one reason for women's comparatively wide discretion in property management in spite of the husband's and his close male agnates' ownership of all family property.

LABOR EXPLOITATION AND RULES OF EXCHANGE

The gendered exchange rules not only skewed the power relations between women and men, but also enabled wealthy families to exploit the labor of poor men. High labor demands and a scarcity of cattle created incentives for multiple strategies for attaching people to local communities. Many families faced the problem of obtaining enough livestock for the marriages of their male members. If a man had a young daughter, he could obtain a loan with her as security. Either her bridewealth when she married would be turned over to the lender or she could be given to him as a wife. Although such arrangements were onerous for poor households, they still enabled the family to retain its labor force. However, as I discussed above, livestock holdings were subject to extinction and slow natural growth. Hence, only households with access to a large labor force could recoup losses. Others who lacked able-bodied workers had to exchange work at other families' farms for cattle.

In this kin-ordered society, as in many others in eastern Africa (e.g., Håkansson 1994b), it was possible for families wealthy in cattle to obtain labor in the form of pawns (*vazoro* [plural] *mzoro* [singular], Chasu)—men who occupied more or less permanent status as dependents. If a young man could not obtain livestock for bridewealth, he had to borrow cows and goats from a wealthy man.[8] This man paid his bridewealth, and the *mzoro* had to perform agricultural and pastoral work for his patron until he could pay back the debt (Kotz 1922: 95). This was expressed as the wealthy buying the poor. The patron took over the client's father's duties to arrange the marriage (Ankermann 1929: 211). The *mzoro* was not detached from his kin group, and the patron only gained rights in his labor capacity, not his whole person.

Hence, by lending cattle to a young man, the same exchange of equivalencies as in a regular bridewealth transaction took place. The labor power of the pawn benefited the growth and strength of the patron family, and his children were not really his until the cattle had been returned. As predicated by the exchange rule of cattle transfers, the sons of a pawn were said to have belonged to the patron, and he received the bridewealth for the daughters. Pare informants explained these relationships to a German missionary as follows: "The slave does not have the daughters without the wife, he does not have the wife without the borrowed cattle." In that sense the pawn replaced aspects of a wife's duties in his patron's household as long as the livestock were not returned. The repayment of the bridewealth to the patron canceled the pawn's labor dues and affiliated his children to him. Just as in a marriage the value of the work performed by the wife was not redeemable at divorce, so was the work performed by the pawn not counted toward his debt. Only cattle obtained from the pawn's lineage or from the work of his wife could release him from bondage.

It is in this institution that we find the link between the political economy and the jural and ideological structures of kinship. It provides the basis for the existence of the economic and political inequalities that characterized many areas of South Pare. From the jural perspective of kinship, pawnship seems to be outside the realm of kinship—a form of extortion that is hidden behind a language of family and marriage (cf. Bourdieu 1990: 126). However, rather than analyzing bridewealth as a result of bounded groups exchanging rights in cattle and women, it may be possible to see marriage processes as one expression within a wider exchange system of values that encompasses rights in people as well as things. Thus, corporate groups and the particularities of marriage are outcomes of exchange processes based on equivalencies that distribute labor and products (cf. Halperin 1994: 86).

In brief, bridewealth in South Pare transferred affiliated children to the husband and his "lineage" and obligated the wife to produce food and nourish her children and husband. In general terms, the transfer of livestock affected the transfer of a women's reproductive powers, her fertility, to the husband's group along with her power to nourish and raise their descendants. If we assume that the exchanges of cattle for children and labor are not intrinsically bound to a prefigured set of social relationships, the patrilineal structure is only one realization of rules of exchange in Giddens's sense (i.e., techniques or generalizable procedures applied in the enactment/reproduction of social practices). Cattle transfers affected the growth of the group through children and food and wealth for further social perpetuation. The prevalence of pawnship, as for any other institution, should not be seen as a fixed and enduring entity, a social cog as it were, but a result of a coincidence of rules and resources. A scarcity of cattle realized the potential inherent in the structure, and a change in the access to cattle wealth would have drastically reduced the prevalence of pawnship (cf. Håkansson 1994b). We can envisage other contexts for exchanges that produce the same result.

Rules of Exchange and the Transformation of Asu Families

The same exchange logic that produced debt pawns in the precolonial period also applies to women's gender identities. As the ability to bear children cannot benefit the patrilineage, daughters' fertility has to be converted into cattle to cause the lineage to grow and prosper. However, this principle does not by itself necessitate marriage, only that the lineage's daughters must enable its growth. Between eastern African patrilineal societies, gender identities differ with respect to women's relationships to their natal lineages. Elsewhere I have shown that whether or not a woman retains membership in her natal lineage establishes her identity as a social person and defines her rights and obligations vis-à-vis her family of birth, including her siblings. In societies where women maintain their descent group affiliation for life, this identity can be used by them to redefine their social position and establish alternative family forms outside traditional marriage (Håkansson 1994b).

In her recent work among the Asu, Karen Porter (1997) shows that this has indeed been the case on South Pare. Today an increasing number of women are opting out of marriage. Many are poor women with children, who are by virtue of their lineage identity able to reside in their natal homesteads. However, such a daughter is at a disadvantage in laying claim on lineage resources by virtue of not having provided bridewealth and a set of indebted affines. Many women, such as nurses and teachers who have personal sources of income, actually plan their pregnancies to establish themselves without a husband. Instead of bringing bridewealth, they use personal income to assist their families, including helping their brothers with bridewealth payments. Thus, they are able to fulfill their obligations to the growth and prosperity of their natal patrilineage outside marriage by reinterpreting the norm that women must marry, utilizing the underlying rule of exchange contained in the bridewealth transaction (Porter 1997: 298–300). In addition, fathers are increasingly giving unwed daughters with children parcels of lineage land, which are explicitly contemporary expressions of the customary father–daughter *kidisa* gift of brass rings (Porter 1997: 233).

CONCLUSION

This study has shown that gender existed as a binary symbol in Asu cosmology that was central as a transformative power in rituals designed to produce fertility, health, and prosperity through exchange and as institutionalized gift transfers. At the same time, the genders existed as social categories inscribed in kinship and age hierarchies that defined access to property, division of labor, and control over persons. However, it would be wrong to separate these into two separate cultural domains of ideology and behavior. Although the gendered rules of exchange established the superiority of male powers over female, the economic consequences of cattle accumulation based on intensive cultivation in turn produced material resources and economic necessities that women could use to increase their own power over people and counteract male dominance.

Gender is not a static category but an expression of powers that could be harnessed through agency in the material world. Agency was based on a combination of the exchange rules expressed in the econo-cosmological model and the resources (material and social) available to actors. Although men were superior to women with respect to their control over both cosmological and material resources, the rules of exchange allowed for more complex relationships of subordination and domination, depending on the social and economic resources available to individuals. Hence, men could become debt pawns, and women could become powerful grandmothers—or today, single mothers.

However, this is not to say that structural properties remain unchanged. Unfortunately, Giddens does not address how rules change other than through large-scale changes in social practices, "de-routinization," by which he means any influence that counteracts the taken for granted character of day-to-day interaction (1994 [1979]: 220f). Although this is not the place for an extended discussion of these issues, it is important to recognize that for the concept of rules to be of theoretical use, how they change must be clearly operationalized.

Despite these difficulties, there is a value in exploring the rules of exchange in economic anthropology. Through this approach it becomes possible to combine institutional and cultural contexts of kin-ordered societies with individual agency without analytically restricting production and exchange to use values and symbolic dramatizations. That is, cosmological schemes reveal the principles that are part of institutional reproduction over time as instanced by the behavior of individuals. Gift economies are differently constituted with respect to exchange principles and gender relationships. This observation does not lead to relativism but to the claim that analysis must focus on processes in order to understand the interrelationship between agency and rules. As Barth (1982: 62) suggested long ago, it is more fruitful to compare social processes than social forms, in that the former specifies the necessary interconnections of elements over time.

NOTES

1. Field research was conducted in South Pare during June–August 1989 and June–August 1995. Archival research was conducted in the Archive of the Evangelical Lutheran Mission in Leipzig, Germany, 1994. The research was supported by the Swedish Agency for Research Cooperation with Developing Countries (SAREC), and the University of Kentucky. I would like to thank Stephen Kitua and the Bombo family for their generous assistance in the field. Thanks are also due to the pastors and administrators of the Evangelical Lutheran Church of Pare for their help with housing and field assistants.

2. This approach is in many ways similar to Fredrik Barth's theory of social organization and change (Barth 1982). For Barth, institutions and social processes are made up of individuals who transact values but are constrained and enabled in their activities by norms that regulate access to both human and material resources.

3. Östberg argues that the expansion of furrows attracted immigrants, who were welcome because they strengthened the community. They made expansion of the irrigation system both necessary and possible. As the Marakwet settlements expanded, their social organization (rights to land and water, the nature of corporate groups, and labor mobilization) became intertwined with their irrigation system. In addition, the presence of pastoralists in the region made any accumulation of cattle by the Marakwet a target for raids, thereby actually preventing any transformation of cultivators to pastoralism. This explanation provides an excellent starting point for the development of a more general model of agricultural intensification in eastern Africa.

4. In Chome, the only chiefdom on the western side of South Pare, the chief was not a rainmaker. He was only a cooling, *kuhoja*, expert but was not in high demand at home. Indeed, Chome chiefs spent much time traveling to Usambara and Kilimanjaro to give cooling rituals. Rainmaking in Chome, as in the rest of the western slopes, was in the hands of clan specialists (Kimambo 1969: 90–91).

5. In his recent excellent analysis of irrigation in neighboring North Pare, Sheridan (2002) shows a similar connection among irrigation, water, and male fertility symbolism.

6. Although women have use rights to plots owned by their natal lineages, Porter (1997: 277) also reports that a woman's land could be passed on to her children but not to her husband. Somewhat obliquely, she writes that a daughter's or a sister's plot was reclaimed by the rightful lineage descendants in the third generation. This may be understood in the light of two facts. Porter mentions that it is common for neighboring lineages to have intermarried for several generations. If we add to this that the early missionary claimed that cross-cousin marriage was common, patrilateral cross-cousin marriage (from the woman's point of view) would transfer female plots to the originating lineage after three of four generations, depending on the number of inter-marrying lineages.

7. If a man was on good terms with his wife, she could assist him in obtaining cattle for a second wife, through the production of crops for exchange for livestock. A mother's accumulation of livestock for her sons' marriages was, of course, also in her husband's interest by increasing his number of descendants.

8. Such cattle loans are expressed as being made by men because of their capacity as formal guardians of family/lineage property. However, wealthy women could also obtain debt pawns, although the transaction formally went though a senior male. The pawn was expected to work primarily for the wife, who contributed the cattle.

REFERENCES

Allen, James de Vere. 1993. *Swahili Origins*. Athens, Ohio: Ohio University Press.

Ankermann, Bernard. 1929. *Das Eingeborenrecht: Ostafrika*. Stuttgart, Germany: Strecker und Schröder.

Barth, Fredrik. 1982. *Process and Form in Social Life*. London: Routledge and Kegan Paul.

Bourdieu, Pierre. 1990. *The Logic of Practice*. Palo Alto, Calif.: Stanford University Press.

Clark, Gracia. 1994. *Onions Are My Husband*. Chicago: Chicago University Press.

Dannholz, Jakob J. 1916. *Im Banne des Geisterglaubens*. Leipzig: Evangelsich Lutherishes Mission.

———. 1989. *Lute luvivi-lwedi* (The Curse and the Blessing; English translation of original German manuscript written between 1912 and 1918, Lute der Fluch). Manuscripts at the Evangelischer Lutherishes Mission, Leipzig, and with Erika Dannholz, Bishofwiesen, Germany.

———. n.d. *Kinderlosigkeit und Säuglingssterblichkeit bei den Wasu in Deutch Ostafrika*. Manuscript in the Evangelical Lutheran Mission Archives, Leipzig.

Donham, Donald. 1990. *History, Power, Ideology*. Cambridge: Cambridge University Press.

Giddens, Anthony. 1984. *The Constitution of Society*. Oxford, U.K.: Blackwells.

———. 1994 [1979]. *Central Problems in Social Theory*. Berkeley: University of California Press.

Gregory, Chris A. 1982. *Gifts and Commodities*. Cambridge, U.K.: Cambridge University Press.

Gudeman, Stephen. 1986. *Economics as Culture*. London: Routledge and Kegan Paul.

Guth, W. 1932. "Die Sippe bei den Vaasu." *Evangelischer Missions Magazin, Neue Folge* 76: 386–91.

Håkansson, N. Thomas. 1988. *Bridewealth, Women, and Land: Social Change Among the Gusii of Kenya.* Uppsala Studies in Cultural Anthropology 10. Stockholm, Sweden: Almquist & Wiksell International.

———. 1989. "Social and Political Aspects of Intensive Agriculture in East Africa: Some Models from Cultural Anthropology." *Azania* 24: 12–20.

———. 1990. "The Appropriation of Fertility: Descent and Sex among the Gusii." In *The Creative Communion: African Folkmodels of Life and Fertility,* ed. by Anita Jacobson-Widding and Walther van Beek, Uppsala Studies in Cultural Anthropology 14, 187–99. Stockholm: Almquist and Wiksell International.

———. 1994a. "Grain, Cattle, and Power: The Social Process of Intensive Cultivation and Exchange in Precolonial Western Kenya." *Journal of Anthropological Research* 50: 249–76.

———. 1994b. "The Detachability of Women: Gender and Kinship in Processes of Socio-Economic Change among the Gusii of Kenya." *American Ethnologist* 21: 516–38.

———. 1995. Irrigation, Population Pressure, and Exchange in Precolonial Pare, Tanzania. *Research in Economic Anthropology* 16: 297–323.

———. 1998. "Rulers and Rainmakers in Pre-Colonial South Pare, Tanzania: The Role of Exchange and Ritual Experts in Political Fragmentation." *Ethnology* 37: 263–83.

Halperin, Rhoda H. 1994. *Cultural Economies Past and Present.* Austin: University of Texas Press.

Jacobson-Widding, Anita. 2000. *Chapungu: The Bird that Never Drops a Feather.* Uppsala Studies in Cultural Anthropology 28. Uppsala, Sweden: Acta Universitatis Upsaliensis.

Kimambo, Isaria N. 1969. *A Political History of the Pare of Tanzania c. 1500–1900.* Nairobi: East African Publishing House.

Kjekshus, Helge. 1977. *Ecology Control and Economic Development in East African History.* Berkeley: University of California Press.

Kotz, Ernst. 1922. *Im Banne der Furcht: Sitten und Gebrauche der Wapare in Ostafrika.* Hamburg: Advent Verlag.

Lebulu, J. L. 1979. "Religion as the Dominant Element of the Superstructure Among the Pare of Tanzania. *Social Compass* 26: 417–59.

Mace, Ruth. 1993. "Transitions between Cultivation and Pastoralism in Sub-Saharan Africa." *Current Anthropology* 34: 363–82.

Mauss, Marcel. 1990. *The Gift.* London: Routledge.

Moore, Henrietta. 1986. *Space, Text, and Gender.* Cambridge, U.K.: Cambridge University Press.

Munn, Nancy D. 1986. *The Fame of Gawa.* New York: Cambridge University Press.

Nurse, Derek, and Thomas Spear. 1985. *The Swahili.* Philadelphia: University of Pennsylvania Press.

Omari, Cuthbert K. 1990. *God and Worship in Traditional Asu Society.* Germany: Verlag der Evangelischer Lutherischen Mission.

Östberg, Wilhelm. In Press. "The Expansion of Marakwet Hill–Furrow Irrigation: A Historical Interpretation from the Kerio Valley, Kenya." In *Islands of Intensive Agriculture in the East African Rift and Highlands: A 500-Year Perspective,* ed. by Mats Widgren and John Sutton. London: James Currey.

Porter, Karen A. 1997. *Kinship and Community in South Pare, Tanzania.* Unpublished Ph.D. dissertation, University of Rochester.

Sheridan, Michael J. 2002. "An Irrigation Intake Is Like a Uterus: Culture and Agriculture in Precolonial North Pare, Tanzania." *American Anthropologist* 104: 79–92.

Soper, Robert. 1967. "Iron Age Sites in North-eastern Tanzania. *Azania* 2: 19–36.

Strathern, Marilyn. 1988. *The Gender of the Gift.* Berkeley: University of California Press.

Taylor, Christopher C. 1992. *Milk, Honey, and Money.* Washington, D.C.: Smithsonian Institution Press.

von Rothenan, D. 1966. *Bodennutzung und Viehhaltung im Sukumaland, Tanzania.* Munich: IFO.

Udvardy, Monica L. 1995. "The Lifecourse of Property and Personhood: Provisional Women and Enduring Men among the Giriama of Kenya." *Research in Economic Anthropology* 16: 325–48.

Weiner, Annette B. 1992. *Inalienable Possessions.* Berkeley: University of California Press.

Wilk, Richard R. 1996. *Economies and Cultures: Foundations of Economic Anthropology.* Boulder, Colo.: Westview Press.

Yoshida, Masao. 1985. "Traditional Furrow Irrigation Systems in the South Pare Area." In *Opportunities for Irrigation Development in Tanzania,* ed. by Adolfo Mascarhenas, James Ngana, and Masao Yoshida, 33–114, Tokyo: Institute of Developing Economies.

3

Woman-Headed Households in Agrarian Societies: Not Just a Passing Phase

Evelyn Blackwood

The concept of the "matrifocal" or "women-centered" household held the center of attention in kinship studies in anthropology in the 1970s and then faded from view. It reappeared in development planning, where it has taken on a life of its own under the name of "woman-headed households." Although anthropologists laid solid groundwork for an understanding of woman-headed households, a number of misperceptions and hidden assumptions persist both in anthropology and development studies concerning woman-headed households. It is time for the issue to be revisited.

The problems I address in this chapter are twofold: the first concerns what I call the "conjugal bias" in household studies.[1] This bias, which assumes that the conjugal couple forms the core and central bond of the household, has limited anthropologists' ability to make sense of other forms of household relationships, in particular those organized around kin ties. The second problem is the assumption that where men are present in households, they will have headship of those houses. This assumption leads to the representation of the woman-headed household as a deviation from the norm, or as a short-term solution to men's absence, rather than as a viable form of household. In an effort to disentangle some of the knots in the analysis of woman-headed households, I draw on my work on rural Minangkabau in West Sumatra, Indonesia, in which the majority of households are headed by women and based on a dominant mother-daughter bond.

I argue for a kinship model of households based on the primary kin relationship in the household rather than on the presence or absence of a man who is the breadwinner or head. By revisiting the concepts of matrifocality and household headship, I rethink the way woman-headed households are categorized and shift the theoretical lens away from conjugal couples and the presence or absence of men to the larger set of women's kin relations upon which such households are constituted.

DEFINING WOMAN-HEADED HOUSEHOLDS

In anthropological and household literature, woman-headed households have been variously defined as households headed by women without (permanent) men partners or by women who are the primary economic contributors (due to inconsistent contributions from men). Anthropological research in the 1950s and 1960s associated woman-headed households with men's absence. For instance, anthropologists who studied Afro-Caribbean cultures categorized households into three types, according to the presence or absence of a male partner. There were stable unions (common law marriages), visiting unions (temporary relationships in which the man occasionally stays with the woman), and single women (no boyfriend) households. Each of these households was defined by the woman's relationship with a man. Visiting union households were said to be "unstable" due to men's irregular presence and contributions to these households. Men's lengthy absences due to labor migration and/or poor economic conditions were blamed for "forcing" these women to take charge of their households. These representations underscore the analytical importance attributed to the conjugal couple in the definition of households by earlier theorists.

Anthropologists who visited questions of woman-headed households in the 1970s focused attention on relations through women in these households (see, among others, Smith 1996; Tanner 1974; Yanagisako 1977; Lamphere 1974). Exploring the variations in domestic networks oriented around kinswomen, these writers developed a more nuanced understanding of gender relations in woman-headed households. Smith (1996), who used the term "matrifocal" to identify these households, argued that in African-descended households in working-class British Guiana, mothers, children, and daughters' children formed a solidary unit that persisted whether or not a husband was present. Because conjugal relations were expected to be less solidary (due to the uncertainties of economic employment for men), they were less important than matrifocal ties in the household. Tanner defined matrifocal households as those in which the mother role was central and women have "relative equality in economic and ritual domains" (1974: 131). Such households, she argued, could occur in any kinship or residence system. Yanagisako's (1977) research on women-centered kin networks in urban industrial societies showed that women often form the core kin relations within and beyond the household, even in societies where men are culturally identified as heads of households. By focusing on women's relations, these works pushed the concept of woman-headed households beyond the limited notion of husband-absent.

Despite anthropological work showing the importance of ties centered on women in matrifocal households, research in anthropology and development studies continues to evoke an image of woman-headed households as households manqué. The persistence of this model is due in part to the analytical separation that emerged between matrifocal households and woman-headed households. Because husbands could be present and even head matrifocal households, theorists argued that matrifocal households and woman-headed households were not the same thing (see Tanner 1974; Smith 1996). Ironically, Tanner herself, whose major ethnographic work was on the Minangkabau, never used the term "woman-headed" to identify Minangkabau households. This analytical separation sidestepped the issue of woman-headed households, leaving unresolved the question of what constitutes these households. Because woman-headed households fell between the cracks analytically, their definition as husband-absent and economically unstable remained in place.

A woman-headed household continues to be seen as one in which women who are single, divorced, widowed, separated, or have long-absent migrant husbands are responsible for the care of their families (Geisler 1993). This scenario suggests that women take charge only in situations when they cannot rely on men to provide sufficient or reliable income (for the Caribbean, see Massiah 1990), or where patriarchal constraints are intolerable (see Tinker 1990; Kabeer 1994; Moore 1988; Obbo 1990). Kabeer notes that, in India, women who are unhappy with household production and consumption priorities may "withdraw cooperation from the male headed households, to live separately and head their own households" (1994: 127). She calls this refusal to participate in the husband's household "voting with their feet." In her reading, the woman-headed household is a rejection of patriarchy, a conscious decision to assert independence. Yet these new households are apparently borne out of necessity and are perhaps only temporary refuges until a more satisfactory conjugal relationship can be established, thus perpetuating the idea that woman-headed households are simply a phase.

Woman-headed households seem to be irrevocably tied to the presence or absence of men, their contributions, or their compassion. In discussing the apparent increase in woman-headed households worldwide in the latter part of the twentieth century, Moore sums up the situation: "the evidence is complex, but it seems that female-headed households are common in situations of urban poverty; in societies with a high level of male labor migration; and in situations where general insecurity and vulnerability prevail" (1988: 63). Her analysis suggests that woman-headed households result from unstable economic conditions, such as a marginal or migrant economy, where men are either absent or unable to contribute adequately to the household. The representation of woman-headed households as strategies to deal with men's absence suggests that the ideal is a household oriented around a conjugal couple. This ideal inadvertently reinforces the normality of the nuclear family and the primacy of the conjugal bond. It suggests that in normal or stable economic conditions, a household will have a husband present and thus an intact conjugal couple who form the core of the household. In order to defuse this model, I build on the theory of matrifocality to explore what else might be going on in woman-headed households. In the following, I examine household relations in a matrilineal society in West Sumatra, Indonesia in order to rethink the question of woman-headed households.

MATRIKIN IN A MINANGKABAU VILLAGE

The Minangkabau living in West Sumatra numbered approximately 3.8 million in 1990.[2] Part of the Indonesian state, they are the largest matrilineal group in the world. Minangkabau matriliny is neither "traditional" (fixed in the past) nor disappearing, but a continually reconstituted system of kinship, inheritance, and land rights vested in women. In this matrilineal society, ancestral property (*harta pusaka*), which includes rice lands, house land, and the big house (lineage house), is passed down from mother to daughters. My analysis is based on research I conducted in the wet-rice farming village of Taram in the easternmost district of West Sumatra. Taram's population in 1989 was approximately 6,800. I focused on one hamlet of 125 households, which I call Tanjung Batang.[3]

Minangkabau households, though varied in composition, in many instances fit the rubric of woman-headed households. Before analyzing these households, however, it is important to understand the way matrilineal ideology organizes household relations. The terms Minangkabau use to talk about household matters are terms of kinship, not family. Big houses owned by elite families are identified with the members of the sublineage (*kaum*) living in it, which usually include a senior woman, her daughters, and her daughters' children.[4] Members of the sublineage extend beyond the big house to include married sons and mother's brothers who reside with their wives' families. The sublineage is also part of a larger lineage (*payuang*) and clan (*suku*). Elite sublineages hold common rights to the house, to ancestral rice land, and to a title for the senior man. Land cannot be alienated (sold) without group consent, but women of the sublineage have different rights in land and houses than men. The practice of matrilineal inheritance means that women are heirs to and in control of matrilineal property. Daughters inherit the rights to land; sons may be given use rights if land is available and their mothers are willing to help them out, but they cannot pass on matrilineal land to their children. Senior women, as lineage heads, have the right to the use, distribution, income, and disposition of the land (see also Pak 1986).[5]

As elder of the lineage, the senior woman controls land, including house, garden, and rice land. The senior man (mother's brother or son) holds the title of the sublineage and is involved in the activities and affairs of his natal kin, but he does not reside with the group. As long as he is married, he lives with his wife's family. As future inheritors of both land and house, daughters share a common interest in their mother's land as well as in the status of their sublineage.[6]

What do these kinship relations mean for conjugal couples in individual households? The data that I collected on Minangkabau households shows that although a few woman-headed households have no husband present, the typical extended household with an intact conjugal couple is woman-headed and organized around the dominant mother-daughter relationship. These households highlight the importance of women's kin ties to the composition and structure of woman-headed households.

THE MATRIHOUSE

To investigate the relationship between matrilineal kin ties and women-headed households, I look at the two main forms of Minangkabau household: extended and nuclear households. Extended households comprised of three or more generations made up 26 percent of all households, and nuclear households of wife, husband, and children made up 35 percent of all households (see figure 3.1).[7] Extended households were usually composed of a senior woman, her husband, her married and unmarried daughters, and her daughters' husbands and children. Despite the fact that some daughters choose to move out of their mother's houses, most senior women have a daughter living with them, who will remain in her mother's house and become the senior woman of the house after her mother's death. I focus on the twenty-eight extended households in 1990 in which a senior woman and her married daughter were present. These households I call matrihouses (meaning matrilineally affiliated houses) to highlight the importance of the generations of women in the household, in particular the mother-daughter relationship.

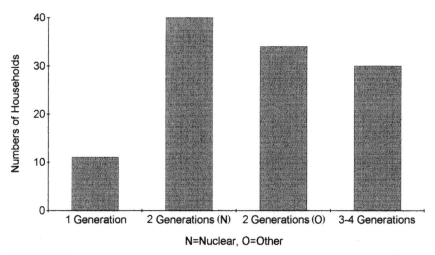

FIGURE 3.1
Household composition.

The extended household or matrihouse does not look like a woman-headed household as they are typically defined, because a husband, either the mother's or the daughter's, is present in most of the matrihouses (86 percent). Going by the standard definition of household head, which is usually determined by a husband's presence or absence, Minangkabau households in large part would be considered headed by men because of the husband's presence. In fact, the Indonesian state supports a Western definition of households as nuclear and man-headed regardless of the particular configuration of households found in the many ethnic groups that make up Indonesia. When registering their families as required by the state, household members must fill out a form that lists "household head" and "wife" as the main two categories for adults (see Blackwood 1995). That is not, however, an accurate representation of household relations. In these households, headship is not a function of men's presence or absence. Rather than relying on such a simplistic rendering of households, the factors related to headship, which include women's kin ties, must take center stage in understanding the nature of woman-headed households.

Factors that I used to determine household headship included: who is the proprietor of the house; on whose lineage land does the house stand (kinship relation); who owns/controls or has access to the land on which household production is dependent (through which kin); and on what other resources (wages, remittances, trade, business) are household members dependent. Another important element of matrihouse relations is the relationships among the women in the household.

In matrihouses, the senior woman controls and manages household land and income from that land, and she expects her daughter's assistance in working the land.[8] A daughter in an extended household shares with her mother the kitchen and food consumed. She raises her children in her mother's house and over time will take on more responsibilities in the household, eventually taking over for her mother. Women in these households say that they are one; they all have the same interests. In seventeen of the extended households (61 percent), mother and daughter operate as a single unit, sharing all the produce from the land. In the other eleven households (39 percent), the daughter controls some of her own land, which she has received either from her mother or a male relative or affine (her father, a titled man [penghulu], or her husband). (See figure 3.2 for sources of all land owned or controlled by the matrihouse.) She uses the income from that land for her own projects, while income from the remaining household land is used jointly. Her husband may provide her additional income as well, which I will discuss more fully later.

A look at the productive labor practices of an extended household will clarify the matrilineal relationship within it. Senior women have access to the labor of their husbands and older children, including unmarried or recently

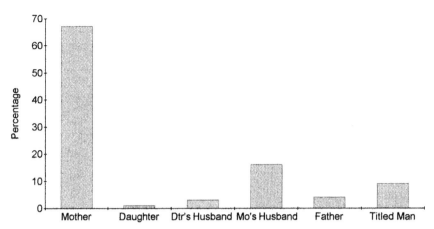

FIGURE 3.2
Sources of land for matrihouses (n=28).

married daughters and sons. Labor arrangements between mother and daughter depend in large part on the life cycle phase or wealth of the family, but generally a married daughter living in her mother's house works with her mother on her mother's land. A daughter's labor on household plots is not recompensed with wages. Where both mother and daughter are of working age, they work their fields together. If the daughter has small children at home, her mother may work the fields, or alternatively, the daughter may work while her mother takes care of the grandchildren. Elderly mothers retire from working in their fields and let their daughters manage the fields themselves. Some wealthy families, who have their land sharecropped for them, only need to oversee the work on the land, sending a daughter to collect the produce and pay the workers at harvest. Married sons assist their mothers with plowing and harvesting, particularly if the father is too old to continue plowing. If a daughter has some land of her own, she may engage in exchange labor with her mother, both working on the other's land for free. In some cases a daughter may work her mother's land for her and give half of the income (split) from the harvest to her mother.

If a daughter has income from her husband or her own land, then this income is usually treated as hers alone to do with as she wants. She may use it to purchase gold jewelry, which then acts as a form of savings against some later need or emergency, such as ceremonies, repairs, or additions to the house. Although it is her own income, besides being used for the needs of her own family, it is also used jointly for the benefit of the whole household. In fact, trying to distinguish between mother's and daughter's interests in the household is often difficult, as the house will ultimately belong to the daughter.

IN-MARRIED MEN

As an in-married man, a husband is considered a permanent guest in his wife's house. Because he does not belong to his wife's sublineage, he is marginal to the affairs of the kin group carried on in that house, such as ceremonial events and matters of the sublineage. He cannot make decisions concerning his wife's lineage affairs, although he may be asked his opinion, especially where it concerns their children. His wife, on the other hand, is concerned with maintaining and improving the status of her sublineage, a concern that her husband shares only peripherally.

Husbands are expected to contribute income or labor to the household. Most of their contributions go toward their children's needs and schooling costs, but they also assist financially in ceremonial events for their wives' matrilineages, particularly if one involves their children. For instance, they will be asked to buy the animals to be butchered for a circumcision or wedding. This assistance is a benefit to the wife's matrilineal group as a whole. A husband has little authority over the children he and his wife produce; nor does he have any control over his wife's land, even if they work it together. If a couple builds a house for themselves and their children, the house is considered the woman's property, even if the husband used his earnings to build it. At divorce, a husband leaves everything behind and returns to his mother's house.

Husbands in matrihouses engage in a range of income-producing activities. Those who are farmers (44 percent are engaged in agricultural work) are expected to provide labor on the household's rice fields (clearing, plowing, harvesting). A number of men work with their wives on land that their wives sharecrop or control themselves. A wife does not pay her husband for working on her land; it is considered his contribution to her household, and he is, of course, fed in her house. Some men provide income by hiring themselves out as agricultural laborers, usually for plowing, but others have salaried or wage labor jobs outside the village. Men from wealthier families tend to have higher-status jobs, such as civil service or contracting; they usually give part of their income to their wives but do not provide any field labor for the wife's household. Others, particularly younger men, work on road construction or building projects for which they are away from home part of the year, returning periodically to visit and give some of their wages to their families.

In addition to providing cash from wage labor, husbands who have access to land through their mothers make some of that land available to their wives. Men's access to land depends in large part on the strength of the tie with their own mothers. Except for titled men, who are usually given one piece of rice land for their lineage duties, men depend on their mothers for use rights to land (although in one case, four sons were given land to share by their father). Men do not have automatic access to land, but approximately 40 percent of men in matrihouses bring to their marriages some rice land. They may use this land in a variety of ways. If a man's mother is wealthy, her son may keep all the income from the field for his wife's family, or he may set aside some for expenses associated with his matrilineage. In some cases a husband and wife may work his land themselves, or the wife may take charge of her husband's land and hire outside labor to do the plowing while the husband engages in other business. An older man may sharecrop the land out, sometimes to a sister or niece who will work the land for him and split the produce with him.[9]

In extended households, husbands' contributions of land (including both mothers' and daughters' husbands) constitute about 19 percent of the land that these households have access to, the bulk of that coming from the mother's husband (see figure 3.2 above). All together, male relatives and affines (fathers as well as husbands) contribute 32 percent of the land that matrihouses control. Consequently, in the majority of matrihouses men's income is supplemental to that of their wives or mothers-in-law.

Husbands, then, provide some income to extended households, but the primary income comes from land owned or controlled by the women of the matrihouse. In my study, only one extended household was supported by the husband's income; this was because the wife had pawned all her land for lineage affairs and had no income left for her household. Whatever the source of income, the husband's money is used to pay for the costs associated with childrearing, so it primarily helps to support the nuclear unit within the larger household. Despite bringing in some land or other income to the wife's household, however, a husband remains a subsidiary member of the extended household.

Whereas women's primary relation is to their matrilineal group, men's relations are divided between their natal and conjugal households. A married son or brother resides in his wife's house, but a small room is set aside in his natal home in case of his return upon divorce or death of his wife. As sons, men are expected to protect the interests and status of the matrilineage. Consequently, men are oriented to two groups, their natal group and their wives' households.

Husbands play a significant role as nonresident members of their own lineage, providing cash, labor, or other assistance if needed. Men farmers split their time between working their mother's land, working on their wives' land, and working for wages. A son provides some labor for his mother, even after marriage, without expecting pay, particularly if he is from a poorer family, but he may stop if a sister has married a man who can take his place assisting his mother. A man who works as a tenant on his mother's land will give half of his income from the land to his mother and the other half to his wife's household. Brothers or uncles who are well-off or have access to rice land (usually because they have few or no elder kinswomen) will give money or rice to their sisters' children when they need help or for projects such as building a new house. Because a man has some discretion in how his earned income is spent, he is often torn between assisting his natal household or his wife's household.

Although husbands are present in these houses, they cannot be considered heads of households. Headship, defined as ownership and control of the house and its resources, belongs to the senior woman.[10] Because of matrilineal inheritance practices, most Minangkabau women own or possess the house, which is almost always on matrilineal land. In many cases, the woman's land is the primary source of income for the family. For the extended household of a senior woman, in which a husband is a permanent guest in her lineage house supported by her rice land, the senior woman is the head of household. Even in poorer households with no land of their own, if the woman provides access to land through her matrilineal kin ties, these houses are woman-headed.

Further, it is the mother's relationship with her daughter, not her husband, that constitutes the core relationship in the extended household. Mother and daughter(s) share ongoing rights in and control over the house, the land, and its produce, which constitutes the primary source of income. Although husbands provide important additional sources of income and labor for their wives' households, these contributions are understood as a husband's duty to his wife's family. His contributions help to support the matrihouse. The conjugal relationship of wife and husband is subsidiary to the matrilineal relationship in the household because as a couple they do not have authority or control over household interests. A normative Minangkabau household is based on the mother-daughter bond.

NUCLEAR PROLIFERATION

The picture of Minangkabau household relations would be incomplete, however, without a discussion of nuclear households. A nuclear household as I define it here is made up of a wife and husband with or without children. In considering nuclear households, I examine wife's versus husband's economic contributions to determine whether women fall under the headship of their husbands or whether the normative ideal of Minangkabau matrihouses takes precedence. My sample includes all nuclear households of one or two generations in the village. In 40 percent of these households, both wife and husband are farmers who work the land together. In the remainder, husbands work as laborers or in the civil service.

Compared to extended households, husbands in nuclear households contribute more land and thus have some control over household property (see figure 3.3). Yet for all nuclear households, their contribution of land amounts to only 23 percent (as compared to 19 percent in matrihouses); women own or have access to 64 percent of household land. The remainder is land that the couple works or controls together.

Where are women getting this land? To obtain an accurate understanding of resources in nuclear households, it is necessary to look beyond the con-

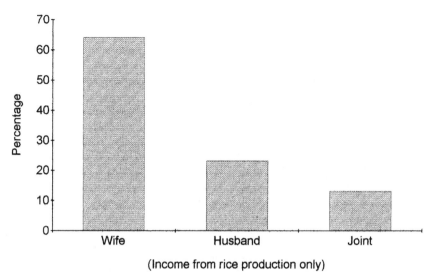

FIGURE 3.3
Income, nuclear households (n=62).

jugal couple to the larger set of matrilineal relations. Most of these women spend the early years of their marriages living in their mother's households with their husbands. During this time couples accumulate savings to build their own houses. When a daughter establishes her own farm household, her mother usually gives her some of the family land in the form of use rights. Once a daughter leaves, mother and daughter do not split the produce from this land. The daughter keeps all of it for her own household. The only exceptions to this pattern were a daughter who sharecropped her mother's land for her, giving her half the produce, and a daughter who managed her own land and also managed her mother's land, splitting the produce with her.

Mothers' contributions of land to daughters make up the largest source of land for nuclear households. Daughters also acquire land on their own either through purchase, pawning in, or redeeming. "Pawning in" entails taking possession of land from someone as security for a loan. Redeeming land means paying back the original loan secured by land that was pawned in the past, in order to take back possession of that land. Daughters acquire cash for land primarily through savings from their own harvests and from husbands' contributions of cash income. Those households that have acquired additional land have husbands with steady wage-earning jobs and wives with adequate ancestral land, meaning that the couple is able to set money aside.[11] Daughters of deceased mothers take charge of all the mother's land, usually splitting it among any living sisters. They may also continue to hold rights to land granted them by their fathers, usually given in the form of a loan to the mother for the life of their offspring.

As with the matrihouse, women in nuclear households control their own land and its income and are considered to be the owners of the house. The figures for women's versus men's land ownership remain relatively consistent from matrihouses to nuclear households (68 percent to 32 percent for matrihouses and 64 percent to 23 percent for nuclear households). Husbands may have separate income or land resources, which they control themselves. But women's greater control of land through matrilineal inheritance rules means that even nuclear households are organized around and dependent primarily on the wife's land.

Woman-headed households constitute 56 percent of all the sixty-two single-family households. The households that do not follow this pattern are land-poor single-family households, in which both spouses contribute more or less equally to household income through agricultural or wage labor, petty trade, or sharecropping. Typically such houses are built from joint contributions or from the husband's income. For women from poor sublineages (with little or no land), their houses may be built on the husband's family land when he has access to some. These houses, which constitute 43 percent of single-family households (23 percent of all households), are "joint" households, meaning neither husband nor wife is head, but both contribute to and make decisions about household resources.[12]

Only one case actually fit the model of a man-headed household in the village. This household was composed of a newcomer family that was in the process of establishing itself in the village. The couple arrived in Taram in 1973, the year they were married. Lacking any kin ties in the village when they arrived, they worked hard to gain the support of a lineage in the village. Now with three children, the wife has no land or income; the husband is the sole wage earner in the family, working as a truck driver delivering goods.[13] The house they live in is rented from the elite lineage that adopted the wife. It sits on the matrilineal land of that lineage. Although this household is currently headed by the husband because he is the primary provider, by establishing matrilineal ties the wife now has connections that may give her and her family greater access to resources in the future. The importance of the matrilineal tie will likely shift her household in the next generation to either a joint household or ultimately a woman-headed household. This case is indicative of a common pattern in which newcomer households work to establish themselves within the matrilineal relationships of the community, eventually producing woman-headed households, the normative ideal for these Minangkabau households.

When women set up nuclear households apart from their mothers, the matrilineal relationship remains embedded in each household. Women still maintain rights to land through the mother, rights that men as husbands lack.

As a husband, a man also lacks rights in produce from his wife's land. Although he has close bonds with his children, they are effectively under the authority of their mother, the senior woman, and the titled man. Women's interests are oriented to matrilineal affairs; much of their surplus income and labor is spent arranging and hosting lineage ceremonies for their own families as well as for members of their sisters' and brothers' families. Sisters also share childcare and work collectively on each other's fields. Thus, nuclear households continue to be part of a much larger network of kin. In these single-family households, husbands are more central and make greater contributions than in matrihouses, but it is still matrilineal relations that structure production, ownership, and access to resources.

Despite the husband's greater prominence in single-family households, he operates within a nexus of matrilineal practices that empower women to appropriate land and resources to their matriline. Husbands are active contributors in nuclear households but do not thereby assume the title of household head. Such a label would disregard the way matrilineal ideology empowers women to control land and resources and the way women use this ideology to configure their houses to their advantage.

THE MATRIHOUSE AND WOMAN-HEADED HOUSEHOLDS

How do households in a matrilineal society help us to rethink the category of woman-headed households? As I pointed out in the beginning of this chapter, representations of woman-headed households tend to portray them as deviations from the normative nuclear family or as short-term solutions to men's absence. Because they are considered temporary substitutes for stable conjugal unions, woman-headed households are not recognized as viable forms of household. The association of woman-headed households with conditions of economic instability underscores the stopgap nature of these households. The implication is that woman-headed households develop only when normative conjugal relations are unsatisfactory and women are forced to seek other means of caring for their families. It is not a desirable or culturally accepted form under "normal" conditions. This woman-headed household model stresses the abnormality of the situation that creates such households.

As the evidence shows for rural Minangkabau, however, woman-headed households are not households manqué. Matrilineal relations situate women and their daughters as central and dominant figures in Minangkabau households. In contrast to the assumptions about woman-headed households, Minangkabau women are not heads by default but have control in every way attributed by researchers to men heads of household. Some Minangkabau researchers have argued that woman-headed households are due to men's migration. Indeed, Minangkabau men (and to a lesser extent, women) are well-known for leaving their home villages in search of fortune (see Naim

1971, 1985). About one in four men migrate from Taram to urban areas, but their ability to leave is dependent primarily on the wealth of their matrikin, who help support the men while they are gone (see Blackwood 2000). Minangkabau women are not making do until their husbands return; in fact, as noted, most households have husbands present. Women support their households through the income from ancestral land and the assistance in labor and resources they receive from their matrikin. Women's headship for these Minangkabau households is not just what happens when men are absent or unable to provide economically. Matrihouses are not the product of economic instability or poverty but the normative form of household for rural Minangkabau.

A similar reading can be made of woman-headed households in the Caribbean, where kinswomen constitute and carry on the household. In working-class British Guiana, the matrifocal, or mother-centered, unit of mothers, children, and daughter's children is the basis of household continuity and security (Smith 1996; see also Bolles 1996). In reality, the households that anthropologists labeled as visiting unions or single-women households are stable households of kinswomen and children in which men play peripheral roles. Such households should not be characterized by what is absent (a contributing man partner) but by what is present: families and households composed of kinswomen—(mothers, daughters, aunts, and children, including sons) who form the primary household relationship.

The term "woman-headed household" is more useful in these cases than the terms "matrifocal" or "woman-centered household," although each has its problems. As Tanner (1974) and Yanagisako (1977) have both shown, a house can be matrifocal, or woman-centered, even if it is headed by a man. "Focality" and "centeredness" simply identify the primary attachments within and beyond the household without saying anything about ownership or control of resources.

Although some use the term "woman-headed household" for those households in which women have "economic responsibility" (see Varley 1996), reliance simply on the identification of who has "economic responsibility" to determine household headship is problematic. Gendered ideologies of power factor into who is culturally identified as "household head," so that headship may not always reside with the biggest contributor. In the Minangkabau case, women provide a large part of household income, and control over that income is also vested in women through matrilineal ideology. In some urban areas of the world, women may provide the bulk of household income, but their husbands are culturally recognized as heads of household (see Benería and Roldán 1987). In nonnuclear households, whether Caribbean or Minangkabau, there may be a number of kin contributing economically; it may even be that a son or daughter makes the major contribution, but the senior woman retains authority over the use and distribution of household income, making her the head of her household. Even though a head may not be providing the most income, she or he may be deferred to in matters of resource management and appropriation. I use the term "woman-headed household" to signify not only that the woman has economic responsibility, but also that she is the dominant figure in the household, either in terms of control over the resources or final authority over household decisions.

The concept of headship remains a problematic concept, however, because it disallows other types of household relations. Woman-headed households as well as man-headed households are limiting concepts that fail to evoke the range of relations occurring within and between households. As shown for some Minangkabau nuclear households, there may not be a single head at all but joint responsibility between wife and husband, a situation that is common in other societies in Asia and Africa as well, where each partner has her or his own resources on which to rely. Household headship also problematically prioritizes conjugal relations within domestic units, because it refers to the headship of either wife or husband. I prefer the term "matrihouse" instead of "woman-headed household" because it signifies that control within the house is through women (passing from mothers to daughters), making the connection between generations of kinswomen and to the senior woman who heads the household.

My model of matrihouses prioritizes kin relations within the household over the conjugal couple. Even nuclear households may have kin ties beyond the conjugal couple that are important to the continuation of the household. The history of the anthropological study of domestic relations, however, has been the history of marriage, conjugal couples, and nuclear families. Anthropologists have mistakenly helped to create the conjugal couple as the linchpin of family and kinship. For instance, anthropologically informed development studies assert that "households are constituted round relationships centered on marriage and parenthood" (Young 1993:114), thus privileging the conjugal bond over other relations within households. Other forms of household that have been labeled "segmented households" illustrate how marital relations are inadvertently prioritized over kin relations. The term "segmented," as used by Kabeer (1994), describes households in which husbands and wives have separate productive activities, but what is missing are the important lineal ties that provide women with their own resources.

Although marriage is, of course, a key social process in all societies, it is important to recognize the conjugal bias that equates domestic relations and households with marriage and child rearing. Recognition of the importance of kin relationships to the formation and maintenance of households helps to shift our conceptual categories away from the (absent) marital one to the primary kin relationship in the household, whether matrilineal (mothers and daughters) or patrilineal (fathers and sons).[14] A kinship model of households emphasizes the relations that descend through the house or extend beyond it through the idiom of kinship rather than the conjugal relations that may be temporary or subordinate to it.

CONCLUSION

My aim in this chapter has been to resolve some of the conceptual issues related to woman-headed households. The Minangkabau case provides some clear solutions because, even when men are present in households, women are heads. These households are not just a passing phase borne out of necessity but arise from the matrilineal practices of rural Minangkabau. Further, these households are organized around a matrilineal relationship represented in the mother-daughter bond. This relationship forms the core of the household; other relationships, including the conjugal one, are subordinate to it.

Rather than prioritizing the marital unit, a kinship model of households recognizes the importance of other ties that women and men develop in creating households and families. There are many possibilities for viewing households and families. The challenge in cross-cultural studies is to avoid simplistic assumptions about what constitutes domestic relations and to improve our understanding of how kin groups operate within households.[15] The assumption that at base most households are nuclear and headed by men would be replaced with the assumption that households are groups of kin operating in a variety of cross-cutting relations, one of which may be the conjugal relation.

ACKNOWLEDGMENTS

This chapter has benefited from the comments of Gracia Clark and the audience at the Society for Economic Anthropology meetings in Bloomington, Indiana, April 20–23, 2000, where I first presented these ideas.

NOTES

1. Thanks to Gracia Clark for helping me clarify this concept.

2. I conducted fieldwork in this area in 1989–1990 and 1996.

3. For a complete account of life in one rural Minangkabau village, see Blackwood (2000).

4. Minangkabau kinship in Taram is divided hierarchically into elites (the original founder clans), client kin (newcomers who have been adopted into elite lineages), and servant kin (families that were formerly owned by elite kin and remain in a subordinate position). Rights to land, titles, and big houses are held only by elites (for more on the Minangkabau ranking system, see Blackwood 2000).

5. Only when there are no female heirs in the sublineage does the control of land revert to the lineage. At the death of the last woman of the sublineage, the senior members of the lineage, both men and women, must decide which of the remaining sublineages will inherit the land. In some cases a senior woman without female heirs who outlives her kinsmen may decide who should inherit the land at her death, in which case the lineage must follow her wishes.

6. For a discussion of the way local, state, and global forces are reorienting households and daughters' desires, see Blackwood (1999).

7. Figures are based on a survey of 115 households in the hamlet of Tanjung Batang, almost all of which were farm households dependent primarily on income from rice fields. The remaining households fell under a variety of different household forms.

8. Lineal rank is also important in household access to resources. Elite households have greater resources and thus are, on average, wealthier than other households. Due to space limitations, I make only brief mention in this chapter of some differences between elite and client households.

9. Approximately 57 percent of all men in Tanjung Batang actually have access to or control land in their own right. This figure is probably higher than the average for the village, however, since more elite men live in Tanjung Batang than in other hamlets in the village. Elite men comprise 75 percent of those men who have use rights to land.

10. Women's headship is also substantiated ideologically in Minangkabau *adat*, which is usually defined as social customs, beliefs, and laws, although *adat* is used by educated urban Minangkabau men to substantiate men's claims to authority and control over the lineage (see Blackwood 2001).

11. I do not have exact figures to show how much income husbands actually contributed to their wives' households due to the fact that people were reluctant to give me information on cash income.

12. By comparison, among elite families, who are the only families with rights to own land in the village, 73 percent of single-family households are woman-headed. The rest are joint households.

13. This pattern is more pronounced in urban areas, where women no longer have control of land and husbands are able to earn better incomes than their wives.

14. Indeed, the conjugal couple in many patrilineal households holds a subordinate role to the patriline of fathers and sons, or brothers. See, for example, Gray (1995), Greenhalgh (1994), and Abu-Lughod (1993).

15. For recent revisions in the study of households, the domestic domain, and women's contributions to social and economic processes, see Brenner (1998) and Carsten (1997).

REFERENCES

Abu-Lughod, Lila. 1993. *Writing Women's Worlds: Bedouin Stories.* Berkeley: University of California Press.

Benería, Lourdes, and Martha Roldán. 1987. *The Crossroads of Class and Gender: Industrial Homework, Subcontracting, and Household Dynamics in Mexico City.* Chicago: University of Chicago Press.

Blackwood, Evelyn. 1995. "Senior Women, Model Mothers, and Dutiful Wives: Managing Gender Contradictions in a Minangkabau Village." In *Bewitching Women, Pious Men: Gender and Body Politics in Southeast Asia,* ed. by Aihwa Ong and Michael Peletz, 124–58. Berkeley: University of California Press.

———. 1999. "Big Houses and Small Houses: Doing Matriliny in West Sumatra." *Ethnos* 64(1): 32–56.

———. 2000. *Webs of Power: Women, Kin, and Community in a Sumatran Village*. Lanham, Md.: Rowman & Littlefield.

———. 2001. "Representing Women: The Politics of Minangkabau *Adat* Writing." *Journal of Asian Studies* 60(1): 125–49.

Bolles, Lynn A. 1996. *Sister Jamaica: A Study of Women, Work, and Households in Kingston*. Lanham, Md.: University Press of America.

Brenner, Suzanne A. 1998. *The Domestication of Desire: Women, Wealth, and Modernity in Java*. Princeton, N.J.: Princeton University Press.

Carsten, Janet. 1997. *The Heat of the Hearth: The Processing of Kinship in a Malay Fishing Community*. Oxford, U.K.: Clarendon Press.

Geisler, Gisela. 1993. "Silences Speak Louder than Claims: Gender, Household, and Agricultural Development in Southern Africa." *World Development* 21(12): 1965–80.

Gray, John N. 1995. *The Householder's World: Purity, Power, and Dominance in a Nepali Village*. Delhi, India: Oxford University Press.

Greenhalgh, Susan. 1994. "The Peasant Household in the Transition from Socialism: State Intervention and its Consequences in China." In *The Economic Anthropology of the State*, ed. by Elizabeth Brumfiel, 43–64. Lanham, Md.: University Press of America.

Kabeer, Naila. 1994. *Reversed Realities: Gender Hierarchies in Development Thought*. London: Verso.

Lamphere, Louise. 1974. "Strategies, Cooperation, and Conflict among Women in Domestic Groups." In *Woman, Culture, and Society*, ed. by Michelle Z. Rosaldo and Louise Lamphere, 97–112. Stanford, Calif.: Stanford University Press.

Massiah, Joycelin. 1990. "Defining Women's Work in the Commonwealth Caribbean." In *Persistent Inequalities: Women and World Development*, ed. by Irene Tinker, 223–38. New York: Oxford University Press.

Moore, Henrietta L. 1988. *Feminism and Anthropology*. Minneapolis: University of Minnesota Press.

Naim, Mochtar. 1971. *Merantau: Minangkabau Voluntary Migration*. Ph.D. dissertation, Australian National University.

———. 1985. "Implications for *Merantau* for Social Organization in Minangkabau." In *Change and Continuity in Minangkabau: Local, Regional, and Historical Perspectives on West Sumatra*, ed. by Lynn Thomas and Franz von Benda Beckmann, 111–17. Athens, Ohio: Ohio University Press.

Obbo, Christine. 1990. "East African Women, Work, and the Articulation of Dominance." In *Persistent Inequalities: Women and World Development*, ed. by Irene Tinker, 210–22. New York: Oxford University Press.

Pak, Ok-Kyung. 1986. *Lowering the High, Raising the Low: The Gender Alliance and Property Relations in a Minangkabau Peasant Community of West Sumatra, Indonesia*. Ph.D. dissertation, Quebec, Canada: Laval University.

Smith, Raymond T. 1996. *The Matrifocal Family: Power, Pluralism, and Politics*. New York: Routledge.

Tanner, Nancy. 1974. "Matrifocality in Indonesia and Africa and among Black Americans." In *Woman, Culture, and Society*, ed. by Michelle Z. Rosaldo and Louise Lamphere, 129–56. Stanford, Calif.: Stanford University Press.

Tinker, Irene. 1990. "A Context for the Field and for the Book." In *Persistent Inequalities: Women and World Development*, ed. by Irene Tinker, 3–13. New York: Oxford University Press.

Varley, Ann. 1996. "Women Heading Households: Some More Equal than Others?" *World Development* 24(3): 505–20.

Yanagisako, Sylvia Junko. 1977. "Women-Centered Kin Networks in Urban Bilateral Kinship." *American Ethnologist* 4: 207–26.

Young, Kate. 1993. *Planning Development with Women: Making a World of Difference.* London: Macmillan.

II

ENTREPRENEURS AS WOMEN

4

Female Entrepreneurship in the Caribbean: A Multisited, Pilot Investigation of Gender and Work

Katherine E. Browne

Women continue to face structural and ideological inequalities across cultures; however, the barriers to women achieving equal status are the result of specific forces, not monolithic constructs. These special forces are associated with assumptions about male breadwinners and female homemakers and can be located at the domestic level, in the workplace, and in state policy. The research presented here involves a preliminary attempt to identify the form and intensity of these assumptions and relate them to patterns in women's entrepreneurship. The focus for this examination involves a pilot study of ninety middle-class women entrepreneurs on three islands of the Caribbean: Puerto Rico (population 3,915,798), Martinique (population 414,516), and Barbados (population 274,540) (CIA 2000).

Female entrepreneurship in the Caribbean offers a particularly useful focus for the analysis of gender and economic outcomes, as women's workforce participation there is among the highest in the developing world (Momsen 1993a: 12). In addition, although the islands of Puerto Rico, Martinique, and Barbados share social histories of both sugar and slavery and the essential features of early integration with the Western capitalist system (Mintz 1977), they vary in ways precisely suited to a comparative analysis of women's status and work. Specifically, these societies demonstrate patterned and significant differences in the degree of female self-employment,[1] the proportion of female-headed households, and the extent of occupational segregation. These patterns are consistent with different social histories characterizing different colonizers (Spanish, French, and British). In addition, the comparative aspect of this work is of special value in the Caribbean where research across cultural and linguistic lines is rare (Hillman and D'Agostino 1992: xv; Mesh 1997: 28),

Reprinted from: *Human Organization* 60(4): 326–42. Copyright © 2001 by the Society for Applied Anthropology.

largely because French, Spanish, British, and Dutch linguistic legacies have balkanized the scholarly literatures. Thus, to create a synthetic base of research across these barriers offers great promise, both in terms of the specific research findings and in terms of the model it may offer future researchers.

In the context of women in development, this study fits into two streams of work. First, the research heeds the call by women and by development scholars to examine gender relations through a household unit of analysis, employing both macrolevel and microlevel data. Second, this research responds to a large and slow-moving paradigm shift related to economic growth in developing countries. An important aspect of this shift involves a growing focus on small-scale entrepreneurs, owners of microenterprises and, specifically, female-owned enterprises, which are noted for their stronger payback rates than male enterprises (Blumberg 1995: 196; Van der Wees and Romijn 1995). The role of microenterprise in planning economic growth has increased in importance, because development efforts at the macro level have generally failed to reverse or even slow poverty in the developing world. This failure has spurred many international development agencies to redirect at least some of their interventions to the microlevel of individuals, groups, and small businesses (Berger 1995: 190; Browne 1996: 225–26).

In spring and summer 1999, a research team of three cultural anthropologists conducted fieldwork in three Caribbean islands as a pilot project on gender and entrepreneurship: Katherine Browne in Martinique, Carla Freeman in Barbados, and Zobeida Bonilla in Puerto Rico. The team completed thirty interviews with female entrepreneurs on each island, for a total of ninety interviews. In addition to structured interviews, this research also incorporates archival data and information supplied by government officials about workplace practices, occupational segregation, and state-level policies and laws. Figure 4.1 shows the research sites from the study.

In spring 2000, the National Science Foundation funded Katherine Browne and Carla Freeman to broaden the scope of this pilot project. The full-scale investigation involves a larger sample, male as well as female entrepreneurs, and a small sample of wage-working women. Fuller-scale data collection began in spring 2001 and will continue for three years. Findings from the 1999 pilot investigation are discussed below.

Pilot research has revealed a number of important findings that suggest both key similarities and differences in female entrepreneurship across these societies. One finding, for example, suggests that the types of women drawn to entrepreneurship vary according to the form of gender role stratification in the home and workplace that exists in their respective societies. These and other findings bear directly on our understandings of how specific patriarchal constraints may lead to specific adaptations among women in the workforce. Findings from this study will also inform development planning efforts, particularly those focused on targeting women and microenterprise develop-

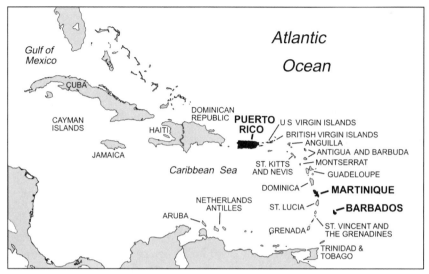

FIGURE 4.1
Caribbean showing the three research sites.

ment. In this chapter, I will review the theoretical grounding for this research, the early findings of the pilot project, and the implications of these findings for the continuing research.

THEORETICAL BACKGROUND

The Status of Women and Work

The proportion of women participating in the world labor force has climbed rapidly since World War II, a climb that is especially evident in Latin America and the Caribbean (Benería and Stimpson 1987; Stichter and Parpart 1990). In this region between 1950 and 1980, the number of working women tripled, but the number of working men only doubled (Berger 1989). In the Caribbean, where women were central economic figures during slavery, recent research demonstrates that they are today among the most active anywhere despite the "developing" status of most of these countries (Momsen 1993a: 12). Still, the strong participation of women in the labor force is overrepresented at the low end of wages and skills and severely underrepresented at the top end and among the self-employed, where many planners believe economic growth is most likely (Benería and Stimpson 1987; Kessler-Harris and Sacks 1987: 75; Momsen 1993a: 3). With such apparent social acceptance of women as full-time economic actors, why have so few achieved economic mobility? Why have so few chosen to create their own businesses?

The answers to those questions are threaded in a complex web of institutional and ideological assumptions about women that trap them in a subordinate status to men in virtually every society. Thus, the international movement of women into the economy has not eroded patriarchal constructs, but has "transformed them instead to meet the requirements of global competition" (Fernández-Kelly and Sassen 1995: 114). According to Nash, social contradictions are the result: "Women's special burden is related to an outmoded patriarchy that no longer sustains the ideology with a material base" (1995: 161). The constraints imposed by the assumptions of patriarchy appear in the differential opportunity structures available for working men and women. For example, the greatest proportion of working women in developing countries has been relegated to low-wage work with minimal opportunities to advance their skills or their earnings (Berger and Buvinic 1987; Blumberg 1995: 195; Rios 1995: 126). Employers realize that women, who are treated as supplementary earners, are willing to take the tedious, low-wage jobs associated with both traditional and offshore assembly and factory work (Acevedo 1995). Although there is no single demographic profile of women recruited for low-wage jobs, women as a group have become the handmaidens of capitalist development in the Third World.

Women and Development

Postwar modernization efforts followed a path that was blind to the role of women or the impacts of development on them (Rios 1995: 125). But in 1970, Esther Boserup published a seminal work that used concrete outcomes from development projects in Africa to challenge the notion that women's status would improve with development. Boserup's alternative theory stimulated a broad new research agenda among social scientists to discover how women were "marginalized" in the production process or "exploited" as cheap labor (Etienne and Leacock 1980; Fernández-Kelly 1983).

Since then, many researchers have attempted to identify the critical factors that empower women. Recent work suggests that these factors cannot be reduced to the fact of earning income but may involve the degree to which this income contributes to the household economy (Benería and Roldán 1987), the degree to which a woman has control of it (Blumberg 1991; Friedl 2000), or the degree to which a woman's income frees her from the burden of primary responsibility for domestic maintenance (Stichter and Parpart 1990: 7). However, in the Caribbean (and increasingly elsewhere), a high proportion of female-headed households and economically active women coexist with an ideology of patriarchy[2] (see Massiah 1993; Scott 1990; Smith 1988: 134). Thus, the status of women in household decision making often remains subordinate, despite their high levels of involvement in paid employment (Momsen 1993a: 1; Moses 1977; Stichter 1990: 59).

Methodologically, researchers now argue that women's position in the economy and their status generally need to be understood in terms of gender relations and, specifically, how these relations at home contribute to differential economic outcomes for women and men (Acevedo 1995; Browne 1997; Espinal and Grasmuck 1997: 104). The present research is explicitly developed to promote these research strategies by using a household unit of analysis.

The Value of Studying Entrepreneurship as It Relates to Gender

Against a Caribbean backdrop in which women are strongly represented in the workforce yet lack the economic mobility and decision-making authority of men, female entrepreneurship offers a unique and underexamined analytical vantage point. A comparative study of entrepreneurship may reveal much about how gender biases at home, in the workplace, and at the state level are differently embedded and negotiated, both across class and across societies. Such a study will advance our understanding of the relationship between economic patterns and gendered institutions and ideologies. In turn, this knowledge may be used to address the needs of planners interested in designing sustainable, relevant, and bias-free development programs for women.

There are several reasons why the focus on entrepreneurship is useful. First, although research suggests that female and male entrepreneurs share basic personality characteristics (confidence, orientation to risk, achievement orientation), women may have a special incentive to be self-employed: to eliminate the barriers imposed by an employer, such as the "glass ceiling" or occupational segregation (McKay 1993: 278; Van der Wees and Romijn 1995: 63; Wells 1998). Moreover, research suggests that women entrepreneurs are motivated by different interests than men and that their patterns of work organization and growth management are also gender-specific (Barahona 1995: 147; Blumberg 1995: 207; Espinal and Grasmuck 1997; GEMINI and Rubio 1991). Therefore, female entrepreneurs provide a powerful focus for asking questions about the role of patriarchal institutions and ideologies in shaping women's opportunities to achieve economic autonomy (production and control of resources) and economic mobility (success in increasing business assets and profits).

Second, in recent years an increasing emphasis on neoliberal, market-oriented solutions to economic problems in developing societies has led to an embrace of the potential role of entrepreneurship. Without exception, the government officials and business leaders in each society in this study greeted the 1999 pilot project with enthusiastic support. Because each island is attempting to promote entrepreneurship, many highly placed contacts have expressed serious interest in our research results. As a single example, CentroUnido, Puerto Rico's largest professional association of business owners, hosted a week-long international summit in the summer of 1999 for female entrepreneurs in Latin America. Moreover, economists and development planners in agencies including USAID, the World Bank, the Inter-American Development Bank, and the International Labour Organization (ILO) agree that the growth of entrepreneurship is now considered vital to a strong economy (Berger 1997; Blumberg 1995: 195; GEMINI and Rubio 1991; ILO 1972, 1994; Van der Wees and Romijn 1995: 45). For this reason, the study of female entrepreneurship where there is strong female participation in the workforce offers practical implications for planners who spend billions of dollars to nurture this segment of a society.

Third, there is little gender-based work on this topic. The literature that does exist is primarily drawn from patterns studied in the United States that are focused on male entrepreneurs and are more often psychological than social in focus (Wells 1998: 31). Entrepreneurial patterns by gender need to be explored in developing economies and other cultural contexts to determine whether women can best help themselves economically by acting entrepreneurially.

PATTERNS AND LEGACIES OF GENDERED WORK IN THE CARIBBEAN

Intra-Caribbean Variations in Labor Force Participation

Puerto Rico, Martinique, and Barbados, colonized respectively by Spain, France, and England, share a history of slavery in a monocrop plantation economy. Today, these islands share three of the highest standards of living in the Caribbean (C/LAA 1991). Each is highly urbanized, with approximately 70 percent of the population situated in urban areas. Each is industrialized, with a middle class and a modern infrastructure providing basic services such as water, electricity, telephone, and television. Each also has a large proportion of women in the workforce. However, the gender-based patterns on these islands reveal fundamental differences in women's access to economic autonomy.

On the surface, women and their work in Puerto Rico, Martinique, and Barbados look very much alike. Of people who are actively working, the proportion of women in the workforce represents 41 percent, 45 percent, and 47 percent, respectively (see figure 4.2). Moreover, in each area, women earn approximately eighty-five cents for every dollar men earn, higher than the average in most developed countries, including the United States. Education levels are high in all areas and are comparable by gender (BSS 1996, 1997; Bureau of Labor Statistics, Puerto Rico 1998; INSEE 1986, 1994, 1995; U.S. Bureau of the Census 1990).

But similarities in female presence in the workforce belie differences in the nature of this involvement. For example, there is a narrower distribution of women's work in Puerto Rico.[3] In Puerto Rico, women also represent a much smaller proportion of those who are self-employed (20 percent) than in either Martinique (30 percent) or in Barbados (34 percent) (see figure 4.3). In addition, 68 percent of women in the Puerto Rican workforce are married, compared to 34 percent in Martinique and 29 percent in Barbados (see figure 4.4). Among working women, female-headed households are far more numerous

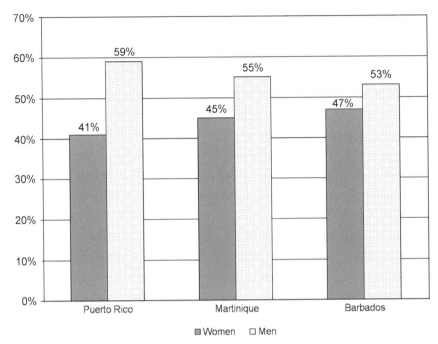

FIGURE 4.2
Ratios of women to men in the workforce, by society.

Source: Puerto Rico Bureau of Labor Statistics, Employment Survey, 1997; Institut National de la Statistique et des Etudes Economiques (INSEE Tableaux Economiques Régionaux, Martinique, 1997; Barbados Statistical Service Labor Force Survey, 1997.

in Barbados (46 percent) and Martinique (33 percent) than in Puerto Rico (20 percent) (see figure 4.5) (Bureau of Labor Statistics, Puerto Rico 1998; U.S. Bureau of the Census 1990; INSEE 1986, 1994, 1995; BSS 1996). Thus, although Puerto Rico, Martinique, and Barbados were each involved in the European quest for New World enrichment through slaves and sugar, the particulars of these histories formed distinct colonial legacies. These legacies are apparent in the differences in gender roles, in household and family-level dynamics, and in how women have been incorporated into the economy.

The Historical Basis of Differences: Spanish, French, and British

In the French and British Caribbean, where more than 90 percent of the population is African-descended, female slaves performed economically central roles for approximately 250 years. Because women's historic economic centrality is tied to gender-blind work practices during slavery, it is not surprising that the strongest workforce participation by women today is in the British and French islands where slavery was long-running and the slave population was dominant (Barrow 1998: xiii).

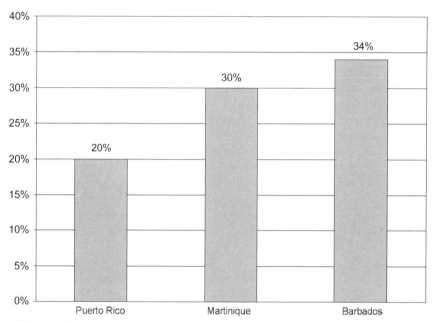

FIGURE 4.3
Proportion of self-employed women among working women, by society.

Source: Puerto Rico Bureau of Labor Statistics, Employment Survey, 1998; Institut National de la Statistique et des Etudes Economiques (INSEE Tableaux Economiques Régionaux, Martinique, 1994, 1995; Barbados Statistical Service Labor Force Survey, 1996.

By contrast, the Spanish relied on indigenous labor and comparatively small numbers of African slaves to work silver and gold mines in mainland America. Spain's Caribbean colonies did not begin monocrop cultivation of sugar until the nineteenth century. The late adoption of this strategy and the small demographic impact slaves had on the Hispanicized settlements led to distinct social formations in Puerto Rico and the other Hispanic areas of the Caribbean (Scarano 1989: 56). The dominant Hispanic ethnicity is especially evident in Puerto Rico, where the small proportion of slaves (who never exceeded 14 percent of the total population) assimilated with the whites and free people of color to such a degree that clear racial boundaries do not exist today (C/LAA 1991; Safa 1995; Scarano 1989: 77).

In the Hispanic Caribbean, as in Latin America, family structures reflect a system in which marriage has become the norm and female-headed households are stigmatized (Findlay 1999). Marriage is clearly not the norm in the non-Hispanic Caribbean, and female-headed households are both more common and less taboo (Safa 1986: 11). Socially distinct patterns are also expressed in the workforce. Of women in the workforce in Puerto Rico, only 20

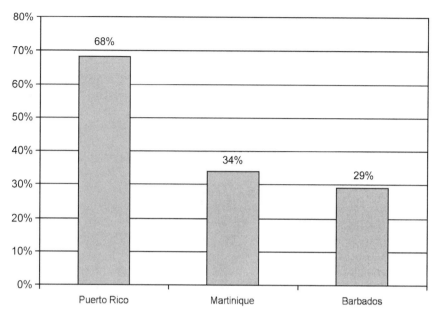

FIGURE 4.4
Proportion of working women who are married, by society.

Source: Puerto Rico Bureau of Labor Statistics, Employment Survey, 1997; Institut National de la Statistique et des Etudes Economiques (INSEE Tableaux Economiques Régionaux, Martinique, 1994, 1995; Barbados Statistical Service Labor Force Survey, 1997.

percent are female heads of household, compared to 33 percent in Martinique and 46 percent in Barbados (see figure 4.5). In addition, in both Martinique and Barbados, the dominant majority of the workforce is composed of men and women who are unmarried (57 percent and 66 percent, respectively), compared to an overwhelming majority in Puerto Rico (68 percent) who are married (see figure 4.4).

Although Martinique and Barbados share more similar histories of sugar and slavery, Martinique tends to sustain stronger gender roles than Barbados. This pattern is apparent in the demographic profiles of working women in Martinique and reinforced by extensive fieldwork experience. On the one hand, Martiniquaise women are less likely than Barbadian women to be self-employed, to be household heads, or to be unmarried. On the other hand, these same women are more likely to be self-employed, household heads, and unmarried than women in the Puerto Rican workforce. Long-term ethnographic experience offers additional, qualitative recognition of the somewhat more constrained gender relations in the household in Martinique than in Barbados. In effect, the ability of women in Martinique to overcome gendered biases and expectations appears to place Martinique in the middle of the three societies, a position in part explained

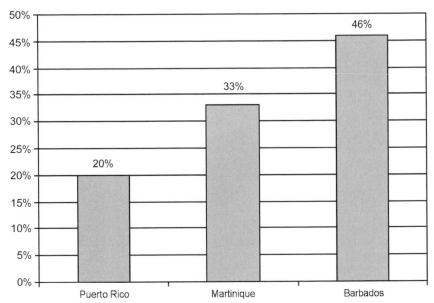

FIGURE 4.5
Proportion of working women living in female-headed households, by society.

Source: Puerto Rico Bureau of Labor Statistics, Employment Survey, 1997; Institut National de la Statistique et des Etudes Economiques (INSEE Tableaux Economiques Régionaux, Martinique, 1994, 1995; Barbados Statistical Service Labor Force Survey, 1997.

by Martinique's Latin social history as well as its cultural assimilation to
France. The French promoted a strong Catholic tradition, maintained unequal access to inheritance for women, and developed laws that compensated mothers (Poirier and Dagenais 1986). Although the British installed
the Anglican Church, its dogmatic restrictions on women were far less pronounced than those that characterize Catholicism. Thus, in Barbados, the
religious manifestations of British hegemony did less than in the French or
Spanish areas to suppress the economic independence of women established during slavery.

   If the social and economic inequality of women in the Caribbean can be
described as following a continuum, these three islands can be plotted at different points, each of the two extremes displaying a stronger (Puerto Rico) or
weaker (Barbados) set of assumptions related to gender that, in turn, condition the nature of economic opportunity as expressed among the entrepreneurial women in a given society. Because each island offers a particular
clustering of characteristics with respect to gender roles, workplace discrimination, and state-level policies, they together form a powerful triad of sites to
test a variety of issues related to gender ideologies, entrepreneurship, and economic mobility.

PROFILES OF WOMEN'S ECONOMIC OPPORTUNITY BY ISLAND

Puerto Rico

When the United States took Puerto Rico in 1898, local women were employed in jobs that were extensions of their work in the household (domestic, seamstress, laundress) (Ortiz 1996: 3). The proportion of women in the labor force during the early years of the twentieth century was about 15 percent. This proportion grew to 24 percent by 1940 as women workers were recruited to fill jobs in the expanding tobacco and needlework industries (Rios 1983). In the postwar period, the United States embarked on "Operation Bootstrap" to diversify the agricultural economy of Puerto Rico and improve the quality of life by investing in basic services and infrastructure, including education, health, and housing (Safa 1995: 13). Tax incentives and other perquisites made available to U.S. firms for locating operations in Puerto Rico have attracted a wide variety of labor- and capital-intensive industries. Gendered stratification of these workforces is apparent in women's dominant representation in labor-intensive, female-typed industries (textiles, garments, electronics, and other assembly operations) that offer only low-wage jobs (Safa 1995: 16; Rivera 1989). As the economy shifted from an emphasis on manufacturing to services, women's participation in the workforce became dominated by low-wage clerical work (Casey 1996), and many such workers rely on welfare to survive (Weisskoff 1985; Rios 1995).

In terms of family life, traditional domestic arrangements in which women keep house, cook, and raise children are still the norm, even for full-time working women (Casey 1996). As one of the foremost scholars on the Hispanic Caribbean has stated, "male control of women's labor and sexuality is maintained through an emphasis on family honor and female virginity fostered by Catholicism" (Safa 1995: 47). Safa (1995: 184) also indicates that in the Hispanic Caribbean, working women continue to associate themselves primarily with their domestic role and to see their work outside the home as an extension of it.

Martinique

The nature of economic and social change in Martinique over the past fifty years is conditioned by its full political incorporation into France as an overseas department in 1946. By 1976, 70 percent of Martinique's economy was based on services and commerce; since that time, no new sectors of productive growth have emerged. The only real job growth has been in the public sector, from 2 percent of the active population in 1954 to 34 percent today. Because of the job security that women in Martinique associate with the public sector, more women are employed here than in any other single sector. Women represent 55 percent of all public-sector employees (INSEE 1986; Audric 1991).

As French citizens, Martiniquais have access to a guaranteed minimum income, family allocations for each child, income supplements, and free health services. The conditioning of economic dependency on the state in Martinique may reduce the need or desire of women to achieve economic independence through self-employment. According to reports by French demographic and labor specialists (Audric 1991: 19–22; INSEE 1994: 43), women's participation in the labor market has been increasing since the late 1960s, when they represented only about one-third of the labor force. However, women are overrepresented among the unemployed (54 percent), are more likely than men to be clustered in the lowest paid formal-sector work (37 percent versus 21 percent), and are underrepresented at the highest levels of employment (INSEE 1994: 55, 44).

Since the 1960s, improvements have been apparent for women, including longer life expectancy, better quality of life, higher levels of education, and lowered rates of fertility. But equality with men in terms of education and workforce participation has not yet signaled an end to gender stratification in the workforce or in the domain of political life. Here, women represent 15 percent of elected officials at the municipal level, but at the highest levels of government, they hold fewer than 2 percent of the elected positions. There are no female senators, and only one in four deputies is female (Gautier 1995: 133).

Barbados

On Barbadian plantations, female slaves were expected to perform the same field labor as men but were less likely than men to be trained for skilled jobs (Beckles 1990: 51). This history established a long-standing expectation that a woman's identity is predicated on work as well as motherhood and domesticity (Sutton and Makiesky-Barrow 1981). Following abolition, Barbadian women emerged as small-scale farmers, as "higglers" (sellers) of produce, and as wage-workers on the plantations (Momsen 1993b).

Although patriarchal gender ideologies were evident in men's higher compensation than women's for the same labor, by the end of the nineteenth century these ideologies were intensified by missionaries who saw social progress in terms of nuclear families headed by male breadwinners (Momsen 1998: 128).

In response to widespread rioting in the 1930s, the British Moyne Commission recommended that local women be trained for marriage and not for work outside the home unless it was necessary (Gmelch and Gmelch 1997: 61). But offsetting historical events increased women's independence: most notably, male migration. From the late 1800s until the 1920s, men left home to seek work in Panama, Cuba, and the United States. A second wave of male migration occurred after World War II when men left to seek work in England, the United States, and Canada. During these periods, women's numbers in the labor force increased (Momsen 1993b: 234).

During the 1960s, women were drawn into low-wage jobs associated with the boom in tourism. Today, Barbados is attempting to use its modern infrastructure to attract information-services industries. Already by 1993, data services firms employed more people than traditional manufacturing operations. In addition to the absence of an official minimum wage for workers, the government of Barbados has supported these offshore firms in strongly discouraging unions from organizing (Freeman 2000).

However, the Barbados government closely monitors working conditions to avoid the exploitation of its workforce by foreign investors. Thus, local labor laws do require that employers provide such compensations as maternity benefits, vacation time, sick leave, and severance pay (Freeman 2000).

A recent report by the United Nations Development Programme (UNDP) ranked Barbados at the top of the developing world on two distinct measures of gender equality: the Gender Development Index (GDI), which assesses whether basic improvements in society have benefited women as much as men; and the Gender Empowerment Measure (GEM), which evaluates the public roles of women in the economy and in political life (UNDP 1995: 84–85). Nonetheless, women in the workforce remain occupationally segregated (Coppin 1995, 1998) and subjected to unequal ideologies of gender (Barriteau 1998: 450).

Methodology

The selection of Puerto Rico, Martinique, and Barbados as research sites was a product of both theoretical and methodological concerns. First, to advance a research project across culturally related areas with distinct colonial and linguistic histories, it was theoretically important to include one society colonized by each of the major colonial powers in the Caribbean: Spain, France, and Great Britain. Second, it was important to locate islands similar in as many other ways as possible to enhance the comparative logic of a single research study conducted in multiple sites. This methodological concern led to the choice of islands that together share the highest living standards in the Caribbean, are strongly urban, and have similarly high proportions of women in the workforce. In short, these islands form an ideal base for comparative research of patterns involving gender and work.

A fundamental premise of this research involves the investigation of multiple sites using common ethnographic methods and identical research instruments. Although there are few anthropological models of multisite ethnography,[4] the potential benefits for applied anthropology are promising. One of the primary benefits involves the opportunity to perform a more comprehensive, "radical" kind of comparison between data sets that are collectively conceived and generated. As anthropologists adapt to the conditions of globalization, it is likely that multisite ethnographic methodologies will become more common.

Key to the radical comparative project envisioned in this study is an emphasis on ethnography. Each of the three anthropologists who conducted the pilot project interviews has long-term, in-depth familiarity with her respective island.[5]

Conducting multisite ethnography, however, poses unfamiliar challenges, including working across language barriers, ensuring that questions on interview guides and census surveys are appropriate and comparable in each context, working with different national data sets that do not track labor patterns in comparable ways, and adapting to each local environment without compromising the project's comparative integrity (see Browne and Freeman n.d.).

One way the ethnographic rootedness of each researcher became important was in identifying prospective female entrepreneurs in each site. None of the islands had accessible, comprehensive lists of women who had started their own businesses, much less lists of those women cross-referenced to the economic sector of their business, the length of time they had been in business, their number of employees, their gross revenues, the location of their business, or their own personal and household demographics. Without a centralized database, there was no possibility of a randomized sample of female entrepreneurs. Each fieldworker tried to vary as much as possible the types of women we interviewed, especially in terms of life stage, marital status, and type of business. We focused the pilot ethnographic research on women who fit broadly under the category of "middle class." Because none of the islands had a database of entrepreneurs, isolating a middle-class sample could only be achieved by exclusion. We attempted to avoid survival-oriented self-employment, such as street vending, on the one hand, and very large businesses (100+ employees) on the other.

The sampling frame of middle-class women reflects a deliberate strategy to focus on the experiences of women who have more economic cushion than poor women and are not necessarily forced by financial need to generate income. This focus enabled us to explore the ethnographic context surrounding entrepreneurial women who are not poor. We selected women who must negotiate middle-class pressures and gendered expectations that operate at the household level and who are engaged in a wide range of entrepreneurial activities. In each field setting, these informants were identified through all means available: personal contacts, government agencies in charge of business registration and development, public and private business lending agencies, and professional associations of female entrepreneurs.

For approximately five weeks during spring and summer of 1999, each anthropologist conducted thirty two-stage interviews with female entrepreneurs from various urban areas on each of the target islands. The first stage involved a comprehensive socioeconomic census survey, which was followed by an in-depth, semistructured interview. Researchers thus generated a total of ninety "double" interviews with female entrepreneurs. In all three sites, the women interviewed represented a wide range of ages, family structures, and types of entrepreneurial endeavors (see table 4.1). A household unit of analysis was achieved through questions posed in the socioeconomic census about the demographic composition of the household, the economic contributions

Table 4.1. Spreadsheet of Sampled Female Entrepreneurs and Their Businesses across Islands (n = 30 per island; 90 total)

Type of Business Owned	Employees	Age	Family Structure
MARTINIQUE			
translation services	1	50	couple
orchid grower	self	45	matrifocal
retail crafts shop	2	30	nuclear
retail florist shop	7	45	single
patisserie fabricator and retailer	10	49	matrifocal
esthetician	3	54	couple
taxi owner/chauffeur	self	37	nuclear
computer services/hardware co.	2	43	couple
retail shoe shop	2	53	nuclear
artisan and retailer of gold jewelry	2	40	single
law partner in family practice	10	50	single
financial/management consultant, Ph.D.	2	35	single
custom export souvenir packages	7	32	single
furniture recovering, custom draperies	6	52	nuclear
printing company	2	27	nuclear
pharmacy	10	50	nuclear
optical shop	4	41	couple
hair salon	3	36	matrifocal
hotel and restaurant	5	50	matrifocal
custom furniture design and building	12	34	nuclear
rapid clothing alterations and makers	5	34	extended
prefabrication of industrial tubes	60	39	nuclear
wholesale cultivator	seasonal	35	nuclear
financial/management consultant, Ph.D.	2	40	nuclear
plastification of luggage	2	56	matrifocal
construction company	8	47	matrifocal
historic bed and breakfast	2	37	couple
serigraph printing shop w/ husband	7	38	nuclear
research and mfg. of medicinal herbs	6	74	extended
sewing supplies (buttons, ribbons, etc.)	2	48	single
PUERTO RICO			
public affairs consultants	7	46	nuclear
balloons co.	2	40	single
funeral home	2	38	single
computer training co.	1	42	single
artist and gallery owner	self	36	nuclear
fire prevention & safety co.	9	44	single
auto parts wholesaler	4	42	matrifocal
computer embroidery for business	seasonal	43	matrifocal
cisterns water storage co.	12	32	couple
casting director	self	55	nuclear
personal services (elderly monitoring; scholarship)	self	45	nuclear
floral design & supply—wholesale	7	32	single
hair salon for children	self	??	single
human resource & mgmt. consultants	9	36	nuclear
retreading tires co.	21	46	nuclear
travel agency	3	50	single

(continued)

Type of Business Owned	Employees	Age	Family Structure
PUERTO RICO (continued)			
realtor/real estate agency	self	49	single
road painting co.	9	37	nuclear
pharmacy owner (has several)	10	49	single
seeds reseller—veg's, herbs, flowers	7	51	nuclear
general construction co.	11	29	nuclear
blocks & cobblestones factory	217	43	single
interior design	self	42	matrifocal
catering	self	29	nuclear
juice mfg.	14	23	matrifocal
psycho-esthetic consulting	self	49	single
plant nursery	self	40	matrifocal
direct marketing & media	35	47	single
plant nursery	self	39	matrifocal
electrician	self	35	female couple
BARBADOS			
graphic designer	1	32	nuclear
architectural firm	3	34	couple
jewelry & fashion design	2	34	matrifocal
clothing mfg. and design	4	30	nuclear
restaurant owner/caterer	5	34	extended
daycare	4	51	nuclear
Rasta jewelry maker	self	33	matrifocal
printer/publisher	8	41	nuclear
beauty cosmetologist	2	34	single
secretarial/admin. mgmt. consulting	4	41	nuclear
hotel	32	40	matrifocal
retail florist	seasonal	68	nuclear
wine bar	25	38	couple
birthday cake bakery	7	42	nuclear
recording studio	seasonal	32	nuclear
café	45	43	female couple
laundry	20	46	couple
clothing & shoe boutique	8	43	nuclear
furniture and housewares rental co.	7	54	single
floral supplier & custom arranging	1	46	nuclear
commercial art gallery	2	37	nuclear
landscape design & consulting	seasonal	30	single
language school	7	56	nuclear
swim instruction business	self	38	female couple
mfr. of canvas awnings & tents	6	37	couple
general construction & roof repairs	3	26	nuclear
street vendor, ice cream cart	seasonal	38	nuclear
basket maker	3	36	nuclear
2 companies: signs; student cards co.	self	29	nuclear
clothing mfg. & retail boutique	14	41	nuclear

of other household members, and specific patterns of household-level responsibilities and decision-making authority. The results of these household-based patterns were factored into the analysis of both the gendered opportunities and the constraints that operate on women who pursue entrepreneurial careers.

Early Results from Pilot Research

The research team is well aware of the hazards of drawing conclusions based on small samples that are not necessarily representative. However, the intensive prior experience of each anthropologist in her respective island offers some support for these early findings. Moreover, once these findings are subjected to the test of larger-scale sampling, the reliability of our pilot sample will become clearer.

Early findings from pilot-level research suggest that the profiles of women who undertake entrepreneurship vary across Caribbean societies depending on both gender ideologies in the household and workplace, and on the welfare orientation of the state. Findings also suggest key similarities among entrepreneurial women across cultural spaces. These similarities include the average ages of women entrepreneurs (40–43) as well as a substantive set of priorities many women share in the ways they conceive of and manage their businesses. In brief, these preliminary findings include the following: 1) depending on the form and strength of gendered ideologies in a given society, the profile of women attracted to entrepreneurship may vary; 2) welfare-oriented states may reduce entrepreneurial risk taking; and 3) across societies, many women entrepreneurs appear to share key priorities in managing their businesses, including a commitment to nurturing employees and building a "family" atmosphere in the workplace.

CROSS-CULTURAL DIFFERENCES

Where Gender Stratification Is Least Negotiable, Women Entrepreneurs May Be "Social Outliers"

According to pilot project interviews, the private lives of entrepreneurial women appear to vary dramatically depending on the strength of a society's prescribed gender roles. In Puerto Rico, where ideologies of gender are the strictest and occupational segregation is strongly pronounced (see note 3), entrepreneurial women appear more likely to be "social outliers" than their counterparts in less gender-stratified societies like Barbados. It is striking that although two-thirds of working women in Puerto Rico are married and live in nuclear households, 63 percent of the female entrepreneurs we interviewed there were unmarried and living alone or in nontraditional households. Nontraditional households in Puerto Rico that appear in our sample include twelve single-person households, six matrifocal (single, female parent) house-holds, and one female-couple household. It seems that in Puerto Rico, many economically ambitious women may choose to avoid the constraints of family structures dominated by a male authority. Other indicators also suggest that entrepreneurial women follow nonnormative patterns: al-though 85 percent of the Puerto Rican population is Catholic (CIA 2000), nearly half of the entrepreneurial women we interviewed said they were not. In addition, more women entrepreneurs here (40 percent) than in ei-ther Barbados or Martinique also engage in "nontraditional" types of work—types of work that remain strongly dominated by men (see table 4.1). Together, the strong proportions of non-Catholic, unmarried women living in nontraditional households, and running nontraditional businesses suggest the possibility of a certain social "marginality" among female en-trepreneurs in Puerto Rico.

Señora Morales[6] runs a marketing firm with thirty-five employees. She typ-ifies many ambitious women in her society who recognize that owning a busi-ness can cost something in terms of a relationship with a man. She explains the dilemma as follows:

> It worries me as a woman not being able to find a partner and get into a stable relationship. But nothing could have stopped me from starting my business. Any man would have to be a very unusual man, not a typical Puerto Rican man.

Señora Reyes agrees. She is a single woman who lives with her mother and brother and runs an auto parts wholesale business she inherited from her fa-ther. She claims that, in Puerto Rico, self-sufficient women present problems for men. She says the expectations of men lead many women like herself to simply avoid being involved:

> Women are becoming self-sufficient and this makes them think less about mar-riage or makes them want to postpone it. I give a lot to my career, so I don't have time to stay home and take care of children. Men don't like it when women dis-tinguish themselves outside the home.

Perhaps in relatively patriarchal societies, the assumptions of male author-ity in a marriage and a nuclear family are not easily negotiated, thus reducing a woman's option to create her own business and requiring ambitious women to organize their lives to avoid such constraints.

Among the small proportion of entrepreneurial women in Puerto Rico who are married, the women we interviewed indicated that they had extraor-dinary husbands who had done a lot to make it possible for them to build their own businesses. Señora Davila, 32, owns a cisterns water storage facility and is married to a doctor. They have no children, but plan to. She clarifies how finding an exceptional man is the solution to avoiding divorce and maintaining a balanced private life:

> I found the ideal man, which doesn't happen to a lot of people. Here, there are only a minority of men who share work in the house. We share everything—chores, decisions. We don't have the kind of relationship where he does certain things just because he is a man. I may have to stay late to go to a meeting so he will cook. That's the key. A lot of women business owners think that when they get divorced, the problem was their business. But that's not it. When you have a business, you need moral support. A husband needs to respect you as a businesswoman.

Señora Burgos is a young artist and gallery owner. She also found an exceptional man who supports her work and is ready to participate in childcare as well as cooking:

> I can leave the house and he will bathe the child, help him with his lessons, or take him to school. So, on Mother's Day, I give him a present, because for me, he is like a mother and a father to my child. As an individual, he has helped me develop into the woman I am. He admires me a lot as a woman, a human being, and as a business woman. All the success that I have now, I would have gotten eventually, but because of him and his support, I have them sooner.

Although marriage and traditional family arrangements may inhibit many women from pursuing entrepreneurship in Puerto Rico, such arrangements may be less likely to constrain Barbadian women. In Barbados, a different social environment for women may draw different kinds of women into entrepreneurship. In contrast to what we observed in Puerto Rico, our sample of entrepreneurial women in Barbados was overwhelmingly married (73 percent) and living as couples or nuclear families (70 percent).[7] The explanation for these cross-cultural differences may be linked to more flexibly constructed gendered relations in Barbadian households. Ms. Clarke is a retired schoolteacher who, at the age of sixty-eight, has built a flourishing retail florist business with a female partner. She echoes the sentiment of other married women in Barbados, "My spouse has never stood in the way of any career choice or advancement."

Many Barbadian women count not only on a spouse's acceptance of their entrepreneurial activity; some also rely on their spouses as partners or regular helpers with their businesses. Others get substantial financial support from their husbands, whose higher incomes offer a security net for their wives' businesses. Thus, having a husband or male partner provides critical financial, moral, or work-related support for many women's businesses.

For example, Ms. Fowler, who left a data entry job to become a specialty baker of birthday cakes, began her business out of her home, with full support from her husband. "He was all for it," she said, because he knew this would allow her the flexibility to better manage transporting children and planning the day. Although she assumes management of the children and the shopping, Ms. Fowler says that when it comes to the household, "my husband and I share all the responsibilities." She also hires a domestic helper to do the cleaning, ironing, and odd jobs. Eventually, she moved the business to a new location, where it has continued to grow. Today, she has seven employees, and her husband has quit his job to become a full partner with her. Interestingly, though, Ms. Fowler indicates without complaint that he has taken over management of the finances and the employees while she manages customer orders and the baking. This situation points up the complicated mix of gender relations for Barbadian women. Despite her autonomous entry into an entrepreneurial venture with support from her husband, Ms. Fowler's successful enterprise is now effectively run by her husband who, according to her, "helped sort things out" and "brought in procedures" to correct various problems.

The larger social environment in Barbados does seem to offer models of encouragement to ambitious women. Three government ministers are women; many female representatives hold national political office; and there are two female Anglican priests. Ms. Thomas, a thirty-eight-year-old married woman who owns a wine bar and restaurant, explains how Anglican religious beliefs have offered support to women, especially compared to the Catholic Church, which has only a small following in Barbados:

> There's the Catholic Church and the Anglican Church. I mean, I think the Anglican Church is definitely pro women helping themselves and doing, being self-sufficient. The Catholic Church tends to promote large families and women at home, not being in the workplace. . . . In this day and age . . . I think the Catholic Church has a very narrow-minded approach to what is going on in the real world.

UN measures citing Barbados as a country with one of the highest degrees of gender equity, however, make many Barbadian women groan. Local informants state that although gender roles may be slightly more relaxed here than in other islands, such as Martinique or Puerto Rico, and although their own husbands and partners may accept their entrepreneurial activities, men still expect women to assume charge of the household and children. Many women we interviewed expressed real frustration in dealing with such continuing assumptions of male authority. They complain that men expect too much from women and do too little themselves. However, the fact that many Barbadian men now participate in a widespread "masculinity" movement, in which the local power of women is contested, suggests that men feel threatened by increasingly powerful women.

So, although Barbadian women do not feel that they are "liberated" from the pressures of double or triple shifts to the single shift most men work, the flexibility they exploit is in the way they are often able to manage the extra tasks expected of them. For many, the solution is to simply hire the help they need at home. More than half of the married women we interviewed hire domestic workers to help manage children, prepare meals, and clean house. Those with young children frequently make use of daycare centers or home-based nannies as well as extended networks of kin. The costs of delegating household management to hired helpers are typically financed by the woman's company as a necessary business expense. So long as these household chores are reliably performed by someone, most Barbadian women business owners whom we interviewed believe their husbands are willing to support their entrepreneurial ventures.

In Barbados, then, where household help and daycare are accessible and affordable for middle-class women and where ideas of masculinity and femininity are slightly more negotiable than in some other areas, perhaps women in nuclear family structures are better positioned than their counterparts in more rigidly gender-stratified areas to pursue an entrepreneurial venture. In fact, nearly half the married women in our sample cited their mates as important to their business, either as full partners, as employees, or as informal but regular helpers (a proportion far higher here than in either Martinique or Puerto Rico). Thus, it may be that many women in such "respectable"[8] family arrangements are able to find effective ways to negotiate the constraints of male authority. Some may also be able to recruit the labor or resources of their partners to help them realize their own business success.

For women in Martinique, as in Barbados, the historically gender-leveling influences of slavery share social space with the European-inherited notions of respectability. But, as in Puerto Rico, the island residents have experienced the long-standing conservative influences of the Catholic Church. Because of these culturally contradictory impacts on gender ideologies today, it is not surprising that local patterns in the profiles of female entrepreneurs may lie between those found for Puerto Rico and Barbados. Compared to their Puerto Rican counterparts, entrepreneurs in Martinique appear less likely to live as single women, to run a nontraditional business, and to be religious heterodox with regard to religion. But, Martiniquaise women entrepreneurs also appear less likely than those in Barbados to be married and living as couples or in nuclear families with children at home and to have husbands who are involved in their businesses.

Although the complexity of this situation precludes further discussion here, the tensions that Martiniquaise women commonly face are illustrated by Madame Arnaud. Madame Arnaud created a printing company at a young age after working for other printing companies and learning the business. She was, unlike many of her counterparts in Martinique, a woman driven to be an entrepreneur. She planned her education and on-the-job experience to position herself to launch her own company. At first her husband was accepting of her ambition, but once they had a new baby, his views changed. By the time of our interview, Madame Arnaud had built her three-year-old company into a small success, with a reliable base of clients and increasing profits. But just a few months following that interview in summer 1999, she decided to sell the business. She explained that although her mother was happy to care for the new baby many hours a day so she could continue running her company, her husband was very upset because she was not home enough. "He asked me to quit being a business owner. He told me, 'You should be a salaried worker,'" she said. Madame Arnaud sold her business and found a part-time job, claiming that family life was too important to compromise it for her personal ambition.

In sum, the private lives of entrepreneurial women across societies suggest contrasting patterns based on the degree of rigidity associated with society's roles for women and men. To the extent that traditional women's roles are strongly enforced, those women who become entrepreneurs may comprise a socially marginal group, including the most self-assured and independent women of society, women who are not daunted by local norms of appropriate female behavior. Those women entrepreneurs in Puerto Rico who are married and have children have found "extraordinary" men, themselves sometimes "marginal," who accommodate and support their wives and who can bear the heat of public disapproval or suspicion.

In a society like Barbados, where many men still persist in holding their wives responsible for work associated with the household and the children, irrespective of their wives' own economic activities, women indicate that their flexibility lies in the way they are able to manage these chores. Thus, although they feel responsible for making sure the tasks are done, doing so frees them to enjoy a broader range of economic opportunities. And, unlike their counterparts in Puerto Rico, Barbadian women appear able to realize their ambitions while remaining within local normative boundaries. Perhaps this more flexible environment for professional women has the effect of recruiting women to entrepreneurship, because they can more readily depend on a spouse's expertise, resources, and support for the enterprise.

The Welfare-Oriented State Reduces Entrepreneurial Risk Taking

During initial fieldwork, we collected limited data from several professional associations of business owners as well as state authorities in each society, ones concerned with labor, business development, and gender. Even in this limited scope of archival research, certain impacts of the role of the state became clear and reinforced the theoretical importance of this macrolevel influence on microlevel entrepreneurs.

One finding from this research involved the link between the overall welfare orientation of the state and the degree to which our informants depended on state assistance to launch their businesses. In Martinique, which has the most extensive welfare-based economy of the three islands and a large, female-dominated public sector, nearly half the women entrepreneurs in the sample got their start through one of many training or aid programs provided by the state. Patterns of reliance on state assistance are also much more pronounced in Puerto Rico than in Barbados. In Barbados, where only two women accessed any state-level support for their business start-ups, the state maintains a small welfare sector and fosters a neoliberal economic orientation.

Another finding related to the type of preparation one has prior to launching a business also suggests that entrepreneurial conservatism appears to derive from a welfare-oriented state. In Puerto Rico, for example, female entrepreneurs average approximately two years more education than the women on the other islands. A different kind of caution appears among our sample of women in Martinique, who are far more likely than women in the other societies to have an accounting background before creating a business. Additionally, many women in Puerto Rico and, especially, in Martinique (compared to very few in Barbados) reveal that they had been prompted to begin their business because they were fired or had a bad experience in their previous work, such as being underpaid or having a conflict with their boss.

Together, the welfare orientation of the state in Martinique and Puerto Rico appears to condition women to be more cautious in undertaking entrepreneurial ventures.

CROSS-CULTURAL SIMILARITIES

At the same time that one set of clustered findings points to the differential effect of gender roles and state policies across societies, other findings reveal areas of similarity among the women in each setting. These similarities seem to derive from a common conflict that most women identify as central: the need to allocate space and time for personal ambition while also allowing space and time to nurture affective relationships, especially those concerning family and children. A striking majority of informants in all three societies expressed a clear commitment to leading with a female style of management and developing a working atmosphere that is nurturing as well as effective. In effect, the tension between women's need to achieve and their need to nurture seems to lead many to construct professional lives that bridge these disparate goals. According to Madame Duville, a young Martiniquaise woman who runs a concrete-tube manufacturing business with a male partner, her male employees regard her as a kind of symbolic mother, a role that provides a degree of continuity between home and workplace:

> The employees are closer to the mother figure and fear the father. The mother from Martinique is overprotective. They see me like that. I don't have any problems with my employees. They are mostly men. If there is a problem, or they need a loan, they will come to me, but not to him [the male partner].

Because workplaces are generally still run by men, many women see their workplace strategies as alternatives to what they encountered as employees in male-run organizations. Women's leadership strategies are often expressly designed to avoid sterile, uncommunicative environments where productivity is a singular goal and little care is taken to attend to employee needs. Instead, many women indicate that they consciously attempt to create a nurturing, family-like atmosphere, where employee efforts and needs are recognized, and where employee loyalty and retention are primary goals.

Madame Charlery fabricates French breads and pastries and owns a retail pastry shop in Fort-de-France, Martinique. She has ten employees. In a society like Martinique, where terms of address at the workplace are commonly formal and hierarchies between the boss and workers tend to be pronounced, she is aware that her female-oriented philosophy is not the norm:

> To succeed in business, you have to be a family. My employees don't call me "Madame" but simply "Michele." I am one of them. I know what it is to be unemployed. I have been there, so I don't feel superior to them.

Ms. Walker, a Barbadian restaurant owner with forty-five employees, described the difference between female and male business owners, saying:

> I think women tend to have more of a heart. In other words, if one of my staff has a personal problem at home, I would be more than willing to let them go and recover, and even I would jump in and cover, you know, but men tend . . . we don't discuss: "You're working and that's it."

In short, women across these islands echo the importance of asserting their own femininity and running their businesses as women not men, developing a "family" atmosphere at work, making it a priority to legally declare their employees and provide them with benefits, responding to the needs of employees with children, and keeping their own schedules flexible enough to accommodate the needs of their own children. For many women, confidence in their own management style derives from a sense of organizational and time-management skills they say come more naturally to them as women.

Señora Cruz, a forty-two-year-old divorced Puerto Rican mother of three, has an interior design business. She believes women have an inherent capacity to respond to diverse needs and to multitask, and that this is what makes them so good in business:

> Women were badly educated because they believed that men should be held up as wow! This magnificent being! But women now realize that we are the "wow" because like in my case, we are mother, father, teacher, tutor, taxi driver. Men can only think of one thing at a time, whereas a woman has to be thinking of a lot of things.

Ms. Johnson is a thirty-two-year-old Barbadian woman who owns a record company, which she devotes to helping her husband realize his work as a composer and singer. But he has no role in managing the company. She said:

> Women are better able to organize, because of that ability to think of a lot of different things at once, because men don't work that way, they aren't going to work in a logical order like that. They'll finish one thing then go to the next . . . even in [the] house, they say let me just finish painting this corner here, and you say, "Well, could we sand here, and while that's drying". . . or whatever. Men don't do that.

CONCLUSION

The findings of this pilot research offer fresh ethnographic and analytical insights into the relationship between the nature of women's entrepreneurship and the strength of gendered ideologies that are manifested in workplaces and households in each society. Just as importantly, though, are those findings that have suggested potential similarities in the kinds of priorities and difficulties women face—sometimes because they are women, sometimes simply because they are ambitious people. Our preliminary findings include three broad insights. First, in societies such as Puerto Rico that are strongly gender-stratified and where male authority is not easily negotiated in households, women with entrepreneurial ambitions may represent "social outliers" who prefer to live alone or in nontraditional households. This situation appears to vary significantly in societies with more relaxed gender roles such as Barbados and, to a lesser extent, Martinique, where ambitious women may be less constrained by traditional household arrangements. A second insight suggests that women in welfare-oriented economies are less risk-oriented and more conservative in their entrepreneurial undertakings than women in other societies. Because women in welfare-oriented societies, such as Martinique and Puerto Rico, are accustomed to relying on the state, they may be less likely to risk as much in the private sector as women who are not so conditioned. A third insight suggests there are cross-cultural similarities among women entrepreneurs, who share a key set of priorities for their business, including the exercise of their femininity to render workplace settings more nurturing and effective.

At this early stage and working with small samples, it would be presumptuous to claim a clear understanding of female entrepreneurship in these three highly complex societies. Analyzing findings across multiple sites is a daunting enterprise. Fortunately, we have the opportunity to deepen our understanding of these complexities and to test our early results with a larger-scale investigation.[9] In fact, the pilot research has helped us reshape the questions and goals that are guiding the second, more extensive phase of data collection, which began in spring 2001 and will continue through 2002. Findings presented here provide a baseline for what lies ahead.

ACKNOWLEDGMENTS

I wish to thank the National Science Foundation (NSF Grant # BCS-9817842) for its generous support of this pilot project and the project that inspired it, dissertation research on the informal economy across class and gender in Martinique. I also wish to acknowledge research support from Colorado State University and the support of government officials in Martinique, Barbados, and Puerto Rico for their patience and willingness to generate customized data sets for use in comparative analysis. I also acknowledge with affection and admiration my research partner, Carla Freeman, with whom I share responsibility for the future full-scale project (NSF Grant # BCS-9911743). In addition, I acknowledge the gracious help of economist Addington Coppin, who prepared data results and analyzed parts of this research. I wish to express appreciation to the manuscript reviewers of *Human Organization* for their helpful comments. Most of all, I wish to thank all the women interviewed for this project who shared their time and insights about the special joys and challenges of entrepreneurial work.

NOTES

1. In keeping with most national and international standards, I use the terms "entrepreneur" and "self-employed" interchangeably. Census data for each island only identify a category of "self-employed" as distinct from wage workers, unemployed, and those not in the labor force. Also, because there is a lack of consensus on the meaning or appropriate operational definition of entrepreneurship (Moore and Buttner 1997: 12; Wells 1998: 29), this research assumes self-employed persons to be entrepreneurs. However, with larger samples of male and female entrepreneurs in the subsequent phase of research, we will attempt to formulate a more useful conceptualization of entrepreneurship.

2. The term "patriarchy" is used to designate "the ideological system of male domination and privilege" (Acevedo 1995: 79), which may become institutionalized in state policy and workplace practice and which is evident in asymmetrical household relations of power and ideologies that define women's roles as economically subordinate to men's.

3. As Blau, Ferber, and Winkler (1998: 350) explain, occupational segregation is defined as "the percentage of women (or men) that would have to change jobs in order to duplicate the distribution of the other group." According to indices of occupational segregation calculated from the ILO Yearbook of Labor Statistics (Blau and Ferber 1992), Puerto Rico is significantly more gender-segregated (36.1 percent) by occupation than Barbados (31.6 percent) and also more gender-segregated than the United States (34 percent). Because jobs are classified differently in France, there are no comparable data available for Martinique. Despite the common usage of occupational segregation as a barometer of persistent inequities in the labor market, there is much debate about the actual utility of such generalized measures (cf. Jarman et al. 1999).

4. In response to decades of anthropological investigation by single ethnographers working in single sites, rapidly globalizing populations and cultural boundaries have led some scholars to promote the idea of multisited fieldwork. See, for example, Mar-

cus (1995) and Hannerz (1998: 247). In a related vein, Erikson and Stull discuss the benefits and challenges of team ethnography (1998).

5. Browne (1996) began long-term research in Martinique on the cross-class informal economy in 1990. She has since returned several times to continue studying the relationship of economic practice and postcolonial identities (2000) and is now completing a book manuscript on this research. In 1989, Freeman (2000) began three years of fieldwork in Barbados among pink-collar women data entry workers as an investigation of the islanders' relationship to the influences of globalization. Her work has also focused on the second careers of wage-working women who become "suitcase traders" to supplement their incomes (2000). Bonilla is a native Puerto Rican who conducted her dissertation fieldwork in the Dominican Republic, focusing on women's health.

6. All names are pseudonyms.

7. "Nuclear family" refers to a male and female parent and children. This percentage includes two nuclear-family households in which one additional relative also resides. "Couples" refers here only to heterosexual couples. There were two female-couple households in the Barbadian sample.

8. "Respectability" is a concept introduced by Peter Wilson (1969) in his 1959 study of a Caribbean island, where he argued that the idea is associated with European values internalized and reproduced by Creole women. This behavior, associated with church-going, keeping a clean house, and working hard, contrasts with the Creole-derived system of status that valorizes sexual, musical, verbal, and physical prowess. Wilson called this value system "reputation" and claimed it is primarily men who seek this form of status. The idea that these dualistic status systems can be separated by gender is contested by a number of more recent studies (Besson 1993; Burton 1997; Freeman 2000).

9. The sample for this subsequent research includes forty female and thirty-five male entrepreneurs, as well as ten wage-working women on each island. Combined with pilot samples of thirty interviews per island, the study totals per island will be 105 entrepreneurs (seventy women; thirty-five men) and ten wage-working women. In this second phase of data collection, Moira Perez, a native Puerto Rican who conducted anthropological dissertation fieldwork in Puerto Rico, is conducting the Puerto Rico research.

REFERENCES

Acevedo, Luz del Alba. 1995. "Feminist Inroads in the Study of Women's Work and Development." In *Women in the Latin American Development Process*, ed. by Christine Bose and Edna Acosta-Belén, 65–98. Philadelphia: Temple University Press.

Audric, Guy. 1991. "Les contrastes de l'emploi." *Antiane Eco: La Revue Economique des Antilles et de la Guyane* 14: 19–22.

Barahona, Iris Villalobos. 1995. "Women's Micro- and Small-Scale Enterprises' Emergence, Features, and Limits: A Costa Rican Experience." In *Women in Micro- and Small-Scale Enterprise Development*, ed. by Louise Dignard and José Havet, 145–57. Boulder, Colo.: Westview Press.

Barriteau, V. Eudine. 1998. "Liberal Ideology and Contradictions in Caribbean Gender Systems." In *Caribbean Portraits: Essays on Gender Ideologies and Identities*, ed. by Christine Barrow, 436–56. Kingston, Jamaica: Ian Randle Publishers.

Barrow, Christine. 1998. Introduction and Overview to *Caribbean Portraits: Essays on Gender Ideologies and Identities*, ed. by Christine Barrow, xi–xxxviii. Kingston, Jamaica: Ian Randle Publishers.

Beckles, Hilary. 1990. *A History of Barbados: From Amerindian Settlement to Nation-State.* Cambridge, U.K.: Cambridge University Press.

Benería, Lourdes, and Martha Roldán. 1987. *The Crossroads of Class and Gender: Industrial Homework, Subcontracting, and Household Dynamics in Mexico City.* Chicago: University of Chicago Press.

Benería, Lourdes, and Catharine R. Stimpson, eds. 1987. *Women, Households, and the Economy.* New Brunswick, N.J.: Rutgers University Press.

Berger, Marguerite. 1989. Introduction to *Women's Ventures: Assistance to the Informal Sector in Latin America.* West Hartford, Conn.: Kumarian Press.

———. 1995. "Key Issues on Women's Access to and Use of Credit in the Micro- and Small-Scale Enterprise Sector." In *Women in Micro- and Small-Scale Enterprise Development*, ed. by Louise Dignard and José Havet, 189–215. Boulder, Colo.: Westview Press.

———. 1997. *Microenterprise Development Strategy.* Washington, D.C.: Inter-American Development Bank.

Berger, Marguerite, and Mayra Buvinic, eds. 1987. *La mujer en el sector informal.* Quito, Ecuador: Instituto Latinoamericano de Investigaciones Sociales, Editorial Nueva Sociedad.

Besson, Jean. 1993. "Reputation and Respectability Reconsidered: A New Perspective on Afro-Caribbean Peasant Women." In *Women and Change in the Caribbean*, ed. by Janet Momsen, 16–37. London: James Currey.

Blau, Francine, and Marianne Ferber. 1992. *The Economics of Women, Men, and Work.* 2nd ed. Englewood Cliffs, N.J.: Prentice Hall.

Blau, Francine, Marianne Ferber, and Anne Winkler. 1998. *The Economics of Women, Men, and Work.* 3rd ed. Upper Saddle River, N.J.: Prentice Hall.

Blumberg, Rae Lesser. 1991. *Gender, Family, and Economy: The Triple Overlap.* Newbury Park, Calif.: Sage.

———. 1995. "Gender, Microenterprise, Performance, and Power: Case Studies from the Dominican Republic, Ecuador, Guatemala, and Swaziland." In *Women in the Latin American Development Process*, ed. by Christine Bose and Edna Acosta-Belén, 194–226. Philadelphia: Temple University Press.

Boserup, Esther. 1970. *Women's Role in Economic Development.* New York: St. Martin's Press.

Browne, Katherine E. 1996. "The Informal Economy in Martinique: Insights from the Field, Implications for Development Policy." *Human Organization* 55: 225–34.

———. 1997. "The Economic Immobility of Women in Martinique: Structural Patterns, Risk, Opportunity, and Ideology." *Research in Economic Anthropology* 18: 183–216.

———. 2000. "Work Styles and Network Management: Gendered Patterns and Economic Consequences in Martinique." *Gender and Society* 14: 435–56.

Browne, Katherine E., and Carla Freeman. n.d. *The Methodological Challenges of Multisite Research: Female Entrepreneurship across Caribbean Islands.* Unpublished manuscript. Author's files.

BSS (Barbados Statistical Service). 1996. *Labor Force Survey Report for 1996.* Bridgetown, Barbados: BSS.

———. 1997. *Labor Force Survey Report for 1997.* Bridgetown, Barbados: BSS.

Bureau of Labor Statistics, Puerto Rico. 1997. *Employment and Unemployment in Puerto Rico: April 1997.* San Juan: Division of Labor Force Statistics, Bureau of Labor Statistics.

———. 1998. *Employment and Unemployment in Puerto Rico: April 1998.* San Juan: Division of Labor Force Statistics, Bureau of Labor Statistics.

Burton, Richard D. E. 1997. *Afro-Creole: Power, Opposition, and Play in the Caribbean.* Ithaca, N.Y.: Cornell University Press.

C/LAA (Caribbean/Latin American Action). 1991. *Caribbean Basin Databook.* Washington, D.C.: Author.

Casey, Geraldine J. 1996. "New Tappings on the Keys: Changes in Work and Gender Roles for Women Clerical Workers in Puerto Rico." In *Puerto Rican Women and Work: Bridges in Transnational Labor,* ed. by Altagracia Ortiz, 209–33. Philadelphia: Temple University Press.

CIA (Central Intelligence Agency). 2000. *The World Factbook.* Washington, D.C.: Author.

Coppin, Addington. 1995. "Women, Men, and Work in Barbados." *Social and Economic Studies* 44(2–3): 103–25.

———. 1998. "A Comparison of Male-Female Earnings across Two Caribbean Economies." *Journal of Developing Areas* 32: 375–94.

Erikson, Ken C., and Donald D. Stull. 1998. *Doing Team Ethnography: Warnings and Advice.* Thousand Oaks, Calif.: Sage.

Espinal, Rosario, and Sherri Grasmuck. 1997. "Gender, Households, and Informal Entrepreneurship in the Dominican Republic." *Journal of Comparative Family Studies* 28: 103–28.

Etienne, Mona, and Eleanor Leacock, eds. 1980. *Women and Colonization: Anthropological Perspectives.* New York: Praeger.

Fernández-Kelly, Maria Patricia. 1983. *For We Are Sold, I and My People: Women and Industry in Mexico's Frontier.* Albany: State University of New York Press.

Fernández-Kelly, M. Patricia, and Saskia Sassen. 1995. "Recasting Women in the Global Economy." In *Women in the Latin American Development Process,* ed. by Christine Bose and Edna Acosta-Belén, 99–124. Philadelphia: Temple University Press.

Findlay, Eileen J. Suárez. 1999. *Imposing Decency: The Politics of Sexuality and Race in Puerto Rico, 1870–1920.* Durham, N.C.: Duke University Press.

Freeman, Carla. 2000. *High-Tech and High Heels in the Global Economy: Women, Work, and Pink Collar Identities in the Caribbean.* Durham, N.C.: Duke University Press.

———. 2001. "Is Local to Global as Masculine is to Feminine? Rethinking the Gender of Globalization." *Signs* 26: 1007–37.

Friedl, Ernestine. 2000. "Society and Sex Roles." In *Conformity and Conflict: Readings in Cultural Anthropology.* 10th ed., ed. by James Spradley and David W. McCurdy, 241–49. Needham Heights, Mass.: Allyn and Bacon.

Gautier, Arlette. 1995. "Women from Guadeloupe and Martinique." In *French and West Indian: Martinique, Guadeloupe, and French Guiana Today,* ed. by Richard D. E. Burton and Fred Reno, 119–36. Charlottesville: University Press of Virginia.

GEMINI (Growth and Equity through Microenterprise Investments and Institutions), and Frank Rubio. 1991. *Microenterprise Growth Dynamics in the Dominican Republic: The ADEMI Case: GEMINI Working Paper No. 21.* Bethesda, Md.: U.S. Agency for International Development.

Gmelch, George, and Sharon Bohn Gmelch. 1997. *The Parish behind God's Back: The Changing Culture of Rural Barbados.* Ann Arbor: University of Michigan Press.

Hannerz, Ulf. 1998. "Transnational Research." In *Handbook of Methods in Cultural Anthropology,* ed. by H. Russell Bernard, 235–56. Walnut Creek, Calif.: AltaMira Press.

Hillman, Richard S., and Thomas J. D'Agostino. 1992. *Distant Neighbors in the Caribbean: The Dominican Republic and Jamaica in Comparative Perspective.* New York: Praeger.

ILO (International Labour Office). 1972. *Employment, Incomes, and Equality: A Strategy for Increasing Productive Employment in Kenya.* Geneva: Author.

———. 1994. *Basic Management Training for Micro-Enterprises: A Training Material Addressing Primarily Women Entrepreneurs in the Informal Sector.* Geneva: Author.

INSEE (Institut National de la Statistique et des Etudes Economiques). 1986. "Les femmes chefs des menages." *Antiane Eco: La Revue Economique des Antilles et de la Guyane* 4: 1–5.

———. 1987. *Les comptes economiques de la Martinique en 1986.* 259 (40). Paris: Author.

———. 1994. *Femmes en chiffres.* Fort-de-France, Martinique: Author.

———. 1995. *Tableaux economiques régionaux de la Martinique: Edition 1995.* Fort-de-France, Martinique: Author.

———. 1997. *Tableaux economiques régionaux de la Martinique: Edition 1997.* Fort-de-France, Martinique: Author.

Jarman, Jennifer, Robert Blackburn, Bradley Brooks, and Esther Dermott. 1999. "Gender Differences at Work: International Variations in Occupational Segregation." *Sociological Research Online* 4(1), at www.socresonline.org.uk/ (accessed September 17, 2001).

Kessler-Harris, Alice, and Karen B. Sacks. 1987. "The Demise of Domesticity in America." In *Women, Households, and the Economy,* ed. by Lourdes Benería and Catharine Stimpson, 65–84. New Brunswick, N.J.: Rutgers University Press.

Marcus, George. 1995. "Ethnography in/of the World System." *Annual Review of Anthropology* 24: 95–117.

Massiah, Joycelin, ed. 1993. *Women in Developing Economies: Making Visible the Invisible.* Oxford, U.K.: Berg Publishers.

McKay, Leslie. 1993. "Women's Contribution to Tourism in Negril, Jamaica." In *Women and Change in the Caribbean: A Pan-Caribbean Perspective,* ed. by Janet Momsen, 278–86. London: James Currey.

Mesh, Cynthia J. 1997. "Empowering the Mother Tongue: The Creole Movement in Guadeloupe." In *Daughters of Caliban: Caribbean Women in the Twentieth Century,* ed. by Consuelo Lopez Springfield, 18–38. Bloomington: Indiana University Press.

Mintz, Sidney. 1977. "So-Called World System: Local Initiative and Local Response." *Dialectical Anthropology* 2: 253–70.

Momsen, Janet Henshall. 1993a. Introduction to *Women and Change in the Caribbean: A Pan-Caribbean Perspective,* ed. by Janet Momsen, 1–12. London: James Currey.

———. 1993b. "Development and Gender Divisions of Labour in the Rural Eastern Caribbean." In *Women and Change in the Caribbean: A Pan-Caribbean Perspective*, ed. by Janet Momsen, 232–46. London: James Currey.

———. 1998. "Gender Ideology and Land." In *Caribbean Portraits: Essays on Gender Ideologies and Identities*, ed. by Christine Barrow, 115–32. Kingston: Ian Randle Publishers.

Moore, Dorothy P., and E. Holly Buttner. 1997. *Women Entrepreneurs: Moving Beyond the Glass Ceiling.* Thousand Oaks, Calif.: Sage.

Moses, Yolanda T. 1977. "Female Status, the Family, and Male Dominance in a West Indian Community." In *Women and National Development: The Complexities of Change*, ed. by Wellesley Editorial Committee, 142–53. Chicago: University of Chicago Press.

Nash, June. 1995. "Latin American Women in the World Capitalist Crisis." In *Women in the Latin American Development Process*, ed. by Christine Bose and Edna Acosta-Belén, 151–66. Philadelphia: Temple University Press.

Ortiz, Altagracia. 1996. Introduction to *Puerto Rican Women and Work: Bridges in Transnational Labor*, ed. by Altagracia Ortiz, 3–32. Philadelphia: Temple University Press.

Poirier, Jean, and Huguette Dagenais. 1986. "En marge, la situation des femmes dans l'agriculture en Guadeloupe: situation actuelle, questions méthodologiques." *Environnement Caraïbe* 2: 151–86.

Rios, Palmira N. 1983. "Women under Colonialism: The Case of Puerto Rico." *Transafrica Forum* 2: 9–20.

———. 1995. "Gender, Industrialization, and Development in Puerto Rico." In *Women in the Latin American Development Process*, ed. by Christine Bose and Edna Acosta-Belén, 125–48. Philadelphia: Temple University Press.

Rivera, Marcia. 1989. "Women in the Caribbean Underground Economy." In *Development in Suspense*, ed. by Norman Girvan and George Beckford, 161–73. Kingston, Jamaica: Friedrich Ebert Stiftung.

Safa, Helen I. 1986. "Economic Autonomy and Sexual Equality in Caribbean Society." *Social and Economic Studies* 35(3): 1–21.

———. 1995. *The Myth of the Male Breadwinner: Women and Industrialization in the Caribbean.* Boulder, Colo.: Westview Press.

Scarano, Francisco A. 1989. "Labor and Society in the Nineteenth Century." In *The Modern Caribbean*, ed. by Franklin W. Knight and Colin A. Palmer, 51–84. Chapel Hill: University of North Carolina Press.

Scott, Alison M. 1990. "Patterns of Patriarchy in the Peruvian Working Class." In *Women, Employment, and the Family in the International Division of Labour*, ed. by Sharon Stichter and Jane L. Parpart, 198–220. Philadelphia: Temple University Press.

Smith, Raymond T. 1988. *Kinship and Class in the West Indies.* Cambridge, U.K.: Cambridge University Press.

Stichter, Sharon. 1990. "Women, Employment, and the Family: Current Debates." In *Women, Employment, and the Family in the International Division of Labour*, ed. by Sharon Stichter and Jane L. Parpart, 11–71. Philadelphia: Temple University Press.

Stichter, Sharon, and Jane L. Parpart, eds. 1990. *Women, Employment, and the Family in the International Division of Labour.* Philadelphia: Temple University Press.

Sutton, Constance, and Susan Makiesky-Barrow. 1981. "Social Inequality and Social Status in Barbados." In *The Black Woman Cross-Culturally*, ed. by Filomina C. Steady, 469–97. Cambridge, Mass.: Schenkman.

UNDP (United Nations Development Programme). 1995. *Human Development Report: 1995*. New York: Oxford University Press.

U.S. Bureau of the Census. 1990. *Social and Economic Characteristics of Puerto Rico: Fertility and Household and Family Composition: 1990*. Washington, D.C.: Decennial Management Division, Bureau of the Census.

Van der Wees, Catherine, and Henny Romijn. 1995. "Entrepreneurship and Small- and Microenterprise Development for Women: A Problematique in Search of Answers, a Policy in Search of Programs." In *Women in Micro- and Small-Scale Enterprise Development*, ed. by Louise Dignard and José Havet, 41–82. Boulder, Colo.: Westview Press.

Weisskoff, Richard. 1985. *Factories and Food Stamps: The Puerto Rico Model of Development*. Baltimore, Md.: Johns Hopkins University Press.

Wells, Sandra J. 1998. *Women Entrepreneurs: Developing Leadership for Success*. New York: Garland Publishers.

Wilson, Peter J. 1969. "Reputation and Respectability: A Suggestion for Caribbean Ethnology." *Man* 4: 70–84.

5

Women, Modernity, and the Global Economy: Negotiating Gender and Economic Difference in Ifugao, Upland Philippines

B. Lynne Milgram

INTRODUCTION

Women in the northern Philippines are refashioning their work in crafts as their rural economies experience dramatic social, political, and economic shifts with globalization. Increasingly, female artisans build on their history of producing and trading textiles, in particular, by applying their skills and experience to the production of other crafts such as wood carving and basketry, goods previously made only by men. Past studies have argued that the hegemony of capitalist market forces has dramatically restructured simple commodity enterprises such that women, particularly, have been marginalized, despite the great diversity among women worldwide (e.g., Boserup 1970; Ehlers 1990). They suggest that this is especially true of women's household production, such as crafts, as female artisans often work for low returns to combine their "productive" work with their "reproductive" tasks. This argument, however, denies women such as these Philippine artisans an alternative engagement with modernity[1] and the agency to effect change beyond the local level.

Recent feminist scholarship in anthropology and economics argues that understanding local transformations with globalizing forces means conducting "multisited" research (Marcus and Fischer 1999: viii–xix) that considers the macroeconomic world of financial and economic statistical indices hegemonic in developing nations but understands that this world "only indirectly maps, or models inaggregate approximations"—the experiential worlds of the peoples whom their policies affect (Marcus and Fischer 1999: xviii–xix; see Eber and Tanski n.d.; Ferber and Nelson 1993). Thus, as Anna Tsing similarly argues, although the global "flow" of goods and technology is valorized, "the carving of the channel" is not (2000: 330).

By positioning the local realities of Ifugao women's lives in craft making and trade within the national Philippine macroeconomic agenda, I seek a gendered and multisited understanding of how female artisans negotiate the impact of structural adjustment policies and the challenge of the global economy. In so doing, this approach reveals a counterposition to the more prevalent studies that focus on changes in men's and women's work in more industrialized economies or in the industrial and agricultural spheres of less industrialized countries (e.g., Ong 1987; Wolf 1992; Ypeij 2000). This chapter thus highlights "the numerous layers of mediation and incommensurability" (Marcus and Fischer 1999: xix) ongoing in globalization and how women navigate these from local community to international arena.

By maintaining their multiple-economic-strategy approach, female artisans build on the historical precedent of relations of reciprocity and their work outside the household to negotiate their status from producer to producer-trader. They organize collective cooperative production and transform their gendered identification with specific crafts, such as weaving, to produce baskets and wood carvings, products previously made only by men. In so doing, these artisans craft their own version of modernity. By simultaneously participating in and reconfiguring modern market institutions, they generate both material wealth and symbolic capital, enabling them to meet economic goals as well as cultural community expectations. Their actions thus dispute models of modernity that hinge on sharp divisions between "domestic" and "public" or between "family" and "economy," as the internal dynamics of Ifugao family life and the cultural expectations of community (e.g., redistributive feasting) continue to be interwoven with the external forces of market exchange and state policy.

Exploring female artisans' different experiences of global forces in Ifugao suggests understanding the economy not as a bounded and unified space with a singular capitalist identity but rather as a "site of multiple forms of economy whose relations to each other are only ever partially fixed and always under subversion" (Gibson-Graham 1996: 15). I argue like Gibson-Graham (1996: 15) that "recontextualizing capitalism in a discourse of economic plurality destabilizes its presumptive hegemony" and enables us to re-envision sites of economic difference where a variety of capitalist, noncapitalist, and class processes interact. Analyzing women's changing socioeconomic roles in crafts reveals the importance of considering how power relations among women and their multiple local to regional to national experiences affect the channels through which they negotiate their productive and reproductive roles within household, community, and larger national arena. Thus I want to suggest, as Tania Li (1999: 295) points out, that it is most important to understand how the practice of power or rule is "worked out in the contingent and compromised space of cultural intimacy" which, in the Philippine case, determines women's power to shape social and economic relations.

In this chapter, I first review the theoretical advances in feminist economics that are relevant to the study of female artisans in Banaue, Ifugao. I then outline the Philippine government's macroeconomic policies and how they are implemented at the provincial level. To explore people's own alternatives to the Philippine government's modernization policies, I focus on women engaged in craft production at both the household and cooperative levels. This discussion highlights the incompatibility between policies instituted over the past two decades and locally based ideas about engagement in capitalist enterprises, ideas that take cultural traditions, values, and women's economic roles into account.

SOCIAL CHANGE, FEMINIST THEORY, AND GLOBAL CAPITAL

Feminist researchers using gendered analyses of social change have critiqued dominant theories of economic development and capitalist hegemony. Early theorists assumed that a move toward individualism and modernity with the advent of capitalism would bring new forms of subordination for women, particularly. They argued that the introduction of new technology more readily available in the public sphere dominated by men would cause women to lose control over important cultural and environmental resources as the majority of their influence and work remains centered in the household sphere (Stamp 1989; Aguilar and Miralao 1984). In some circumstances this is certainly the case; but it is the way this steamroller model of capitalism and modernity has been "thought" that has made it so difficult to imagine alternatives—a world of economic difference (Gibson-Graham 1996: 5).

Since the 1980s, feminist economists have been problematizing the neoclassical economic paradigm, a paradigm heavily influenced by individualistic assumptions and explanations of the market economy. They argue that with its current focus on mathematics and econometric analyses, neoclassical theory purports to be more scientific and rational than theories that utilize a more descriptive or case study approach (Nelson 1996: 27; McCloskey 1993). Arguing that most economic discourses are "capitalocentric" (Gibson-Graham 1996: 6), that capitalist economies may not be as prevalent as mainstream economics assume, these critiques advocate developing alternative models—models that "liberate a heterospace" of both capitalist and noncapitalist economic forums that reflect people's "real-life" experiments (Graham-Gibson 1996: 5). These include local assumptions rooted in cooperation, empathy, and collective decision making (Eber and Tanski n.d.; Sequino, Stevens, and Lutz 1996; Strober 1994; Waring 1988).

Feminist scholars argue that a major weakness of neoclassical economic theory is that capitalism is portrayed as unified, singular, and total rather than as uncentered, dispersed, plural, and partial in relation to other spheres of society (Ferber and Nelson 1993). Theorists employing models that rule out alternatives, namely the coexistence of multiple economic practices, privilege individualism, self-interest, and the ideal of "perfect competition" as "natural" values that need not be questioned. In such a world "rightfully owned" by capitalism (Gibson-Graham 1996: 120), any actions not wholly capitalist or non-commodified become capitalism's "other" (Gibson-Graham 1996: 122). Such models of economics preclude strategies of real opposition by relegating to the backwoods of "tradition" and "premodernity" societies such as Banaue, Ifugao, where social and cultural relations and values continue to be rooted in reciprocal and community networks, as well as in economic negotiations. Neoclassical economic analysis has ignored such alternative forums and their potential for configuring different forms of social organization, policy, and action (Benería 1999: 72).

By focusing on communities such as Banaue, it becomes evident that neoclassical theory's implied equivalence of the economy to the market and assumption that markets are the most ideal means of allocating resources fail to apply (Benería 1999: 65). Central to feminists' critique is the assertion that "models of free individual choice are not adequate to analyze behavior fraught with issues of dependence, interdependence, tradition, and power" (Ferber and Nelson 1993: 6).

Exploring the dialectal relationship between internal cultural constraints of communities and external market forces, feminist economists highlight loci of economic activity that neoclassical theorists neglect, including households, local communities, and nonprofit sectors (Karim 1995; Illo 1995). Devoting particular attention to households as traditional sites of women's economic activity, they argue that in terms of both value of output and numbers of people involved, the household sector cannot be called marginal (Albelda 1997; Folbre 1988). Their research on households and other local economic sites directly contradicts the neoclassical description of markets in which decisions are made freely by individuals acting alone, a description that denies the integral roles of community and family members based on different social and economic bonds and expectations.

Gendered analyses of the effects of economic development and globalization on rural women in Southeast Asia, in particular, have shown the limitations of viewing male-headed peasant households as the basic unit of production (Brenner 1998; Illo 1995; Milgram 1999, 2001). Insights from these studies conclude that women in rural societies play much larger roles in agriculture and household-based production, such as crafts, than previously recognized. As Atkinson observes for the highland Wana in Sulawesi, Indonesia, "the conjugal relationship is about work" and "both spouses are expected to be hardworking contributors to their productive unit" (1990: 68). Rural women generate income through artisanal and agricultural production, wage labor, and trade, negotiating a complex network of different economic activities to mitigate the effects of shifting demands. As Karim (1995: 28) argues, the marginalization of the "domestic" sphere by neoclassical economists has overlooked how such activities for women in Southeast Asia encompass economic and commercial value beyond the normal consumptive needs of the family and household:

> So-called "domestic" activities are often part of a continuous chain of produc-tive enterprises linked to a woman's need [and ability] to obtain independent sources of income.

Throughout the Philippine Cordillera, women's labor thus makes a significant contribution to the well-being and economic productivity of their households and plays a fundamental role in maintaining the peasant economy and repro-ducing cultural capital.

Philippine studies have also shown that increasing global competition, trade liberalization, and the adoption of structural adjustment programs have had unequal effects on men and women in different areas (e.g., Balisacan 1995; Chant 1996; Morton 1996). Research indicates that those in low- and middle-income households are the most likely to be negatively affected and that women face disproportionately negative consequences from the adjust-ment strategies that have been implemented (Chant 1996: 297). Central to the analysis of the effects on women of structural adjustment policies is the recog-nition of women's triple role—their responsibilities in household production, reproduction, and community maintenance (Ofreneo and Habana 1987). In-creased participation in income-generating activities in both the formal and informal sectors often lengthens the workday of many women; the elimina-tion of food subsidies and the rising prices reduce women's spending power as food providers; and rising prices further affect the purchasing power of women's earnings more negatively than men's, as women are concentrated in low-wage jobs often within the household and on a part-time basis.[2]

Structural adjustment policies are the product of macroeconomic perspec-tives that have "no human face"; they focus almost exclusively on promoting "economic efficiency and bringing an economy to a stable and sustainable growth path" (Balisacan 1995: 33). They do not take into account the processes of reproduction, the maintenance of human resources, and the value of unremunerated work, in which women are more intensively involved than men. Even when macroeconomic perspectives consider reproduction, they fail to carefully examine households to understand the different positions of women and men within them. They thus ignore the implications of house-holds as sites for renegotiating gender roles with the advent of global capital.

In Ifugao, female artisans, especially, reconfigure homogeneous national capitalist policies into sites of economic difference that accommodate the in-teraction of multiple economic and class processes. Through their engage-ment in commercial crafts, they pursue different channels to transform global forces into local forms that they can operationalize to benefit both their per-sonal positions and those of their families.

A Dynamic Setting: Banaue, Ifugao, and Women's Positions

Ifugao is located in the Gran Cordillera Central mountain range, which extends through much of northern Luzon. The main economic activity in Ifugao, as throughout the Cordillera, is subsistence wet-rice cultivation carried out in irrigated pond-fields. In some areas, such as Banaue, the high elevation (1,500 meters) and cool climate means that cultivation is limited to one rice crop per year. With no mixed agricultural production base and no agricultural surplus for commercial sale, most families must engage in other nonagricultural cash-earning activities such as wage labor or crafts. These crafts are sold to tourists coming to view the region's spectacular rice terraces.

The region of the Gran Cordillera Central resisted Spanish domination for 300 years (1565–1898). It became part of the Philippine state through negotiation rather than conquest during the American colonial period, 1898–1946. Early American policy in this region stressed local control over local economy and resources. Although this policy was later reversed, it set the precedent for the autonomy of the indigenous population (Jenista 1987). This has meant that many of the community's cultural and economic elements have remained dynamic and provide the basis of unique local development. For example, the production of crafts for domestic and ritual use exists in a commercial market economy which was introduced in the early 1900s and which accelerated after World War II, and particularly since the 1970s, with growing tourism. The pluralism of Banaue's socioeconomic practices thus provides a provocative context within which to situate the changing dynamics of craft production and the ensuing negotiation of gender and economic relations with the advent of globalization and capitalist market forces.

Throughout the Cordillera, the ideology of gender equality has set the historical precedent for many women's continuing engagement in a variety of intrahousehold and extrahousehold economic activities. The region's bilateral kinship system and women's right to own land through inheritance laws that honor seniority rather than gender mean that there are few restrictions on women's participation in income-generating work both within and outside of the community. Although some household tasks are assigned by age and gender, many are highly interchangeable, and some men assume more domestic responsibilities if their wives are successful in business (Bacdayan 1977). Most Cordillera women also have extensive experience managing and controlling household finances—pooling, collecting, and allocating the family's earnings. Such circumstances enable many women to maximize their earning potential and, often, simultaneously enhance their symbolic and social capital by sharing their good fortune through culturally prescribed channels of gift giving and sponsorship of special events.[3]

Within the Cordillera ideology of equal rights, however, men and women continuously renegotiate gendered roles and power relations as they redefine their work and positions in a rapidly commoditizing society. In Ifugao, moreover, it is also important to consider the differences among women, rather than seeing them as one homogeneous group equal to a similarly homogeneous group of men. Depending upon factors such as their social class (landed elite, tenant, or landless) and their education, some women as artisans and traders may have more of an advantage than others to gain prestige and increase income through their involvement in craft production and trade.

Globalization, Women, and Structural Adjustment in the Philippines

Following the Second World War and Philippine independence in 1946, different political parties dominating the Philippine government sought to "modernize" the domestic economy through protectionist policies. In the 1970s, during the Marcos administration, the reinsertion of the Philippines into the global economy was carried out as a response to the internal limits of import substitution. In an officially propagated export fever, export-processing zones were, and continue to be, actively established in major Philippine urban centers targeting the manufacture of garments, electrical equipment, and handicrafts for export. The growth of small and medium-sized industries, through the promotion of foreign investment, is part of an export-oriented and "outward-looking" pattern of development being pursued upon the recommendation of the World Bank and other international lending agencies (Pineda 1995: 153–54). At the same time, officials began implementing policies to achieve modernization more effectively than in the past. These included monetary devaluations, privatization of industry, a policy of austerity (massive cutbacks in government social spending), and deregulation of markets and prices (Chant 1996; Morton 1996).

As a consequence, for example, subcontracting and the use of outworkers in small and medium-sized industries in southern Luzon has continued to grow since the implementation of these policies in the early 1980s. Studies have documented the multileveled subcontracting practices prevalent in both agriculture (e.g., bananas, market gardening, pig raising) and industry (leather, garments, toys, food processing, electronics, and handicrafts) and how women, particularly, at the bottom of the subcontracting ladder, are often the most exploited in home-based production (Pineda 1995).

With regard to handicrafts, however, this subcontracting pattern is primarily applied to the most marketable products, such as rattan baskets and furniture and wood carvings, the large majority of which are obtained from craft producers living in lowland areas within easy access to existing road transportation (bus and truck). The importance of being able to distribute raw materials and collect finished products in a timely manner has largely excluded the participation of artisans in the northern Cordillera provinces. The ten- to twelve-hour drive between Manila, Baguio City, and Banaue, and the unreliability of the roads (the only available mode of transportation), especially during the long, rainy season, has meant that the national government's push for local production to conform to global capitalist practices has been differentially implemented in provinces such as Ifugao. The Philippine government agenda then trickles down unevenly to Cordillera artisans, depending upon the efforts of the provincial offices of the Department of Trade and Industry (DTI).

In 1992, for example, the Ramos administration instituted the Presidential Council for Countryside Development with the mandate to "fast-track the development of the countryside" and specifically the nineteen poorest provinces, of which Ifugao is one (DTI 1992: 1). Within this initiative, the National Economic Enterprise Development (NEED) program was founded to "focus on handicraft production for export development. The NEED program identifies raw materials and skill potentials for entrepreneurs in target provinces and initiates skills training, enterprise development and marketing networks to maximize the use of local resources" (DTI 1992: 2).

Under this umbrella, DTI offers different programs, but all are oriented to small entrepreneurs already established in business, and as such they present barriers to those in part-time household production. In crafts, the vast majority of these small businesses are in the wood carving industry. Wood carving made the leap to the commercial export market in the 1950s when many Ifugao wood carvers moved to Benguet province in the south to work on road building projects after the end of the Second World War. Weaving, on the other hand, even that done for commercial sale to regional and national tourist markets, remains almost exclusively a woman's craft, practiced part-time, at the household level.

In response to the needs of such household production and as part of DTI's Five-Year Development Plan, 1993 to 1998 (Bunolna 1993; PDC 1993), a special initiative was mounted to identify and assist as many as six small "anchor firms" in different handicraft media (weaving, wood carving, baskets, paper, furniture, ceramics) in each of Ifugao's eleven municipalities (Bunolna 1993: 19). A specific goal was to "target at least one small exporter of loom weaving" (Bunolna 1993: 23) in the municipality of Banaue, which is particularly renowned for its cloth production. Through this special program, the beneficiary would receive skills training in weaving and dye technology, and consultations with the Product Design and Development Centre in Manila on the current and popular product styles and colors.

In Banaue, DTI identified Paul Bannug's[4] weaving business as the "anchor type enterprise" they would sponsor (Bunolna 1993: 14). Paul, forty-two years old with three children, had been weaving on an upright (*tilar*) loom since 1990. While still a teenager, he had helped his mother and sister prepare the yarns for cloth production and later had assisted in selling their weavings in the town craft stores. Following the devastating earthquake of 1990, the DTI supplied aid to ten Banaue weavers by giving them upright looms for cloth production. Paul's mother received one of the looms. As these looms require large amounts of yarn for production, they did not suit the backstrap weaving practices of most household producers, who can afford to buy only small quantities of yarn at one time and who try to produce differently colored and patterned products to satisfy the local market for variety in woven products. Many of these upright floor looms thus sat idle for some years.

Paul attended the skills training sessions on loom weaving, cloth dyeing, and product design run by DTI and continued to weave on his mother's upright loom. In 1992, using his family's land as collateral, Paul obtained a loan from the local bank to establish a loom weaving business. He purchased four looms not being used by his neighbors and added a room onto his roadside house to accommodate this new equipment. He then hired five local weavers to produce the yardage he had designed.

When I first met Paul in 1995, his business had already encountered difficulties. The first weavers he had hired quit after working for him for seven months; they complained that Paul did not pay them sufficiently for their labor or that he paid them in kind, not in cash, and that he begrudged them days off to celebrate family ritual occasions. This pattern was again repeated the following year with different artisans. Currently, the weavers in Paul's village refuse to work in his business. With such unstable working relationships, Paul was unable to complete and deliver a large order he had received from a well-known Manila department store. From 1995 to 1998, Paul relied on the periodic labor of his sister and two cousins to fill the infrequent orders he received from Baguio City craft shops in the regional tourist center.

The DTI staff agree that Paul's business practices are problematic and concede that in 1996 they tried to eliminate him from their list of beneficiaries, as he had done little with the extensive training they had invested in him. The DTI's gaze, however, continues to be gender-blind. To these government officials, Paul operates Banaue's only "commercial" loom weaving business that manufactures products with the potential for export. The fact that the majority of local weaving is done by women on backstrap looms in household production has been totally overlooked by DTI in facilitating accessibility to their programs. Staff explain that they continue to encourage Paul to acquire personal communication skills and to improve his business management practices.

Such action, moreover, is indicative of how DTI is operationalizing the Philippine government's macroeconomic agenda. Staff currently confirm that they are first targeting the larger producers or traders, primarily men, in the hope that the benefits of such initiatives will eventually trickle down to individual artisans. Thus DTI field officers have done little to support local collective production or to establish more accessible marketing options. Instead, they have chosen to devote their energy and funds to events such as national craft trade fairs, in which the high cost of booth rental fees (9,000 pesos or

US$250) excludes all but the wealthiest entrepreneurs; these fairs, however achieve a high public profile.

The DTI remains convinced of their vision of modernity, as evidenced in their treatment of empirical evidence. On the one hand, they use favorable economic results such as traders' attendance at their fairs to validate their neoliberal policies based on the success of only selected craftspeople; on the other, they interpret unfavorable results as evidence of Ifugao artisans' timid implementation of the neoliberal model. Because most independent craftspeople can make only limited use of DTI-initiated projects, many are formulating their own economic tactics rooted in relations of social reproduction to reconfigure global forces into local forms.

OPERATIONALIZING OPTIONS IN CRAFTS:
THE MAPOD WEAVING COOPERATIVE

Banaue women have responded to the advent of global capital by intensifying the use of resources under their control. Building on their historical precedent of working in crafts as both producers and traders, women strive to hold on to a way of life that is fundamental to their identities by exploring new opportunities in crafts.

Without access to DTI's programs, some women have organized themselves into weaving cooperatives. In these groups, women have developed leadership skills, provided much-needed economic support to their households, and reinforced strong social networks through cooperative work. In response to the Ramos administration's initiative in Ifugao, in 1994 a local NGO (nongovernmental organization) provided startup loan funds to help establish a weaving cooperative in a Banaue village. At weavers' requests, the agency provided the construction materials for a building to house the weaving cooperative; one member contributed the land for the building and the others contributed the labor for the actual construction. With an initial loan to cover the cost of weaving materials and the purchase of six looms, the Mapod Weaving Cooperative of fourteen members was in operation by early 1995. Like many new enterprises, the cooperative suffered initial growing pains. Loan repayments were due before buyers for their products could be found and before weavers could establish a regular production schedule. With the strong leadership of a few board directors, however, cooperative members are now repaying their loan, albeit in smaller than expected amounts, and in 1997, the collective was able to raise the 2,000-peso (US$60) fee to formally register themselves as a cooperative. The cooperative is now eligible to apply for provincial grants targeting formally organized artisan livelihood enterprises.

The Mapod Weaving Cooperative produces handwoven cotton yardage from which they manufacture a variety of functional products such as bags, backpacks, and garments. They sell these items to tourist craft shops in Banaue and in Baguio City, and directly to tourists visiting the cooperative.

Much of the woven yardage is uniquely designed such that the spatial organization of the woven and tie-dyed (ikat) motifs coincide with the final construction of the product; this design innovation contributes to the organization's efforts to claim a niche in the competitive market for Ifugao textiles. Weavers feel they have more control over their earnings, as they are paid an agreed-upon fee per finished item; the fee varies depending upon the product (e.g., garments, bags), not upon the whims of wholesale buyers.

The cooperative, however, is still negotiating how it can mitigate the effects of the fluctuating demand for crafts. During the long, rainy season (May to November), the sales of weavings locally are slow, as few tourists visit the Cordillera region. This means that at those times when the cooperative does not have sufficient funds to purchase yarn for members' cloth production, the stock of accumulated weavings is low. Thus, when buyer demand is at its height during the tourist season from December to mid-May, or when the cooperative receives a large order on short notice, the organization may not have sufficient yardage in stock to meet these demands. In addition, at such times, the cooperative's one sewing machine is not sufficient for members to manufacture large orders within a limited time frame.

To overcome this seasonal cycle, cooperative members have decided to diversify their income-generating activities by selling rice. In 1998, they applied the profits they made from selling weavings to purchase rice in bulk. They sell the rice in smaller per-kilo amounts that are more easily affordable by local artisan-cultivators. The profits from the rice sales have been rechannelled into low-interest loans to cooperative members. This, in turn, has stimulated membership. Cooperative members support the practice of paying loan interest, as these funds contribute directly to the organization's capital to purchase yarns for future cloth production and, hopefully, for a second sewing machine. The availability of yarn encourages women to weave throughout the year, thus keeping products in stock while strengthening their allegiance to their self-managed organization.

The cooperative also provides an important context in which older women work with younger women to teach them to weave as well as how to organize alternatives to the status quo of livelihood enterprises. For example, older weavers have started training younger members to sew the cooperative's specially designed products. In the process of working across generational lines, women conserve the kinship networks of support that have been so important to their cultural and material survival. Indeed, weavers supplied the initial cooperative membership by drawing on those women with whom they worked in reciprocal labor exchanges in rice cultivation. Thus, capital production here is rooted in relations of social reproduction.

Women in the cooperative also benefit from being able to rely on more than just the members of their extended families for moral and material support and for advice in making social and economic decisions. Because a cooperative reduces the tendency for members to be isolated in their homes, women working in such organizations can expand the network of people with whom they interact to learn how to use their household and extra-household resources in different social and economic spheres.

To promote their sales beyond the local and regional levels and to achieve more autonomy within the current market structure, the cooperative has recently taken steps to enter the global craft market on its own terms; it has established connections with the Community Crafts Association of the Philippines, or CCAP. The Community Crafts Association of the Philippines, a nongovernmental organization, is in contact with international craft distributors who participate in fair trade networks; to further promote their services they have established a listing on PEOPLink, a website devoted to marketing fair trade crafts produced worldwide. Alternative Trade Organizations (ATOs), adhering to fair trade practices, buy goods directly from small producers to eliminate the layers of middlepeople and the multiple mark-ups. Fair trade guarantees producers a locally appropriate price for their products to enable them to earn enough money to remain on their land and support their families. ATOs do not work to maximize shareholders' profits, but rather to foster a more democratic and equitable system of international exchange, one that confronts the dominant "disciplinary authority" of current global markets (Grimes 2000; Littrell and Dickson 1999).

In the Mapod Weaving Cooperative then, women's participation in fair trade networks and their efforts to diversify their work options harmonize with feminist critiques of markets (e.g., Eber and Tanski n.d.; England 1993; Folbre 1996; Strassman 1997). Their actions challenge the hegemony of neo-classical economic discourse, highlighting women as significant agents of social change in the Philippine Cordillera.

BASKETRY AND WOOD CARVING: NEW SPHERES
FOR WOMEN'S PRODUCTION AND TRADE

In addition to establishing craft cooperatives, female artisans have developed new, innovative products in response to the growing global demand for crafts. Female artisans, in particular, are designing new crafts that combine weaving, basketry, and wood carving in functional household products such as containers and trays. Weavers who periodically lack capital to buy yarn for cloth production work in these cross-media crafts either full- or part-time, depending upon the demand. One craft is not more prestigious than the others, but the growing export market for embellished wood containers means that unlike weaving, demand is not as firmly tied to the seasonal fluctuations in local tourism, and thus, these crafts provide a more continuous source of work and a higher rate of pay than that from cloth production. Women, however, do not necessarily learn their new craft skills from other family members, as they do with weaving. Rather, artisans may learn basketry and carving from any knowledgeable community member willing to teach them, thereby broadening their network of contacts within the community.

In Ifugao, as throughout Southeast Asia, weaving has been symbolically associated with women's production, and carving and basketry with that of men (Gittinger 1989). Through their current involvement in the latter craft forms, then, female artisans in Banaue are actively renegotiating their gendered association solely with cloth production to fashion an alternative modernity. Rather than abandon low-paying crafts like weaving to pursue better-paying factory work, as the unidirectional neoclassical economic model would have us assume, female artisans in Banaue build on the precedent of an interchangeability of household tasks to reconfigure the gender division of labor in productive craft work.

In so doing, women have used these new crafts to open different channels through which they can meet the challenges of structural adjustment policies that do little to recognize local alternative models of self-development. Earnings from different spheres of craft production can increase the security of total household income and may indeed enable families to improve their personal positions within the community both socially and economically. Although the majority of female artisans engaged in these new craft forms are working on a piecework basis, this arrangement can still offer advantages to producers. As these crafts often pay more than weaving, they allow artisans to maximize their earnings through the flexibility to work in different crafts according to market demand. The knowledge of and earnings from these new skills can facilitate the shift from petty commodity producer to producer-trader.

Ruth Mataag, for example, thirty-two years old and a widow with three children, supports her family with her craft business. When her husband died in 1993, she took her savings from her basketry piecework to start her own business. She works hard to develop a good relationship with four urban buyers to ensure that she obtains continuous orders. Ruth tries to obtain commissions for decorated bowls and trays rather than small containers, as she can complete the former in less time and thus realize a better profit. With a small rice field that provides her family with six months' worth of rice each year, Ruth has been able to continue her business without accruing debts.[5]

As with other local crafts in Banaue, however, there may be a drop in demand during the rainy season from mid-May through November. To overcome these obstacles, these new businesswomen like Ruth have agreed to cooperate in setting standard prices. They will not sell their products to shop owners for less than the standard price during the low season and will negotiate as a group to determine price increases for their goods. Like her fellow businesswomen, Ruth must continually negotiate with the carvers, male and female, for prompt delivery and stable prices. But negotiating market relations constitutes only one-half of doing business in Ifugao.

In the Philippines, trade is a dialectic relationship between partners operating at various levels of the production-marketing network: between artisans and local traders or shop owners, and between local traders and regional and national buyers (Anderson 1969; Dannhaeuser 1983). Known as a *suki* relationship and acknowledged as the very foundation of Philippine entrepreneurship (Davis 1973: 179), its aim is to ensure reliability in a changing economic environment that is often erratic and negotiated without written contracts. Its form is one of personalized relations, marked by "subjective values and extralegal sanctions which encourage individuals to meet obligations to others" (Davis 1973: 211). As Anderson (1969: 642) emphasizes, such "economic personalism" is the "social cement" necessary for economic success; "technical competence is less crucial."

In building up their social network of *suki* relationships, traders try to develop new personal ties or activate existing relations of kinship and neighborhood. Traders like Ruth explain that when artisans approach them with requests for help, in order to nurture and maintain the loyalty of their producers they have to explore every avenue to "remedy artisans' problems." Artisans most often request cash to pay for unexpected medical expenses or for sacrificial animals, usually pigs, which are required for the many local Ifugao rituals. In personalized trade agreements such as these, the importance of an entrepreneur's trading reputation and his or her need to ensure a steady supply of products when required means that community expectations have left avenues of resistance open to artisans. Entrepreneurs such as Ruth customarily redistribute a portion of their surplus, usually in the form of gifts of food or cash advances, to maintain good businesses relationships. Thus, while operationalizing new economic opportunities in the global market for crafts, producers and traders are simultaneously entrenched in patterns of reciprocal exchange of goods and services. In a similar gesture of goodwill, Ruth often gives samples of new products to her urban buyers, or she may discount the final balance due her in order to promote future orders.

Such exchange relations problematize understanding the market as the unfettered circulation of money and commodities—one that breaks down traditional social hierarchies and distinctions and bypasses the constraints of culture or history. It disputes the premise that the market, governed by the logic of capital, gradually comes to govern the logics by which society itself operates. This image of the market, as this case study of Banaue's craft industry highlights, while compelling, has its limitations. In the upland Philippines as elsewhere, the market is entangled with local social, political, and cultural forces in ways that do not fit well with neoclassical theory of capitalist development and modernization.

CONCLUSION

Exploring contemporary craft practices in Banaue offers a gendered and local understanding of some of the impacts of economic change in the upland Philippines. On the one hand, women confront the global economy through their collective methods of survival. As both defenders of traditions and as innovators, artisans make the transition into market relations that extend and modify traditional definitions of self and community without completely abandoning those definitions. By producing and marketing weavings in craft cooperatives, women reaffirm their connection to a place and to valued local practices, and they strengthen their families and communities while expanding economic and, potentially, political rights for themselves and other women. (See also Eber and Tanski n.d.)

Similarly, women's movement into producing baskets and wood carvings, crafts previously made only by men, illustrates how female artisans actively expand their identification with different types of crafts; they combine production in both "hard" (male) and "soft" (female) material-based crafts to best operationalize opportunities in the global craft market.

Despite these shifts in women's work, I do not argue that, in all cases, such initiatives can provide sustainable development for all women in the context of global capital. This belief belies the tremendous structural forces at play against them and the extent to which globalization has transformed social relations on many basic levels.

Rather, I want to highlight the dilemmas that accompany the concepts of globalization and modernization. Gibson-Graham (1996: 145) points out that the "local" or "localization," as in household or community cooperative production, is often posited as global capital's only alternative—the way in which "global processes can . . . be pinned down in certain localities and become the basis for self-sustaining growth in those places." She cautions, however, that while localization may encompass alternatives or resistance to global capital by the local, any models enveloping this premise must also make room for the penetration of globalization and capitalist practices by the local: "making global capitalism lose its erection becomes a real possibility if we reject the naturalization of power that is conferred upon capitalism" by such neoclassical paradigms (1996: 146). I suggest, then, that by considering other-than-capitalist practices and the multiple channels through which women fashion economic difference, we can engage in a critical study of economic change that includes in its agenda preferential options for subaltern majorities. We can come to understand how women, through their agency, operationalize capitalist practice as one among many forms of economy.

ACKNOWLEDGMENTS

Field research for this chapter was conducted from November 1994 to September 1995, from January to July 1998, and from June to July 2000 and 2001.

Financial support for this research was provided by the Social Sciences and Humanities Research Council of Canada (SSHRC), Doctoral Fellowship, Post-Doctoral Fellowship and Standard Research Grant, and by the Canada/ASEAN Centre (Association of Southeast Asian Nations), Academic Support Programme. I also wish to thank the editor of this book, Gracia Clark, and the anonymous reviewers for their thoughtful comments on this paper. In the Philippines, I am affiliated with the Cordillera Studies Center, University of the Philippines, College Baguio, Baguio City. I thank my colleagues at CSC for their generous support of my research. To the residents of Banaue, I owe a debt of gratitude.

NOTES

1. Following Brenner (1998: 10) and Appadurai (1996: 18), I use the term "modernity" to reflect the overlap of meanings that is common in discussions of this concept. Modernity implies something experienced subjectively by individuals through their awareness of becoming part of a new way of life, but which also reflects the changes in social institutions and social relations so closely associated with modernity such as the rise of capitalism, industrialization and global markets, the expansion of the state into everyday life, and increasingly complex divisions of labor and class.

2. In addition, during recessions, women's employment prospects in higher-waged manufacturing jobs tend to deteriorate and their jobs are likely to be threatened more than men's, because many women are employed in less skilled occupations easily replaced by machines (Chant 1996: 297–301).

3. Current research on gender relations in Southeast Asia has argued that women's control of household finances and their prominence in community economic activities is not necessarily accompanied by so-called high status. Throughout island Southeast Asia, spiritual potency and public oratory skills, attributes controlled by men, are accorded the highest status and prestige (Atkinson 1990; Brenner 1998). Thus, Western economic models that seek to improve women's positions solely by increasing economic opportunities are not as effective as their advocates would have us believe. The tension between women's control of economics, but exclusion from political and religious spheres, is ongoing. Women thus make extra efforts to accumulate cultural capital by distributing gifts and sponsoring rituals to negotiate community prestige.

4. All personal names of individuals identified herein are pseudonyms.

5. As a self-employed basketry producer-trader, Ruth's income per day is as high as 130 pesos compared to 40 pesos per day earned in weaving (in 1998). The exchange rate in 1998 was US$1.00 = 35 Philippine pesos; in 2001 it was US$1.00 = 44 Philippine pesos.

REFERENCES

Aguilar, Filomeno V., and Virginia A. Miralao. 1984. *Handicrafts, Development, and Dilemmas over Definition (The Philippines as a Case in Point).* Handicraft Project Paper Series No. 1. Manila: Ramon Magsaysay Award Foundation.

Albelda, R. 1997. *Economics and Feminism: Disturbances in the Field.* New York: Twayne Publishers.

Anderson, James N. 1969. "Buy-and-Sell and Economic Personalism: Foundations for Philippine Entrepreneurship. " *Asian Survey* 9: 641–68.

Appadurai, Arjun. 1996. *Modernity at Large: Cultural Dimensions of Globalization.* Minneapolis, Minn.: University of Minnesota Press.

Atkinson, Jane Monnig. 1990. "How Gender Makes a Difference in Wana Society." In *Power and Difference: Gender in Island Southeast Asia,* ed. by J. M. Atkinson and S. Errington, 59–93. Palo Alto, Calif.: Stanford University Press.

Bacdayan, Albert S. 1977. "Mechanistic Cooperation and Sexual Equality among the Western Bontoc." In *Sexual Stratification: A Cross-Cultural View,* ed. by Alice Schlegel, 270–91. New York: Columbia University Press.

Balisacan, Arsenio M. 1995. "Anatomy of Poverty during Adjustment: The Case of the Philippines." *Economic Development and Cultural Change* 44(1): 33–62.

Benería, Lourdes. 1999. "Globalization, Gender, and the Davos Man." *Feminist Economics* 5(3): 61–83.

Boserup, Esther. 1970. *Women's Role in Economic Development.* New York: St. Martin's Press.

Brenner, Suzanne April. 1998. *The Domestication of Desire: Women, Wealth, and Modernity in Java.* Princeton, N.J.: Princeton University Press.

Bunolna, Jacinta N. 1993. *Medium and Short Term Trade and Industry Plans, Province of Ifugao, 1993–1998.* Report. Lagawe, Ifugao: Department of Trade and Industry.

Chant, Sylvia. 1996. "Women's Roles in Recession and Economic Restructuring in Mexico and the Philippines." *Geoforum* 27(3): 297–327.

Dannhaeuser, Norbert. 1983. *Contemporary Trade Strategies in the Philippines: A Study in Marketing Anthropology.* New Brunswick, N.J.: Rutgers University Press.

Davis, William G. 1973. *Social Relations in a Philippine Market: Self-Interest and Subjectivity.* Berkeley and Los Angeles: University of California Press.

DTI (Department of Trade and Industry). 1992. *Presidential Council for Countryside Development Summary Report.* Lagawe, Ifugao: Department of Trade and Industry, Provincial Government of Ifugao.

Eber, Christine, and Janet M. Tanski. n.d. *We Are Struggling to Unite All Mexico and the World: Women and Development in San Pedro, Chenalh, Chiapas, Mexico.* Unpublished manuscript.

Ehlers, Tracey B. 1990. *Silent Looms: Women and Production in a Guatemalan Town.* Boulder, Colo.: Westview Press.

England, Paula. 1993. "The Separative Self: Androcentric Bias in Neoclassical Assumptions." In *Beyond Economic Man: Feminist Theory and Economics,* ed. by M. A. Ferber and J. A. Nelson, 37–53. Chicago: University of Chicago Press.

Ferber, Marianne, and Julie Nelson, eds. 1993. *Beyond Economic Man: Feminist Theory and Economics.* Chicago: University of Chicago Press.

Folbre, Nancy. 1988. "The Black Four of Hearts: Toward a New Paradigm of Household Economics." In *A Home Divided: Women and Income in the Third World,* ed. by D. Dwyer and J. Bruce, 248–62. Palo Alto, Calif.: Stanford University Press.

———. 1996. "Debating Markets." A debate with Peter Dormon, Donald McCloskey, and Tom Weisskopf, *Feminist Economics* 2(1): 69–85.

Gibson-Graham, J. K. 1996. *The End of Capitalism (As We Knew It): A Feminist Critique of Political Economy.* Malden, Mass. and Oxford, U.K.: Blackwell Publishers.

Gittinger, Matteibelle, ed. 1989. *To Speak with Cloth: Studies in Indonesian Textiles*. Los Angeles: University of California, Museum of Cultural History.

Grimes, Kimberly M. 2000. "Democratizing International Production and Trade: North American Alternative Trading Organizations." In *Artisans and Cooperatives: Developing Alternative Trade for the Global Economy*, ed. by K. M. Grimes and B. L. Milgram, 9–25. Tucson, Ariz.: University of Arizona Press.

Illo, Jeanne Francis. 1995. "Who Heads the Households in the Philippines." In *The Filipino Woman in Focus*, ed. by Amaryllis T. Torres, 235–54. Manila: University of the Philippines Press.

Jenista, Frank L. 1987. *The White Apos: American Governors on the Cordillera Central*. Quezon City, Philippines: New Day Publishers.

Karim, Wazir Jahan. 1995. "Introduction: Genderising Anthropology in Southeast Asia." In *"Male" and "Female" in Developing Southeast Asia*, ed. by Wazir J. Karim, 11–34. Oxford, U.K. and Washington, D.C.: Berg Publishers.

Li, Tania Murray. 1999. "Compromising Power: Development, Culture, and Rule in Indonesia." *Cultural Anthropology* 14(3): 295–322.

Littrell, Mary Ann, and Marsha Ann Dickson. 1999. *Social Responsibility in the Global Market: Fair Trade of Cultural Products*. London: Sage Publications.

Marcus, George E., and Michael M. J. Fischer. 1999. *Anthropology as Cultural Critique: An Experimental Moment in the Human Sciences*. 2nd ed. Chicago: University of Chicago Press.

McCloskey, Donald N. 1993. "Some Consequences of a Conjective Economics." In *Beyond Economic Man: Feminist Theory and Economics*, ed. by M. A. Ferber and J. A. Nelson, 69–93. Chicago and London: University of Chicago Press.

Milgram, B. Lynne. 1999. "Crafts, Cultivation, and Household Economies: Women's Work and Positions in Ifugao, Northern Philippines." In *Research in Economic Anthropology* 20, ed. by Barry Isaac, 221–61. Stamford, Conn.: JAI Press.

———. 2001. "Situating Handicraft Market Women in Ifugao, Upland Philippines: A Case for Multiplicity." In *Women Traders in Cross-Cultural Perspective: Mediating Identities, Marketing Wares*, ed. by Linda J. Seligmann, 129–59. Stanford, CA: Stanford University Press.

Morton, Alice L. 1996. "Assessing Policy Implementation Success: Observations from the Philippines." *World Development* 24(9): 1441–51.

Nelson, Julie A. 1996. *Feminism, Objectivity, and Economics*. London: Routledge.

Ofreneo, Rene E., and Esther P. Habana. 1987. *The Employment Crisis and the World Bank's Adjustment Program (Philippines)*. Quezon City, Philippines: University of the Philippines Press.

Ong, Aihwa. 1987. *Spirits of Resistance and Capitalist Discipline*. Albany: State University of New York Press.

Pineda, R. Vergara. 1995. "Domestic Outwork for Export-Oriented Industries." In *The Filipino Woman in Focus*, ed. by A. T. Torres, 153–67. Manila: University of the Philippines Press.

PDC (Provincial Development Council). 1993. *Provincial Development Plan 1993–1998*. Lagawe, Ifugao: Provincial Development Council, Province of Ifugao.

Seguino, Stephanie, Thomas Stevens, and Mark A. Lutz. 1996. "Gender and Cooperative Behavior: Economic Man Rides Alone." *Feminist Economics* 2(1): 1–21.

Stamp, Patricia. 1989. *Technology, Gender, and Power in Africa*. Ottawa, Ontario: IDRC.

Strassman, Diana. 1997. "Expanding the Methodological Boundaries of Economics." Editorial, *Feminist Economics* 3(2): vii–ix.

Strober, Myrna H. 1994. "Can Feminist Thought Improve Economics? Rethinking Economics Through a Feminist Lens." *American Economic Review* 84(2): 143–58.

Tsing, Anna. 2000. "The Global Situation." *Cultural Anthropology* 15(3): 327–60.

Waring, Marilyn. 1988. *If Women Counted: A New Feminist Economics*. San Francisco: Harper San Francisco.

Wolf, Diane. 1992. *Factory Daughters: Gender, Household Dynamics, and Rural Industrialization in Java*. Berkeley: University of California Press.

Ypeij, Annelou. 2000. *Producing against Poverty: Female and Male Micro-Entrepreneurs in Lima, Peru*. Amsterdam: Amsterdam University Press.

6

Between Family and Market: Women and the New Silk Road in Post-Soviet Kazakhstan

Cynthia Werner

For centuries, caravan traders transported goods across the steppes and deserts of Central Asia in multiple directions along the legendary Silk Road. Precious commodities such as silk, ivory, gold, and fur exchanged hands numerous times as they traversed distances of up to 7,000 miles. The oasis towns of Central Asia profited greatly from such trade until the fifteenth century, when the decline of the Mongol empire and technological advances in shipbuilding brought political instability to the region and encouraged alternative trade routes. Within Central Asia, trade was further disrupted in the twentieth century with the formation of the Soviet Union and its nearly impenetrable border with the outside world. Since the fall of the Soviet Union, the bazaars of Soviet Central Asia have once again filled with foreign goods. On the New Silk Road, the old commodities, such as silk and gold, have been replaced by "modern" global commodities, such as ready-made clothing, packaged foods, and electronic goods (Khasanova 1998). And, the earlier forms of transportation—horses and camels—have been replaced by "modern" ones, including airplanes, trains, and buses. Nevertheless, the nature of this trade is imbued with the spirit of the ancient Silk Road: the trade fills local markets with highly coveted luxury goods; the commodities cross through numerous middlemen before they reach their final destination; and the merchants gain exposure to other lifestyles through travel.

In a place where Marxist-inspired policies have long rankled patriarchal customs, one of the most striking aspects of the New Silk Road trade is the predominance of Central Asian women in the marketplace. In particular, they dominate the exchange of commodities that play a special role in women's lives. This includes the cloth and clothing that women exchange as gifts, and the food products that women use to feed their families and honor their guests. The merchant women who sell these goods spend long hours outside of the household, buying and selling goods in public marketplaces. In addition, they travel unsupervised to markets in distant towns where their activities are less constrained by local talk. Although the recent development in market trade is clearly a post-Soviet phenomenon, the mobility and freedom that these women now experience should be viewed as an important legacy of Soviet rule. For seventy years, the Soviet state tried to "emancipate" women by providing education and employment opportunities. These policies were relatively successful, yet Western scholars repeatedly point out the "double burden" of Soviet women (Buckley 1989, 1997). Although Soviet policies encouraged women's participation in the workplace, they did little to change gender roles at home. So, even after working long hours outside of the home, Central Asian women remained responsible for the domestic tasks of cleaning, cooking, and childcare.

This chapter examines the role of women in the New Silk Road trade and the impact of these activities on the merchant women and their families in southern Kazakhstan. In order to understand the rise of small-scale trade, it is first necessary to look at the economic transition in post-Soviet Kazakhstan. Then, in order to illustrate the scope of trade that is managed and/or operated by women, the chapter turns to the history and organization of several small-scale businesses. And, finally, in order to explain the full impact of these trade activities, this chapter examines the gender roles, household economies, and family relationships of merchant women.

THE ECONOMIC TRANSITION IN POST-SOVIET KAZAKHSTAN

Shortly after the Soviet Union dissolved in December 1991, the leaders of newly independent Kazakhstan initiated the transition from a socialist planned economy to a capitalist market economy. In 1993, the government introduced a new national currency and a comprehensive structural reform program. The reforms include the liberalization of prices for consumer goods; the reduction of state subsidies for transportation, housing, and other services; the privatization of some state-owned enterprises; and the downsizing of other state-owned enterprises. Although Kazakhstan has great economic potential, with vast oil and mineral reserves and a small but educated population, the current economic situation in most households is not very good.

I conducted research in a small town that previously served as the administrative hub for nine state farms specializing in the production of the Astrakhan sheep. The town is located about three hours northwest of the city of Shymkent. There are currently about 8,300 people living in this town. More than 96 percent of the residents are Kazakh-speaking Kazakhs. They all live in homes with electricity, although none of the homes have running water and few have telephones, refrigerators, or automobiles. About half of the households could be described as nuclear family (two-generation) households, and the other half could be described as extended family (three- and four-generation) households. The extended family households are typically patrilocal.

As elsewhere, the transition process in this town has been characterized by a sharp decline in the average standard of living and a growing disparity between wealthy and poor households. In 1994, 1995, and 1998, most of the villagers I interviewed complained about increased unemployment, delayed payment of salaries, and high inflation. With the dissolution of several prominent state enterprises in the region, including the state farms, the nurseries, and the bread factory, many villagers lost their regular source of income. Those who are still employed by the remaining state enterprises are often paid six to eight months behind schedule. And, with rising costs, the value of these salaries rarely provides enough to offset basic expenses.

The transition process has delivered several serious blows to Kazakh women in particular. First, although women have experienced high rates of employment in Soviet Kazakhstan (up to 49 percent of the registered labor force), the post-Soviet state has eliminated more jobs in female-dominated sectors than in male-dominated sectors. Between 1990 and 1994, the number of jobs occupied by women decreased by 22.7 percent, compared to only 10.2 percent for men. Approximately 700,000 women were laid off during this period. This figure does not even include the number of women who have been placed on part-time status or who have difficulty returning from maternity leave (Bauer, Boschmann, and Green 1997). Second, the post-Soviet transition has brought serious cutbacks to the heavily subsidized system of nurseries. From 1989 to 1994, the total enrollment in Kazakhstan's nurseries declined from 52 percent to 28 percent of preschool children (Klugman et al. 1997). The employability of women is strongly influenced by the existence of childcare options. As nurseries become less available and more expensive in the post-Soviet period, working women have to become more dependent on social networks for childcare and/or find jobs such as trading, in which they can bring their children to the workplace.

In the post-Soviet period, rural Kazakhs have been developing new strategies to cope with these new strains on household economies and women's lives. Before the transition, most rural households were already pursuing complex survival strategies by combining the wages of at least one state employee with the domestic production of vegetables and livestock. In the post-Soviet period, most households have tried to cut expenses by further increasing the production of food for domestic consumption. In addition, many households have turned to new sources of income from private farming, handicraft production, or small-scale trade.

PATTERNS OF TRADE ON THE NEW SILK ROAD

The expansion of bazaar trade signifies a sharp break with the Soviet period when the state controlled the production and distribution of almost all goods. Although small neighborhood and village bazaars did operate in the past, they were largely limited to fresh produce or used consumer goods. Anybody who was involved with the speculative trade of other goods was either profiting at the expense of the state or illegally selling goods from abroad. In contrast, many Kazakhs view small-scale trade as the most viable option for survival in the post-Soviet period.

In rural areas, this is especially true for the towns and villages that have central marketplaces and have easy access to railways and big cities. The town where I worked was ideally situated for the development of trade. As an administrative center, there were already two semiweekly, state-run bazaars in place, one specializing in livestock and one specializing in food products and household goods. A third privately owned daily bazaar was opened in 1994 to accommodate the increased volume of trade. The town also benefited from its relative proximity to several cities; the cities of Turkestan, Shymkent, and Tashkent are two, three, and six hours away by bus, respectively. Each of these cities can also be reached by train, as the main railway connecting Moscow and Tashkent conveniently stops in a smaller village about ten miles away.

As the lure of the bazaar attracts individuals from various backgrounds, it is difficult to characterize the new class of village merchants. In the town where I worked, one could find merchants in three local bazaars, dozens of kiosks, and numerous street corners. Some merchants work daily, but others resort to trade on those occasions when they need some extra cash. Many of the part-time merchants in particular are still full-time employees in other sectors. Some merchants sell home-produced goods, such as fermented horse milk, but others exclusively buy and resell consumer goods. Among the speculative traders, a few travel across national borders to buy goods in Uzbekistan or Iran, while most buy goods in the wholesale markets of nearby cities in Kazakhstan.

Although men can be found selling things in the local bazaars, they are clearly outnumbered by women, especially when it comes to older and elderly merchants. One day, I counted the number of merchants sitting in one of the three town bazaars. On that particular day, there were seventy-five merchants working in the daily bazaar. Fifty-six percent of them were adult women, 16 percent were girls, 19 percent were adult men, and 9 percent were boys. It is important to point out that these figures do not include the merchants who work exclusively at the semiweekly livestock bazaar, which is dominated by men. In contrast to the livestock bazaar, this daily bazaar contains a wide variety of food products and household goods, the trade of which is dominated by women. Although merchants typically specialize in either food or clothing, most merchants sell a variety of goods within their particular specialty. On that particular day, 40 percent of the merchants were selling fruits and vegetables, 32 percent were selling clothing, 30 percent were selling rice and pasta, 28 percent were selling candy and cookies, 20 percent were selling home-produced goods, and 4 percent were selling meat.

The gender differences in the marketplace can be explained from both economic and cultural perspectives. From an economic perspective, there are more women in the bazaars because more women have been laid off in the post-Soviet period, and they were laid off earlier (Bauer, Boschmann, and Green 1997). In interviews with both male and female merchants, however, an alternative, cultural explanation emerges. According to some informants, Kazakh men just don't handle money as well as women. They say men are more capricious when it comes to cash, either spending it on alcohol or loaning it to undeserving friends. In their opinion, this is why women usually manage the household income and why women belong in the marketplace.

CASE STUDIES OF MERCHANT WOMEN AND THEIR BUSINESSES

The following portrayals of merchant women illustrate the nature and dynamics of bazaar trade in rural Kazakhstan:

"Zhanar," a fifty-six-year-old wife and mother of four, sells a small assortment of home-produced and retail goods in front of the central bazaar. Trained as a nurse, she is now on an extended leave with the local hospital, where she is still officially employed. She started working as a merchant in 1995 with the sale of homemade dumplings in the town bazaar. For a while, Zhanar received a lot of business from local organizations that would contract her services for special events, such as birthday parties and holidays. By 1997, none of the local organizations could afford such luxuries anymore. Now, her business is limited to the sale of eggs, candy, soap, socks, tea, and *kozha*, a local drink made by adding corn and sour cream to boiling water. Although she produces the *kozha* herself and buys the eggs from a neighboring family, the other goods come from the nearby city of Turkestan. As her volume of trade is so small, Zhanar generally relies on her merchant friends to purchase goods for her. They do not charge her for this service. Her children also help out with the business, by helping her carry things by foot from her house to the bazaar and by running home for extra goods when necessary. Zhanar works at the bazaar seven days per week, unless she has a social obligation, in which case one of her older children will sit at the bazaar for her. Compared to other merchants, her expenses are relatively low. She has no transportation costs, as she lives so close to the bazaar and does not travel herself to the other bazaars. She also does not have to pay for a license because of the small volume of her trade. Like the other merchants, however, she does pay a daily fee to the bazaar manager and a retail tax to the tax collector. She claims that the business is successful, although the profits only cover a small percent of her household expenses.

"Gulnara," a fifty-five-year old wife and mother of eight, works full-time as a schoolteacher and part-time as a merchant. Gulnara started to engage in trade shortly after her first daughter "eloped" with her boyfriend in 1994. (In

Kazakhstan, elopements, which are typically ritualized as kidnappings, are generally followed by exchanges of in-law gifts and payments of bridewealth and dowry.) In addition to Gulnara's teacher income, her husband receives a good salary from the department of culture where he works, and her family manages to save money by producing their own fruit and vegetables. They are generally well off compared to others in the town. However, she and her husband were completely surprised by their daughter's elopement, and they simply did not have enough cash to buy the expensive gift and dowry items. So, Gulnara decided to try her luck selling things at the bazaar. In her first effort, she bought a sheep in town, had her husband slaughter it, then got on an overnight train to Tashkent, Uzbekistan, where she sold the meat in the central bazaar. In one day, she managed to make one-fourth of her monthly salary, which had not even been paid for several months. But as the work was difficult and time-consuming, she decided to change tactics. Using a portion of the profits as capital, she traveled to the nearby city of Turkestan and purchased an array of inexpensive clothing. She then recruited her teenage daughters to sell these items in the town bazaar, while she continued to work in the school. The profits, however, were only trickling in. So, eventually, she decided to turn to a third strategy: she decided to travel with several other merchant women to Almaty and then to Baikonyr, two cities that are each a full day's train ride away. She borrowed money from friend and relatives. She was gone for more than a month. Unfortunately, after subtracting expenses for housing and transportation and paying back her loans, Gulnara only received a small profit (1,500 *tenge*), about three times the profit of the first sheep that she was able to sell in just one day. After her daughter's wedding, she stopped trading goods.

"Raikhan," a sixty-six-year-old wife and mother of six, operates a relatively large business across the street from the central bazaar. She sits there with her goods seven days per week. Depending on what direction they are coming from, villagers might reach her small kiosk before they arrive at the central bazaar. For decades, Raikhan was a full-time mother and housewife. She started her business in 1995 by selling rice in the daily bazaar. But, now her business has expanded to include tea, preserved fruits, butter, cigarettes, matches, soap, and laundry detergent. Her husband helps her with the business by purchasing goods at the wholesale bazaar in Turkestan and by driving her and her things to work every day. At home, she lives with her husband, her grown son, his wife, and her six grandchildren. Unlike some of the other women, Raikhan has the advantage of having a "daughter-in-law in hand" (*kelin kolynda*), which means that she can pass a lot of the housework on to her daughter-in-law. In fact, she admits that the merchant lifestyle is much more peaceful than her home life, because the young children are always fighting with each other and running underfoot. At work, she enjoys gossiping with friends and passersby while making a decent amount of money. Her business income, however, only makes up a portion of the household income, which also includes her husband's salary, her pension, and her son's income as a private taxi driver. Like most merchants, she was unwilling to specify her net profit, yet notes that her trade income provides her household with enough money to buy food and coal.

Finally, "Maira," a seventeen-year-old girl, sells fruits, vegetables, and toys in the daily bazaar. As an unmarried girl, she still lives with her parents and siblings where she helps with household chores. She has been working as a merchant for two years with her mother. Her mother is responsible for going to Shymkent or Turkestan twice per week to buy products, while Maira is responsible for sitting in the town bazaar seven days per week to sell things. Sometimes her mother sits with her in the bazaar. In addition to paying taxes and bazaar fees, she and her mother pay a small fee to store their products in a locker every night. In general, Maira is satisfied with her job, especially on the days that she sells a lot of things, but she gets bored sitting at the bazaar day after day. In the future, she hopes to attend the university, but for now her family cannot afford the "bribe" that is necessary for admission. Since both of her parents are now unemployed, the only source of household income is the profit from speculative trade. Her family manages to reduce household expenses by producing some of their food in their garden, but they no longer provide their own meat, as they have gradually slaughtered all of their livestock for food and cash.

IMPACT OF TRADE ON WOMEN AND THEIR FAMILIES

Taken together, the stories of these four merchant women and their families illustrate the nature and scope of small-scale trade in post-Soviet Kazakhstan. I now want to highlight some of the ways in which this trade is affecting gender roles and family relationships. I have borrowed several insights from the literature on "working women" and "working daughters" in Asia and the Middle East. Authors such as Janet Salaff (1995), Diane Wolf (1992), Homa Hoodfar (1997), and Jenny White (1994) have examined the extent to which wage employment improves women's position within the household and transforms patriarchal gender roles. As these authors cautiously point out, women's income may benefit other household members, but income alone does not necessarily transform women's status within the household.

In the case of rural Kazakhstan, merchant women are bringing in significant amounts of income, which they generally contribute to the household pool. All of the women I spoke to started their businesses because their household needed more money for basic survival and networking expenses. Some households rely exclusively on the income derived from small-scale trade, but others receive income from multiple sources. Regardless, the income from small-scale trade represents a significant portion of household income, especially at a time when state salaries and state pensions are delayed for months. The majority of merchant women, however, rely on other household members to help them with their work. Their husbands and children provide assistance with the purchasing, transporting, and selling of goods. Thus, although the women who sit daily in the bazaar do the most time-consuming aspect of the job, the business itself is viewed within the family as a collaborative venture.

Although trading is a time-consuming and tiring job, Kazakh merchant women do report several perceived benefits. First, many of the women enjoy the social atmosphere of the bazaar. The social isolation of nonworking women varies from family to family. Although some women socialize regularly with friends and relatives and share household tasks with daughters and daughters-in-law, others are much more socially isolated at home. In particular, young wives who grew up in different towns from where they currently live have fewer social contacts. In contrast, merchant women are anything but isolated. During nonpeak hours, they have plenty of time to catch up on local news with other merchants and their customers.

A second perceived benefit, acknowledged by several merchant women, is that they have fewer responsibilities at home because of their work responsibilities. This is also the case for women who are employed in other sectors. And, this is especially true in nuclear family households with older children and in extended family households with other adult women. In these types of households, the nonworking women and older children do the bulk of the cleaning, cooking, and childcare. Although nonadult sons are unlikely to perform certain "female" tasks, they do help with child supervision and general housecleaning. Adult men, on the other hand, are much less willing to cross these gender boundaries, even if they are completely unoccupied with other tasks and there is nobody else at home to do these things.

Finally, some merchant women relish the travel and shopping opportunities involved with this line of work. This is especially true for those women who have traveled across national borders to purchase goods in Russia, Uzbekistan, Turkey, and Iran. Just as international tourists boast about their experiences, these transnational traders benefit socially from their firsthand knowledge of distant places. But, even those who don't travel so far can benefit socially from their knowledge of and frequent access to consumer markets in nearby cities. Merchant women often have the opportunity to gain social credits by purchasing consumer goods for their nonmerchant friends and relatives. Depending on their relationship with the intended recipient, they may provide these goods at reduced or no cost. As I have written in other papers (Werner 1998), social networks, which are critical in Kazakhstan, are often maintained through the exchange of women's labor, such as food production. Since merchant women have less time to devote to these traditional exchanges of labor, supplying friends with consumer goods provides them with one alternative means to maintain their social networks.

In addition to these perceived benefits, women's involvement in small-scale trade sometimes comes with social costs. In particular, as women spend long hours outside of the home, this trade can have negative effects on children, who may receive less supervision, and on marital relations, which may become strained. The case of Jazira, a thirty-five-year-old mother of four, illustrates both of these social costs. When I met her in 1998, she was ready to end her marriage and take away two of her four children. In her own explanation of the events leading up to this, her problems had started five or six years earlier when the economic situation in her village changed for the worse. She was living with her husband and his parents in a small village where almost all of the adult men and more than half of the adult women were employed by the state farm. In the early 1990s, everybody in the village was finding it more difficult to make ends meet. Then, in 1996, things got even worse when the state farm privatized; her household lost its primary source of income. Having received a small parcel of land from privatization, her husband and father-in-law started to increase the production of subsistence crops. Meanwhile, Jazira herself started to bring extra income into the household by engaging in small-scale trade. At first, she traded clothing and packaged goods in the local bazaar.

After earning small profits for a few months, Jazira decided that she should temporarily move to the city of Almaty where she could earn greater profits. Although Almaty was a twelve-hour train ride away, she made arrangements to share an inexpensive apartment with friends who were resorting to similar tactics. Her husband and her in-laws were not sure if this was a good idea. They were all concerned that her children would miss their mother. Although they knew that there was no guarantee of financial profit, they agreed that they could use any extra money. With some reluctance, her mother-in-law agreed to take care of her grandchildren while Jazira worked in Almaty. Every few weeks, Jazira returned to the village to visit her family and to bring home a portion of her profits. Things were going fine until one day, when her husband unexpectedly showed up at her bazaar stall in Almaty and harshly announced that he knew she was having an affair with another man. He yelled at her in front of her friends and then beat her for the first time ever. As she retold these events, she insisted that the accusation was a lie and that she was seeking a divorce because she refused to live with a man who did not trust her and who beat her after hearing such a rumor.

She had thought seriously about all of the consequences of this divorce. She would have to move permanently to Almaty. She could only afford to take her two school-age children, as the cost of daycare was too high to take the others. And, given her "family situation," she knew she would have some problems getting remarried. For these reasons, her parents were giving her a very hard time. Despite the beating, her husband was a good man, they argued, and besides that, he was the son of their close friends and this would put a strain on their friendship. Although nobody in her family supported her, Jazira did go ahead with the divorce proceedings and moved permanently to Almaty with the two children.

In conclusion, the impact of the New Silk Road trade on women and their families varies. For the women, benefits include greater social interaction, reduced household chores, and increased physical mobility. For most families, the income that a merchant woman brings into a household to pay for basic foodstuffs outweighs the strains that these activities place on family relationships. In other families, such as Jazira's, the cost of trade can extend as far as family dissolution.

REFERENCES

Bauer, Armin, Nina Boschmann, and David Green. 1997. *Women and Gender Relations in Kazakstan.* Manila: Asian Development Bank.

Buckley, Mary. 1989. *Women and Ideology in the Soviet Union.* Ann Arbor: University of Michigan Press.

———. (ed.) 1997. *Post-Soviet Women: From the Baltic to Central Asia.* New York: Cambridge University Press.

Hoodfar, Homa. 1997. *Between Marriage and the Market: Intimate Politics and Survival in Cairo.* Berkeley: University of California Press.

Khasanova, Markhamat. 1998. "Kazakhstan: Foreign Trade Policy." In *Central Asia: The Challenges of Independence,* ed. by Boris Rumer and Stanislav Zhukov, 169–207. Armonk, N.Y.: M. E. Sharpe.

Klugman, Jeni, Sheila Marnie, John Micklewright, and Philip O'Keefe. 1997. "The Impact of Kindergarten Divestiture on Household Welfare in Central Asia." In *Household Welfare in Central Asia,* ed. by Jane Falkingham, Jeni Klugman, Sheila Marnie, and John Micklewright, 183–201. New York: St. Martin's Press.

Salaff, Janet W. 1995. *Working Daughters of Hong Kong: Filial Piety or Power in the Family?* New York: Columbia University Press.

Werner, Cynthia. 1997. "Household Networks and the Security of Mutual Indebtedness in Rural Kazakstan." *Central Asian Survey* 17(4): 597–612.

White, Jenny. 1994. *Money Makes Us Relatives: Women's Labor in Urban Turkey.* Austin: University of Texas Press.

Wolf, Diane. 1992. *Factory Daughters: Gender, Household Dynamics, and Rural Industrialization in Java.* Berkeley: University of California Press.

III

LOVE AND ENTITLEMENTS

7

Neoliberalism and Newar Economics of Practice: Gender and the Politics of Consciousness in a Nepalese Merchant Community

Katharine N. Rankin

INTRODUCTION

Feminist scholars have made remarkable gains over the past three decades in placing the needs and perspectives of women on the development planning agenda. Early research documented the significant—if not majority—role women play in subsistence agricultural systems and noted that development planners overlook this role when they target their interventions exclusively to men. As efforts to expand women's access to resources and programs failed to significantly change women's material condition, however, feminist scholarship shifted from "women" to "gender relations" as a focus of analysis in an attempt to bring power relations between women and men more clearly into view. The empirical evidence of persisting gender inequity—as well as the global networking among feminist practitioners enabled by the periodic UN Conferences on Women—have inspired efforts within individual nation-states to bring gender policy to bear systematically on unequal power relations. At the programmatic level, these efforts have commonly manifested in various models of "microfinance" that aim to correct discrimination in the formal financial system by expanding women's access to credit.

Implicit in the latter models of development, which have proliferated at lightning pace and with ample donor funding in the past decade, is the expectation that economic opportunity can help women overcome their subordinate social position and ultimately transform oppressive gender ideologies. Yet, in practice, these important goals and optimistic expectations are often compromised by significant institutional constraints to gender transformation. Ethnographic evidence increasingly suggests that the social processes through which microfinance programs are implemented may, in fact, entrench, rather than challenge, existing social hierarchies (Fernando 1997; Mayoux 1995; Rankin 2001a, 2001b).

In this chapter, I contend that the possibility for altering the distribution of material resources in ways that do transform gender relations requires foremost an analysis of the dialectical relationship between gender ideology and material reality (see also Agarwal 1994). To this end, I engage Pierre Bourdieu's notion of an "economics of practice" to explore the cultural processes through which value is created in both material and symbolic domains and how competing regimes of value in turn structure social organization and behavior. Focusing for the purpose of illustration on Sankhu—a merchant community of the Kathmandu Valley, Nepal—the chapter explores the role of prestige systems in mediating social opportunity. Gender ideologies rooted in the "honor economy" preclude, for example, women's rights to landed property, and the distribution of property ownership and control directly shapes ideological constructions of gender and norms of behavior for men and women.

The analytical focus here on gender ideology in turn begs questions of equal relevance to gender planning about women's consciousness of hierarchical social relations. The chapter thus explores the ways in which ideological constructions occupy the minds and lives of women as common sense—resulting in behavior that appears as acquiescence to domination.[1] Rejecting notions of false consciousness, however, the chapter also discusses the extent to which Newar women do recognize the established order as an arbitrary human construction and have manipulated available material and symbolic resources to advance their interests in quite strategic ways within socially acceptable parameters. Thus, for example, women have invested their dowries, culturally coded as women's own property, to amass considerable material wealth for their families while adhering to Hindu norms of seclusion, modesty, and chastity. This discussion highlights the critical resources available within culture, should planners and policy makers learn how to recognize them.

The chapter ultimately considers how contemporary neoliberal economic ideology and associated "open market" policies articulate with the Newar economics of practice. In particular, it highlights the regressive tendencies generated for women as new patterns of commodification and attendant consumer cultures undermine their rights to dowry wealth. In the face of these cultural transformations, discrete capital access programs alone may not be adequate to challenge dominant gender ideologies limiting women's autonomous control over finance capital. Rather, these trends suggest that planners could effect more structural and sustainable impact by creating the institutional and social spaces to channel women's existing levels of consciousness into collective forms of social criticism and action. The chapter thus proposes a model for gender planning that focuses foremost on cultivating locally situated social criticism as the surest foundation for "development"—in contrast to the dominant approaches that emphasize market deepening and capital access with little regard for the cultural politics of social change.

THE ECONOMICS OF PRACTICE AND THE POLITICS OF CULTURE

The emphasis here on the significance of culture for planning and economic development requires at the outset an understanding of economic value as culturally given, rather than as an inherent property of commodities.[2] Arjun Appadurai (1986) has pioneered by suggesting that the key to understanding value lies in the realm of culture, as it conditions how objects circulate in different "regimes of value." By examining the *contexts* of exchange, it is possible to think of capital as any form of wealth intended for exchange or investment. Through an analysis of "symbolic capital," for instance, Pierre Bourdieu extends economic analysis beyond material processes to encompass forms of value in demand within specific social situations. His "economics of practice" thus accounts for the social and cultural dimensions of profit and exchange:

> the theory of strictly economic practice is simply a particular case of a general theory of the economics of practice. The only way to escape from the ethnocentric naïvetés of economism without falling into populist exaltation of the generous naivety of earlier forms of society is to carry out in full what economism does only partially, and to extend economic calculation to *all* the goods, material and symbolic, without distinction, that present themselves as *rare* and worthy of being sought after in a particular social formation—which may be "fair words" or smiles, handshakes or shrugs, compliments or attention, challenges or insults, honor or honors, powers or pleasures, gossip or scientific information, distinction or distinctions . . . (Bourdieu 1977, 177–78).[3]

Within an economics of practice, then, "symbolic capital" refers to the "sum of cultural recognition . . . which an individual . . . could acquire through skillful manipulation of the system of social symbols." Where honor is a central form of capital, then much of social practice must be interpreted in terms of producing and exchanging, hoarding, or squandering honor. This chapter refers to investments that generate such nonmaterial forms of wealth as "social investments." The notions of "economics of practice" and "regimes of value" thus reject a view of culture as distinct from economy—as a bounded or purely localized system of meanings in which every act of exchange presupposes a complete cultural sharing of assumptions.

Two further analytical possibilities emerge from this discussion, the first of which has to do with conventional understandings of macroprocesses such as globalization, economic liberalization, and modernization, all of which imply linear processes, from local to global, "fettered" to liberal, traditional to modern.[4] With regard to neoliberalism, the approach here rejects the notion of cultural homogenization typically imputed to economic globalization and instead focuses on how powerful external forces are inserted in particular cultural political contexts. I thus refer to the "articulation" of local cultural forms with global political-economic processes in order to emphasize the ways in which such processes are firmly rooted in historical and cultural foundations: globalization, it must be said, is always locally constituted. Viewing local-global articulations in terms of competing and conflicting "regimes of value" specifically challenges the notion—endemic even within the realm of gender planning—that one can merely replace "traditional values" with "market values."

Second, thinking in terms of culture as a form of production highlights questions about just who is doing the producing, as well as the social and cultural differentiation within an apparently uniform community. As such, it is possible, following Bourdieu, to bring the study of symbolic forms to bear on social struggle—to recognize in logic of symbolic capital a mechanism for establishing dominance and power and for maintaining unequal social relations. Here it is useful to invoke Jean Comaroff's and John Comaroff's distinction between "agentive" and "nonagentive" forms of power to specify the role of ideology and hegemony within the politics of culture. In the former, dominance requires conscious command and defense over various modes of cultural production, such as patterns of socialization and gender norms and beliefs.[5] To the extent that the established social order is accepted in the minds and lives of social actors as the natural state of the world—a nonagentive manifestation of power—such ideological constructions may be said to have achieved a temporary state of hegemony. In such cases, write Comaroff and Comaroff:

> Power . . . hides itself in forms of everyday life. . . . This kind of nonagentive power proliferates outside the realm of institutional politics, saturating such things as aesthetics and ethics, built form and bodily representation. . . . (Comaroff and Comaroff 1991, 22)

At the level of individual consciousness, this condition in which there is a correspondence between objective order and subjective experience Bourdieu calls "doxa," a realm of social life within which "what is essential *goes without saying because it comes without saying:* . . . tradition is silent, not least about itself as a tradition" (1977, 163, emphasis in original). For that part of culture in which hegemony prevails, individuals adopt dominant ideologies as cultural common sense—as their own worldview—and thus collude in the maintenance of social structures that oppress them. Yet the power of culture to blind people to their own oppression is always limited by the possibility that those in subordinate positions will recognize the established order as an arbitrary, human construction. As "the contradictions between the world as represented and the world as experienced become ever more palpable, ever more insupportable," there is the possibility that people will develop a critical consciousness of the social order as a constructed political order (Comaroff and Comaroff 1991, 26).[6] Women could have not only "feminine consciousness"— that which is construed in accordance with normative gender beliefs—but also "feminist consciousness"—a critical understanding of patterns of subordination, limitation, and confinement (Keohane and Gelpi 1981). For planners, the challenge then becomes how to facilitate collective expressions of feminist, or critical, consciousness.

The remainder of this chapter explores the economics of practice and the politics of culture through ethnographic research in the merchant community of Sankhu, located in the Kathmandu Valley and populated by people of the Newar ethnic group. Within Nepal, Newars have historically been most associated with commerce and long-distance trading; Newar society is stratified by the most elaborate caste system in Nepal, but its attitudes toward women's participation in commerce are liberal relative to those of the politically and numerically dominant Parbatiya.[7] As such, this society provides an interesting context in which to consider social differentiation in processes of cultural production. Today the residents of Sankhu palpably feel the transition to "open market" policies—especially through the emerging labor and commodity markets these policies generate—but the structuring force of caste and gender ideologies still prevail in significant ways, shaping the experience of macroeconomic change.

THE NEWAR "HONOR ECONOMY"

Among Newars, as within many other South Asian societies, prestige systems play a powerful role in regulating local economics of practice and, in so doing, constructing caste and gender hierarchies.[8] Honor, or *ijat*, operates as a most significant currency in the Newar marketplace of value.[9] Newars begin life with a certain amount of honor that is handed out according to caste and family of birth. High castes automatically start with a lot of honor, but low castes by nature "are only capable of a limited fund of *ijat*" (Miller 1992). Regardless of caste standing, however, one's honor must be continually defended and replenished by meeting numerous religious and social obligations. As a result—and in spite of their reputation for business acumen and greed—Newars impress even their Parbatiya and Tamang neighbors with their propensity to engage in feasting, carnival, festival, lavish personal spending, and generous civil and religious charity.[10] Indeed, Newars' reputation for excessive consumption is captured in the Nepali proverb that taunts "*Newar bigriyo bhojle*" (feasting has ruined the Newars).

Feasting in particular enables one to accrue *ijat*, because feasts punctuate most important social obligations. Occasions for feasting come around with remarkable frequency and impose no small burden on household budgets. First there are the life cycle rituals: depending on one's caste, religious affiliation, and gender, up to seven rituals associated with birth; two initiation rituals; betrothal; marriage; three old-age initiations to the status of gods; and the thirteen- to forty-five-day intensive series of mortuary rites. Each of these entails not only the requisite feast, but also elaborate, costly, and time-consuming preparations for the ritual itself, involving both the prescribed configuration of kin and a full entourage of ritual specialists. The ancestors, too, must be worshipped—fed, clothed, housed, and comforted as integral members of the social group—through mortuary rites performed regularly by the living. These occasions for worship also require the preparation of a feast to which the appropriate kin and ritual specialists must be invited.

Community and national festivals propitiate deities ranging from the local patron goddess Vajrayogini, to the gods of the distinct lineage groups. These festivals, which number approximately fifty during the calendrical year, each entail a domestic feast of some measure as well as varying levels of household participation in their collective community-wide dimensions. Even ghosts— the spirits of those who have died and never passed to the land of the dead— must be appeased with their own special offerings and dietary observances. Failure to perform any of these rituals or prepare the associated feasts does not just incur the wrath of gods, ancestors, and ghosts; more importantly, one's honor is at stake and, as we will see, there is a lot to lose.

Most of these obligations are organized and enforced under the auspices of the characteristic Newar *guthi* associations. As corporate bodies that enable households to fulfill their social and religious obligation through group action, *guthis* play a crucial role in regulating social life in Newar communities.[11] Every household should belong to at least two *guthis*, through which, at a minimum, worship of lineage deities and performance of mortuary rites are accomplished. *Guthi* members adhere to a rigid organizational structure that facilitates monitoring behavior to ensure compliance with social norms: responsibility for managing *guthi* functions (including the rigorous round of feasting) rotates annually among the membership, and authority within the association is vested in senior members; the leadership enforces a rigid system of penalties and fines intended to punish noncompliance with *guthi* rules or absence from *guthi* functions.

In the calculus of the *ijat* economy, *guthi* membership ensures the sound social standing of individuals and households who meet the arduous round of obligations. We can grasp the value of such standing by considering the extraordinarily high costs of foregoing *guthi* participation and feasting obligations—tantamount to excommunication from Newar social life—as the following comments of a *guthi*-less merchant caste man suggest:

> If you don't do your *guthi* work, then society really holds you in contempt. Our *guthi* has many members; my grandfather eventually had to drop out because he could not afford to offer the feast when his turn came around. After that everything, including our business, became difficult; it was even hard to arrange for me and my brothers' marriages because the first thing they always ask: which *guthi* do you belong to?[12]

For the wealthy, then, the honor economy requires that finance capital be transmuted into symbolic capital through social investments in religious piety, hospitality, feasting, life cycle rituals, and *guthi* membership (Rankin 1996). Profits transformed into social investments establish a sound reputation on the basis of exemplary religious devotion. As such, the Newar feast and other modes of social investment express a strong ethic that profits earned through business acumen must be warranted by the generosity and disinterest with which they are dispersed. For those lacking in finance capital, moreover, it is the honor generated through meeting social obligations that best guards against the threat of destitution. The honor that accrues from fulfilling social obligations is one's best economic guarantee—the shame in forsaking them, one's surest demise.

The value that *ijat* holds for Newars lies in the significance of social networks for the ways in which they find economic security. In its prescriptions for the distribution of private wealth, *ijat* also mitigates extreme class disparities characteristic of societies in which more commoditized regimes of value prevail. Yet this leveling effect comes at the cost of considerable social control and regulation of individual behavior. In addition to the onerous demands its regimen of social investments places on household financial and human resources, the honor economy functions agentively to maintain and defend caste and gender hierarchies. From the perspective of high castes, many forms of association with those situated lower on the caste hierarchy—from commensality to marriage—bring *bejat* (shame) of such insufferable magnitude as to entrench even illegal forms of caste discrimination.

The honor economy also expresses—indeed produces—Newar gender ideology. Put starkly, men's *ijat* depends crucially on their relationships with women—who not only perform the onerous domestic labor entailed in keeping up social obligations, but also exhibit qualities of moral, sexual, and social propriety. Although for men *ijat* functions in some ways as a possession (one either has it or one does not), for women, honor operates as something more like a "character trait" that reflects not only on themselves, but also on their household or patriline (see Liechty 1995). It is primarily through sexuality and ritual pollution (as opposed to integrity in maintaining social investments) that a woman's honor is gauged; if not properly managed, women's sexuality and regular episodes of ritual pollution (through menstruation and childbirth) can compromise the pedigree of an entire household or lineage.

Ijat also has a more material dimension bearing on the position of women in Newar society. A man's honor rests as much as moral integrity in matters of ritual and female sexuality as on accumulating appropriate levels of material wealth. In this regard, Newar gender ideologies again play an instrumental role. Women are ritually associated—in marriage, initiation rites, and daily worship—with the goddess of wealth, Laksmi. In relation to this association with the protection of wealth, women's very appearance is considered to reflect a household's honor. Only a shameful household, for instance, would allow their women to walk around "bare," without jewelry or the appropriate standards of dress, or even accept a bride who does not meet certain standards of beauty.

As repositories of household honor, women's actions and appearance thus require considerably more collective surveillance (and individual self-regulation) than that of men. Recent brides, for example, face the greatest restrictions, as their sexuality is at once most crucial and most threatening to the patriline. Thus, they may not leave the house unaccompanied or without the permission of their husband and mother-in-law. The only legitimate destination is their natal home or the home of some other consanguineal relative, from which they can return only with an escort and only upon being sent for by their husband. On a visit to her natal home in Sankhu, one recently married Shrestha (merchant-caste) woman described the extent of such restrictions within her natal household in the city of Patan:

> They [husband and mother-in-law] don't send me outside at all. Not even to the store. If we need anything, he [husband] gets it, or my mother-in-law gets it. I expect they won't send me out for such errands for maybe one or two years. Usually a family won't let a new bride outside the house. They say they have to protect their honor.

Likewise, although anyone may fall prey to vicious and powerful gossip networks in Sankhu, women of any married status can assume themselves to be an automatic and special focus of public discussion, regardless of their actions—how do they look, what are they wearing, with whom are they walking, where are they going?: "Sometimes," confessed the oldest unmarried daughter from a Joshi (priest/astrologer-caste) household, "I really wish I could just run away and hide in the jungle." Gossip operates so forcefully that even married women with children whose sexual loyalties are established and who therefore, theoretically at least, have more mobility, self-regulate their movement in public spaces—traveling only through back, narrow *gallis* (lanes) instead of main thoroughfares, limiting conversation to only those whose acquaintance they have made through their marital household, walking briskly and purposefully, not sauntering. For high-caste women especially, there are many quarters of town that they literally will not see in their lifetime.

Restrictions on women's mobility and a sexual division of labor that limits women's work primarily to subsistence production and household commercial enterprises allow men to accumulate material and symbolic capital at the expense of, or at least on the backs of and to the exclusion of, women. They are thus examples of cultural practices that defend the social order and represent it as natural and moral. The association of women's sexuality and mobility with household *ijat* serves as a particularly forceful deterrent to independent participation in kinds of market activities that require much social interaction or movement outside the household. Nor can women easily motivate the kinds of social investments, such as hospitality and religious patronage that justify and expand opportunities for individual gain. Through the honor economy, we can thus recognize a dialectical relationship between gender ideology and social opportunity: ideological constructions of gender influence women's ability to compete in the honor economy, and the disadvantages women face in the accumulation of symbolic capital reflect how they are represented and expected to behave.

THE POLITICS OF CONSCIOUSNESS

Gender constructions and women's perceptions at times converge in a manner that suggests acquiescence, or even blindness, on the part of women to the ideologies that subordinate them. In everyday speech and action, women willfully give expression to their ascribed low status—such as when they address their husbands honorifically or bow down in respect to their husbands each morning before taking tea; or the myriad ways in which they self-regulate in matters of purity and pollution. Beyond these mundane manifestations of consent, moreover, are practices and behaviors that bear more significant political and, indeed, material consequences.

Consider, for example, women's participation in customary ideas and practices surrounding inheritance (*angsa*). In Nepal, women have legal rights to inherit their father's property if they remain unmarried beyond the age of thirty-five. Yet among Newars, as well as other strongly patrilineal societies in Nepal, social conventions dictate that landed property should pass exclusively to male heirs and that women should not enjoy the kind of autonomy from their kin that direct ownership of landed property would entail. Indeed, many Newar women meeting legal criteria for inheriting an equal share of their fathers' property decline to exercise this right and prefer to remain as a dependent in their brother's household. When a controversial bill came before the national Parliament to reform inheritance laws in favor of the rights of daughters, there was widespread dissent in Sankhu among both men and women.

If we probe the motivations of individual women in electing to place themselves in dependent positions vis-à-vis men, however, we find that women's choices reflect strategic concerns for their own security. As one middle-aged and single low-caste woman explained to me, if a woman rejects the dependent status associated with being female, she risks falling outside the networks of obligation that constitute Newar society and provide the ultimate protection against poverty and ill health:[13]

> Sure, I have a right to a share of my brother's inheritance. Still, I am not planning to take it. I'll just give my share to my brother. See, if I take my share, he and his wife might not take care of me later. Then who knows what could happen.

Some sense of "what could happen" to an economically autonomous woman can be obtained through the stories of the fate met by women in Sankhu who *have* pursued legal rights to inheritance. One widely circulated story recounts the experience of a woman who had recently died of physical complications related to malnutrition. Once she had become unable to cultivate her own land, she no longer had any source of income or means to meet her basic subsistence requirements. Yet she also had no grounds to make demands on her brothers, whose only obligations, in both legal and social terms, were to family members residing in their own households. As she never married and had no children, she died alone—in a physical isolation that ultimately reflected the loss of social citizenship she had long endured as an independent woman.

When women choose to comply with normative gender beliefs, then, they are not always unaware of the nets of power in which they are entangled. Their compliance with cultural practices signaling their subordination and dependence on men—even down to the small gestures of submission—does not necessarily mean that they accept those practices as legitimate and moral. Their actions suggest consent, not blindness; practical dominance, not total hegemony.[14]

Evidence of individual gender consciousness can also be found in the way women take advantage of contradictions within gender ideology to further secure their own material well-being. For example, although Newar women do not customarily inherit property, they do receive significant family assets in the form of a dowry (*kvasah*) presented to them on their betrothal and departure from their natal to their marital home.[15] Conventions surrounding dowry contradict the ideology of women's dependence embedded in patrilineal patterns of inheritance (*angsa*), for in the Newar context dowry is unequivocally valued as "women's own property." The accumulation of a suitably large dowry is actively underwritten by the bride's natal family through a feast held in her honor. Invited guests must contribute to the bride's dowry, at a scale meticulously specified by the type of invitation received. Once she is in her marital home, a woman's dowry has a special status as her exclusive private property. As one low-caste woman incontrovertibly stated:

> A woman should have total control over her *kvasah*, including in her husband's household. Others are not allowed to touch it without her consent. Say her father-in-law has to attend a wedding feast for the daughter of a close neighbor; he may offer to purchase an item from his daughter-in-law's dowry to put down as a dowry gift for the other girl, but he may not just take it. He must pay his daughter-in-law for it—and at a good market rate.

In the event of divorce, moreover, convention further dictates that all *kvasah* items must be returned to the woman (with the cost to the husband's family for the wedding sometimes being subtracted), according to a list meticulously compiled by the woman's family at the time of betrothal: "Even if a man has used just one notebook from his wife's dowry," a Shrestha woman emphasized, "he must pay for it or replace it." Here *ijat* works as an effective sanction, as breaches to these norms would bring immediate shame upon a household: as one senior woman put it, "if we were to sell our daughter-in-law's dowry, our honor would be lost. . . . The neighbors would say, Oh, they don't have enough to eat; they had to sell the dowry!"

Within joint family marital households, women generally exercise careful vigilance to keep their dowry wealth out of circulation—if not hidden entirely from view. They thus take full advantage of the "ideological space" within customary ideas about dowry for the accumulation of certain kinds of private wealth. Relative to men's rights to *angsa*, in fact, *kvasah* affords Newar women some distinct benefits. Although a man can never exercise complete autonomy in the dispensation of his inherited property (to which his sons, brothers, and parents always have some legal claim), a woman is legally accountable to no one with regard to her *kvasah*. The strength of a woman's (otherwise dependent and subordinate) position, that is, lies precisely in the fact that she, unlike men, has no prescribed social debts or obligations to tie up her private property.

Women, in fact, rarely allow their dowry to sit idly. As one woman from a relatively poor household explained to me, "If you just keep your dowry packed up like a bank note in a picture frame, what good is that? You have to put it to some good use." It turns out that women commonly invest earnings from surplus dowry in money lending—an enterprise that does not compromise their ability to meet full-time domestic responsibilities in the household and family commercial enterprises (which might come as a surprise to those who design capital access programs). Even women from families that are not well-off can give accounts of how they had tripled or quadrupled dowry investments, as one woman described for the case of her aunt:

> When my aunt died, she did not know how to write her own name; she did not even know the alphabet; she really didn't know anything. But anyway, up to the time of her death, she used to keep a small fortune in her closet—money she'd earn from investing. She'd give someone a loan; interest would come; she'd reinvest the interest [through moneylending], and so on. From that wealth she provided her daughters with a nice dowry, and when she needed money for her own purposes, she could always take it from her savings.

The contradictory values of *angsa* (inheritance) and *kvasah* (dowry/women's own property) thus "coexist in a mutually subversive complimentarity," the recognition of which can then become the basis of critical consciousness (Parish 1997). Although women often appear to be complicit in their own disadvantage to the extent that they assume postures, behaviors, and roles that mark their own subordination, the discussion here suggests that they comply not for moral, but for predominantly strategic and material reasons. And they do not comply without casting a critical eye on the system as a whole, without understanding its arbitrariness and its contradictions. These observations suggest that even in the most rigidly hierarchical societies, critical consciousness operates within culture as much as conformity, or doxa. For planners and development practitioners, the point to emphasize here is that potential for critical consciousness lies in the everyday thinking of subaltern actors. The first step to facilitating collective projects for emancipatory social change is thus to seek out such perspectives and recognize in them the potential for locally situated social criticism.

NEOLIBERALISM AND NEWAR ECONOMICS OF PRACTICE

To imagine such a role for planning in more programmatic terms, however, requires an understanding of how neoliberalism, and its programs of economic liberalization, articulate with the Newar economics of practice. Given what we know about the structuring role of gender ideologies, that is, we can consider how local logics of accumulation and investment might interact with the commoditization and emerging labor markets associated with Nepal's new economic orthodoxy—imposed, as in other Third World countries, through structural adjustment programs and other forms of donor conditionalities on country lending. What new regimes of value and structuring ideologies emerge in these contexts, and what kinds of social relations result as cultural common sense assumes new parameters? In light of the concern here with progressive planning, what emancipatory and regressive political tendencies can be seen in these articulations of local cultural economies with state economic policies?

It is worth noting that in Sankhu, low castes have successfully engaged new service-sector jobs as channels to middle-class status in a manner that has posed a formidable challenge to their low status within caste ideology. For the new hotels, offices, and carpet factories of Kathmandu all require a whole range of services compatible with low caste occupations and services that are below the rank and dignity of high castes.[16] Thus, for instance, untouchables from Sankhu have found employment as janitors, office "peons," and septic tank cleaners.[17] Their new incomes enable them to participate as consumers in the new commoditized regime of value unleashed by open market policies accompanying structural adjustment programs. Currency deregulation, financial reforms, loosened licensing procedures, and new facilities for direct foreign investment have all contributed to a veritable flooding of domestic markets with imported consumer goods (which, as Liechty [1997] explains, first became available to mass society only in the 1950s with the lifting of century-old import bans and sumptuary laws). In the first decade of economic liberalization, the flow of imports—and the ubiquity of commodities in everyday life—skyrocketed, increasing nearly ninefold between 1985 and 1995. The commodity economy, of course, knows no caste distinctions; within its calculus low castes can use their purchasing power on equal footing with anyone else who possesses financial capital. Low castes are thus able to climb toward the ranks of a newly consolidating urban middle class organized around a social logic of consumption.

Honor remains the crucial currency within this new cultural logic, but strategies for building honor rely increasingly on the display of modern commodities—rather than on building relationships and meeting social or religious obligations. Class is thus emerging as an idiom of social life that competes with the logic of caste by structuring hierarchy around competition in the calculus of commodity consumption instead of around initial endowments of *karma* and ritual purity. Historically, economic and caste status in Newar society have tended to converge—with dominant castes enjoying relative material advantages.[18] Caste and class are becoming increasingly distinct idioms of social life, however, as people find means to pursue their ambitions through new regimes of value. For low castes in particular, the emerging logic of class provides an alternative framework for social mobility.[19]

The political possibilities opened up for women in the current macroeconomic conjuncture seem less promising. New commodity cultures associated with trade liberalization and the recent proliferation of imported consumer goods, for instance, intersect with gender ideology in ways that subvert the progressive dimensions of *kvasah* for women. Young women report spending more of their private wealth on fashion as a means of pursuing and upholding the status of "being modern" for themselves and their households (see also Liechty 1995). Because consumption of modern commodities figures so centrally in an emerging class-based regime of value, women, as bearers of household honor, simply cannot afford to ignore the latest trends in clothing, makeup, and hairstyle—however much they may experience the recent fascination with fashion as oppressive or trivial.[20]

Using *kvasah* for purchases of consumer goods on a regular basis clearly leaves fewer resources for income-generating investments. Even more significant for women's financial autonomy is the rapid pace at which consumer commodities lose their value. Fashions change, clothes wear out, and electronic goods and accessories eventually break down: as Liechty (1995, 310) argues, "their nature and meaning are perishable." As women invest more in modern commodities, then, the value of their *kvasah* declines over time.

At the same time, there is some evidence that even the meaning surrounding *kvasah* may also be transforming within the new commoditized regime of value. For many joint families in Sankhu, marital gifts provide the first occasion for acquiring modern furniture and other consumer goods crucial for marking out claims to middle-class status. As a result, dowries these days are increasingly encompassing kinds of moveable property whose use is in demand by the wider extended family of a woman's marital home: sofa sets, televisions, steel storage cabinets, and other commodities required for households to function at minimally accepted standards of modernity. In a society where the calculus of class and commodity consumption is gaining new currency, it is increasingly common to find such dowry items appropriated for collective use—and display—in the more public spaces of the household. These tendencies directly undermine normative beliefs about *kvasah* as women's property. One high-caste woman compared these trends in Newar towns to the coercive North Indian dowry system, in which the groom's family extorts dowry items from the bride's family, sometimes after the marriage itself, and sometimes involving violence against the woman:

> *Newar Woman (NW)*: It is really an Indian custom for a woman's marital family to use her dowry or for dowry to even include items that are in demand by men. At first it was not like that in Nepal. There did not use to be a lot of *pressure* [on a bride's family] to give a lot of dowry.[21] In India, and also in the Marwari society here in Nepal, the *tilak* system prevails. What happens in this system is that in order to marry their daughter, the bride's family must give as much dowry as has been requested by the groom's family . . . motorcycle, motor, house, whatever—the bride's family must give it.
>
> *Katharine Rankin (KR)*: Has this custom influenced Newar society in any way?
>
> *NW*: In Newar society, wealthy families have tried to institute this practice.
>
> *KR*: You haven't seen this in the Newar towns, though, have you?
>
> *NW*: What is happening in Newar towns now is that dowry items more often come to belong to whoever uses them [instead of exclusively to the bride]. So even in Newar towns, the groom's family may demand dowry items: Bring a TV, bring one of those steel cabinets, bring this, bring that. Some people have started looking for dowry items with their sons' weddings in this way.
>
> *KR*: Do they really request particular things?
>
> *NW*: Some don't really, but some do. . . . Now among the rich Newars, they have gone so far as to expect the bride's side to clean the house on the groom's side, paint it, repair it, and so on before the wedding. The groom's side leaves all of the house preparations, decorations, curtains, everything—it is all considered to be part of the dowry. They'll consider it part of a woman's dowry to decorate the groom's house on the occasion of her marriage![22]

Here we find a form of Sanskritization[23] particularly pernicious to women. As the basis for honor shifts from old forms of social investment to participation in a commodity-based regime of value, households find the surplus necessary to finance the requisite consumer goods in forms of finance capital normatively earmarked as women's property. Dowry itself is no longer gendered exclusively female—with significant implications for women's financial autonomy within marriage or beyond divorce.

New labor market opportunities, meanwhile, have not challenged gender ideologies restricting women's mobility in the same manner that they have begun to erode the status prescriptions of caste hierarchy. Even though Newar households have begun to look more favorably on sending their daughters to school, upon marriage the customary concern with seclusion still prevails. Within the emerging class-based regime of value, "educated women" in marriage are increasingly valued among Newars as icons of modernity, but education has not generally opened up new employment opportunities for women that could challenge ideological constraints on women's mobility (see also Shtrii Shakti 1995). As Liechty (1995) argues with regard to Kathmandu middle-class culture more generally, Sankhu Newars have thus modernized the concepts of *girl* and *daughter* in accordance with the development discourse on "girl child education," but it is beyond marriage, in the context of the husband's family, where the new freedoms of economic liberalization and political democracy fail to challenge established gender relationships. For women, then, "being modern"—whether through keeping up with fashion, receiving dowries comprised increasingly of modern consumer goods, or schooling for the sake of becoming an acceptably "educated bride"—may be experienced as yet another form of male domination.

THE CULTURAL POLITICS OF SOCIAL CHANGE

These findings offer several conclusions about the cultural politics of social change and a facilitative role for planning in promoting gender transformation and social justice. First, social groups do not "modernize" or "develop" in unilateral or predictable ways with the deepening and expansion of markets. Rather, they change through dialectical and culturally specific processes of material and ideological transformation. "Market" values do not merely replace "traditional" values; rather, new regimes of value articulate with old ones, creating different opportunities and constraints for differently positioned social groups. It follows that access to markets generally and access to credit specifically does not in itself guarantee social opportunity. Rather, cultural ideologies, and the various ways they articulate with processes of macroeconomic change, play a particularly important role in structuring opportunity. In Sankhu, women have always actively engaged in "microcredit," specifically by lending out dowry wealth. The recent consolidation of consumer cultures oriented around a commoditized regime of value has disrupted local capital access systems for women in two ways: it has shifted some dowry wealth out of financially liquid forms, and it has undermined the Newar gendering of dowry as "women's own property." When they fail to recognize such cultural ideological shifts, as they so often do, planners (implementing microfinance programs or, indeed, any development intervention) could end up unwittingly reproducing, even exacerbating, existing social hierarchies.

At the same time, the findings here present planners with some rather optimistic evidence about the scope for critical resources within culture to inform social change. We have seen that even though women's practices suggest compliance with subordinating gender ideologies, their compliance is strategic; women recognize prescribed gender roles *as* ideology and function within its constraints to reduce the risk of social isolation, chaos, and material deprivation. Women also manipulate the contradictions in gender ideology to enhance their economic and political security in ways, ironically, that the honor economy constrains men from pursuing. As Bina Agarwal (1994) suggests, however, the shift from individual recognition and resistance to more critical, collective forms of action is crucial for engaging existing levels of consciousness toward ideological change. The kind of individual resistance and recognition described here are only the seeds for a politically more potent, collective action against structures of oppression.

It is toward this transition from "individual, covert" to "collective, overt" consciousness and action that planners could most effectively direct their initiatives. In the absence of processes that build collective consciousness and a will for overt challenges to dominant gender ideology, credit in itself can never offer a panacea for women's subordination, even in the Newar context with its history of women's "microlending." Regardless of the sectoral focus of their programs, therefore, it is incumbent on planners to play a role in creating the social spaces and developing the institutional means for collective reflection on individual experiences of resistance—to attend to the *process* by which women participate in development programs and not merely to what women "get" in the form of program output (numbers of loans disbursed, savings generated, and so on). Such procedural considerations could create possibilities for women and others in subordinate social locations to negotiate their differences and develop a collective social criticism of dominant cultural ideologies. This kind of locally situated social criticism could provide a foundation for articulating social justice from the standpoint of the oppressed—and mobilizing for progressive social change.

ACKNOWLEDGMENTS
Research for this chapter was conducted under the auspices of a Fulbright-Hays Research Grant. I am grateful to Madan Gopal Shrestha and Raju Shrestha for their assistance with interviews and translations. For comments on earlier drafts of this chapter, thanks go to Chris Cavanagh, Gracia Clark, Stuart Corbridge, Susan Christopherson, Amrita Daniere, Kathryn March, and Norma Rantisi. This chapter is an earlier version of a much-revised paper, "Cultures of Economies: Gender and Socio-Spatial Change in Nepal," published in *Gender Place and Culture* 10(1).

NOTES

1. Here I closely follow Parish's (1997) similar analysis of low-caste consciousness in Newar society.

2. Arjun Appadurai (1986) and Pierre Bourdieu (1977) may be noted especially for drawing on Simmel (1907) for discussions of the cultural politics of value.

3. As will become clear below, expanding an understanding of capital to encompass symbolic forms does not preclude an analysis of their coercive and exploitative dimensions—following Bourdieu, that is, one can engage a Marxist analysis of culture and social practice.

4. On this point, see Roseberry (1989, 11).

5. I thus use "ideology" in the sense advanced by Raymond Williams, as "a relatively formal and articulated system of meanings, values, and beliefs, of a kind that can be abstracted as a 'world view' or 'class outlook' of a particular social group (1994, 596). The dominant ideology of any period or place will, of course, be that of dominant groups. To the extent that subordinate populations have collective identities and attempt to assert themselves against a dominant order, however, they may also have ideologies—their own explicit and *articulated* world view—through which they attempt to critique the established orthodoxy and control the cultural terms in which the world is ordered. Subordinate ideologies are implicit or immanent in contradictory consciousness, but may or may not be realized as the explicit expression of heterodox—alternative, critical—possibilities. Though I hold out the possibility, and the hope, that contradictory consciousness in Newar society may eventually consolidate more agentive forms of antihegemonic power, I use "gender ideologies" here to evoke prevailing ideas about gender that advantage men over women.

6. "The contradictions of life in a society structured by hierarchical values of caste and gender, that is, are such that 'self' and 'worldview' can never coalesce into a single, coherent vision" (Parish 1997).

7. Parbatiya literally means "hill people" and is used, by Newars at least, to refer to Hindu groups that South Asianists commonly call "Indo-Nepalese" or "Indo-Aryan"—namely, Brahmans (Priests), Chetris (Warriors, including the Shah and Rana lineages), and their associated Untouchable artisan castes (Tailors, Leatherworkers, and Blacksmiths).

8. The term "honor economy" is drawn from Liechty (1995). For a similar discussion of the regulating function of honor among caste Hindus in Nepal, see Cameron (1998).

9. Newari words are transliterated according to the conventions of Manandhar (1986) and Nepali words according to the conventions of Turner (1931).

10. Tamangs are the largest Tibeto-Burman ethnic group in Nepal.

11. On *guthis*, see also Gellner (1993), Nepali (1965), and Quigley (1995).

12. See also Satya Mohan Joshi's story, "Guthi" (1992), which recounts the suicide of a farmer-caste man from Kathmandu who cannot bear the shame of being financially unable to host the annual *guthi* feast.

13. For similar findings throughout the South Asian subcontinent, see Agarwal (1994).

14. See also Parish (1997) for a similar analysis of low-caste consciousness in Newar society.

15. Technically, *kvasah* is translated as "women's own property," including earned income. As dowry usually comprises the bulk of women's own property, however, the term is often used synonymously with *dowry*. For a similar account of Tamang women's strategic use of personal property, see March (1998).

16. Carpet factories are perhaps the most significant generators of new employment for Sankhu residents. Hand-knotted "Tibetan" carpets had surpassed tourism as the largest source of foreign exchange in Nepal by 1992. Two years later, Nepal became the fourth largest exporter of carpets, with 200 large producing units and more than 5,000 small-scale carpet factories having been registered in 1991 and 1992 alone. Many of these production facilities are concentrated on the western edge of Kathmandu, within ten kilometers of Sankhu.

17. "Peon" is a term, originating with the British in colonial India, for office servants who perform menial tasks ranging from cleaning to running errands. To say that new market forms present opportunities for low castes in Sankhu, however, is *not* to suggest that the terms of the emerging employment opportunities—of the janitors in five-star hotels, for example—are in themselves ideal or just.

18. I do not mean to suggest absolute congruence between caste and class, but rather that low castes have typically faced greater odds against becoming rich. Certainly also, as we have seen, high castes have faced the risk of descending into poverty if they do not meet their social obligations.

19. On tension between religious and class idioms of social life in Kathmandu, see Liechty (1998).

20. On women's experience of fashion as oppressive and trivializing, see Rankin (1999).

21. Words set off by asterisks indicate that the speaker has used an English, as opposed to Newari or Nepali, word. I have followed Liechty (1998) in adopting this convention.

22. On the North Indian system and a comparative analysis of dowry systems throughout South Asia, see Agarwal (1994). On a similar trend of extorting dowry in the Parbatiya context, see Miller (1992).

23. The term "Sanskritization" was developed by M. N. Srinivas (1962) to designate the tendency of lower-caste groups to imitate Brahmans in the hope of improving their status, particularly in the prohibition of meat-eating and liquor consumption, and in the emphasis on Vedic and Sanskrit religious texts. It has been generalized to refer to both Brahamanical and non-Brahmanical models for emulation within the caste system; here, the emulation is of North Indian high-caste practices.

REFERENCES

Agarwal, Bina. 1994. *A Field of One's Own: Gender and Land Rights in South Asia.* Cambridge, U.K.: Cambridge University Press.

Appadurai, Arjun. 1986. "Introduction: Commodities and the Politics of Value." In *The Social Life of Things: Commodities in Cultural Perspective*, ed. by A. Appadurai. Cambridge, U.K.: Cambridge University Press.

Bourdieu, Pierre. 1977. *Outline of a Theory of Practice.* Cambridge, U.K.: Cambridge University Press.

Cameron, Mary. 1998. *On the Edge of the Auspicious: Caste and Gender in Nepal.* Chicago: University of Illinois Press.

Comaroff, Jean, and John Comaroff. 1991. *Of Revelation and Revolution: Christianity, Colonialism, and Consciousness in South Africa.* Chicago: University of Chicago Press.

Fernando, Jude. 1997. "Nongovernmental Organizations, Micro-Credit, and Empowerment of Women." *Annals of the American Academy of Political and Social Science* 554: 150–77.

Gellner, David. 1993. *Monk, Householder, and Tantric Priest: Newar Buddhism and Its Hierarchy of Ritual.* New Delhi: Foundation Books.

Joshi, Satya Mohan. 1992. "Guthi." In *An Anthology of Short Stories of Nepal,* trans. Kesar Lall and Tej R. Kansakar. Kathmandu: Foundation for Literature.

Keohane, Nannerl O., and Barbara C. Gelpi. 1981. Foreword to *Feminist Theory: A Critique of Ideology,* ed. by N. O. Keohane, M. Z. Rosaldo, and B. C. Gelpi. Chicago: University of Chicago Press.

Liechty, Mark. 1995. *Fashioning Modernity in Kathmandu: Mass Media, Consumer Culture, and the Middle Class in Nepal.* Ph.D. dissertation, Philadelphia: University of Pennsylvania.

———. 1997. "Selective Exclusion: Foreigners, Foreign Goods, and Foreignness in Modern Nepali History." *Studies in Nepali History and Society* 2(1): 5–68.

———. 1998. "Consumer Culture and Identities in Kathmandu: 'Playing with Your Brain.'" In *Selves in Time and Place: Identities, Experience, and History in Nepal,* ed. by D. Skinner, A. Pach, III, and D. Holland. New York: Rowman & Littlefield.

Manandhar, Thakur Lal. 1986. *Newari-English Dictionary: Modern Language of Kathmandu Valley.* Delhi: Agam Kala Prakashan.

March, Kathryn S. 1998. "Two Houses and the Pain of Separation in Tamang Narratives from Highland Nepal." *Oral Tradition* 12(1).

Mayoux, Linda. 1995. *From Vicious to Virtuous Circles? Gender and Micro-Enterprise Development.* Geneva: U.N. Research Institute for Social Development, Occasional Paper no. 3.

Miller, Sarah. 1992. *Twice-Born Tales of Kathmandu: Stories that Tell People.* Ph.D. dissertation, Ithaca, N.Y.: Cornell University.

Nepali, Gopal Singh. 1965. *The Newars.* Bombay: United Asia Publications.

Parish, Steven. 1997. *Hierarchy and Its Discontents: Culture and the Politics of Consciousness in Caste Society.* Delhi: Oxford University Press.

Quigley, Declan. 1995. "The Guthi Organizations of Dhulikhel Shresthas." *Kailash—A Journal of Himalayan Studies* 12(1–2): 5–62.

Rankin, Katharine N. 1996. "Planning for Equity: Ethical Principles from Newar Representations of Finance." *Studies in Nepali History and Society* 1(2): 395–421.

———. 1999. *The Cultural Politics of Markets: Economic Liberalization and the Challenge for Social Planning in Nepal.* Ph.D. dissertation, Ithaca, N.Y.: Cornell University.

———. 2001a. "Governing Development: Neoliberalism, Microcredit, and Rational Economic Woman." *Economy and Society* 30(1): 18–37.

———. 2001b. "Planning and the Politics of Markets: Some Lessons from Financial Regulation in Nepal." *International Planning Studies* 6(1): 89–102.

Roseberry, William. 1989. *Anthropologies and Histories: Essays in Culture, History, and Political Economy.* New Brunswick, N.J.: Rutgers University Press.

Turner, Ralph Lilley. 1931. *Dictionary of the Nepali Language.* New Delhi: Allied Publishers.

Shakti, Shtrii. 1995. *Women, Development, Democracy: A Study of the Socio-Economic Changes in the Status of Women in Nepal (1981–1993).* Kathmandu: Shtrii Shakti.

Simmel, Georg. 1907 [1978]. *The Philosophy of Money,* trans. by T. Bottomore and D. Frisby. London: Routledge and Kegan Paul.

Srinivas, M. N. 1962. "A Note on Sanskritization and Westernization." In *Caste in Modern India and Other Essays,* 42–62. Bombay: Asia Publishing House.

Williams, Raymond. 1994. "Selections from Marxism and Literature." In *Culture/Power/History: A Reader in Contemporary Social Theory,* ed. by N. B. Dirks, G. Eley, and S. B. Ortner. Princeton, N.J.: Princeton University Press. Originally published in Raymond Williams. 1977. *Marxism and Literature.* Oxford, U.K.: Oxford University Press.

"Why Would She Fight Her *Family*?" Indian Women's Negotiations of Discourses of Inheritance

Srimati Basu

When I tell people that my research is on Indian women and property, per-haps the commonest query is "So, do women have any property rights in India?" to which my favorite response is "They have property rights; they just don't have much property!" I want to explicate that remark more fully by talking about the cultural fears and desires that frame Indian women's legal rights and their dislocation from family property, the meanings of property as well as the meanings of power and resistance. The backdrop is a situation in which women have substantive (though not fully equal) legal rights to inheritance in the postcolonial era but rarely lay claim to the na-tal family property they are legally entitled to, most often citing ideological hindrances.

An unpacking of refusals of property shows not a passive acceptance of cul-tural prescriptions but rather the negotiation of material, social, and emo-tional needs, a complex mix of consternation, affection, and optimized survival strategies. They provide a way to examine the ways in which gender and kinship are mutually constituted, and the ways in which the boundaries between the so-called domestic and politico-jural realms are not only porous but indeed symbiotic (Collier and Yanagisako 1987). As Brettell argues in her analysis of nineteenth-century property bequests in Portugal, property trans-actions "both shape and are shaped by relations between men and women, parents and children, brothers and sisters," constituting "moments when the rights and obligations between people are negotiated" (1991, 447). Thus, no-tions about kinship and gender fundamentally undergird the intergenera-tional transfer of wealth, and "an understanding of cultural constructions of gender difference are [sic] of utmost importance" for interpreting property transmissions (1991, 462). Women's availing themselves of inheritance rights is not necessarily a marker of "modern" consciousness, and attitudes to inher-itance may be considered a diagnostic of cultural norms; Moors shows in a

study of Palestinian women that awareness of property rights may be widespread, particularly in urban contexts, but women pursue taking family property only in vulnerable socioeconomic positions or in culturally prescribed
ways (1995, 49–50).

These refusals of property show the limitations of both power and resistance (Abu-Lughod 1993). Women, although partly constituted within and
limited by dominant ideologies about their disentitlement to natal property,
are not simply manipulated by them; they also contest such beliefs in overtly
rebellious or subtly resistant ways. With regard to property transmission,
some women show a desire to assume equal social and financial responsibility toward parents and to maintain empowering connections with the natal
family, but others separate themselves from the natal family except for receiving occasional gifts, and are possessive about other women's claims to "their"
affinal property. All these positions are related to the tradeoffs within the total system of distribution of resources; they are not the result of passivity but
rather markers of what women feel able to do while balancing their notions of
kinship against material exigencies.

HINDU WOMEN'S INHERITANCE: ILLUSION OF RADICAL CHANGE

One of the mechanisms through which systems of property transmission perpetuate gender and class hegemonies is the invention of "tradition," the transformation of the past to serve contemporary ends. In many postcolonial states,
this has taken the form of a struggle between ideas of liberty and equality associated with modernity and "authentic" national ethos. This negotiation between discourses of liberty vs. alleged "Indian traditions" marked the debates
over colonial and postcolonial Indian lawmaking and continues to suffuse contemporary judicial rhetoric (Parashar 1992). Parashar argues that although
women's interests are frequently invoked in these contexts, these invocations
mark philosophical stances rather than a comprehensive approach to improving women's situations; the negotiations have primarily been about political
contests for power between old and incoming regimes in the new nation.

The Hindu Succession Act, passed in 1956, exemplifies a law that purported
to be centered on women's interests while consolidating existent property
regimes. It ostensibly radicalized women's lives, because it gave widows the
right to absolute as opposed to usufructuary maintenance and made provision for daughters to be heirs in cases of intestate succession of self-acquired
property. The Act was very far from being a testimonial to gender equity: it did
not challenge the greatest sites of privilege such as the Mitakshara coparcenary[1] or the exemptions to equal inheritance for agricultural land (Agarwal
1994). It was centered on north Indian Brahmanical patriarchy and inscribed
the rights of matrilineal communities as marginal for questions of "Hindu"
succession. Even within north Indian communities, it eroded the property

rights of widows, who had customarily been entitled to marital property despite remarriage, by making remarriage a condition whereby all Hindu widows would have to forego property (Chowdhry 1994; Agarwal 1994).

And yet, the passage of the Act occasioned widespread anxiety among legislators. "The purity of family life, the great ideal of chastity and the great ideal of Indian womanhood" were at stake, according to Pandit Thakur Das, a member of the legislative assembly; he contended that property rights for women were an example of "equality run mad" (quoted in Kapur and Cossman 1996, 56). This statement is typical of responses that resist property law reform, which invoke the destruction of the "Indian family" as an inevitable outcome of granting property rights to women. The President, Rajendra Prasad, declared that he would veto the Act unless the notion of the coparcenary was retained (Agnes 1996, 64). Even B. R. Ambedkar, who as Nehru's Law Minister was the prime champion of post-independence legal reform and resigned in protest when the overall package of reform—the Hindu Code Bill—did not pass in its original comprehensive form, opposed drastic reform because he felt this could "perturb many families." He fully supported the theoretical idea of daughters being included as heirs in case of intestate succession, but when the Select Committee of the Constituent Assembly suggested that daughters and sons be treated as equal with respect to the quantum of inheritance, he "described this alteration as an effort by his enemies to make the entire reform process appear ridiculous, and thereby cause the entire reform process to be abandoned" (Parashar 1992, 124).

The Hindu Succession Act (1956) stands as a prime signifier for the contemporary position of Indian women with respect to personal law. It includes some changes that give Hindu women greater access, while veiling the significant patriarchal and patrilineal scripts on which it is grounded. Ironically, these light changes cast as far-reaching reforms are also used as ideals against which laws of other communities (e.g., so-called Scheduled Tribes) are judged (Basu 1999a). The bottom line is that at best the Hindu Succession Act (1956) improved the situation for some women, particularly widows, in some communities, thereby emphasizing that women's best economic options lay within marriage. But Hindu women rarely use the provisions of the Act to claim natal property, as this chapter discusses at length. A significant issue is also the ways in which the provisions of the Act are reinterpreted by judges according to their own cultural perceptions. In other words, the Hindu Succession Act (1956) demonstrates the ways in which the discourse of modernization and development is deployed with relation to gender.

THE PARAMETERS OF PROPERTY OWNERSHIP

Women's putative claims to natal property are often inscribed in images of overreaching greed, selfishness, lack of empathy and love for the natal family, and a desire to cause family conflicts. For example, one of the women I talked to, Sushila, described what she imagined her brother, sister-in-law, and other relatives saying if she ever tried to claim her legal share of natal family land in the village: "*wo ayee hak lene*" (there she comes, to claim her rights). The phrase brilliantly captures the pun on "*hak*" as well as the translated term "right." (The Urdu "*hak*" can be translated as "right" both in the sense of legal rights and in the sense of right as true or correct.) Even while "*hak lena*" or "taking rights" has a strong pejorative connotation in this context—implying greed, a selfish focus on individual rights, and a monetization of family relations—ironically, the notion that availing oneself of one's "rights" is the right or correct thing to do by legal guidelines cannot be erased. This tension between the fairness represented in enforceable legal equity and the invaluable family ties that allegedly rise above legality may explain the hostility directed towards the "*haklenewali*," the woman who would claim her "rights." The transgression lies in her "demand" to break cultural taboos in favor of legal guidelines. These specters of property-seeking women are important vehicles of maintaining socioeconomic hegemonies; they are used not only to deter potential heirs, but are actually inversions of how family conflict, overreaching greed, and love and empathy operate. The myth that women are waiting to seize their rights, grab property, and destroy their natal family base is frequently used to set up legal avenues disinheriting women without their knowledge, to indefinitely delay the divisions, and, most often, to offer women token amounts in lieu of substantive property.

The specter of the *haklenewali* seems to have been effective: not only has there been no dramatic transformation in social hierarchies, but in fact there has been little change in inheritance practices in over forty years of the Hindu Succession Act's existence. Numerous studies show that the inheritance provision for daughters is rarely availed of: women generally turn down shares of natal inheritance.[2] Why are they averse to taking advantage of legal provisions that would benefit themselves and their nuclear families? Women frequently cite reasons relating to gender roles, kinship, and family responsibilities to justify this situation.

The situations described in this chapter are based on the interviews I conducted in New Delhi between 1991 and 1993, in three neighborhoods I call KE, KC, and SN.[3] The sample included an equal number of middle-class and poor urban families. Among the women I interviewed, no women who had brothers had received or expected to receive natal property (typical of other studies of inheritance practices). The most common rationale given for refusing property shares (said by 41.7 percent of all the women and by 50 percent of women in the highest income group in this sample) was that the women did not want to precipitate family rifts and to sever social relationships with their brothers. But the responses also covered a variety of other reasons that reflected or resisted dominant ideologies. In this chapter, I want to examine some of these reasons in detail, to analyze the sites of women's compliance and resistance as sites where the meanings of gender and kinship are both invented and solidified.

Before exploring women's negotiations of property decisions, I will provide a quick map of women's property ownership and of the significance of property in this sample. In what positions were these women likely to become actual property owners? Marital property was the most likely route: in this sample, some of the middle-class women, many of whom had contributed gold for purchasing their residential homes, had titles in their names, and a large number of the poor women had temporary huts in their residential colonies registered in their names, although these had dubious legal or monetary value. Neither group had legal ownership or control over their husbands' family property in the husbands' lifetimes. As widows, a few women became de facto owners and managers of family property or received a share of affinal property if they had lived in joint patrilineal households. No women with brothers had been given any natal property; a few brotherless women expected to inherit. One other atypical route was for the chain of inheritance to be diverted in favor of women in cases where they had been caregivers to elderly neighbors or relatives who would not customarily have been their responsibility.

It is important to mark different meanings of property here. The middle-class women may have had insignificant amounts of natal or affinal family property, but having ownership of or access to residential property in a middle-class area ensured them access to prime educational resources and employment opportunities on par with men of their households. Many women, particularly in the middle-middle-class area, availed of these opportunities and earned amounts equivalent to men in their households. On the other hand, men who lived in the squatter colony often owned large amounts of rural property, having moved to the city for more cash income than was available to them in their villages while some of their family members kept up the farming. However, they lacked access to the prime jobs in the urban economy due to education-related and class-related reasons and were drawn into the informal sector or into low-level formal sector jobs, an example of one of the postcolonial processes of class formation. Most women in these poorer households had neither land nor permanent housing in their names, nor education or formal sector employment, and they were involved in the worst-paying and most marginal informal sector jobs, a result of the compounded effect of gender and class subalternity.

Multilayered Attitudes toward Natal Property and Women's Property

Most women cited a variety of reasons for not taking natal family property (table 8.1), indicating a complex reaction to the issue. However, the responses could be grouped into certain broad categories reflecting prevailing ideologies

Table 8.1.   Respondents' Attitudes toward Taking Property (in Percentages)

Attitude Toward Taking Natal Property	KE N=14	KC N=16	SN N=30	Total N=60
1 Don't want, it causes rifts with brothers/sisters-in-law; want smaller share to prevent rift	50.0	37.5	40.0	41.7
2 Get dowry/lifelong gifts instead	28.6	25.0	50.0	38.3
3 Share husbands' wealth and affines' property instead	50.0	25.0	40.0	38.3
4 Could get property in sonless family	14.3	6.2	36.7	23.3
5 Want natal family's prosperity instead	7.1	37.5	16.7	20.0
6 Women should take natal property	0	18.8	26.7	18.3
7 Can't get property as per "custom"	0	12.5	26.7	16.7
8 Not enough property for multiple shares	7.1	12.5	23.3	16.7
9 Property goes to givers of eldercare	14.3	25.0	0	10.0
10 Should take if woman is poor or in trouble	7.1	18.8	0	6.7
11 Have own wages instead	21.4	0	0	5.0
12 Other	35.7	18.8	10.0	18.3
13 Do not know/Unknown	7.1	6.2	0	3.3

about women and property. At one extreme were the responses that reflected the allegedly progressive and "feminist" paradigm that women should take family property and people should not distinguish between sons and daughters (item 6 in the table). The opposite extreme was represented by views that did not challenge or question dominant ideology at all, in which it was claimed that "custom" was the barrier against women getting natal property (item 7). "Custom" was an opaque concept in such responses, combining inheritance norms, family dynamics, and diverse ethnic, regional, and religious practices.[4]

As the descending order in table 8.1 shows, women's responses evoked different paradigms for achieving a fair social distribution of resources. Most numerous was the fear that taking natal property would lead to rifts with brothers and sisters-in-law (item 1, brought up by 41.7 percent of the women in all), that leaving women's share as part of their natal family's assets allowed family relations to be harmonious and supportive. Next in importance were responses that brought up the idea that marriage placed women in a different mode of entitlement: that women got dowry and other gifts instead of property (item 2, evoked in 38.3 percent of the responses); and that daughters "got" marital and affinal, rather than natal, resources (item 3, also mentioned by 38.3 percent of the women). Although 23.3 percent of the women believed that women could get property in Hindu families if they were brotherless, per alleged scriptural prescriptions (item 4), others saw themselves as being generous (rather than afraid) in being able to keep their natal family more prosperous by not withdrawing their share (item 5, 20 percent). In addition to these rationales based on the idea of women's separation from the natal family at marriage, other paradigms invoked property being a reward for eldercare (item 9, 10 percent of responses), or property as a compensation for a daughter's economic hardship (item 10, 6.7 percent of responses).[5]

The tensions within the responses are further demonstrated in the discrepancies between tables 8.1 and 8.2, in the difference between women's reactions to their own natal property versus their views on how they would distribute property ideally. Many of the same rationales appear in both, but in different proportions. In all, 66.7 percent of the women supported ideas of not discriminating between children by gender in distributing property (item 1), whether by including them all as heirs or choosing heirs based on need or ability rather than gender. In sharp contrast to table 8.1, in which only 18.3 percent of women in all contemplated taking natal property in equal shares, 53.3 percent in table 8.2 thought that ideally both daughters and sons should get property in equal shares (item 1a). However, alongside widespread support for giving property to children regardless of gender (table 8.2, item 1), a substantial proportion of women preferred sons as heirs (item 2, 40 percent in all) or as preferred heirs (item 3, 30 percent in all). Among the diverse rationales for leaving property to males, the idea of giving property to sons to prevent family rifts was brought up by 13.3 percent of women (though this was considerably less than the 41.7 percent seen in table 8.1), along with ideas of women getting dowry and affinal property, other popular attitudes in table 8.1.

Table 8.2.   Respondents' Attitudes toward How Property Should Be Distributed Ideally (in Percentages)

	Ideal Distributions of Property	KE N=14	KC N=16	SN N=30	Total N=60
1	**All children should be equally entitled**	**64.3**	**75.0**	**63.3**	**66.7**
1a	Equally among all children; to all children in very wealthy families	50.0	43.8	60.0	53.3
1b	According to children's needs/abilities	14.3	37.5	10.0	20.0
1c	Parents should give to all children; refusing share is daughter's choice	0	25.0	3.3	8.3
2	**Should go to sons**	**28.6**	**43.8**	**43.3**	**40.0**
2a	To sons, while daughters get from affines	21.4	37.5	10.0	20.0
2b	To sons, while daughters get dowry	0	18.8	20.0	21.7
2c	To sons, per "custom"; to sons, to prevent family rifts	7.1	6.3	20.0	13.3
2d	Daughters should not demand share; can take property if offered by brothers	0	12.5	6.7	6.7
3	**Should go to daughters and sons, but unequally**	**28.6**	**25.0**	**33.3**	**30.0**
3a	Small token to daughters only; immovable property only to sons, other shared	28.6	18.8	20.0	21.7
3b	To daughters, if family sonless	0	6.3	16.7	10.0
4	**To giver of eldercare**	**7.1**	**25.0**	**10.0**	**13.3**

Eldercare was evoked as an ideal standard by a similar number of women overall (table 8.2 item 4, 13.3 percent versus table 8.1 item 9, 10 percent).

Like the notion that women contributed to family prosperity by not subtracting their shares (item 5, table 8.1), ideas that women need not be entirely sidelined from family property were articulated by several respondents in contemplating ideal divisions of property, even as they confirmed male preference; they suggested giving daughters some moveable assets in the parents' lifetime, or allowing them the option of refusing (table 8.2, items 1c, 2d, and 3a). Along with the much larger number of respondents in table 8.2 who wanted daughters to be equal heirs, this indicates that women went along with customary notions of women's being disentitled to natal property in their present circumstances, but envisaged bequeathal of property to women in an ideal situation.

Equal Love: Conceptions of Equitable Distribution

If parents gave both daughters and sons something then both might think that their parents loved them.

—*Reena, SN*[6]

Notions that daughters should be equally included in property distributions were the commonest way in which women conceptualized ideal inheritance (Table 8.2, 53.3 percent, and also evoked by 18.3 percent of the women in delineating their own attitudes to natal family property, Table 8.1). This idea was often visualized in association with images of property as a vehicle of love, as typified by Reena's comment above. The youngest woman in my sample, eighteen-year-old Reena was still in seventh grade and with no marriage imminently in sight, and her response was unencumbered by many of the "social" obligations or considerations that married women in particular took upon themselves. Yet though atypical in those ways, Reena's response matched the theme running through women's ideas about giving and getting equal property: showing and earning love.

Women's rights to property are often viewed as being a "modern" and feminist demand, appearing proportionate to education and high social class (connoting more "enlightened" views) and irrelevant to the majority of women. The voices of Reena and many women in her neighborhood refute the eliteness of the above claim. Despite the overwhelming impression that Indian women tend to refuse natal property, it is important to remember that a large number of the women in this study supported the idea of equal property, especially when it came to visualizing how they might distribute property ideally without restraints (53.3 percent), as opposed to what they could actually see themselves demanding (18.3 percent). Moreover, in either case, women from SN were the ones who supported equal distributions of property in far greater proportions (as high as 60 percent, followed by KE with 50 percent, Table 8.2). In this sample, high education and class were definitely not correlated with ideals of women being equal inheritors of property, and it was not women's own "backwardness" or disinclination that was keeping them from sharing natal assets.

Furthermore, the images used by SN women revealed a significantly different paradigm for claiming property, evoking neither the alleged brashness of rights-based claims nor the pathos of victims' needs associated with demands for legalization of women's rights to property. Instead, inheritance issues were coded in emotional and affectional terms. For example, several of the women who unqualifiedly supported equal property for sons and daughters used their experiences of motherhood and images of the womb as a symbol of equal entitlement for all children. As Meena, age twenty-two and the mother of two daughters, put it:

> If parents make equal shares of everything for all their children, then no one can say they have been given less or more, they can say that the parents having given birth to them all gave them all equal shares. After all, daughters and sons come from the same cells in the body, not different places, and one feels the same empathy/tenderness [darad] for both.[7]

A comment from Paro, a thirty-three-year-old mother of two sons and a daughter, is another example of women connecting the dispensation of property to their mothering/parenting duties:

> It would be nice if everyone could get a share since they are all equal [barabar] to the parents; we don't clothe one and keep the others naked or feed one sweets and starve the other.[8]

In these images, the economic dimensions of property were muted; women's profound connections to their natal families were emphasized. Although it is impossible to tell if this was a conscious strategy on the women's part, this line of argument provided a much more comfortable entry to the discourse on property, because it did not evoke the specter of the woman rudely claiming her "rights." In defiance of dominant ideologies that proclaim women's complete severance from the natal family upon marriage, it also emphasized the importance of ties of birth for women and hinted at the need to feel recognized by natal kin through gifts of property.

In contrast, women from KE and KC often used calculations of relative amounts in justifying their choices, focusing on a more precise financial division. Ritu, a thirty-five-year-old lawyer with one son, said, "Parents should divide property equally, or proportionately depending on marriage expenses. But nowadays they spend a lot on sons' weddings too, so it should be equal."[9] Uma, a twenty-seven-year-old mother of one son, proud of her dowryless wedding and aware of her lesser claims on her mother's house compared to her brother, contended that if she had daughters she would prefer to give them no dowry but equal shares of property instead.[10] Forty-two-year-old Indira asserted, given her experience of her own lavish wedding and also her expectation of property, that things bought for weddings were gifts and should not be taken into account in the dispensation of property.[11] Although the absence of womb imagery from these responses cannot be tied to a class-based conclusion, here equity of assets was far more of a direct concern. Although talking about women's "rights" was just as socially taboo in these milieus, tangible economic fairness apparently could be voiced as a standard.

However, despite the 53.3 percent of respondents who visualized and voiced culturally acceptable metaphors for women to get property, only 5 percent in all actually felt they would be able to pursue their justifiable claims. Only one woman from KE (7.1 percent of KE responses) and two from SN (6.7 percent of SN) were absolute about pursuing shares, and four women overall (6.7 percent) expected to get property because of the serendipity of brotherlessness. Others who thought they were entitled to shares felt inhibited either because there was not enough property to divide, or because they felt the simultaneous pull of contrary ideologies such as having gotten dowry already. Though it is important to note that women themselves were often supportive of daughters' equal rights to natal property, ultimately few could realize these professed ideals in the face of other cultural pressures.

Naihar Tut Hi Jaye (The Natal Home Is Broken for Me):
Fears of Natal Abandonment
Babul ki duya-e leti ja
Ja tujhko sukhi sansar mile
Maike ki kabhi na yad aye
Sasural me itna pyar mile[12]

Take your father's blessing/prayer as you go;
Go, and [may you] get a happy household;
May you never remember your mother's home;
[Because of] all the love you receive
at your in-laws' place.

A significant number of women (41.7 percent in all, Table 8.1) also evoked the theme of a daughter's love and love for a daughter in delineating their rights to property by calling upon apprehension rather than affection, saying they would not claim full or any shares of natal property because they were afraid this would sour relations with their brothers or cause their brothers' wives to hate them, and that as a result they would no longer be welcome in their natal homes. This attitude marks one of the dominant metaphors mediating women's refusal of property (Teja 1993, 70; Hershman 1981, 75), that of the greedy shrew or the *haklenewali*. There was also a close connection between these feelings and the apparently obverse ones, the desires for continuing to be part of the natal family by actively contributing to its prosperity or being available for its crises (table 8.1, 20 percent). Significantly, these attitudes articulate women's desire for closeness with the natal family with an agency that is invisible in, and indeed contrary to, the discourse on women's needs and feelings.

The opening phrase heading this section (quoted from a well-known folk song) and the song that follows it in the film (sung in the persona of the bride's father) are examples of the dominant discourse whereby the wedding is represented as the event that marks the watershed of the woman's pleasures, affections, loyalties, and memories.[13] Ties to the natal family are supposed to be severed, and the woman is to become an inseparable part of the affinal family. The *bidaii* ceremony, when the bride leaves her parents' home after the wedding, is an occasion of bittersweet sadness over the cutting of deep emotional ties.

Without dismissing the parents' sorrow at this rite of passage, made worse by rituals of eternal severance, it is difficult to miss the fact that the mourning veils the consolidation of patriarchal property relations. As Kolenda (1984) demonstrates in her study of two Hindu communities, groups (often north Indian) that ritually sever the woman's natal connections upon marriage tend to pack her off with dowry and little subsequent inheritance, but those who have no concept of "losing" the woman upon marriage and who believe couples "belong" to both families often give land to daughters to persuade them to live nearby and help the family. Among the communities studied here, the woman's complete change of identity underlined by Hindu wedding rituals that permanently alter her name and caste (and even religious and funerary affiliations), along with the concept of *kanyadan,* the gift of the daughter, symbolize her severance. Thus, property comes to be the brother's, because he remains "in" the family.

Yet, contrary to these hegemonic expectations, many women do not internalize this severance from the natal family in the ways represented by the songs; if they cry "the natal home is broken for me," they do so with regret, longing to keep that tie unbroken, to retain their connections with the family associated with love, as opposed to the affinal family, which represents the realm of dutiful work (Jeffery and Jeffery 1996, 155). Numerous studies that examine north Indian Hindu women's relationships to their natal families emphasize repeatedly that women challenge the notion of "losing" their natal families and affirm profound emotional connections with them.[14] Raheja contends that women's assertions of their natal connections are not just about sharing the wealth and resources of their families, but "a poetic discourse on power and the possibility of women's resistance to patrilineal authority and patrilineal pronouncements on female identities . . . contesting the power relations that make them so vulnerable when they marry and go away" (1995, 26).

One of the commonest traces of such love for the natal family is seen in fear, that claiming property will break the last residual ties with the natal family and that women will no longer be welcome in their brothers' homes. The "*haklenewali*," the woman who "takes her rights," is evoked here as the specter to be avoided if all natal links are not to be broken. In claims such as "where the sister takes her share all those things [gifts, respect] are not there any more, they say 'now you've got your share so go away, why are you back here again?'"[15] the connection to the natal family can be seen as a concrete fund, and taking property exhausts that link, such that women are cut adrift from customary gifts, emergency shelter, and even affection.

The severe wrath faced by women claiming property described by my respondents (that are beyond the purview of this chapter) show that these were not idle threats. To prevent such rifts, some women tried to leave a residual share in the natal family fund by not separating their portion, as among Rehana's aunts who told their brothers to keep the land and farm it, and that they would visit and take crops once in a while.[16] But several others (20 percent of the middle-class women, plus 3.3 percent of poor women) legally signed over their portions to the brothers to emphasize the affectional connection over the material one. This was usually done at the brother's request to show good faith, but was in fact a legal safeguard, an official insurance against the woman's claims surfacing later.[17] It is important to note that, given the paucity of actual gifts or sustained help from the natal family (as described in a later section of this chapter), no economic consideration was usually expected in return; women usually made such "gifts" because of the fear of loss of the emotional space represented by the natal family, the fragile realm already threatened by marriage and residential separation.

Bringing up property and hence monetizing the brother-sister relationship was seen as undesirable,[18] that is, brothers resented any financial claims made by sisters and could apparently be munificent based only on "pure" love. Brothers' relationships, on the other hand, were not perceived to be adversely affected by having to divide property. At most, according to Rani,[19] "between brothers the quarrel is about a bigger or smaller share, but when sisters are involved it'll turn into such a quarrel that they won't even want to see each other's faces anymore."

However, such notions of brotherly love being untainted by economic transactions were not borne out by the many stories about brothers' resentment over having to share resources (Jeffery and Jeffery 1996, 45). These incidents also gave the lie to the ideal of the joint family having unified interests in building up a common stock of property. For example, Meena's husband was waiting for his father to pass away before he bought rural land in his own name (they had three *bighas* in her name), hoping to get his share of the ten *bighas* controlled by his father without being the only one sending home money for land, and having to share what he purchased with the others.[20]

Similarly, Sushila said that her father-in-law wanted them to buy rural land, but she urged her husband not to buy it while the father-in-law was alive, because all the brothers would take shares of it.[21] Medha's husband kept sending money to his brother for buying joint family land in the village, but the brother continually spent the money on himself; Bindu's brother-in-law mortgaged her husband's land in his absence.[22] In KC, too, several cases of family discontent among brothers were reported: Seema and Renu's elder brothers-in-law sold their fathers' property in rural Punjab and ex-West Pakistan and kept nearly all the money, and Sharmila's father and uncles had long-standing disputes with their stepbrothers over which rooms each brother would get in the family house.[23] In all these cases, the breakdown of alleged joint family values and the entrenchment of the separate interests of "nuclear" or individual units were clear.

Yet even in cases of disputes involving brothers' shares, the source of discord was often perceived to be other women's greed; that is, the spectral figure of the property-hungry woman was made the repository of blame even where males contested over property.[24] As Medha narrated, she worked hard to get their new *jhuggi* (informally acquired temporary hut) registered in her name (her husband already had one in his name), but her brother-in-law got the formal ownership while she was briefly away. When she chided her husband over allowing this to happen, he told her that the *jhuggi* was still "in the family" and that wives try to destroy love among brothers by such requests.[25] Her wish to have property was overrun by the ideal of brotherly solidarity.

Fear of incurring the wrath of brothers' wives figured prominently in women's reasons for staying away from natal family property. It was alleged that mothers could no longer give gifts once sisters-in-law were there because they claimed rights over all possessions, and that women would no longer be welcome in the natal home managed by sisters-in-law if they had asked about property.[26] The putative jealousy of daughters-in-law has a rational basis: if women are supposed to get property only through their in-laws, as daughters-in-law they might well feel possessive toward their only sanctioned (albeit indirect) access to resources (Jeffery and Jeffery 1996, 142). Some women did indeed express resentment at the idea that their husbands' sisters might diminish the property of their in-laws, such as Pushpa who said about her sisters-in-law "Why should they take anything? I'm not going to give them anything from my share."[27] But the jealous sister-in-law can also be regarded as the metonymic transformation of the wrathful brothers themselves (the wrath supposedly brought on by sisters demanding property). With sisters-in-law being the only "strangers" to women in the natal home, it seemed emotionally more comfortable for women to scapegoat them as the disapproving ones, thus preserving parents and brothers as sources of love and generosity, and denying the collusion of their own relatives in erasing their natal connections.

Women's fear of estrangement motivating their refusals of natal property is a widely articulated belief, but there is also a positive face of that desire: women's active urge to contribute to the well-being and prosperity of that family. Ritual connections with brothers observed by north Indian women, such as the wearing of two toe rings for the husband and brother to symbolize natal and affinal connections (Wadley 1995, 97) or the similar mourning rituals for husbands' and brothers' deaths (Raheja 1995, 34), signify the most profound of emotional ties. Thus, in what Moors terms the "problems of dependence and the pleasures of identification," women may not take shares of inheritance as a way to retain rights in their natal families, "to share in its status and feel a special closeness to their natal household," which "enhances their status and by implication her own and accentuates their obligations towards her" (1995, 53–54).

As Table 8.1 shows (item 5), 20 percent of the women claimed that they wanted their brothers to have all the property not because they were afraid of soured relations, but because they did not want to diminish the resources of the natal home further and wanted it to flourish as much as possible. Whether these women had independent financial resources to help their families or not, they could contribute passively by "not taking." As Pramila put it, women want that "*mera naihar bana rahe*" ('my natal home remain prosperous/well-endowed');[28] they take pride in this first home being joyful and smoothly run, and indeed draw esteem from preserving that part of themselves.

The related notion that the natal home should continue to exist as a site of love and indulgence in a world of duty and work also powerfully propels the distribution of property. A woman without natal family members to visit described herself to Jeffery and Jeffery (1996, 201) as "toasted on one side." As Seema put it, "the son should be given some more property so that he can give his sister enough love to make up for her parents' absence at every festival, every important day, every occasion."[29] Lata also stressed the seemingly contradictory idea that her daughter would lose if she and her brother divided up and sold the parents' apartment in KE, because she would no longer be able to come back to the emotional space represented by a natal home.[30] In these instances, the poignancy of feeling toward the natal family completely undercuts the ritual, patriarchal prescription of severance and reveals women's ambitions for and dependence on ties of blood.[31]

Property over Time: Dowry and Long-Term Help in Relation to Property

Another popular notion about the ultimate fairness of the social distribution of resources is that marriage is the path for daughters to "get" affinal property[32] and that daughters also get parental property through gift-giving rituals associated with weddings, childbirth, and other festive occasions. Of the respondents, 38.3 percent claimed that they would refuse natal property because they had been given dowry and continued to be given presents, and

38.3 percent also mentioned that once married, they were supposed to "get" property through husbands' families (Table 8.1). The idea of equity according to this scheme is that daughters ultimately get as much as sons through a life-time of gifts, and even more because of access to affinal wealth.

This myth of equivalence between dowry and premortem inheritance can be disproved by contrasting dowry payments with total wealth. In many middle- and upper-middle-class families in my sample, sons' weddings often cost as much as daughters' when total food and entertainment and jewelry costs were calculated. Furthermore, except for cases of landlessness (in which case dowry was still given), even the smallest unit of property (except for informally acquired temporary huts or *jhuggis*) was worth several times more than the higher-priced dowries mentioned. For instance, although Medha's wedding did cost Rs.1–200,000 and included a Rs.30,000 cash dowry, she reported that her father had at least 100 *bighas* of rural property, including cash crop and commercial land, so her three brothers would get far more than her wedding expenses if there was a customary division.[33] Even when several male shares needed to be made of more modest estates, the value of property was always much greater (except in extreme cases, e.g., Uma's sister-in-law's wedding negotiations in which many families sought Rs.2,000,000 cash[34]).

Another vivid proof of the mutual exclusivity of dowry and inheritance is in the expensive weddings of women in sonless families, in which women who fully expected to inherit natal property also got as many or more wedding presentations than other women in the community. Both Indira and Vimla described unusually elaborate gifts and entertainment at their weddings, given to them because of their fathers' wishes to display status as prominent businessmen and not at the request of their in-laws.[35] Shobha also claimed that people in her village who had given property to brotherless daughters usually gave at least as much, if not more, dowry/gifts than others.[36] In these cases, inheritance was a supplementary distribution of assets and was not affected by the amount given at marriage, but dowry was related to establishment of kin ties and demarcation of status.

When inheritance consisted of "joint family" living quarters or land for subsistence agriculture, there was no immediate monetary profit for males from the inheritance, whereas dowry always resulted in out-of-pocket expenses; but property was a heftier chunk of resources nonetheless. The contentions of 38.3 percent of the respondents that they would not take property because they had already been given dowry (or expected to get presents), or attitudes such as Gita's (who had no daughters but unmarried adult sons herself)—"if there is such a law [for daughters to always get shares], then why did we need to get our daughters married at such great expense?"[37]—revealed a common ideological connection drawn between dowry and property. However, this could not be supported in economic terms and was rather a rationale to justify disinheritance.[38] Dowry cannot be regarded as equitable premortem inheritance unless it is assumed that women are inherently entitled to smaller shares of family resources, or that they should get less because they "take" liquid assets rather than immovable property.

The idea of women receiving natal property in addition to dowry plus affinal resources invoked a fear that women would thereby get "a double share" and impoverish the brothers. This assumed that not all nuclear units would get property from both sides, that women's inheritance of natal property would not become ubiquitous. But these fears were also tied to legitimate concerns that enforcing women's property rights might lead to in-laws pressuring women to claim exact inheritance from the natal fund, that is, an extension of dowry harassment. The position of daughters-in-law at the bottom of the chain of control makes manipulation and coercion in such cases likely.

This angst was used to manipulate women in various ways. As a mother-in-law in a household with very meager resources and despite having a son who was keen to get his in-laws' help in raising their living standard, Harjinder used this fear to enforce her authority over her daughter-in-law in forbidding her to take natal property. She claimed that they would lose social dignity if the in-laws (i.e., she) were perceived to be taking things continually from the daughter-in-law's parents.[39] On the other hand, Renu narrated an incident of clear dowry harassment in which her niece's in-laws were pressuring her wealthy brother-in-law and his wife to give them money for adding on to their house.[40] Significantly, the (niece's) in-laws were using the rhetoric of women's right to receive natal property to validate their claim on their daughter-in-law's parents, and the parents were using the facts of the in-laws' harassment to raise the accusation of dowry demands and deny the daughter property. In such family situations when young married women had little control over any financial resources, it was hard to postulate a realistic empowering way for daughters to claim and retain control over natal property. Given the current structure of domestic control and hierarchies between bride-givers and bride-takers, the prospect of increased harassment of women and their families if there were fewer taboos against women's property is hardly unrealistic. However, being excluded as heirs to natal property does not strengthen women's material situation either. These situations show that rather than women being conduits for property transfer, they need to be able to assert control over critical resources.

Many women pointed out that parents had to spend a lot of money not just for daughters' weddings but also for the years afterwards, sending gifts when grandchildren (particularly grandsons) were born and at other festive times, with an especially large role during the marriages of grandchildren. Parents' responsibility in this matter was supposed to be transferred to a woman's brother. However, in this sample, women's natal families or brothers rarely helped with the major expenses of their children's weddings. Kalpana voiced a common contention[41] that wedding contributions from the woman's relatives were more like gifts, and that sisters usually reciprocated with equal amounts at brothers' children's weddings, unwilling to impose on brothers to that extent or to be that indebted.

Besides gifts, other kinds of economic assistance from natal families were also rare in the middle-class areas, despite ideological assertions about the family's long-term responsibility for their daughter's well-being. From KE, only 21.4 percent of fourteen women (14.3 percent of whom were widowed early) were given occasional financial assistance by their brothers, and one woman (3.3 percent, from a sonless family) was helped substantially by her father. From KC, there was only one case (6.3 percent) of a mother helping out with childcare, one of a brother giving gifts when the sister visited, and one of general financial help.

The extent of help was much greater in SN. Ten percent of thirty women reported widows being extensively helped by their natal families, 36.7 percent mentioned getting gifts from brothers on a regular basis, 10 percent relied on the parents for financial assistance for living expenses, and one (3.3 percent, with husband and children) lived in her mother's household.[42] Perhaps most importantly, 20 percent of respondents described living in their natal homes for several months in the year, especially during lean times, using the natal families' resources to ensure their survival and that of their husbands and children. This latter circumstance is one of the few genuine examples of foregoing a concrete property share in exchange for short-term economic benefit over years. Such family help was largely absent in middle-class families except in unusual circumstances like widowhood but was a more realistic possibility in poorer families who had fewer taboos of financial help between parents and daughters.[43]

Yet, help given to married daughters was likely to be a source of conflict, because brothers resented sisters getting a substantial share of what they believed to be their assets, despite the sister's financial need or the disparity in wealth between the families. Even though help given was rarely equivalent to an inheritance share, any alienation of resources became grounds for family rifts. For example, Preeti's maternal grandfather, who was quite wealthy and had a high-paying job in addition to substantial semi-urban land in Uttar Pradesh, had given Preeti's parents a house and land in addition to regular monetary help, largely because her father had never been able to hold down a good job. After the grandfather's death, the maternal uncles, who were also independently wealthy due to their own jobs, said that there was no legal validity to the gift and took the property back; Preeti's father and brother lacked the financial resources to challenge this usurpation.[44] In contrast to the ideal that daughters are looked after by their natal families for life, in times of trouble or joy, brothers could be quite resentful of *any* transfers of property to sisters, and women had good cause not to seek help from natal families for fear of causing rifts and severing connections.

In times of financial need, married women did not usually turn to their natal families for help.[45] But women who were outside of marriage, such as single or divorced women, clearly had a much greater need for the resources of the natal family, having no access to marital or affinal resources. In these cases, some families made provisions for daughters, but in others, property was still believed to be fundamentally a male entitlement and was only grudgingly or temporarily put in women's control.

In contrast to very rare instances of married women sharing inherited property with their brothers, single or divorced women were more likely to receive some property from their families. With no male heirs in Kanta's maternal family, her mother had foregone a share of property (two apartments and some cash) in favor of an unmarried sister, who was seen to deserve special protection from the parents.[46] The parents of a divorced friend of Kavita's had built a set of separate rooms for her in their house in Indore, ostensibly so that she need have no dependence or conflict with her brother or sister-in-law.[47] Within Sharmila's affinal family, her husband had been saying that when the family property, a house, was divided or sold, a share should be given to one unmarried sister, though the other (married) sisters were apparently not to be given anything.[48] In these cases, families clearly recognized the special vulnerabilities of women who had no access to the means that were believed to be women's paths to wealth.

However, families were far from unanimous about the support extended to women in such situations. In the case of Sharmila's affines, it was not known how the other brothers felt about the one sister getting a share, but in a similar instance, when Kavita's paternal grandmother tried to give shares to two widowed daughters, her sons vehemently resisted attempts to have their shares curtailed even by a small amount, even if it meant helping their sisters.[49] Jaya's mother-in-law, widowed early in life, was given property and looked after by a relatively well-off sister, but the father and brothers had been unwilling to do more than give crops, or occasionally, cash.[50] These situations reflected an ambivalence about the daughter who could get no property through a husband yet who, nonetheless, could not be given a full entitlement; some family members contended that this custom should be set aside in these exceptional circumstances, but others were unwilling to curtail habitual male privileges.

Even women who had not encountered any such situations hypothesized that women without access to marital or affinal wealth would not get rights to natal property easily, although their families might try to make some alternate economic arrangements for them. Rani speculated that "even if a woman is not married her parents or brother are not going to be happy giving her a share, they will say 'let her get married,' and if she does not, they can say 'stay with us and we will look after you,' but nobody will want to give property."[51]

Bina felt that parents-in-law might look after widowed women, and parents and brothers were supposed to be responsible for widowed or deserted women, but "nowadays in case the share gets less, they [brothers] try to further educate those sisters," hoping to make sisters employable so that they no longer "needed" to be given property.[52] These comments reveal that women realized property was viewed as a profound male entitlement whatever the woman's situation, giving the lie to the idea that women do not usually get natal property because they "get" shares from in-laws. Given that women had little hope of receiving assets from the natal family whether married, unmarried, or married but poor, and with the only potential sources of regular support being affinal or marital resources or personal income, it is thus not surprising that women opted to stay within marriage even when there were severe marital troubles.[53]

In sum, the ideology of dowry and ongoing gifts to women being equivalent to inheritance does not bear up in practice. Not only are marriage expenses (whether for sons or daughters) and other ritual gifts relatively less in value compared to property, but there is little expectation of other help from the natal family for children's marriages, annual gifts, or more serious economic crises. With nonfamilial sources of financial help counted as most important, and marriedness being crucial to financial well-being, it is not surprising that dowry gifts come to be regarded as the major socially sanctioned path of receiving some resources from the natal family. If not for dowry, women would have no assets other than personal savings and resources of the nuclear household.

SURROGATE SONS: BROTHERLESS WOMEN INHERIT PROPERTY

Among Indian communities with patriarchal inheritance norms, transmission of property through daughters in sonless families has been a historically popular device for keeping assets in the family line.[54] Among certain ethnic groups, daughters' full inheritance in sonless families is explicit in customary law.[55] In many other communities, the frequency of this practice, though not formally articulated in law, can be inferred from family histories of uxorilocal residence.[56] A geographical transfer of "home base" to live among women's natal kin is the hushed secret of many family chronicles. In terms of the gender codes enshrined in property relations, it is fascinating to note that in such cases the husband of the property-owning daughter is culturally depicted as an emasculated, slothful, and ridiculous figure, presumably because his lack of paternal property is a profound signifier of powerlessness (Hershman 1981, 75–79; Jeffery and Jeffery 1996, 123). It is seen as impolite and cruel to remind him of his "unusual" and "unmanly" residential situation. The very term "*gharjamai*," literally meaning the domestic or at-home son-in-law in several north Indian languages, is significantly asymmetrical, with no parallel term for women who live with their in-laws and "whose enjoyment of affinal property is therefore naturalized."

In the present study, brotherlessness was indeed one of the rare situations in which women received natal family property. All of the five brotherless respondents (8.3 percent of total respondents) whose parents had property had already inherited or expected to inherit (this included two women from SN; one other SN woman who was brotherless had no parental property). In the past few generations, daughters (rather than sons-in-law or nephews) seemed to have become preferred heirs. Uma's grandmother, for instance, had inherited her parents' rural house in Bihar as the only daughter, and it had always remained in her name.[57] The nine *bighas* in Punjab farmed by Ganga's father for a lifetime had all been given by her sonless maternal grandfather to his daughter.[58] In a recent case, a couple from SN had just bought some rural land fairly cheaply from a woman who had inherited her natal family land and cash in the absence of brothers but who was selling it because her postmarital residence was far away from the land.[59]

The preference for daughters as heirs in sonless families can also be connected to other cultural changes such as the erosion of notions of joint family unity and a greater attention to individual "nuclear" branches. Shobha's comment on this subject, "those who don't have sons give property to their daughters; they think that if their own daughter stays there then no-one else can seize it,"[60] hints at this contemporary emphasis on one's immediate family that has superseded ideologies of preserving joint family property in male hands as the ultimate goal.

Whether or not women were brotherless, many of them believed that this was one of the few ways in which property could come to women; 23.3 percent of women, mostly from SN (table 8.1), brought this up as a criterion, and 10 percent mentioned it even in contemplating shares for women in ideal divisions of property (table 8.2). In fact, many women from SN were insistent that brotherlessness was the only legal way for women to get property. Sushila, who had gotten a share of her father's savings along with her stepsiblings, declared that "the legal right [to property] is for those who are the only daughters and have no brothers or if they have only one brother who has no children. Once the brother has children then the woman has no right any more."[61] Even Medha, who believed she should be able to share some of her father's substantial property with her brothers, proclaimed that daughters' rights did not even "develop" ("*hak banta nahi*," alternatively translatable as "rights were not even 'created'") when there were sons in the family.[62] They based these assertions on situations in their villages or among their kin. This mode of inheritance for women was interpreted as the "new" and modern reform that had come about under the postcolonial state, that is, the preference for daughters as heirs over distant male relatives or sons-in-law that was more common in the previous century was regarded as being *the* new law of "property for women."

In this inscription of the property rights of brotherless daughters as both an exception to the rule and one of the only rules, the spectral quality of women's property entitlements is highlighted. Propertied women can be ideologically contained within this rationale, with no spillover into "normal" families with sons. The absent presence of male heirs mediating this standard is best revealed in the niches of these proposed transmissions, where women's ownership of property is repeatedly marked by surrogate male presences. For example, Vimla's parents wanted her to have their house, and often said to her, "you are our son." She took this to connote not just that she would take their property but that she would also be responsible for their eldercare "like a son," feeling she could not have taken property if there had been a brother, except in the unlikely situation that he was very wealthy and she very poor.[63]

Furthermore, Vimla was the surrogate heir not just in her brother's but also in her son's place. Even though she had a sister, she was treated as the only designated heir; her sister had indicated that she did not want any natal property because her in-laws had a lot of land, and also that she thought of the natal property as being for Vimla's son, the only male grandchild (Vimla also had a daughter). Similarly, although in Indira's natal family, women had been offered property even when they had brothers (predictably, the divorced aunt had accepted part of her share, and the other aunts had written away their shares "because they did not need it"), Indira considered herself to be the main heir to her father's considerable wealth. This was not only because of the prosperity of her sister's in-laws but mainly because her elder son had been raised by her parents, and her father loved and depended on her husband "like a son."[64] In these cases, the women inherited not only "as" sons but also "for" sons, underlining rather than erasing the fundamental male entitlement to property. Significantly, this also made the so-called modern form of the practice a mirror image of the ancient scriptural notion of the *putrikaputra*.[65]

Women's inheritance of property in sonless families is a vivid example of an apparently sanctioned path for women to inherit with little radical potential. Here, women's access to property depended on genetic accidents, and even actual ownership was haunted by ghosts of unborn and future male heirs. Meanwhile, this route of property transmission appeared in discourse as a sanctioned modern way of giving women property, and the rarity and subversiveness of the practice were muted.

Property as Payoff: Eldercare and Other Family Responsibilities

Both daughters and sons should be given something. But furthermore the son, or daughter, who looks after the parent the most should be given the property, because usually all the others have separated themselves, are living and eating by themselves and do not even ask about the parents. Just when it is time for the parents to give things [before dying], they all show up and start calling them "mother" and "father"; then all they have to do is to put them on the funeral pyre, feed some people at the funeral to hide their shame, and get ready to take the property and live it up (Parvati).[66]

An alternative paradigm to viewing inheritance as the transmission of family wealth over generations is the commonly recurring standard of eldercare: that elderly parents give children property as a reward for tending to their physical, financial, and emotional needs. Though only 10 percent of respondents overall (none from SN, table 8.1) pointed to it as a rationale for property division, one SN woman had actually received all of her mother's property in exchange for caregiving, and many other instances of eldercare awards across generations were cited by the respondents. Though not the commonest basis of property division, this was nonetheless an important path of noncustomary property devolution.

Parvati, a widow of age fifty, who was often perturbed by her four sons' allegedly selfish lack of attention to her needs, framed the concept of eldercare-based property division in the gender-neutral way cited above. But the rationale of eldercare was more commonly used to justify male inheritance, by invoking the customary gendered division of labor among siblings whereby sons are supposed to be responsible for elderly parents' financial needs, medical crises, and even funeral costs. Ironically, the consistent application of the eldercare principle has the potential to be especially significant for women, who more often take on caregiving, marking one of the negotiable spaces for women to get property in defiance of norms of male inheritance. And yet, the standard of eldercare can also be one of the most intransigent bases to deny women property, if customs against accepting help from married daughters set the standard. To understand whether property indeed devolves precisely in proportion to eldercare, or whether this rationale is simply a screen to justify giving property to sons, explicit eldercare rewards and the barriers to women assuming these responsibilities need to be examined closely.

Using property as a reward for services rendered or for potential responsibilities (as 1.7 percent of the respondents did) is, of course, the obverse of the view that property is a gift of love toward all children (and also distant from the perception that ancestral resources are carried on through inheritance). Parvati's comment makes explicit the vulnerability and fear of abandonment that runs through the idea of using property to pay caregivers, fears especially tangible for people with meager resources. For instance, Durga related that her mother was afraid to cash in the remainder of her natal family's land in Bangladesh, fearing that if she went with her sons and they took the money, they might then abandon her and she would no longer have the inheritance to hold over them.[67]

Although women were likely to be more neglected in this respect because they typically owned less property, men also felt the vulnerability of age and tried to use their property to obtain financial or social security. Lakshmi's grandfather wanted to divide up his land among his sons in exchange for Rs.250 per month as "*khoraki*" ("maintenance," literally, money for food) from each son, but they were unwilling to give this money for what they perceived to be a family entitlement, while the son whom he was staying with thought he should get more land if he was going to bear the entire financial "burden."[68] Without extended families and usufructuary rights to count on, the elderly without liquid cash were increasingly vulnerable; disposition of family property was one of their few avenues of power.

The above dynamics illustrate that eldercare is far from being the natural, loving duty it is ideologically proclaimed to be; rather, "payment" for eldercare more often shows traces of disintegration of usufructuary rights in family land and a greater reliance on concepts of individual property and conditional inheritance. In addition to financial vulnerability, physical frailty also appears as a frequent cause for concern: expectations of caregiving frequently evoke images of bodily fluids, a recurrent theme being that the person who does the actual work of taking care of an elderly relative without bladder or bowel control is the true heir.

Numerous examples of women receiving property in return for taking on eldercare, in preference to customary male heirs, bear evidence of male heirs' abandonment of the elderly despite lip service to sons' responsibility in this area. A dramatic instance in which property was left to nonkin or neighbors who had been caregivers was that of Kavita's mother looking after a widow in their neighborhood, who left her land to Kavita's mother and brother.[69] Another atypical example was that of Jaya's mother-in-law who, although widowed early and largely supported by her natal kin near their place, had brought her (the mother-in-law's) father-in-law over to her home and looked after him in his last years. She was rewarded with his entire property, but his son, Jaya's uncle, was disinherited for staying away from his father and living near his own in-laws.[70] In other cases, it was daughters who had looked after mothers and been given family assets; for example, Uma's paternal aunt who had lived in the rural home in Bihar with Uma's grandmother was treated as de facto owner of that house and property, but Uma's father had opted to live in the city and travel abroad.[71] In these instances, women's caregiving conferred direct economic benefits, to the extent that customary heirs had been disinherited.

In one of the clearest cases of commodification of eldercare, Bindu's mother had come to live with her and her family and had given Bindu her savings of Rs.15,000 because Bindu had agreed to look after her.[72] None of the other sons or daughters received anything. Bindu's mother had lived earlier with one of her sons, but when he died, the other married sons had not been willing to assume responsibility for her. Thus, Bindu received the privileges of being a default/surrogate son along with the work, and she felt she had lived up to taking the money by paying entirely for her mother's funeral (typically a son's job), and taking care of all her mother's food, clothing, and also bodily care while she was alive.

Given the gender division of labor whereby women are responsible for domestic work, including the management of intimate body fluids as part of childcare and eldercare, it is not surprising that women had the advantage in getting unexpected eldercare awards, by extending their caregiving to people not included in the customary scheme. (Within the customary scheme, women are expected to be caregivers to parents-in-law, and their husbands are given property in "return.") In terms of the standard as contemplated by Sushila (twenty-five years old and with a four-year-old male child), "whoever is going to clean up my urine and feces and is going to put up with taking care of me, that's who I want to give everything to,"[73] women stood to get the upper hand.

Several of the women mentioned related the provision of eldercare to inheritance and wanted daughters to be included as equal heirs, making similar connections about the superior quality of daughters' caregiving. For instance, Maya, with two married sons and a married daughter, proclaimed that "she [the daughter] plays an equal role in taking care of her parents, helps in their troubles; she comes by when her mother feels sick, so she should have a share."[74] Madhuri, having experienced only daughterhood and not marriage or parenting, was even more extreme, saying "when do sons help nowadays, it is the daughters who take much more care of parents; they might get some share of property but they help more than sons do."[75] If property division were indeed proportionate to eldercare, women could thus have a favorable claim based on their physical care (if not financial assistance).

However, as the portrait of property divisions showed, women rarely inherited any property, and the examples of property awards cited above were highly atypical; only one of the sixty respondents (plus women in 6.7 percent of the respondents' families) had inherited anything in this manner. Much more commonly, eldercare was supposed to be the province of the sons, and property dispensation was believed to reflect that responsibility, whether or not particular sons got property specifically as a result of eldercare.[76] Ritu and Vimla's husbands, for example, had both been the youngest sons and caretakers of their parents and inherited the parents' residences by family consensus.[77] However, eldercare was not necessarily the only basis for distributing property in those families; Vimla's husband's brothers (and not his sisters) had received other property from their father. On the whole, all males were heirs and all females disinherited. As with many other families, one brother was responsible for the bulk of the caregiving, but all the males shared the property under the banner of sons undertaking eldercare. Among the kin of the SN women, it was very common for a parent to be living with one of the sons in the village, while other sons gave some crops or cash but were clearly not the primary caretakers; however, all males expected equal shares of land. Lakshmi's family dispute, narrated above, is a vivid case in point showing that, although some property awards may have been related to eldercare, shares of property were rarely distributed in proportion to the amount of caregiving.

The persistent trope of the daughter's emotional and financial severance from her natal family upon marriage and the son's continuing responsibilities and privileges to and from that family strongly affect women's refusals of property, viz. the belief that daughters have no claims if they do not assume any corresponding responsibilities. Brothers' sole right to property is often seen by sisters themselves as a justifiable return for all the duties that are habitually assigned to the sons. As Kiran, a relatively newly married woman with an infant son living in the husband's "joint" family, said:

> My brother is the one who is going to be useful to my father and be with him in his times of joy or sorrow, so that is why he should have it [property]. We are away in our own homes. If my father runs into any problems, my brother is the one who will have to worry about it. We can maybe go there, but we can't help if they need money.[78]

Kiran's comment was typical of many women, who implied that they should forfeit property because they were unable to help their parents due to lack of financial resources, residential patterns, and most strongly, ideological restrictions. Kiran explained, "Among us the 'duties' have been fixed. We can worry about them [parents], if they really need help we could think about helping them in the time of trouble, but we are supposed to be 'attached' to our *own* [i.e., affinal] homes first." Suman also pointed out that her natal family had recently had many crises involving divorce, illness, etc., and although she was worried, she had not felt able to leave her allegedly primary responsibilities—her tasks in the nuclear family—to be with her parents in another city. However, her brothers had to go, as their presence was expected in hard times.[79]

As a parent receiving assistance, Seema felt that her son ought to be rewarded and encouraged not just for physical and emotional support, but also as financial compensation for his assets that were diminished by helping the parents.[80] Her son had contributed large sums to the renovations of their house (which he would inherit, thus protecting his own assets) but also to his sister's and his own weddings. Thus, she felt that "since the son helps the parents with everything, and the daughter is in her own home not doing anything and saving on their [sic] own, while the son could also be saving on his own and could put aside a lot, I think that gives him slightly more rights." Here, the expenditure of time, energy, money, and even loss of the "freedom" to look after one's nuclear unit solely was sought to be compensated by property.

What is unfair in this customary division of duties is not that those who do actually expend resources are duly compensated, but that daughters are not permitted to share in eldercare (and hence property) per ideological pro-scriptions. In many cases this ban was framed in terms of the Hindu wedding ritual of *kanyadan*, translated as "gift of a virgin[81] daughter," in which the giving away of the daughter constitutes a high holy act for the father.[82] This is supposed to be the supreme selfless gift, to which the bulk of other material gifts are merely supplementary. As I learned from some of the middle-class women (21.4 percent of KE and 31.3 percent of KC respondents), the act was interpreted in their families as one in which the daughter is given away along with the dowry with no rights retained in her, and so parents accept nothing from her—stark symbols of woman-as-property.[83] In the strictest form of this custom, parents do not even drink water at their daughter's marital home; the "modern adaptation" of this is to eat a piece of fruit or drink a cup of tea, and usually leave a payment for large meals or extended stays, even if the stay is for an emergency in the daughter's home and at her request.[84] Women from families observing this practice made an explicit connection between *kanyadan* customs, eldercare responsibilities, and property inheritance. Bina said:

> If we don't even eat at our daughters' homes then why do we have to give them things? . . . The son is doing all the work for us and we have given the daughters what we wanted already, so why bring them into the remainder that we haven't given?[85]

Both the privileges and responsibilities of eldercare were thus blocked by the act of a Hindu woman's marriage itself.

It appears quite significant that no women from SN brought up notions of *kanyadan* and the resultant blocking of any help from daughters. No similar taboos were ever mentioned; in fact, there were several instances when married women gave their families ongoing financial and other help. In contrast to KE, where no cases of helping natal families were mentioned, and KC, where two women narrated instances of sisters helping with family weddings and other financial crises and one woman gave her parents some financial support, there were several kinds of help proffered by the SN women. Among 13.3 percent of thirty respondents and in many other households in the neighborhood, the woman's parent, brother, or sister lived in her nuclear family. In 10 percent of cases, women paid for natal family funerals, debts, and legal expenses out of their own earnings; Medha described her motivation in doing this as wanting to be by her brother's side helping him through troubled times, an act of love and support.[86] Besides financial help, other assistance was provided by Deepa and her sister, who would take turns staying with their father in the village a few months at a time, doing the cooking and domestic work because there were no women in their natal household.[87] There were clearly no cultural proscriptions against the women's natal family members staying or eating.

Although there were fewer restrictions on sources of help among SN families, no women had been given shares of property, despite their assistance. Also, a much smaller percentage of SN women as compared to KC women (only 10 percent as compared to 25 percent, Table 8.2) believed that eldercare should play a role in the dispensation of property. The conclusion may be drawn that in this group, eldercare was a matter of assisting one's natal family based on social and affectional ties and not on financial considerations. Several women who had helped their families professed to believe in equal love and equal duties of sons and daughters, but also cited numerous barriers to claiming their own natal inheritance (e.g., potential rifts with brothers). Thus, their own support was not necessarily tied to a calculated consideration of property. Even among the women from KE and KC who had helped natal families, there were only two instances of women wanting to claim natal property, including one brotherless woman. Here, too, eldercare was generally not undertaken in expectation of receiving property (except in the case of sonless property, when eldercare *was* seen as a necessary duty).

Although relatively few respondents mentioned the ideological relevance of eldercare in delineating how property should be distributed, several instances of actual inheritance showed that women did inherit property in dramatically unusual ways as a result of caregiving. However, because of strong ideological proscriptions, women did not usually provide eldercare except to their affines and did not typically expect inheritance in return when they did so. Though only some of the sons (and daughters-in-law) actually did the caregiving in most cases, the rights of *all* male heirs to inheritance were nevertheless proclaimed to be connected to eldercare. The issue of eldercare thereby functioned as a screen for disentitling women from property; that is, sons inherited more in accordance with ideological prescriptions about sons undertaking the bulk of eldercare, whether or not they actually did any caregiving.

Medha's Case: Complex Negotiations

Women's feelings about natal property revealed a complex mix of fears and strengths, pragmatic indifference and generous assistance, love and alienation. A detailed analysis of one response, Medha's attitude to taking natal property,[88] provides one of the most vivid illustrations of the discursive complexity over property. It shows that women's refusal of natal resources is not necessarily a mark of being consumed by dominant ideologies while also revealing the difficulty of structuring lives free from the deep hold of patriarchal power relations.

Unlike most Indian girls in rural areas, Medha had grown up with dreams of opportunity. Her grandfather, who owned a large amount of rural property, had indulged her as a child, often saying playfully that she could stay at her parents' all her life, could study instead of getting married, and work as a nurse or teacher. Not surprisingly, this had not come to pass, and she had married and borne three daughters by the time she was twenty-one. However, she still cherished those visions of independence and valued the experiences provided by her job. Having passed her matriculate (school-leaving) examination, she was the most educated woman in SN (though low on the educational scale compared to KE and KC), one of the few SN women with formal employment, and an enthusiastic community worker.

A strong believer in the importance of women having property/assets of their own, Medha had been trying to get a *jhuggi* in her own name, had her own bank account, and had also used some savings to buy jewelry for herself and her daughters. Her appreciation of her need to be economically self-sufficient was further enhanced by the scant reliance she could place on marital and affinal assets; her wages were crucial for the nuclear family because her husband stopped giving her food money when he went on drinking and gambling binges, and although they expected to inherit some farmland that was presently jointly held between her husbands' brothers, she did not trust her brother-in-law, who had cheated her out of her wedding jewelry and also pocketed the cash dowry. She also felt a strong affection and responsibility toward her natal family, to the extent that she kept her full income secret from her husband, being committed to certain expenses he did not approve of, such as helping her natal family with legal or funeral expenses.

Thus, Medha was completely aware of the value of financial resources, had few illusions about getting control over any property through her husband or in-laws, and had a strong responsibility toward her natal family, showing herself to be a woman who did not passively accept notions of women's access to financial resources mediated through husbands or support notions of women's severance from the natal family upon marriage. Yet she did not believe that daughters stood to gain by taking equal property shares. As she formulated it:

> It might be good if people gave completely equal shares of money to all their children, but I think that one should not take equal shares from the brother. The brother has to make a living from that small area, and why should the sister take an equal share when she has a right to a part of her in-laws' property too? I also think that if I take a smaller share then he will look after me with more care. For example, if five shares are made of the property they will be very small shares, but instead if three shares are made for three brothers, the fourth is shared by sisters and the fifth is redistributed among the three brothers, then the sisters will have rights over all three brothers. She can stay with any of them and they might all look after her.

It appears from these words that Medha was unable to conceive of a system of property distribution in which each couple could get property from both sides of the family, or visualize a gender-neutral world in which women could have equal economic power and responsibility and would not need looking after.

Or rather, she could not realistically see this happening, and thus her plan was to choose the most empowering avenue in the present scenario.

As she planned it, she could take advantage of some natal family property while giving up some to secure brotherly insurance, thereby simultaneously raising the living standard of her own nuclear unit and not causing her natal home to be visibly impoverished. To this end, she contemplated asking her eldest brother to give her and her husband two shops on a strip of land that he was planning to develop commercially. These shops would be quite valuable and would certainly assure them a materially better life than they had now, but they would be a very small portion of her father's total assets. Even to do this she would have to contend both with her brother, who was more willing to give them less valuable agricultural land, and also with her husband, who wanted her to claim ownership over a larger portion because her family was wealthier than his.

Medha preferred to have use rights over the shops so that they could make a good living and not to accept the other land with less profit potential; but she also wanted to be careful not to take so much that she lost her brother's support or gave her in-laws a reason to deprive her husband of his or their share. This conceptualization of property rights for women hovered between acceptance of customary patriarchal notions (e.g., women "getting" property through affinal families or women getting lifelong help rather than dowry), active negotiations to maximize immediately profitable assets, and the long-term insurance of "use rights," which could be constructed as being less alienable than ownership (as long as she didn't commit dire cultural transgressions). Her vision of property distribution shows the ways in which women may be practically or emotionally unable to be free of constitutive ideology, yet able to negotiate solutions that optimize their needs rather than passively accepting "custom."

As Merry contends in her analysis of the contemporary significance of law, the very notion of individual resistance to regimes of power is double-edged, often harming the resister in the very act of opposition, but also "disrupt[ing] those modes of conceptualizing and categorizing the world which lie at the heart of modern processes of power" (1995, 18). Medha's strategy, though contrary to her own maximal financial gain, nevertheless represents a keen evaluation of the structures of power governing her life, a "reshap[ing of] the way communities and identities are understood" (Merry 1995, 23). In that sense, her negotiations of property, which altered customary patterns only in minimal ways, were nonetheless acts of ideological contestation.

CONCLUSION

In delineating how property should be divided, some women echoed the patriarchal ideology that seemed contrary to their material interests but often revealed their own dissociation from such beliefs, while underlining their socioeconomic powerlessness. Furthermore, in naming connections between inheritance and factors like eldercare, dowry, or long-term financial help, women demonstrated a process of cultural sense making in which they weighed their realistic possibilities of intervention against financial options. Without a broader change in socioeconomic relations, it would be difficult for women to proffer substantial help to the natal family and get property in return, and thus, dowry from the natal home along with the "protection" supposedly offered through marriage was the safest economic route, whereas radically different actions could leave them too vulnerable. Most remarkably, the images used by these women, particularly images of love from and toward parents, demarcated a realm of feeling escaping from and indeed contrary to dominant discourse, a construction of entitlements very different from and yet at least as powerful as the notion of individual jural rights. Thus, what appeared to be a jumble of deluded attitudes from women toward property were often complex attempts at optimizing material survival and bridging emotional alienation within a system giving them limited agency and subjectivity; as Moors puts it, "women may well see advantages in 'giving up property,' for property does not necessarily mean power" (1995, 256).

Ultimately, it is useful to remember that these women did not inherit either natal or affinal property. In celebrating the spaces of discursive leakage, one ought not to forget the resilience of hegemonic discourse. Despite exceptional cases of women receiving family property and subtle negotiations by women to retain natal ties, patriarchal principles of inheritance remain stable. Studies of women and land have shown a positive correlation between owning even a small piece of land and a dramatic sense of empowerment with regard to legal rights, credit or income generation, healthcare, etc. (Agarwal 1994). In this study, however, women neither received much family property nor expressed the wish to get much. Although some did appear to negotiate to create space for themselves, we ought to bear in mind how little property or substantial economic assets they actually owned, and how that limited their opportunities and aided their impoverishment and dependence. In that light, the rationales for refusing property that were optimized tradeoffs in women's minds had little revolutionary momentum, especially given their economic dependence. Under this form of patriarchy, feelings of love and loyalty toward parents and the natal family were enacted in ways that bolstered male privilege. The preferred paths for women to obtain resources were said to be paid work or marriage, despite the recognition that this would necessarily perpetuate socioeconomic dependence, given that women were in a subordinate position in the labor force as a whole, and also the notorious insecurity of marriedness as a form of property.

Although women got little material property, they did gain some cultural property through acquiescence to these norms of property ownership. Claiming material property from one's natal family was associated with losing kinship ties and contributing to the decline of the natal family. Although gaining property was ephemeral at best, losing connectedness with one's natal family (in the course of getting said property) was perceived as fundamentally alienating, and there was too much to lose here with too little to acquire in its stead, given that at best most women could hope to acquire only very small shares of property. Opting for cultural over material property, even at the cost of extreme deprivation or violence in married life, thus appeared safer and more sensible. And yet, this "preference" is itself poignant and problematic, because it represents both the positive claiming of cultural capital and the difficulties of resisting family pressures.

NOTES

1. In this system of land division, males become cosharers or coparceners to family property by birth. The ancestral property is known as the coparcenary, and is managed by the senior male, or *Karta*.

2. Agarwal 1994; Basu 1999b; Magu 1996; Sethi and Sibia 1987.

3. I worked in three neighborhoods in New Delhi, India. The first was KE (Kailash Enclave): an area of "'Middle-Income' Housing" created in the 1960s, a middle-middle-class area of senior government employees and office workers, professors, accountants, and small business owners. Of the women, 67.1 percent had a bachelor's degree or higher (35.1 percent had more than a BA/BSc); 35.1 percent of women were in paid employment or self-employed. The second was KC (Kalka Colony): a "'Refugee Resettlement' Area" built in the 1960s, a lower-middle-class area of small shop owners, mid-level government workers, teachers, and factory workers. Of its women, 44.8 percent had a bachelor's degree or higher (6.5 percent had more than a BA/BSc); 17.8 percent of women were in paid employment or self-employed. The third area was SN (Siddharth Nagar): a squatter colony developing in phases since the 1950s. It is occasionally razed by police as illegal structures, yet simultaneously the huts are also recognized through identity cards. Residents include vendors, laborers in construction sites, security guards, and lowest-level government workers. One woman (0.99 percent of the neighborhood) had finished high school; 11.9 percent had paid employment. The KE and KC neighborhoods contained a lot of families who had been refugees from West Pakistan in the 1950s. The SN neighborhood had ongoing two-way rural-urban migration. A variety of ethnic groups were represented in the sample, but respondents were almost all Hindu.

4. In Sethi and Sibia's study of rural Jat women, 87.5 percent of women were aware of changes in Indian property law but two-thirds were unfavorably inclined toward women availing of those rights. The only favorable responses to women taking property were from women who had more than a high school education, but even 60 percent of women in that group did not agree that women should take property. Sethi and Sibia attribute this pattern to a "strong force of tradition" (1987, 107–11).

5. There was no strong statistical correlation between age and attitudes toward taking natal property. Certain variations in responses between neighborhoods did seem connected to socioeconomic circumstances, for example, differences in education, prevalence of particular ethnic groups, or rural versus urban upbringing.

6. Interview 3.21, SN, 12/30/92.
7. Interview 3.28, SN, 1/7/93.
8. Interview 3.22, SN, 1/4/93.
9. Interview 1.11, KE, 12/13/91.
10. Interview 2.14, KE, 2/24/92.
11. Interview 1.10, KE, 12/11/91.
12. From the film *Neel Kamal* (1968) directed by Ram Maheswari. Music director: Ravi; Lyrics: Sahir Ludhyanvi; Singer: Mohammed Rafi. The song originally accompanies scenes of a bride leaving her natal home, but appears as a refrain later in the movie when she begins to suffer at her in-laws' house (i.e., the representation of the song in the film marks both the ideology of severance and its inherent pitfalls).
13. See Sharma (1980, 137) and Chanana (1993) for a further discussion on the significance of wedding songs. The ideology of the woman's severance from the natal family has been documented in various studies (Sax 1991, 77–81; Raheja and Gold 1994, 83–85; Jacobson 1977, 264–65).
14. Jacobson 1977, 276–77; Sax 1991, 83–98. Raheja and Gold analyze how some Uttar Pradesh women subvert proverbs and songs to critique and resist patriarchal kinship norms (1994, 74–104), pointing to women's depth of love for their natal families and widespread skepticism about their affines.
15. Bharti, a married woman with two brothers, Interview 1.7, KE, 12/9/91.
16. Interview 3.19, SN, 12/27/92.
17. These signed releases sealed the woman's refusal of property even where the brother did not fulfill his part of a specific bargain.
18. Hershman says that an old Sikh man told him that the brother-sister relationship represented true love, as opposed to the husband-wife relation, which had to deal with everyday economic matters. However, Hershman also repeats a common jest of the area that brothers had become more carefully attentive to sisters since the laws changed, showing that people were often well aware of the conflicting economic interests of brothers and sisters, and chose to manipulate it using the emotional dimension (1981, 175–91).
19. Interview 1.9, KE, 12/10/91. Rani had one brother, and her husband had no sisters; both claimed to have no disputes in their families.
20. Interview 3.28, SN, 1/7/93.
21. Interview 3.17, SN, 12/28/92.
22. Interview 3.13b, SN, 12/24/92; interview 3.3, SN, 12/8/92.
23. Interview 2.2, KC, 2/4/92; interview 2.12, KC, 2/17/92; interview 2.9, KC, 2/11/92.
24. Hershman 1981, 63; Sharma 1980, 183. Sharma points that even when women do quarrel, it is usually about their husbands' shares (i.e., their greed can only be secondhand).
25. Interview 3.13b, SN, 12/24/92.
26. Raheja (1995, 51) provides an example of a song graphically articulating this fear.
27. Interview 3.11, SN, 12/21/92.
28. Interview 3.20, SN, 12/30/92.
29. Interview 2.2, KC, 2/4/92.
30. Interview 1.2, KE, 12/3/91.

31. In the rural areas, the natal home is literally a much freer and more comfortable place for women, because (even married) daughters do not have to veil themselves or not speak to elders or nonfamily like daughters-in-law have to. Besides, the load of domestic work is usually negligible while they are visiting, although in some cases daughters specifically come home to help with crops. Sharma (1980, 19) also shows the central difference between natal and affinal worlds for women, an opposition not particularly significant for men.

32. The most influential proponents of this approach are Goody and Tambiah (1973), who characterized dowry as the woman's equitable share of property that was given to her at marriage, over which she had some measure of control, and which often served as a starting economic base for the couple. Numerous scholars (Agarwal 1994, 134–40; Bossen 1988, 140; Ebrey 1991, 3–4; Schlegel and Eloul 1988, 301–3; Sharma 1993, 351–52) and Tambiah himself (1989, 425–26) question the relevance of this definition in the north Indian context. Tambiah points to evidence such as the difference in dowries between sisters and variations according to the status of the groom. Tambiah's revised concept is that the Indian model of dowry may best be visualized as "double transmission" (not equal) of property through sons and daughters, with the woman's dowry/property share contributing to the joint family unit and coming to the conjugal unit only if joint family resources are divided (1989, 426). Furthermore, such dowry may be viewed as the means by which the groom's family acquires upward socioeconomic mobility.

33. Interview 3.13b, SN, 12/24/92.

34. Interview 1.14, KE, 2/24/92.

35. Interview 1.10, KE, 12/11/91; interview 2.13, KC, 2/17/92.

36. Interview 3.9, SN, 12/14/92.

37. Interview 3.5, SN, 12/9/92.

38. In contrast to claims by scholars such as Harrell and Dickey (1985) that dowry is a different and parallel form of property transfer as compared to inheritance, Sharma claims that giving dowry is a convenient way of deflecting the question of inheritance, that is, that dowry is really a form of *dis*inheritance [emphasis mine] (1980, 47–48).

39. Interview 2.10, KC, 2/12/92.

40. Interview 2.13, KC, 2/17/92.

41. Interview 2.4, KC, 2/6/92.

42. Some women had multiple responses.

43. Jeffery and Jeffery (1996, 89–90) record numerous examples of women receiving help from natal families for their children's needs. In fact, cash and goods given by the natal family was cited by women as their "income" (1996, 189).

44. Interview 3.26, 1/6/93.

45. Most married women claimed they relied on the resources of the nuclear unit (e.g., husbands or sons). Nonfamilial sources of help such as banks, moneylenders, and friends or neighbors were also very significant. Women contemplated turning to in-laws for help more often than to parents.

46. Interview 1.12, KE, 12/14/91.

47. Interview 2.6, KC, 2/7/92.

48. Interview 2.9, KC, 2/11/92.

49. Interview 2.6, KC, 2/7/92.

180

SRIMATI BASU

50. Interview 3.1, SN, 12/7/92.

51. Interview 1.9, KE, 12/10/91; interview 1.9, KE, 12/10/91.

52. Interview 2.1, KC, 2/3/92.

53. Of the thirty-five cases of marital disputes cited among family and close friends of the respondents (twelve from KE, eleven from KC, and twelve from SN, including cases of problems with the in-laws, problems between the couple, or situations of male bigamy), there were 28.6 percent of cases of reconciliation and 20 percent of remarriage following the divorce (in 31.4 percent of cases, the dispute was ongoing or an informal separation had taken place). In other words, only 22.9 percent of cases had resulted in the woman formally severing the marriage without entering into another conjugal relationship, indicating that women were not wont to depend solely upon their own earnings or rely on dubious help from the natal family. In the absence of good economic opportunities or inheritance for women, being married was indeed one of the few ways to enjoy property with any security.

54. Adoption of other blood relatives like nephews, sons-in-law, or nonrelatives within the caste as "sons" is the other primary device for securing property in the Indian context. Well-known political examples (e.g., Lord Dalhousie's "Doctrine of Lapse," which prevented sonless rulers from adopting so that their kingdoms could "lapse" into British domain), show the preference for this practice. Many Bengali folktales end with a sonless king offering the poor but deserving stranger "half the kingdom along with the princess," rather than the princess herself succeeding the king.

55. Mitra (1989) on the Santals.

56. In Hindu *shastric* texts this is framed as the "appointed daughter" or *putrika-putra*, variously interpreted as "the daughter appointed as son" or "the son of an appointed daughter" (Agarwal 1994, 87).

57. Interview 1.14, KE, 2/24/92.

58. Interview 3.14, SN, 12/24/92.

59. In Hershman's study (1981, 79), it was usually nephews rather than sons-in-law who inherited; Sharma (1980, 55) found that brotherless daughters did inherit in line with the new laws, but often tended to sell the property to male cousins at a low price, thus maintaining goodwill with natal kin.

60. Interview 3.9, SN, 12/14/92.

61. Interview 3.17, SN, 12/28/92.

62. Interview 3.13b, SN, 12/24/92.

63. Interview 2.13, KC, 2/17/92.

64. Interview 2.13, KC, 2/17/92.

65. See footnote 56.

66. Interview 3.15, SN, 12/25/92.

67. Interview 3.18, SN, 12/28/92. Durga's mother's situation is a vivid illustration of a trend recently uncovered by researchers (Chen and Dreze 1992; Gulati and Gulati 1993), one in which widows with even minimal property tend to be treated with more care and respect in their families, compared to widespread neglect of widows without property.

68. Interview 3.6, SN, 12/10/92.

69. Interview 2.6, KC, 2/7/92.

70. Interview 3.1, SN, 12/7/92.

71. Interview 1.14, KE, 2/24/92.

72. Interview 3.3, SN, 12/8/92.

73. Interview 3.17, SN, 12/28/92.

74. Interview 3.30, SN, 1/8/93.

75. Interview 2.11, KC, 2/12/92.

76. Wadley's research shows that the most important economic resources for women were land, which they rarely got control over, and sons, through whom they could have a place to live and eat and be protected from the ill treatment of the affines and the natal family (1995, 114). In the present study, a son often, though not always, took on eldercare.

77. Interview 1.11, KE, 12/13/91; interview 2.13, KC, 2/17/92.

78. Interview 2.8, KC, 2/11/92.

79. Interview 1.5, KE, 12/5/91.

80. Interview 2.2, KC, 2/4/92.

81. Like the contested Hebrew-to-English translation of the word "virgin" as in "Virgin Mary," here too the word "*kanya*" can mean both "young daughter" and "sexually virgin." In the case of child marriages, the meanings usually converge.

82. In some families this may be done by the maternal uncle and is a sign of the mother's family's participation.

83. As Trautmann puts it, "The idiom of *kanyadan* is the patrilineal idiom of complete dissimilation of the bride from her family of birth and her complete assimilation to that of her husband" (1981, 291).

84. Interestingly, food or drink or visits are acceptable when a grandson, the daughter's son rather than the daughter, is an earning member and the ostensible host.

85. Interview 2.1, KC, 2/3/92.

86. Interview 3.13a, SN, 12/23/92.

87. Interview 3.25, SN, 1/5/93.

88. Interview 3.13b, SN, 12/24/92.

REFERENCES

Abu-Lughod, Lila. 1993. "The Romance of Resistance: Tracing Transformations of Power Through Bedouin Women." In *Women's Studies: Essential Readings*, ed. by Stevi Jackson et al., 102–3. New York: New York University Press.

Agarwal, Bina. 1994. *A Field of One's Own: Gender and Land Rights in South Asia*. Cambridge, U.K.: Cambridge University Press.

Agnes, Flavia. 1996. "The Politics of Women's Rights." *Seminar* 441: 62–66.

Basu, Srimati. 1999a. "Cutting to Size: Property and Gendered Identity in the Indian Higher Courts." In *Signposts: Gender in Post-Independence India*, ed. by Rajeswari Sunder Rajan. New Delhi: Kali.

———. 1999b. *She Comes to Take Her Rights: Indian Women, Property, and Propriety*. Albany, N.Y.: SUNY Press.

Bossen, Laurel. 1988. "Toward a Theory of Marriage: The Economic Anthropology of Marriage Transactions." *Ethnology* 27(2): 127–44.

Brettell, Caroline B. 1991. "Kinship and Contract: Property Transmissions and Family Relations in Northwestern Portugal." *Comparative Studies in Society and History* 33(3): 443–65.

Chanana, Karuna. 1993. "Partition and Family Strategies: Gender-Education Linkages among Punjabi Women in Delhi." *Economic and Political Weekly* 28: WS25–34.

Chen, Marty, and Jean Dreze. 1992. "Widows and Health in Rural North India." *Economic and Political Weekly* 27: WS81–93.

Chowdhry, Prem. 1994. *The Veiled Women: Shifting Gender Equations in Rural Haryana 1880–1990*. Delhi: Oxford University Press.

Collier, Jane Fishburne, and Sylvia Junko Yanagisako. 1987. *Gender and Kinship: Essays toward a Unified Analysis*. Palo Alto, Calif.: Stanford University Press.

Ebrey, Patricia Buckley. 1991. Introduction to *Marriage and Inequality in Chinese Society*, ed. by Rubie S. Watson and Patricia Buckley Ebrey, 1–24. Berkeley: University of California Press.

Goody, Jack, and S. J. Tambiah. 1973. *Bridewealth and Dowry*. Cambridge, U.K.: Cambridge University Press.

Gulati, Mitu, and Leela Gulati. 1993. "Remnants of Matriliny: Widows of Two Kerala Villages." *Manushi* 76: 32–34.

Harrell, Stevan, and Sara A. Dickey. 1985. "Dowry Systems in Complex Societies." *Ethnology* 24(2): 105–20.

Hershman, Paul. 1981. *Punjabi Kinship and Marriage*. Delhi: Hindustan.

Jacobson, Doranne. 1977. "Flexibility in Central Indian Kinship and Residence." In *The New Wind: Changing Identities in South Asia*, ed. by Kenneth David, 262–83. The Hague: Mouton.

Jeffery, Patricia, and Roger Jeffery. 1996. *"Don't Marry Me to a Plowman": Women's Everyday Lives in Rural North India*. Boulder, Colo.: Westview Press.

Kapur, Ratna, and Brenda Cossman. 1996. *Subversive Sites: Feminist Engagements with Law in India*. New Delhi: Sage.

Kolenda, Pauline. 1984. "Woman as Tribute, Woman as Flower: Images of 'Woman' in Weddings in North and South India." *American Ethnologist* 11: 98–117.

Magu, Poonam. 1996. "The Hindu Succession Act—Has It Really Helped Women?" *Legal News and Views* 10(8): 1–3.

Merry, Sally Engle. 1995. "Resistance and the Cultural Power of Law." *Law and Society Review* 29(1): 11–26.

Mitra, Manoshi. 1989. "Women in Santhal Society: Women as Property; Women and Property." *Samya Shakti* 4/5: 213–27.

Moors, Annelies. 1995. *Women, Property, and Islam: Palestinian Experiences, 1920–1990*. Cambridge, U.K.: Cambridge University Press.

Ocko, Jonathan K. 1991. "Women, Property, and Law in the People's Republic of China." In *Marriage and Inequality in Chinese Society*, ed. by Rubie S. Watson and Patricia Buckley Ebrey, 313–46. Berkeley: University of California Press.

Parashar, Archana. 1992. *Women and Family Law Reform in India: Uniform Civil Code and Gender Equality*. New Delhi: Sage.

Raheja, Gloria Goodwin. 1995. "'Crying When She's Born, and Crying When She Goes Away': Marriage and the Idiom of the Gift in Pahansu Song Performance." In *From the Margins of Hindu Marriage: Essays on Gender, Religion and Culture*, ed. by Lindsey Harlan and Paul B. Courtright, 19–52. New York: Oxford University Press.

Raheja, Gloria Goodwin, and Ann Grodzins Gold. 1994. *Listen to the Heron's Words: Reimagining Gender and Kinship in North India*. Berkeley: University of California Press.

Sax, William S. 1991. *Mountain Goddess: Gender and Politics in a Himalayan Pilgrimage*. New York: Oxford University Press.

Schlegel, Alice, and Rohn Eloul. 1988. "Marriage Transactions: Labor, Property, Status." *American Anthropologist* 90(2): 291–309.

Sethi, Raj Mohini, and Kiran Sibia. 1987. "Women and Hindu Personal Laws: A Sociolegal Analysis." *Journal of Sociological Studies* 6: 101–13.

Sharma, Ursula. 1993. "Dowry in North India: Its Consequences for Women." In *Family & Marriage in India*, ed. P. Uberoi. Delhi: Oxford University Press.

———. 1980. *Women, Work, and Property in Northwest India.* London: Tavistock.

Tambiah, Stanley J. 1989. "Bridewealth and Dowry Revisited: The Position of Women in Subsaharan Africa and North India." *Current Anthropology* 30(4): 413–35.

Teja, Mohinderjit Kaur. 1993. *Dowry: A Study in Attitudes and Practices.* New Delhi: Inter-India.

Trautmann, Thomas R. 1981. *Dravidian Kinship.* Cambridge, U.K.: Cambridge University Press.

Wadley, Susan S. 1995. "No Longer a Wife: Widows in Rural North India." In *From the Margins of Hindu Marriage: Essays on Gender, Religion, and Culture*, ed. by Lindsey Harlan and Paul B. Courtright, 92–115. New York: Oxford University Press.

9

Decision Making and Flows of Income and Expenses among Households with Factory-Employed Members

Aurora Bautista-Vistro

INTRODUCTION

The goals of industrialization and economic development are very major current concerns of developing countries such as the Philippines. This chapter attempts to examine, from both the macrolevel and the microlevel perspectives, the responses of the household in the context of an ongoing rural industrialization program and globalization process. This research shares the view that "transnational production and globalization of capital, which are the main driving force in rural industrialization processes, affect the lives of men and women in both common and different ways" (Lamphere, Ragone, and Zavella 1997).

This chapter approaches the study of households by "focusing on how domestic consent is produced and maintained and on the conditions under which subordinate household members are likely to challenge and redefine the rules," an approach which is also called "intra-household bargaining and contestation" (Hart 1992). It examines ways in which negotiations take place between those who are wage earners and those dependent on their wages within the context of household roles. It examines decisions made by factory workers in apportioning their earnings to meet their personal needs, as well as the proportion that they contributed to the household pool of resources. It explores further the motivations or sanctions used by other household members on the factory workers to make them contribute to the household.

The Regional Development Plan of the provinces of Cavite, Laguna, Batangas, Rizal, Quezon, and Aurora (CALABARZON) growth area presents a test case of Philippines rural industrialization programs. Located in Southern Luzon Island of the Philippines, the growth area has been viewed as the "industrial power house of the Philippines" (*Board of Investment CALABARZON Brochure*, n.d.). The CALABARZON development program was launched during the Philippine Assistance Program in 1989 (Philippine Regional Profile

1996) and was originally conceived of as a project to transform agro-based rural economies to industrial/urban based economies:

> It has been reformulated to encompass all the sectors: economic sector (agriculture, livestock, fishery, manufacturing, mining, tourism, and services), infrastructure sector (water, transportation, telecommunication, energy, and utilities) and social sector (education, health, livelihood development, and others) (JICA 1991).

The research area is located in Barangay Ambulong in the municipality of Tanauan, province of Batangas, in Southern Luzon, Philippines. This chapter begins by looking at the macrolevel responses by households in the research site. It presents data generated from a census of households with members employed in factories and relates this to data on employment patterns and different industrial sectors found in the CALABARZON area. The research also looks at microlevel responses within the household. It focuses on the dynamic interactions that take place between the individual employed in a factory and other household members. It discusses interrelationships between an individual's household position, gender roles, expectations, and obligations. It examines the process of decision making and negotiations by different members of the household within the context of pooling household resources and the resulting flows of income and expenditures for the household.

In conducting this research, several data gathering techniques were used. The research began by conducting a census of all households with factory workers, looking at household structure and composition as well as the relative position of the household member working in the factory and the employment status of other household members. The census was conducted by a research assistant from the research area from November 1998–January 1999. A total of eighty-three households had at least one household member working in a factory at the time of census. From this list, twenty-two households were selected for intensive interviews of the household member working in the factory and at least one other household member. In households with older parents, where the son or daughter works in the factory, parents, working sons and daughters, and other dependent siblings were interviewed. Among households where either the husband or wife works in a factory, interviews of both spouses were conducted. Interviews for the case studies began in February 1999 and ended in December 1999.

A sample survey of all households in the community was also conducted beginning August 31, 1999 to November 9, 1999. There was a dearth of information on employment conditions in the community from existing censuses and surveys that have been done in the past five years. There were 249 households surveyed out of a total of 672 households listed in community health records. The topics covered in the survey included employment data, household composition, household expenditures, decision making, and pooling of household resources.

In September 1999, toward the last few months of the case interviews, focus group discussions were held with three groups: women working in factories, mothers with young children, and fathers and mothers with adult sons and daughters working in factories. Issues raised were pooling of household resources and contributions by working sons and daughters, differences in expectations from sons and daughters regarding contribution to household, household composition, nuclear and extended family structures, and perception of factory employment.

THE LOCALE

The Province of Batangas

The province of Batangas is the most populous of the provinces in the CALABARZON region, with a total population of 1,658,567 in 1995 and an average annual growth rate of 2.2 percent. The average household size was 5.2 persons (National Statistics Office [NSO] 1995a). In the past twenty-five years, Batangas province has moved from being a predominantly agricultural economy to more service-oriented industries. Labor force participation rate as of October 1998 was pegged at 64.3 percent, with the employment rate at 92.7 percent and the unemployment rate at 7.3 percent (NSO 1999).

The Barangay of Ambulong

A *barangay* is the smallest political subdivision in the country. A city or municipality is composed of several barangays. It is the barangay that is used as the basic geographic enumeration area for purposes of enumeration in the Labor Force Survey of the NSO of the Republic of the Philippines. The municipality of Tanauan lies in the northeastern fringe of Batangas province. The municipal annual growth rate is 2.1 percent, and the average household size is 5.88 persons (NSO 1995b).

Barangay Ambulong is located 11 kilometers from the town proper of Tanauan municipality. Part of the barangay rests on the banks of Taal Lake, and its farthest boundary leads to the municipality of Talisay, Batangas. There are a total of 758 households with a population of 4,699 as of the 1995 mid-decade population census conducted by the NSO. Average household size was 6.47 persons (NSO 1995b). However, as of May 1999, an actual count of 672 households was recorded for Barangay Ambulong. This was used as the baseline data in conducting a sample survey for this research. Sample size for the survey was 249 households or 37.05 percent.

THE HOUSEHOLD IN BARANGAY AMBULONG

Defining the Household

Studies of households have faced issues on whether the household is to be examined as a corporate social unit with members acting in their own self-interest or as a unit with members all behaving in an altruistic way to further the interest of the group as a whole. Refinements on the study of households include bargaining models, Marxist and neo-Marxist models, a dual systems model, and the incorporation of gender (Hart 1992).

The Labor Force Survey of the NSO of the Philippines defines a household as:

> an aggregate of persons, generally but not necessarily bound by ties of kinship, who live together under the same roof and eat together or share in common the household food. Members comprise the head of the household, relatives living with him, and other persons who share the community life for reasons of work or other consideration. A person who lives alone is considered a separate household (NSO 1998: xiii).

The sample survey conducted sought to explore the standard definition used by the national census and surveys and note down the local concepts and practices that put into question some elements of this definition of the household. One limiting aspect is the part of the definition that specifies "living under the same roof." The Ambulong case included eight of the 249 households (or 3 percent), who stated that some members, even if they were not living under the same roof, were still considered part of the household. Another limiting phrase is the part that specifies that members "eat together or share in common the household food." It was observed in the research area that food was often shared beyond the household. The practices of *libanan* or *lahok-lahok* (food sharing) among neighboring households were often observed, particularly during the midday meal. Children would carry bowls going from one neighbor to another in search of food. They take the viands or the cold rice shared with them back to their own homes to consume these food items with other members of that household. The locations of some households were also observed to cluster around natal families. The local term *isang pisa* (grouping of houses) describes that condition. Married children regardless of sex set up their own households near or around their parents' house. Neighboring households tend to be made up of closely related kin. This situation of neighboring households of closely related kin has resulted in some houses being structurally connected, sharing common walls, thus making it difficult to distinguish one household from another. Within the clustered houses some buildings are used communally, such as bathing and toilet facilities and water pumps.

Another limit to the census definition is limiting household membership categories to include only that of "head of household" and that of "relatives living with him, and other persons who share the community life for reasons of work or other consideration." This specifies the household composition to be organized in reference to the household head. Implicitly it points to only a single individual who is perceived to be the "head."

Household Composition and Structure

The Ambulong data show that household membership is not merely the category of household head and all other members related to the head. The case studies and the sample survey on composition of households and their members' corresponding roles, responsibilities, and expectations reflect the household as being composed of the following:

- *Household Head* is a position held by a majority of fathers. They are heads by the nature of their being "oldest male member" of the household for a majority of the respondents. Other characteristics that defined local perceptions of the head of household are being "primary income earner" and "person in charge of household " as defining features, but these made up less than 20 percent of the sample survey.
- *Household Money Manager* is held by a majority of mothers and is defined as the person who physically holds the money used for household expenditures. Household resources, particularly income earned by different members of the household, may be pooled and used to purchase food or to pay for lighting, water, medical expenses, educational expenses of dependent children, and clothing needs. Fewer than 10 percent of those responsible for managing the household income pool were fathers or adult offspring.
- *Offspring as Main Income Provider* is a category that emerges from the study as daughters in particular are finding employment in factories in the economic zones. Some daughters are the sole support or the only source of regular income for a household.
- *Other Working-Age Offspring (Seasonally Employed, Unemployed, or Not in Labor Force)* is another category for offspring in households. Working-age sons may find seasonal employment in vegetable farming, fishing, and construction jobs. Working-age daughters are vending vegetables or fish. Those who are unemployed may be found doing household work (particularly daughters), and helping in farm cleaning or raising farm animals (for sons). School-age sons and daughters also contribute both labor and money to the household pool through vending activities. Young school-age daughters may vend rice cakes or vegetables before or after school. Young school-age sons are tasked with caring for farm animals such as goats and cows and collecting animal fodder.

- *Extended Family Structure (Married Offspring Living within the Natal Household).* It is ideal for newly married couples to reside with either the man's or woman's family in the first few years of marriage, until the birth of the first or second child. It is only then that the young family decides to build their own house and set up a separate household.

THE HOUSEHOLD RESPONSE TO RURAL INDUSTRIALIZATION

The nature of the linkages of the household to the macro forces are examined here in relation to the employment and unemployment patterns that result from the thrust of rural industrialization and globalization. In the CALABARZON region, the factories that have been set up within the Philippine Economic Zone Authority (PEZA) or economic zones reveal a pattern of investments by product sector that show that the top three industries are "electronic components and products, with 54.5 percent of all factories, electrical machinery with 22.10 percent and transport and car parts with 9 percent" (*PEZA Brochure* 1996). The census data and sample survey reflect similar patterns, particularly for the electronics sector. The similar proportions suggest that households in the research area have members who are able to gain entry and be employed in factories throughout this sector. The "garment and textile" sector, as revealed in the census and sample survey, represents a larger percentage of households with members employed in this sector. However, this finding is not reflected in the CALABARZON data, as few of these garment factories are located within the economic zones. These factories are usually outside the economic zones and are mostly subcontractors of some other larger multinational garment or textile producer. Most garment and textile factories began in the late 1980s before the start of the CALABARZON development program.

Impact of Availability of Factory Work on Households

The breakdown of census data on household with members employed in factories by age and sex reveals that more than 53.39 percent of all factory workers are females between the ages of fifteen and twenty-four. The next 22 percent are females between twenty-five and thirty-four years old, and a little less than 10 percent are females between the ages of thirty-five and fifty-four. Almost all males employed in factories, or about 15 percent, are between the ages of fifteen and thirty-four.

These figures show that females have better chances of being absorbed by the ongoing rural industrialization occurring in the area. The "electronic components and products" sector prefers hiring women, particularly young, single women between the ages of fifteen and twenty-four. Older women, between the ages of twenty-five and fifty-four, are still employable, as they have options to work in garment and textile factories, where neither marital status nor age sets limits for employment opportunities. Interviews with several factories within the economic zones support the above findings. Job openings within the economic zones advertise and specify requirements for their applicants to be single women who have completed a high school education, in the age range of fifteen and twenty-four.

In the research area, the most visible effect of these factory employment opportunities is the situation of female employment and male unemployment or underemployment. In a related work, Kathyrn Ward (1990) raised the issues of contradictions and tensions in the home as a result of women's economic contribution. She looked also at the contradictory effects of empowerment of women and at household survival strategies.

This preference for young, single females has led to an emerging feature of having daughters and some mothers as sole support for whole households. Of the twenty-one sole supports of households in the study, nineteen are females, with twelve of them having the position of daughter and seven having the position of mother in their households. There are only two males who act as sole support of their households. Even among households with two or more income earners, daughters are more likely to be employed in factories. There were six households where two or more sisters worked in factories, and only one household where two male members (brothers) worked in factories.

Fathers and sons find themselves more often in the position of being unemployed. More men depend on finding employment in the construction of houses, buildings, roads, and bridges. Finding employment in construction, however, is seasonal and irregular. Hiring out one's labor for fishing and farming activities are also both seasonal and irregular sources of income. There are twenty-seven out of eighty-three households, or 32.53 percent in the census, of households with factory-employed members, with male members who classify themselves as unemployed.

Notices for job openings within factories travel more by word of mouth than through notices in print advertisements. Recommending one's kin or neighbors to apply for a factory position is common. Other factories send notice to the Department of Social Welfare municipal office, which then in turn relays the message down to the barangay level. Some factories routinely send notices of job openings directly to all barangay heads around the factory site. They have called this the "barangay training program."

The requirements for applying for factory work are a high school diploma and a "barangay clearance" that serves as a letter of recommendation for the applicant by the barangay head. A screening process follows, which involves tests, a medical examination, and the interview of the applicant. Some factories send out interviewers to the place of residence of prospective employees to confirm information given by the applicant. Some interview parents before "permanent" status is awarded.

There are factories reportedly limiting the personnel they allow to move into "permanent" status. They set employees to work only on a contractual basis, which means that they work only for a period less than six months to complete a contract. This is also referred to as "contractualization" of labor. A new batch of applicants is then hired. This situation brings about a high turnover rate within the factory and, for workers from the research site, a cycle of unemployment. Male members of the household find it more difficult to get permanent positions in factories in the economic zones. Women reportedly do not experience contractualization to the same degree, as they are more likely to be made permanent. The reason why women move from one factory job to another is to find better pay and working conditions.

POOLING OF HOUSEHOLD RESOURCES

The survival of the household rests upon the contributions of different members through a pattern of pooling resources of both labor and income. This section looks at the process of pooling household resources as well as at patterns of income flows and expenditures. It also looks into the ways by which different household members make differential contributions to the household pool. The dynamics by which income pooling takes place become more visible through a process of modeling the flow of income and expenditures.

Key to understanding the dynamics within the household are the findings on the expectations and responsibilities of the "household head," "household money manager," and "income-earning sons and daughters." The "household head," usually defined as the oldest male member and usually the "husband/father," ideally will not want anything to do with managing or even physically holding money. He will relinquish control of the money that he earns. He may decide to hand over all his earnings, or keep only a portion for his personal needs like tobacco and alcohol and hand over the bulk to his wife. In a related study by Stirrat on Sri Lankan fishing households, he showed the "dissonance in male dominance and women's control of money" (1989). The men engaged in fishing but would have nothing to do with holding money or controlling money they earned, as they saw cash as "dirty." It was the women who had control over cash. The "money manager," usually the "wife/mother," will physically hold the money that all income-earning members contribute to the household income pool. The census has shown that there are wives/mothers who are sole supports of households. In these households, women remain as money managers but may have their husbands sharing the responsibility of making food purchases for everyday needs.

The different members of the household, depending on their age, employment status, and marital status, each contribute and make demands on the household pool of resources. Individual members who are employed and receive wages in the form of cash make decisions on the proportion that will be contributed to the household pool, as well as set a budget for their own personal expenses and for gifts and contributions to other individuals.

The mother/wife who has control over the household income pool then allocates resources in two ways. She makes sole decisions on some purchases and payments and negotiates with other household members on other items. An individual who contributes to the household pool occasionally will also negotiate with the wife/mother. Dependent children and other household members who are not earning also negotiate with the mother for their own individual needs.

The practice of having one member as "money manager" and "wife/mother" physically holding the money of the household accounted for 88 percent of households in the survey. A portion of the wages earned is given to the wife/mother on a regular basis by members who are working regularly, or this may be done on just a few occasions by those who work on temporary types of jobs on a daily basis. The contributions by different members, whether regular or irregular, go into a common household income pool. This household pool is held by the mother, and her control over this resource involves either making sole decisions on purchases or negotiating with different members of her household. The benefits from the pooled household resources are shared and accrue to different members depending on their individual needs. The survey revealed that this pooling of income was done only by 50 percent of 249 households, because in other households, only one person was earning for the whole household so pooling income was not possible. More so for the 10 percent of all households in the survey that reported that no household member was earning wage income. Households are able to survive in these conditions, as forty-nine households or 20 percent reported that they received contributions from members who are not living under the same roof. The occurrence of members living under one roof and not contributing was only in 1.2 percent of all households.

Contributions to the household pool of resources are made on a voluntary basis. The term *kusa* (out of one's own volition) best describes how mothers feel about how their children who are already earning income contribute to the household pool. There seems to be an understanding that those who earn and are still single contribute what they earn to help out their parents in meeting the needs of all the members of the household. Most working sons and daughters feel compelled to help out their parents, because they perceive their contribution as essential to keeping the household running. They reason that they saw their own fathers giving their earnings to their mothers. Older siblings entering the workforce see and have experienced the difficulties encountered by their parents in raising their large families. Younger siblings, once they begin earning, want to make the lives of their now-older parents more comfortable. It is more likely that the youngest offspring, or one who remains single, will continue supporting their parents in old age.

The responses of households to factory employment opportunities were examined through the flows of income and expenditures within the household. Related studies documenting decision making and money flows, allocations, and control elements of household pools of resources are found in the works of Wilk (1989) and Roldan (1987). The study by Roldan was based on patterns of monetary distribution and control among industrial home workers in Mexico City. The elements of differing goals, decisions, and choices made within the household (Barlett 1989) occur in many cultural contexts. Wilk pointed out: "economic change leads to alterations in boundaries, in the economic bargains and balances between household members, in the allocation of labor and resources to different funds and in the economic roles taken by different people" (1989). Furthermore, in modeling material flows and decision-making processes, one can "distinguish the degree to which the household budget and household processes are structured" (Wilk 1989).

The model in figure 9.1 provides a general model by which households (nuclear with sole support, nuclear with two or more income earners, and extended family types) are patterned. The categories of expenses that each individual member makes decisions on are designated in this model as "Personal Expenditures." After setting some aside for personal expenditures, a portion is given as "Contribution to Household Pool." This amount is given to the "mother" as household manager. She in turn will use this money to pay for expenses of the household. Some expenses are her "Sole Decision," but others she negotiates with other members of the household. A third portion, decided on particularly by single working offspring, is the category "Gifts and Contributions to Father/Mother/Other Siblings."

The model in figure 9.2 presents the types of expenses that each individual makes, which include "Personal Expenditures" involving transportation expenses, food expenses for food consumed at the place of work, personal care, and personal effects such as toiletries. Other more incidental expenses are for recreation, such as birthday gatherings or parties, movies, and purchases of alcoholic beverages, usually by young men. There is the "Contribution to Household Pool," and lastly "Gifts and Contributions to Other Household Members." In this last portion, the working son/daughter gives a separate amount to the father for his personal use, which goes mainly toward the purchase of alcoholic beverages, tobacco, recreation, and purchase of cooked food for the household. The working sibling also contributes separately to the other siblings, who may still be in school and need additional amounts of money for special school projects or outings with their friends. They also give gifts or contribute directly to their married siblings, who may have unexpected expenses for health or education. Gifts to mothers are more likely to be purchases of personal care products, clothing, or shoes.

Nuclear-Type Households Where Factory-Employed Offspring Is Sole Support

In the situation in which only one member of the household is employed and receives income on a regular basis, this individual, likely to be a single adult female, makes decisions on three levels regarding the apportioning of

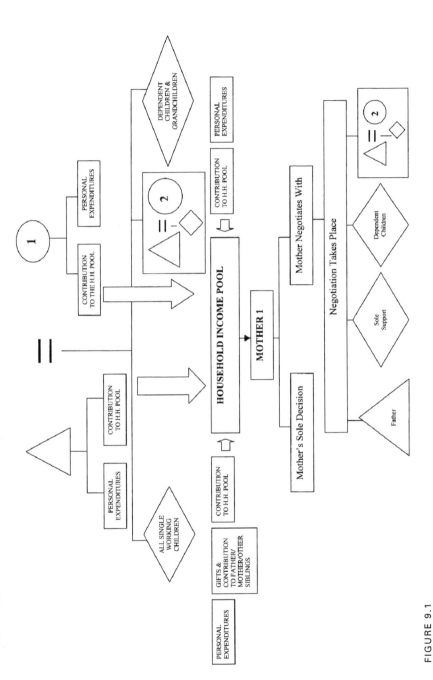

FIGURE 9.1
Extended family with two or more income earners.

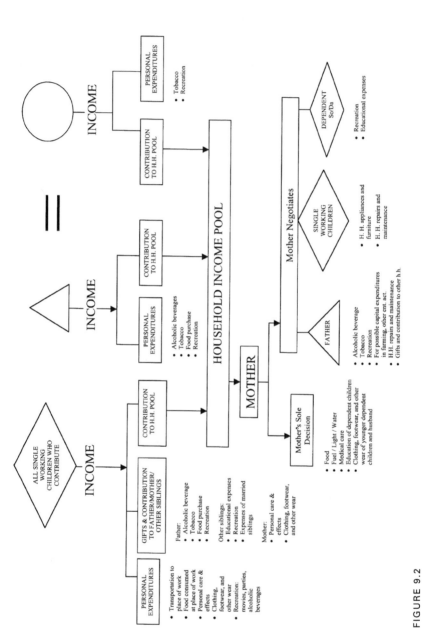

FIGURE 9.2
Nuclear family with two or more income earners.

her income. This person sets aside money for personal expenditures, contribution to the household pool, and gifts and contributions to other household members.

Nuclear-Type Households with Two or More Income Earners

Among nuclear-type households where there are two or more income earners, the flow of contributions and expenses is similar to previous models on sole supports. In this case, all single working offspring who contribute decide also on three levels: personal expenditures, contribution to the household pool, and contributions to other household members. There may also be cases when father or mother also are earning, and they decide mostly on two levels. Personal Expenditures for father may include purchases of alcoholic beverages, tobacco, purchased food, and recreation. Personal Expenditures for mother may include tobacco and personal care and effects, clothing, or footwear.

Extended Family-Type Households

Among extended family-type households, the pattern follows the nuclear family with two or more income earners. The difference lies in the contributions of married children. Married children's contribution to the pool is in the form of food, not money. Items such as rice, vegetables, meats, coffee, and sugar are purchased by the younger married couple and contributed to the household to be consumed by all other members.

Each income earning household member makes the decision as to how much is to be contributed. Mothers do not make a direct request to the income earning member to contribute to the household pool. Mothers reportedly accept whatever is given by their children as their contribution to the household pool. To complain openly and directly to the person contributing is viewed and judged negatively. On occasions that the contributor to the household pool gives less than usual, the person who is the giver makes the first move to inform the mother why a lesser amount is given.

AREAS OF SOLE DECISION AND NEGOTIATION IN HOUSEHOLD POOLED RESOURCES

Wives and/or mothers engage in sole decision making and negotiations with reference to the household income pool under their control. They make purchases assumed to be essential for the smooth running of the household without consulting any other member of the household. Negotiation as a concept means discussion between members on how the common household resource is to be utilized. This includes discussion on ways to augment, increase, and reallocate household resources. Negotiation also involves incentives and sanctions employed by a wife and/or mother in relation to the other household members. The diagram in figure 9.2 also details the types of expenses that a mother makes sole decisions about and those that she negotiates with other household members.

Mother's Sole Decision-Making Areas

The money that is held by the wife/mother is allocated primarily for food purchases. Rice, coffee, and sugar are most likely the only items bought in bulk and not on a daily basis. Other essential household items purchased besides food include laundry needs and toiletries. The management of household resources also calls for allocation of payment for fuel, light, and water; medical care; the educational expenses of dependent children; and clothing and footwear of younger dependent children and the husband.

Wife Negotiates with Husband

As mentioned earlier, husbands ideally and literally "surrender" their earnings to their wives. The wife gives back an allowance to her husband for his personal use. The term *allowance* is commonly used by women interviewed to mean the amount of money they give their husbands upon his request. Allowance is a catch-all term, which may mean money to be used for transportation expenses to and from work, or simply for the purchase of alcoholic beverages and tobacco. Some women give their husbands an allowance even without their husbands asking for it. The women feel that men should readily have some amount of money in case of an emergency and to avoid "loss of face" or being "ashamed" in front of their peers when they have to decline an invitation for a *barikan* (a gathering of men for the purpose of drinking alcoholic beverages) because they have no money at hand to contribute to that gathering. This may also be the explanation as to why adult working children all give gifts of money to their father for his personal use.

However, interviews with men revealed that men already set aside an amount from their earnings before handing over the rest to their wife. Some declare the amount that they take from their actual earnings, but others do not inform their wives of the amount they have set aside. The men feel that having some amount of money at hand is important in case of emergency situations. Besides alcoholic beverages and tobacco, men make food purchases that they want to consume at home along with other members of the household.

Among farmers and fishermen, the daily earnings from sales of produce or catch are handed over to their wives. Men discuss and negotiate with their wives for their future capital needs in either farming or fishing inputs. Upon agreement with their wife as to how the future capital needs are to be met, the wife then needs to budget and allocate funds for this future need. Some women may find ways to augment the household resources by looking for other income-generating activities, like vending, trading, or even making loans, just to meet these future needs. Some women will discuss with their working children the financial requirements of their father. Fathers seldom directly approach their children to discuss money matters and financial needs.

Mother Negotiates with Single Adult Working Son/Daughter

As earlier stated, mothers do not directly confront a household member who does not contribute to the household pool. One's contribution is ideally *kusa* (voluntarily). Upon further probing, mothers reveal that they make known the needs of the household openly to all members. A mother may complain about a forthcoming need that she may not be able to cover. She may also let her other children in the household know about the situation. Working offspring then will hear about the financial difficulties through their siblings. It will be up to the working offspring then to find ways to contribute or further help out.

The working offspring who provides the biggest support to the household is readily given praises by the mother. That individual is praised and his or her virtue of being hard-working is more often recounted to neighbors, visitors, and even within the household. It is possible that a mother uses this as an indirect way of giving incentives to her other children to contribute more. Mothers do not complain directly to the noncontributing or very irregularly contributing working son/daughter. However, the mother may speak negatively about that individual to others. A mother may complain that her working son/daughter is being selfish, lacks skill in managing finances, or is even being lazy.

The cases when a mother negotiates with her offspring who contribute to the household pool lie predominantly in the purchase of household furnishings and equipment. The working son/daughter informs the mother of his or her interest in purchasing small household appliances like televisions, videocassette recorders, electric fans, cooking ranges and refrigerators, household furnishings like living or dining room sets, or beds. They must negotiate with mother for her approval of making the purchase. Mothers appreciate having the opportunity to own these items, but they worry that the payment for these may become a burden to their children. Most of these purchases can be made on an installment basis or on credit, which has to be paid on a weekly, bimonthly, or monthly basis in a retail appliance store or is deducted directly from the salary when purchases are made through the factory cooperative store.

The case of household repairs and maintenance is also an area for negotiation between mothers and working offspring. The mother has to inform her son/daughter to allocate for some future date money that can be used for repairing some parts of the house, or the offspring gets mother's approval to use some of his or her earnings toward the repairs in the household. A mother will again employ indirect methods of making known to the working offspring the condition of the house and the needed repairs.

Relatives of either husband or wife usually approach the wife when they seek help in the form of a loan. Neighbors borrowing rice or making small loans will also approach the mother in a household. However, for larger loans, the wife/mother usually makes the request from a married sibling, distant relation, or neighbor, asking for the loan with either the father or the working son/daughter. There are occasions when the income-earning household member will also make requests from the mother for money, when the budgeted amount for personal expenditures will be consumed before the next payday. The working household member must then borrow from the mother, most likely to cover transportation expenses until the next salary payment.

Mother with Other Dependents, Married Offspring, and Grandchildren

Mother and dependent children also negotiate the allocation of household resources, particularly for educational purposes beyond tuition and travel expenses to and from school. School activities, such as field trips, special programs, graduations and awards ceremonies, and school dances will involve extraordinary expenses, and participation in these has to be negotiated. Extracurricular activities, such as joining basketball leagues or attending birthday celebrations, involve travel expenses and some pocket money. In all of these activities, the dependent child will make known his or her interest in participating in the activity. Permission will be sought from the mother, and information on estimated expenses for such activity will be given. The mother must find ways to allocate for such activities, and only then can she give her approval.

Married offspring living in the same household may on occasions also make requests from the mother for loans, for unexpected expenses that the younger couple will not be able to meet. The married son/daughter will be the one to approach his or her mother and inform her of their need. The mother may allocate funds for the needs of the married offspring's family from the household pool of resources, or she may inform other siblings or make the information known among other siblings, so they may want to directly contribute and make the loan to the person/family concerned. These negotiations are conducted within the mother's role as the person who maintains stronger social networks within and among their kin and community.

CONCLUSION

Households have responded to rural industrialization by having daughters play a more active role in providing a steady source of income from factory wages. The resulting dynamics between household members working in factories and other household members may continue to be seen as altruistic, when those employed contribute a part of their wages so that the other members who are unable to find work may survive. This study, however, recognizes that individual members of the households make decisions that are not always solely on the "altruistic level." The individual member has personal needs and goals, but also some level of altruism, wanting to help and contribute to meeting the needs of the household. The dynamics are presented here through models of flows in income and expenditures, along with details of the items that individual members decide and negotiate about.

The process of pooling of income by different household members can be seen as a survival strategy by households in this situation, in which employment opportunities are selective based on one's sex and age. Rural industrialization may result in empowerment of some household members, particularly young, single daughters. The opportunity for women to find employment in factories in economic zones has allowed women to have more control over meeting their individual needs. Daughters have become more valued, as their contributions are seen as significant and even necessary for the survival of the household. The position of being a significant contributor to the household income pool also increases an individual's chance to negotiate with the mother or the money manager over the purchase of small household appliances like television sets or radios or plans for general household repairs or construction work. Households often find themselves in situations in which only one member ends up supporting all the other members, and daughters have become sole supports of households as such. Young, single males end up dependent on the household income pool instead of having the opportunities to contribute to the pool, as finding employment is proving to be difficult. The notion of increased empowerment of young, single women as a result of the move to rural industrialization needs to be weighed in relation to present conditions that result in unemployment, particularly for male members of a household.

ACKNOWLEDGMENTS

This chapter is part of a dissertation research project entitled *Household Dynamics in the Context of Rural Industrialization and Globalization*. Findings from this research were based on fieldwork conducted between October 1998 and December 1999. Initial research began in January 1995 and continued intermittently through March 1997. I thank the University of the Philippines Faculty Fellowship Program, which has given me the opportunity to do field research full time. Funding for this dissertation research has been made possible through the University of the Philippines Dissertation Aid Grant and the Philippine APEC Study Center Network Dissertation Grant. Much appreciation is owed for the hospitality and support of Mr. and Mrs. Peter Garcia and the different Barangay Health Workers in Barangay Ambulong, Tanauan Batangas. A Fulbright-Hayes Doctoral Enrichment Grant for 1997–1998 provided the opportunity to pursue a specialization in Economic Anthropology at Boston University and at the same time work on developing a working bibliography and concept paper for this dissertation. Special thanks to Dr. Sutti Ortiz for her guidance and encouragement throughout the doctoral enrichment program at Boston University and her continued support throughout the years. Special thanks to Dr. Realidad Rolda and the other faculty and staff of the Department of Anthropology, University of the Philippines, who have been supportive throughout my doctoral program.

REFERENCES

Barlett, Peggy F. 1989. "Introduction: Dimensions and Dilemmas of Householding." In *The Household Economy: Reconsidering the Domestic Mode of Production*, ed. by R. R. Wilk. Boulder, Colo.: Westview Press.

Board of Investment CALABARZON Brochure. n.d. Manila, Philippines: Department of Trade and Industry, Republic of the Philippines.

Chant, Sylvia, and Cathy McIlwaine. 1995. *Women of a Lesser Cost: Female Labour, Foreign Exchange, and Philippine Development*. Quezon City, Philippines: Ateneo de Manila University Press.

Feldman, Shelley. 1992. "Crises, Poverty. and Gender Inequality: Current Themes and Issues." In *Unequal Burden, Economic Crises, Persistent Poverty, and Women's Work*, ed. by L. Benaria and S. Feldman. Boulder, Colo.: Westview Press.

Hart, Gillian. 1992. "Imagined Unities: Construction of the Household in Economic Theory." In *Understanding Economic Process*, ed. by S. Ortiz and S. Lees. Monographs in Economic Anthropology No. 10. Lanham, Md.: University Press of America.

JICA (Japan Institute for Cultural Affairs). 1991. *Master Plan Study on the Project CALABARZON*. Executive Summary Report. Manila, Philippines: Department of Trade and Industry, Republic of the Philippines.

Kung, Lydia. 1978. *Factory Women in Taiwan*. Studies in Cultural Anthropology No. 5. Ann Arbor, Mich.: University of Michigan Press.

Lamphere, Louise, Helena Ragone, and Patricia Zavella. 1997. Introduction to *Situated Lives: Gender and Culture in Everyday Life*, ed. by L. Lamphere, H. Ragone, and P. Zavella. New York: Routledge.

Lamphere, Louise, Patricia Zavella, and Felipe Gonzales, with Peter B. Evans. 1993. *Sunbelt Working Mothers: Reconciling Family and Factory*. Ithaca, N.Y.: Cornell University Press.

NSO (National Statistics Office). 1998. *Census Facts and Figures*. Manila, Philippines: Author.

———. 1995a. *Mid-Decade Population Census*. Manila, Philippines: Author.

———. 1995b. *Census of Population, Report No.1-D Population by Province, City/Municipality and Barangay: Southern Tagalog*. Manila, Philippines: Author.

———. 1998. *Integrated Survey of Household Bulletin (ISHB) Series No. 93*. Manila, Philippines: Author.

———. 1999. *Batangas' Most Requested Statistics*. Manila, Philippines: Author.

Ong, Aihwa. 1987. *Spirits of Resistance and Capitalist Discipline: Factory Women in Malaysia*. Albany, N.Y.: SUNY Press.

Philippine Economic Zone Authority (PEZA Brochure). 1996. Manila, Philippines: Philippine Economic Zone Authority.

Redclift, Nanneke, and Enzo Mingione. 1985. Introduction to *Beyond Employment: Household, Gender, and Subsistence*, ed. by N. Redclift and E. Mingione. Oxford, U.K.: Basil Blackwell.

Roldan, Martha. 1987. "Class, Gender, and Asymmetrical Exchanges within Households." In *The Crossroads of Class and Gender: Industrial Homework, Subcontracting, and Household Dynamics in Mexico City*, ed. by L. Benaría and M. Roldán. Chicago: University of Chicago Press.

Stirrat, R. L. 1989. "Money, Men, and Women." In *Money and the Morality of Exchange*, ed. by J. Parry and M. Bloch. Cambridge, U.K.: Cambridge University Press.

Tiano, Susan. 1987. "Maquiladoras in Mexicali: Integration or Exploitation?" In *Women on the U.S./Mexico Border: Responses to Change*, ed. by V. Ruiz and S. Tiano. Boston: Allen and Unwin.

Ward, Kathyrn. 1990. Introduction and Overview to *Women Workers and Global Restructuring*, ed. by K. Ward. New York: School of Industrial and Labor Relations, Cornell University, ILR Press.

Wilk, Richard R. 1989. "Decision Making and Resource Flows within the Household: Beyond the Black Box." In *The Household Economy: Reconsidering the Domestic Mode of Production*, ed. by R. Wilk. Boulder, Colo.: Westview Press.

Wolf, Diane L. 1992. *Factory Daughters: Gender, Household Dynamics, and Rural Industrialization in Java*. Berkeley: University of California Press.

IV

MIGRATION ENGENDERED

10

"Male Wealth" and "Claims to Motherhood": Gendered Resource Access and Intergenerational Relations in the Gwembe Valley, Zambia

Lisa Cliggett

INTRODUCTION

The story of women's economic marginalization as a result of development and transitions to capitalist, cash-oriented economies is not a new one. Scholars from a range of disciplines have detailed the many paths towards the creation of women's economic dependence throughout the world (e.g., di Leonardo 1991; Mikell 1997). In this chapter, I join this body of literature in telling the history of how Tonga women of Zambia's Gwembe Valley have lost access to valuable wealth and become increasingly dependent on men for access to material resources that ensure their livelihood. However, demonstrating the transition of women's economic autonomy to dependence is not my main purpose in this chapter.

I use the context of women's economic marginalization to examine gendered strategies for mobilizing support from relatives as men and women age. In particular, Gwembe women employ a range of methods for encouraging assistance from children and other relatives that include performing the "rhetoric" of motherhood—behaviors and conversations that emphasize the sacrifices mothers have made throughout a child's life, and highlight the mother's entitlement to support from children. Gwembe men, alternatively, spend most of their adult lives attempting to accumulate material wealth which, in their old age, they can use to marry younger wives and encourage support from a range of dependents.

Beyond documenting these different strategies older men and women employ in harnessing support in their old age, this chapter reveals some of the historical processes in the Gwembe Valley that shaped gendered access to resources. In particular, this chapter highlights the household- and kinship-level dynamics that influence who has access to resources like land and cattle, and how men and women have benefited from these resources in different ways. Using data collected during fieldwork in the Gwembe Valley from 1994 to

1998 and from the Colson-Scudder longitudinal Gwembe Tonga Research Project, I argue that it is these gender differences in access to resources and investments in these resources that have led to the very different strategies in how aging parents mobilize support from their children and kin.

THEORETICAL FRAMEWORK

Understanding the relationship between parents and children benefits from considering the notion of individual actors within a socially constructed kinship group. The argument presented in this chapter draws on practice-centered theory that sees individuals as empowered to make choices within their social structures (Bourdieu 1977; Giddens 1976). Rules and norms shape and constrain behavior, but individuals can test the boundaries of those rules and norms through their individual and social actions. The norm of caring for elders in African societies offers an ideal example of how individuals do and do not adhere to these cultural ideals.

During the Southern African drought of 1994–1995, while I was conducting ethnographic fieldwork in the Gwembe Valley, a man abandoned his grandmother in his homestead as he and his two wives and all their children moved to their lakeside gardens to protect crops from invasions of hippos, cattle, and birds. Typically, when a dependent (such as an elderly mother, aunt, uncle, or disabled relative) remains in a homestead, an adolescent child or one of the wives will remain in the homestead in order to care for the dependent woman or man. In this case, the man's nuclear family abandoned the whole homestead and his grandmother with it. Daughters of the elderly woman eventually rescued her, but the abandonment itself suggests that the norm of caring for and respecting elders does not always reflect actual behavior. As this example illustrates, caring for elders is not inevitable or "natural" behavior; individuals make choices as they move through their social worlds.

Notions of the household economy as outlined by Robert Netting and Richard Wilk draw on this sense of practice theory—that individuals test boundaries of rules and norms by their individual and social actions, simultaneously shaping, and being shaped by, those structures (Netting, Wilk, and Arnould 1984; Wilk 1989, 1991). Netting and Wilk see households as a place of action where individuals work both together and apart in their productive and reproductive activity, as the story about the abandoned grandmother shows. Gender differences between husbands and wives, brothers and sisters, and fathers and mothers also illustrate the range of cooperative and noncooperative behaviors within domestic groups.

Theories of intergenerational wealth flows proposed initially by the social demographer John Caldwell help to frame the lifecycle component of the argument presented in this chapter. Caldwell argues that until certain economic conditions are met in developing countries, children represent a material benefit for parents, particularly in old age, and this accounts for high fertility in those places (Caldwell 1976, 1982). In other words, in "nonindustrial" settings, parents have many children because raising children is relatively cheap, and as the parents age, they will benefit from those many children in the form of caregiving and material support.

FIELD SITE AND METHODS

The Gwembe Valley carries the reputation throughout Zambia as a drought-prone, isolated, and impoverished area. Annual hunger seasons, combined with cyclical droughts, often make subsistence tenuous. Over the past two decades, droughts and "hunger years" throughout Southern Africa have occurred more frequently, and in 1992–1993 and 1994–1995, two of the worst droughts since the 1920s hit Zambia's Southern Province (Savory 1996). In addition to these aspects of hardship, the Zambian nation has suffered from economic decline since the mid-1970s when copper prices (Zambia's largest export) on the world market dropped, causing an economic crisis throughout the country. Since that time, Zambia's economy has fluctuated, with a general downtrend most recently exacerbated by the World Bank and International Monetary Fund's (IMF) structural adjustment program (SAP) launched in the early 1990s. SAPs attempt to improve efficiency of "developing" countries' economies, most often by encouraging cuts in government spending and subsidies of basic needs for the majority of the population. These programs, including Zambia's recent experience with the SAP, often result in a rapid rise in costs for basic foods and household needs and increasing unemployment while government offices and government-owned industries (in the case of Zambia, all industries) attempt to "restructure" their operations.

These national-level economic conditions affect both urban and rural populations through increased prices for staples like maize (for food and seed), fertilizer, and other household supplies; staffing and supplying medical clinics and schools; employment options in all locations; and maintenance of infrastructure such as roads and transportation systems. In these austere economic conditions, everyone faces the challenge of daily survival in conditions of increasing scarcity. For the people of the Gwembe Valley, these conditions trigger familiar responses, such as gathering wild foods that satisfy hunger (but not taste preferences), tapping into larger and larger support networks (such as migrants living in areas with better harvests), and trimming down expenses and consumption (Colson 1979: 21–22). In these times of hardship, the elderly often find themselves in tenuous positions at the fringe of the productive domestic unit, at risk of being "trimmed out" and receiving less than their basic needs. Given such conditions, the elderly must become key players in their own survival, negotiating their position and rights to valuable resources with relatives and kin.

Many scholars of social change and African studies know of the matrilineal Gwembe Tonga people due to the research Elizabeth Colson and Thayer Scudder have conducted over the past forty years (Colson 1960, 1971; Colson and Scudder 1988; Scudder 1962; Scudder and Colson 1978, 1981). Their original research agenda focused on cultural continuity and change in the face of massive upheaval caused by the building of Kariba Dam on the Zambezi River and subsequent resettlement of approximately 60,000 Gwembe Tonga. In 1956, Colson and Scudder initiated the "before" study of Gwembe Tonga life ways, and in 1962, after resettlement, they returned to their original sites in order to understand the process of change and adaptation. Since that time, Colson and Scudder have returned to these original field sites approximately every three years and continued systematic data collection on a vast array of sociocultural, economic, political, religious, and demographic information.

In 1994, I joined Colson and Scudder's Gwembe Tonga Research Project (GTRP) as part of the "next generation" that would increasingly manage the project as Colson and Scudder began the process of retirement. In the spring of 1994, I went to Zambia and settled in Sinafala village to begin approximately eighteen months of anthropological research on support systems for the elderly among the Gwembe Tonga people (Cliggett 1997a, 2001a). I made my home base in Sinafala village, located along the lakeshore in Gwembe central and chose Mazulu village, at the north end of the Gwembe Valley, as a comparison site. Sinafala and Mazulu offer good opportunities for comparison for a variety of reasons. Prior to relocation, the two villages neighbored each other, and residents of each village maintained a variety of kinship and social networks. After relocation, those relationships persisted, and they continue to this day (although significantly altered because of the physical distance between the villages). In addition, Sinafala, a village approximately six hours from a paved road by public transport, represents a community relatively distant from town and the day-to-day impacts associated with urban life, but Mazulu, situated fifteen minutes from a major road and transportation route, offers a comparison community with much greater integration into the national economic and political systems on a daily basis. These characteristics offered the opportunity to look at social support networks in two similar populations but with differing economic contexts.

I also conducted extensive interviews in two migration destinations for Gwembe villagers: Chikanta, a frontier farming area on the plateau northeast of the Gwembe Valley, and Lusaka, the capital of Zambia and the primary migration destination for those people seeking wage employment. The data presented in this article come primarily from Sinafala village, although I found the behavioral patterns I describe in all of my research sites, as well as in other areas where I visited briefly.

At the beginning of fieldwork in 1994, I initiated contact with ninety-two individuals aged fifty-five or older, in three different research sites. Lusaka, my urban research site, had no permanently resident elderly people; Zambians attribute the small population of elderly people living in urban areas to the high cost of urban life and the lack of institutional support for seniors in the absence of kin networks. When men or women reach their senior years, they typically return to home villages or establish new farms in frontier land, abandoning their urban homes (see also Ferguson 1999). Although I worked with Gwembe villagers in Lusaka, this population consisted of the children of elderly people living elsewhere.

The Gwembe central village, Sinafala, housed forty-five of the ninety-two elderly people with whom I worked intensively. In 1994–1995, Sinafala had a total population of approximately 500 people. By the end of my fieldwork in 1995, three of these elderly people in Sinafala had died. Mazulu village, with a 1994–1995 population of approximately 400 people, housed another thirty-seven of my study group (by September 1995, five elderly people had died). The frontier farming region northeast of the valley became a popular migration destination for many Gwembe people in the 1980s, including children of many aging villagers. In 1994–1995, I found ten elders living in Chikanta; these aging men and women had left Sinafala village, or retired from urban centers where they had wage employment, to settle with relatives in the frontier. The migrant destination of Chikanta poses challenges for identifying a "total population," because the region covers a vast area and the residents include migrants from many areas of the country. However, our GTRP data shows that in 1994–1995, approximately 150 migrants from Sinafala, or descendents of those migrants, lived in the Chikanta region. In all three sites, the group of elders with whom I worked constituted the total population of people age fifty-five or older.

The methods of data collection that I employed included extensive open-ended interviews; focused discussions on resource access, support networks, and gift exchanges; and surveys to collect detailed information about family members, residence patterns, and frequency of contact with nonresident kin. I interviewed all ninety-two elderly people in their homesteads and also interviewed most of their children, both in the village and, in the case of migrant children, in their homes in town or other rural areas. With the help of my research assistant, I conducted most of these interviews in Citonga, the local language all Gwembe Tonga people speak.

In addition to the formal data collection techniques I used, I also simply observed the ebb and flow of daily life. I lived in a homestead with a man and his three wives and their thirteen resident children. Sharing meals with this family and other villagers offered a multitude of opportunities to witness village life in action, including many moments of resource distribution, a primary aspect of my research agenda.

THE ARGUMENT

The Gwembe Tonga Research Project and the questions we ask in this specific ecological setting are part of a broader context of cultural and political ecology. Specifically, development-induced relocation and its aftermath profoundly influenced the Gwembe's past and present. But many other pressures play key roles in the social history of this area. The multitude of microlevel pressures, such as village and chieftaincy political struggles and household and kinship power dynamics, all influence local people's choices, decisions, and behavior.

In the Gwembe, as elsewhere throughout the world, household- and kinship-level dynamics influence who has access to what resources and how they can use them. During my year and a half living in the Gwembe, I saw women mobilizing their relationships to children by calling on concepts of "mother" and the reproductive experience as evidence for their right to demand support. Older women offered the statement, "Don't they know that I'm a human who gave birth to them?" as enough reason for children to give them material assistance in their old age.

Men, on the other hand, most often used their control of resources, especially plow and draft animals, to extract assistance and support from their children. One of the wealthiest men in Sinafala managed to keep four adult married sons living in his homestead and thus contributing to the domestic group in a variety of ways. According to both the father and the sons, these sons exchanged their labor in farming their father's vast fields for the use of his cattle and plows in their own fields.

Another case study reveals a conflict between father and son over use of the father's farming implements and the son's personal cash income. Lazwell and his new wife of four months lived in his father's homestead. His father gave him use of his plow and two cattle in exchange for the labor put into his father's fields. A unique opportunity to build a brick house in the village gave him a small sum of cash as payment for the job. When his father demanded a portion of those earnings, Lazwell refused, claiming that his father had no right to the income and that he already worked in his father's fields. As the heated discussions continued and the conflict grew to include relatives outside the homestead, Lazwell's father finally stated that Lazwell no longer had use of his cattle or plows, and in addition, Lazwell's wife could no longer use any of the cooking pots of her mother-in-law. Faced with the prospect of having no farming implements for the fast-approaching planting season, Lazwell chose to migrate to a frontier farming area where he would work in his cousin's fields in exchange for the use of the cousin's cattle and plow. Such conflicts frequently lead to some kind of migration, whether to town, distant farming areas, or nearby regions with matrilineal kin (Cliggett 2000). Colson (2000) also suggests that the recent shift in witchcraft accusations from more distant male kin to fathers is associated with these types of conflicts between fathers and their offspring. These conflicts also demonstrate the authoritarian nature of the fathers' relationships with their sons in particular, but other relatives as well (for a discussion of the dynamics between brothers and sisters, see Cliggett 1997; 2001a). Cultural notions of gender and obligation certainly influence these differences in styles of interaction between men and women and their children. The Tonga typically see men as strong, aggressive, and warrior-like, and they view women as more sentimental, nurturing, and protective.

Assistance and obligation are also deeply embedded cultural forms in Tonga society. The long history of food scarcity in the Gwembe Valley has encouraged patterns of pleading (begging) and equally strong social controls that encourage compliance with such pleas. One type of social control comes in the form of spirit beliefs. If an old woman goes to a homestead and asks for food, the people of the homestead will very likely give her a dish of porridge and sauce because of their fear that her bad spirits (*zyelo*) will make children sick when they are angered.

However, the differences between mother-child and father-child relationships are not simply culturally constructed notions of intergenerational relations. Very real differences in material wealth exist between men and women, and these differences influence the leverage with which elderly parents can negotiate their support in old age. In order to understand the contemporary situation of gendered strategies in elderly support, we need to look at the history of women's and men's access to wealth, starting with the role of land and the increasing importance of cattle.

The Changing Value of Land

Prior to the forced relocation of the Gwembe Tonga people, the majority of the population farmed on the alluvial soils of the Zambezi River, using the horticulturalist technology of hand-held hoes and digging sticks. Cereal crops (predominantly millet and sorghum, but increasingly maize), vegetables, and tobacco made up most of their crops. On portions of this land, both dry and rainy season harvests were possible. Alluvial gardens on the riverbanks maintained their fertility over time due to annual flooding and generally allowed two harvests per year. Consequently, these gardens on the riverbanks were highly valued. Corporate matrilineages held communal access rights to this land, but individuals within lineages and clans often competed for the same land, particularly as the population grew. Colson and Scudder document many dramatic stories of witchcraft and murders attributed to disputes over land from that time period (Colson 1960, 1963, 1964; Scudder 1962, 1969).

In the 1950s, a few men began clearing bush areas for larger fields that they plowed with oxen. These fields allowed for more extensive cultivation of bulrush millet and also solved the problems of population increase and of decreasing fertility of some fields (Colson 1960, 1971; Scudder 1962). In contrast to the alluvial gardens that did not require clearing, these "bush fields" required extensive woodland clearing. The men who cleared these fields had rights over the land. Upon a man's death, the matrilineal inheritor of the man's property expected to claim rights to the land. The same inheritance distribution occurred with river land, except that although only men had rights to the large cleared fields (because they had done the work of clearing), women, as well as men, had rights to the alluvial gardens, and daughters, as well as sons, could inherit these riverside gardens (Colson 1963). In the Tonga inheritance system, men are primary inheritors of men's property, and women usually inherit from women. The growth in bush fields meant that men gained access to land that women had little chance to inherit or clear on their own.

After relocation in 1959, the imbalance in women's and men's access to land, and the preference for ox-drawn plows, increased because people were forced to rely more heavily on cleared fields. Most women depended on their husbands for fields and plows in the new location, rather than clearing bush themselves and planting such large areas with a hoe (Colson 1999). In effect, the Tonga agricultural system changed almost overnight. Close to 60,000 people replaced intensive agriculture on alluvial soils with extensive farming on fields cleared from the bush, using ox-drawn plows.

Communities that resettled close to the lake made gardens along the lakeshore. Some of the older women informants described to me how they "grabbed" garden plots next to the lake when they found them and used the familiar hoe to plant. However, because the lake level can change unexpectedly due to variability in rainfall and inconsistent dam releases downstream, these lakeshore gardens, although more fertile than their counterparts on higher land, can be precarious. With little warning, a rising lake will drown grain seed, and a retreating shoreline can reduce the groundwater table, thus drying out germinating seeds. These days, people rely more on rainy season fields, cleared from the bush and plowed with oxen, for their subsistence. Shore gardens, usually planted by women, are most often used during the dry season to grow vegetables that supplement sauces eaten with the carbohydrate staple.

Although Tonga are matrilineal and inheritance ideally follows through the matrilineage (*mukowa*), there is also a patrilineal link (*lutundu*) between fathers and their children that provides the basis by which a father claims his sons' and daughters' labor. This link also allows for children to make claims to their father's property upon his death and the inheritance of his property. Since relocation, the tendency to inherit from fathers has increased, particularly since the passage in 1989 of the new inheritance laws, giving children and wives more legal access to a deceased man's property. The fact that the men who cleared the fields from the bush in the resettlement areas owned the fields facilitated this transition to patrilineal inheritance. Children could expect to inherit land from their fathers because the fathers held original, and individual, rights to that land. However, the rights to land could fall to the clan if a man died without allocating the fields he cleared to his children prior to his death.

In addition to increased reliance on large, rain-fed fields and an increasing tendency to inherit from fathers, the growing reliance on cattle and plows for farming accentuated the ties children have to their fathers. Fathers depend on children's labor in fields. In exchange he gives them land and lets them use his plow and oxen for their own farming. The increasing importance of huge cleared fields made plows and oxen critical resources for farming, so that young men were willing to work for their father in exchange for access to farm implements. In effect, the role of patrilineal ties grew in importance as plow farming became the norm. This echoes other Africanist scholars' work suggesting that matrilineal societies often rely on hoe farming but patrilineal societies are plow-based (Goody 1976; Murdock 1949; Schneider 1979).

Most adult women did not have their own fields after relocation, both because clearing the bush demanded male labor and because local gender perceptions allowed women to expect that husbands would provide fields (Colson 1999: 32). Although women could gain access to land via their husbands, both before and after resettlement a field was not allocated to them as "owners," merely as wives farming on behalf of their husbands (Colson 1999: 32). Upon the death of a man, relatives can challenge his wife's right to use his land. A son can claim his father's land on behalf of his mother, but if there are no sons present to help a mother, she risks losing access to the fields completely. In these cases, an old woman becomes dependent on her kinsmen and community for productive land.

One elderly widow in Sinafala village told me about her annual practice of "begging" for land from different relatives and villagers, four years in a row. She said that people were willing to lend her a field once in a while, but that after her using the field for one year, the owner would say "Oh, I'm going to plant that field this year," and they would tell her to ask someone else for some land. Her two sons lived in the capital city, and without their support, she had little help in advocating for extended use of any land.

Over the past four decades, men have continued to clear new fields because of the decreasing fertility of the land originally cleared at resettlement. Gwembe people do not use fertilizer on their fields, but they do have a good sense of how long particular fields require fallowing in order to restore fertility. However, fallowed fields are vulnerable to requests for use from kin and neighbors. For this reason, men are likely to keep rights to older fields, whether fallowing or not, which they can lend to relatives including children, wives, aunts, and cousins. One result of continually clearing new land while simultaneously farming old fields is the increasing loss of soil fertility and the growing problem of erosion, which can be seen as one walks through the village and surrounding areas (Cliggett 2001b; Petit, Scudder, and Lambin 2001).

The changing environment plays a part in the current role of land in the Gwembe.

In the past, land was highly valued, and conflict over land was common. Today in some communities with no remaining woodland to clear, land is still worth fighting for. Colson (2000) tells of a recent murder between two half-brothers over rights to an unclaimed field. But conflicts like this are not as frequent as they used to be, particularly in Sinafala where some virgin woodland remains.

My informants told me that land was not as important as it was when they first settled in the relocation areas. Village fields become less productive over time due to overuse and erosion. In some cases young men don't want their fathers' fields because they are too small for their dreams of cash cropping. When villagers decide they want new fields, they either clear a bit of remaining woodland or migrate to frontiers where they can claim up to 100 hectares of virgin woodland.

Unless soils are clearly high-quality, rainy season fields in the village have become less and less desirable to new generations of farmers. For communities where land used to be highly valued and desired, these changes suggest that the importance of village land has decreased. Unlike the generations before them, young adults told me they were not concerned about land inheritance anymore. When I asked people what they hope to inherit from elders now, they all agreed; they want cattle.

The Value of Animals

Owning animals is both an investment strategy and a symbol of wealth for Gwembe Tonga people. This point became clear to me when I learned that many people in Sinafala do not view one of the local shopkeepers as "wealthy." Jackson has two wives, which is also a sign of prosperity, children in secondary school, a cinder block home, and at least three small businesses that he runs out of his home. In my subjective opinion, Jackson was very well-off; he had a steady income and could feed and clothe his family more than most other villagers could during the drought of 1994–1995. But he did not have any cattle at the time of my fieldwork. For this reason, I was told, Jackson was not a wealthy man. Although cattle don't provide a regular income like a business would, they do provide security for financial emergencies, and also a respected social position.

All Tonga desire cattle, but access to animals is not equal. Women and young people experience more difficulty in accumulating cattle than do older men. This is due largely to the bridewealth system, which gives the majority of cattle to the father of a girl, and to the historically male wage earning possibilities, which give men access to cash with which to buy cattle.

In the Tonga bridewealth system, husbands make cattle payments, most of which goes to the father of the girl. The maternal uncle sometimes receives one or two head of cattle or oxen, and recently mothers have begun receiving the share that would go to her brother. The husband making the payments often goes to his own maternal uncle to ask for a cow toward the payment, and sometimes a mother will give her son one of her animals.

The system is somewhat unbalanced; fathers can increase their cattle herds by three to five animals through the marriage of a daughter. Mothers and their brothers may receive one or two cows for the same marriage. At the same time, fathers rarely help their sons with marriage payments, but mothers and their relatives are expected to assist a young man if possible. In contrast to men's ability to accumulate cattle quickly, women usually obtain cattle through inheritance or as a gift from a matrilineal relative. A brother can give a woman a cow as his investment toward marriage payment of his nephews (the woman's sons).

These days it is more common for mothers to be given a share of the marriage payments for her daughter. And sometimes brothers give cattle to sisters, so that the options for women acquiring cattle may be increasing. But for the population of senior women during the mid- to late 1990s, obtaining cattle has been difficult throughout their lives.

In effect, men have more, and more lucrative, options for accumulating cattle than do women. Men can build a herd of cattle through the bridewealth system, purchase with wage earnings, and inheritance. Women can inherit cattle or receive them through a gift from a relative (and, increasingly, women are given a portion of their daughter's bridewealth). In Sinafala during mid-1995, senior women (above age fifty-five), on average, had fewer cattle than did men of the same age group (table 10.1), and women also had fewer goats (table 10.2). In addition, homesteads with any resident man over age fifty-five had more cattle and goats than did homesteads with women, but no men, over age fifty-five (table 10.3).

What does ownership of animals mean to daily life in the village? Cattle owners are respected within their community, and they have a secure savings account. I saw distinctions between respected women, and women who were pitied

Table 10.1.   Cattle Ownership in Sinafala by Gender (1995 Data)

	Women	Men
Total Population (age 55+)	33	10
No Cattle	13	0
	(40%)	
More than 1 Cow or Ox	20	10
	(60%)	(100%)
Average Number of Cattle per Person	4	8

Table 10.2.   Animal Ownership in Sinafala by Gender and Animal
(1995 Data)

	Women	Men
Total Population (age 55+)	33	10
Number of Goats	24	6
	(73%)	(60%)
More than 1 Goat	9	4
	(27%)	(40%)
Average Number of Goats per Person	5	10
Number of Chickens	14	8
	(42%)	(80%)
More than 1 Chicken	19	2
	(58%)	(20%)
Average Number of Chickens per Person	10	4

for their poverty in various forms of assistance within the village. When I no-
ticed one young man giving one aunt only a plate of mealie meal but giving
her sister a whole bucket of maize, he explained to me that the first aunt was
poor, and he gave her that plate out of charity. The other aunt, a relatively
wealthy and respected woman, had the potential to help him in the future, so
he was willing to give her more maize now. This example supports the argument that material resources influence who supports whom in the village; the
change in the value of land and cattle plays a significant role in who has access
to what resources.

Table 10.3.   Homestead (Extended Family Group) Animal
Holdings In Sinafala by Gender and Animal (1995 Data)

	Women	Men
Total Number of Homesteads with 1 Resident Woman or Man age 55+	28	10
Homesteads with Cattle	24	10
	(86%)	(100%)
Average Number of Cattle per Homestead	9	14
Homesteads with Goats	15	6
	(54%)	(60%)
Average Number of Goats per Homestead	9	12
Homesteads with Chickens	25	9
	(89%)	(90%)
Average Number of Chickens per Homestead	12	12

THE LAND-FOR-CATTLE EXCHANGE

As described above, after relocation, land started to lose value. At the same time, cattle ownership increased, and cattle became one of the major local currencies. These changes were taking place from the late 1960s into the 1970s. By the end of the 1970s and the early 1980s, most of my informants agreed that cattle ownership was the number one source of wealth and that desire for land was not so frequently an area of conflict. The exception to this is lakeshore, or tributary, fields that still exist in some communities; the good soil fertility of the lakeshore and riverbank fields make them highly desirable and worth an argument.

Two of the major differences between land ownership and cattle ownership are mobility and gendered access. Cattle, a highly mobile form of property, can be hidden, sold for cash, and given to relatives and friends nearby and far away. In fact, it is common practice to distribute one's herd of cattle among relatives in different regions, as part of risk management in drought-prone regions. Also, when a conflict arises over who should donate animals for slaughter at a funeral, a man who has shared his herd out among a number of relatives in different areas will be more able to claim poverty because the community will not know exactly how many animals he truly owns, and thus he can avoid obligation to slaughter more animals than he feels are his share. The ability to keep one's wealth somewhat hidden is a primary benefit of animal ownership.

Other benefits of animal ownership include income from the sale of milk, renting the animal out for plowing, and the ability to establish support networks and cooperative relationships over distance. A number of men in Sinafala periodically give an ox to a brother or cousin in one of the distant frontier farming areas to help with plowing. The frontier area has frequent outbreaks of cattle-borne diseases, so maintaining a herd in that region is impractical. But using one or two cattle at a time permits completion of farming tasks without risking loss of a herd, and in the sharing of the cattle, brothers reaffirm their supportive relationship. That relationship often benefits the cattle owner in the form of food assistance during droughts and poor harvests. Due to better rainfall patterns and good soils, the frontier region produces a larger and more reliable harvest. Gwembe villagers with links to the frontier know they have a form of insurance through those relationships, and providing use of cattle strengthens those links.

In contrast to cattle, land is fixed in location, and in effect, fixed in social relations. Land, although used and managed by individuals, belongs to a broader group of relatives—usually the matrilineage. Land should not be sold for cash or given for permanent use to someone outside the defined kin group, although this occurs and is disguised as "sale of improvements" such as clearing. A particularly disturbing exception to this rule is the increased sale of valuable lakeshore land by chiefs to outsiders, such as Afrikaners or Europeans, for commercial developments like fishing enterprises, crocodile farms, and tourism. Aside from this kind of alienation, for the most part land remains in the hands, and in the sight, of owners and users. Land cannot be hidden when conflicts erupt over use or wealth, and land cannot be used to establish insurance networks over long distances.

The other key difference between land and cattle is women's and men's access to the resources. Over the past forty years, women's access to cattle has been limited by a male-focused bridewealth system, lack of significant cash earning options (compared to male migration for wage earning, income from cash crops, and control of resettlement compensation payments), and gendered inheritance practices that keep cattle in the hands of men. In contrast, prior to relocation, women had relatively open and equal access to land, which was highly valued. In contrast to Schneider's (1979) argument that land-based societies are more hierarchical than cattle-based societies, the Gwembe Tonga scenario suggests that the transition from wealth in land to wealth in cattle fostered gender inequality and increased hierarchy.

In this cattle-for-land exchange, men increasingly own cattle, which is increasing in importance for both wealth and status. Land, which used to be a source of women's wealth and status, has lost both its real and its perceived value—land is losing fertility, and young people do not value it in the same way that their parents did.

If we consider what these differences in resource accumulation mean for an older person trying to mobilize support from a child or nephew, we see that older men have the material advantage. In Caldwell's (1982) study of intergenerational resource flows, he suggests that it is the potential to inherit from a parent or other "elder" that motivates young people to provide support. Among the Gwembe Tonga, children typically stand little chance to inherit much wealth from their mothers, but potentially quite a bit from a wealthy uncle, or these days with changes in inheritance systems, from a wealthy father. This begs the question, are older women now destitute?

THE RISE IN BEER BREWING AS WOMEN'S INCOME

Not surprisingly, women have developed their own mobile property in the form of cash from beer sales. This relatively new form of economic activity has supplemented other cash-generating options and has the potential to be highly profitable due to men's increasing desire for drink. In Colson and Scudder's book on the importance of beer in the Gwembe (1988), they describe the rise in production for sale from the mid-1960s until the late 1970s, due primarily to the boom in the fishing industry after relocation. This was the same time that cattle were becoming the major source of men's wealth. Beer brewing gave women a source of income independent of their husbands. Thus, women were developing a cash income at the same time that men were accumulating cattle. These two very different forms of resources have different potential for investment.

Over time, women can purchase cattle from their beer profits (women can make a profit of between $10 and $15 for one batch of beer) and attempt to join the men in accumulation of material wealth and status. But it is more common for cash to be invested immediately into family needs such as school fees and uniforms, medical costs, clothing, or household supplies. Through their less visible and less prestigious material wealth, women continually participate in behaviors that reinforce the cultural construction of the nurturing, protective mother. That is, they invest their income in "mothering" (Clark 1999: 720). This leads us back to the question of women and men's differing strategies in encouraging support from their children.

CONCLUSION: BACK TO INTERGENERATIONAL TRANSFERS

As I have described here, changes in resource ownership in the Gwembe Valley over the past four decades, particularly in land and cattle, have led to a situation in which older women have become marginalized from prestigious and highly valued material wealth, while men of the same generation have increased their holdings—which is not such a new story. But I am asking what this means in terms of how men and women negotiate their relationships to children, and how they mobilize support as they age.

If a father hopes to keep his children near him and extract some of their labor, he is wise to allow controlled use of his equipment. His best strategy for security in old age is to have amassed enough cattle that he can still attract younger wives and their children.

If she does not have cattle, a woman has little material base with which to encourage a child's support at the time she most needs it—in her own old age, when she is more likely to be divorced or widowed. Instead, she uses metaphors of the mother-child relationship. But in using such rhetoric, she also reminds the child of her earlier investments—including the breast milk she gave during infancy and the school fees, clothing, and encouragement she gave while the child grew. In contrast to men, a woman's best security in old age is to have lived out the cultural norm of a nurturing, caring mother. With small investments in her children over time, she can establish a framework for reciprocal support in her old age.

As of the late 1990s, the majority of Gwembe women aged fifty-five and older did not have easy access to cattle or other forms of substantial material wealth with which to influence their personal relationships. However, with changing patterns in bridewealth payment and inheritance, younger women in the Gwembe may have more options for cattle ownership throughout their lifetimes, consequently improving their ability to control important material wealth by the time they reach their senior years. As the opportunities for women to control property increase, certainly their options for mobilizing social networks will also change, raising the possibility for new styles of gendered strategies of elderly support that will deserve additional investigation.

Ultimately, the analysis of historical changes in access to resources suggests that gender differences in material wealth over the life course play out in men's and women's social worlds in meaningful ways, whether or not women have access to important wealth. Examining the outcomes of differential access to wealth in men's and women's later life reveals important understandings of the life cycle, extended family support systems, and also the creativity inherent in women's and men's negotiations within their social networks.

REFERENCES

Bourdieu, Pierre. 1977. *Outline of a Theory of Practice.* Cambridge, U.K.: Cambridge University Press.

Caldwell, John. 1976. *The Socio-Economic Explanation of High Fertility.* Canberra: Australian National University Press.

———. 1982. *Theory of Fertility Decline.* New York: Academic Press.

Clark, Gracia. 1999. "Mothering, Work, and Gender in Urban Asante Ideology and Practice." *American Anthropologist* 101(4): 717–30.

Cliggett, Lisa. 1997. *My Mother's Keeper: Changing Family Support Systems for the Elderly in the Gwembe Valley, Zambia.* Ph.D. dissertation, Bloomington, Ind.: Indiana University.

———. 2000. "Social Components of Migration: Experiences from Southern Province, Zambia." *Human Organization* 59(1): 125–35.

———. 2001a. "Gender, Subsistence, and Living Arrangements for the Elderly in the Gwembe Valley, Zambia." *Journal of Cross Cultural Gerontology* 16(4): 309–32.

———. 2001b. "Carrying Capacity's New Guise: Folk Models in Anthropology and the Longitudinal Study of Environmental Change." *Africa Today* 48(1): 3–20.

Colson, Elizabeth. 1960. *Social Organization of the Gwembe Tonga.* Manchester, U.K.: Manchester University Press.

———. 1963. "Land Rights and Land Use among Valley Tonga of the Rhodesian Federation: The Background to the Kariba Resettlement Programme." In *African Agrarian Systems,* ed. by D. Biebuyck, 137–54. London: Oxford University Press.

———. 1964. "Law and Land Holdings among the Valley Tonga of Zambia." *Southwestern Journal of Anthropology* 22: 1–8.

———. 1971. *Social Consequences of Resettlement.* Manchester, U.K.: Manchester University Press.

———. 1979. "In Good Years and in Bad: Food Strategies of Self-Reliant Societies." *Journal of Anthropological Research* 35(1): 18–29.

———. 1999. "Gendering those Uprooted by 'Development.'" In *Engendering Forced Migration: Theory and Practice,* ed. by Doreen Indra, 23–39. New York/Oxford: Bergham Books.

———. 2000. "The Father as Witch." *Africa* 70(3): 333–58.

Colson, Elizabeth, and Thayer Scudder. 1988. *For Prayer and Profit: The Ritual, Economic, and Social Importance of Beer in Gwembe District, Zambia 1950–1982.* Palo Alto, Calif.: Stanford University Press.

Di Leonardo, Micaela, ed. 1991. *Gender at the Crossroads of Knowledge.* Berkeley: University of California Press.

Ferguson, James. 1999. *Expectations of Modernity: Myths and Meanings of Urban Life on the Zambian Copperbelt.* Berkeley: University of California Press.

Giddens, Anthony. 1976. *New Rules of Sociological Method.* New York: Basic Books.

Goody, Jack. 1976. *Production and Reproduction: A Comparative Study of the Domestic Domain.* Cambridge, U.K.: Cambridge University Press.

Kabeer, Naila. 1998. *Reversed Realities: Gender Hierarchies in Development Thought.* London: Verso.

Mikell, Gwendolyn, ed. 1997. *African Feminism: The Politics of Survival in Sub-Saharan Africa.* Philadelphia: University of Pennsylvania Press.

Murdock, George P. 1949. *Social Structure.* New York: Macmillan.

Netting, Robert, Richard Wilk, and Eric Arnould, eds. 1984. *Households.* Berkeley: University of California Press.

Petit, Carine, Thayer Scudder, and Eric Lambin. 2001. "Quantifying Processes of Land-Cover Change by Remote Sensing: Resettlement and Rapid Land-Cover Changes in South-Eastern Zambia." *International Journal of Remote Sensing* 22(17): 3435–56.

Savory, Tomas. 1996. *Moorings Farm Rainfall Records from 1914 to Present.* Private Archive. Monze, Zambia.

Schneider, Harold K. 1979. *Livestock and Equality in East Africa.* Bloomington, Ind.: Indiana University Press.

Scudder, Thayer. 1962. *The Ecology of the Gwembe Tonga.* Manchester, U.K.: Manchester University Press.

———. 1969. "Relocation, Agricultural Intensification, and Anthropological Research." In *The Anthropology of Development in Sub-Saharan Africa* (Society for Applied Anthropology, Monograph No. 10), ed. by D. Brokensha and M. Pearsall, 206–35. Lexington, Ky.: University Press of Kentucky.

Scudder, Thayer, and Elizabeth Colson. 1978. "Long-Term Field Research in Gwembe Valley, Zambia." In *Long-Term Field Research in Social Anthropology,* ed. by G. M. Foster, T. Scudder, E. Colson, and R. V. Kemper, 227–54. New York: Academic Press.

———. 1981. *Secondary Education and the Formation of an Elite: The Impact of Education on Gwembe District, Zambia.* London: Academic Press.

Wilk, Richard, ed. 1989. *The Household Economy.* Boulder, Colo.: Westview Press.

———. 1991. *Household Ecology: Economic Change and Domestic Life among the Kekchi Maya in Belize.* Tucson, Ariz.: University of Arizona Press.

Age, Masculinity, and Migration: Gender and Wage Labor among Samburu Pastoralists in Northern Kenya

Jon D. Holtzman

INTRODUCTION

Migration studies have long been characterized by a profound tension between an emphasis on the economic and noneconomic facets of migration. The predominant thrust by scholars of migration, in Africa and elsewhere, is to view migration fundamentally in economic terms (e.g., Nolan 1986; Amin 1974). This is in many ways reasonable, given that economic factors are, generally speaking, fundamental motivations for migration, while the fact of migration has economic implications in both sending and host communities. Nevertheless, there are important reasons to go beyond this. As a variety of migration scholars have noted (Sassen 1988; Portes and Bach 1985; Glick Schiller, Basch, and Blanc-Szanton 1992), it is possible through an emphasis on the economic aspects of migration to reduce complex, cultural human agents to little more than traveling units of labor. Both older and more recent studies have, indeed, suggested that the motivations of actors involved in various forms of migration may be highly complex, encompassing a range of factors economic and noneconomic alike (Cliggett 2000; DuToit 1975; Mayer 1961; Haenn 1999; Stone 1997). Finally, regardless of the causes of migration, it is a process intertwined with important social and symbolic meanings, constructing new meanings and forcing reinterpretations of old ones.

Fundamental to considerations of the social and symbolic aspects of migration are questions of gender. Cultural constructions of gender (regardless of whether the migrants are women or men) play a central role in determining the form and meaning of migration—who migrates, why, and the ways in which migration coalesces with both new and historically justified forms of identity. Nevertheless, as in studies of international migration (Hondagneu-Sotelo 1994, 1999), studies of rural-urban migration rarely consider gender as a central structuring factor in the migration process. Where, as is often the case, it is young men who are centrally involved in the process of migration, there is the particular hazard of falling back on easy assumptions concerning the naturalness of their journeys, particularly to the extent that it coalesces with western models and mythologies of young men striking out to cities or other unknown environs. Certainly, rural-urban migration in Africa has been and continues to be dominated by young men—though certainly there are many contexts in which women and older men may be heavily involved. Yet even where labor migration is undertaken by the same commonplace demographic category of junior males, it is necessary to interrogate the differing motivations for migrants. Although in one context wage labor may be a necessary rite of passage in order to earn bridewealth (e.g., DuToit 1975) in others labor migration may be a frivolity of youth that elders may seek to stop so that a young man will properly settle down to the responsibilities of marriage (Hutchinson 1996). Although in some cases labor migration may be a strategy to avoid long-standing forms of social control (Cliggett 2000; Mayer 1961), in others it may merely be a manifestation of them (e.g., Meillassoux 1981).

Certainly there are commonalties among many of these cases that should be considered. Many of these sending communities share the characteristic of being societies where male prestige and wealth is accrued to a great extent through age and where, conversely, problematic features of juniorhood drive wage labor. Yet the specific ways in which juniorhood may be problematic and the specific responses are contingent on the particular configurations of gender and age in these societies—particularly the masculine roles and identities of young men, which have received increasing attention within contemporary anthropology (e.g., Guttman 1997; Herzfeld 1985; Herdt 1994).

In this chapter, I will examine migratory wage labor within the specific masculine roles and identities of Samburu pastoralists in northern Kenya. My goal in doing this is less to account for wage labor per se than it is to explicate its position within particular Samburu configurations of age and gender. Since Kenyan independence in the mid-1960s, and increasingly in recent decades, wage labor has become a central pursuit of Samburu, undertaken primarily by junior males—*murran* (the age set of bachelor warriors), and to a lesser degree junior elders (Holtzman 1996). Though there is no question that at a macrolevel, Samburu labor migration is driven by widespread declines in their economy of subsistence pastoralism, the particularities of its manifestation must be understood through close attention to the social, material, and symbolic aspects of the masculine roles and identities of the young men participating in wage labor. Interestingly, Samburu accounts of wage labor center to an unusual degree around issues of food: Wage laborers go to help their families eat, to allow themselves to eat, or to remove the burden of feeding them from their families. The extent to which this constitutes the "real" reason for labor migration, rather than a justificatory account that serves to mask true motivations, is debatable (Holtzman 1996). What is more important to this chapter, however, is the extent to which this explanation meshes with the roles and identities of Samburu junior males who are the principal labor migrants. The "economic need" for food that drives wage labor is, I argue, constituted through the cultural construction of junior males in relationship to their domestic groups, particularly in their capacity as female-centered sites of food allocation.

Nutritional shortfalls are a real aspect of contemporary Samburu life, but who is affected by them, who should respond, and how they should respond is constructed in a social and cultural space in which gender plays a central organizing role. Where food access for all is problematic, for young men it is particularly tenuous. Key rituals that serve to initiate murran into manhood concern food, and fundamental to the masculine identity of murran is distance from domestic consumption, particularly in time of want. These aspects of masculine identity, I argue, centrally shape both objective aspects of migratory wage labor and cultural understandings of them. In making this argument, I will further suggest the relationship of labor migration to other traditional and recently adopted activities for young men—cattle raiding, long-distance herding, and boarding school—which, despite fundamental differences both among these and between these and wage labor, coalesce around the shared characteristic of removing young men from domestic food allocation from which they are culturally prescribed to be apart.

BACKGROUND

The Samburu are seminomadic pastoralists of north-central Kenya. Closely related to the better-known Maasai, they speak a mutually intelligible dialect of Maa. Historically, the Samburu have been among the wealthiest known livestock keepers, and have survived almost exclusively on the products of their animals (Spencer 1965, 1973). Samburu social organization is characterized by an age set system, the most striking feature of which is the institution of murranhood. For a period of seven to fourteen years following initiation, young men live as murran, bachelor-warriors, who may not marry and should distance themselves from domestic life. Until recently, no agriculture was practiced, and pastoralism was the sole economic pursuit. Wide-ranging transformations concomitant with integration within the colonial and independent Kenya state—characterized most strikingly by a widespread decline in the herding economy—have forced many Samburu in recent decades to augment pastoralism with nontraditional pursuits. In well-watered areas this has included, for some, small-scale agriculture; for many women, brewing has become an important means to augment pastoral income (Holtzman 1996,

1997; Straight 1997). The new economic activity with perhaps the most broad-ranging importance, however, is wage labor, principally migratory. In labor histories conducted with 1,127 Samburu men in four locations in Samburu district, 51.8 percent of adult males had participated in migratory wage labor at some time, with 26.3 percent actively doing so at the time of research. Wage labor is undertaken predominantly by younger men, either murran or, to a lesser degree, junior elders, a substantial percentage of whom were still unmarried at the time of the research.

Migratory wage labor is a relatively recent development, particularly in its current form. During the colonial period, wage labor was largely avoided by most Samburu. In the 1920s and into the 1930s, "native" employees in the district were largely Turkana who—in stark contrast to Samburu—were even alleged to sneak onto conscripted Samburu road gangs in hopes of gaining future employment (CPK 1934). Local employment in the game department and police increased in the 1940s and 1950s, though movement of Samburu outside the district was highly restricted due to its designation as a "special and closed district." Small numbers of Samburu were allowed to travel to work on European-owned farms in neighboring Laikipia District, though this was looked down upon by most Samburu as being the purview only of individuals from impoverished families of poor reputation. More widespread was employment as soldiers in the King's African Rifles, though accounts are conflicting concerning the extent to which this was voluntary, at least until the late 1950s (Holtzman 1996).

Participation in wage labor increased significantly following independence. Restrictions on movement were eliminated, and education also increased considerably. Although Samburu continue to have rather low educational levels, a limited knowledge of Kiswahili can be a significant help in gaining employment outside the district. In addition to these factors that facilitated Samburu entrance into the wage labor market, the need to seek employment became more pressing, as Samburu pastoralism suffered a variety of setbacks beginning in the years just prior to independence. A severe drought struck in 1961, which devastated Samburu herds. In the mid-1960s, the "Shifta war" resulted in widespread raids by heavily armed Somalis deep into Samburu territory. In the 1970s, Turkana "Ngoroko" bandits caused similar disruptions in the western parts of the district. Finally, in approximately 1976, an East Coast Fever epidemic spread down from the highest areas of the Leroghi plateau, devastating Samburu herds.

As Samburu have been increasingly pushed to seek employment, urban networks have developed to help migrants find jobs and to provide housing and social support while they seek work. Of perhaps greater significance, however, is the extent to which migratory wage labor has become perceived as normal. Among the Kimaniki age set, initiated in 1948, few worked outside the district as murran, except in the armed forces or police. Those who did seem to have come from poor families that not only lacked animals, but the skills and discipline to manage livestock properly. Among the next age set, the Lkishilli, initiated in 1960, participation by murran increased significantly and became fairly widespread. With the Lkirroro (initiated in 1976), however, participation in wage labor became the predominant pattern, with 81.8 percent of Lkirroro having engaging in wage labor at some time. In this context, wage labor has become a normal (though not required) part of murranhood.

CONTEMPORARY MIGRATION PATTERNS

Data on current and past wage labor were collected through a series of surveys and interviews administered between March 1992 and July 1994. Between April 1993 and February 1994, complete labor histories were collected for 1,127 jurally adult males (murran and elders) in four sites in Samburu district. All adult males in these four sites were surveyed (except for a small number who refused to be interviewed or were not available and had no close relative who could provide the information). Whenever possible the individual would be interviewed himself, but if he was living outside of the district or was not available upon repeated attempts, a close relative was surveyed on his behalf. Respondents were asked to list the type, location, and dates of all employment, including short-term employment and closely related nonwage labor activities (such as engaging in the livestock trade) that they are currently engaged in or have been engaged in in the past.

Samburu are employed within a range of jobs, though generally low-skill and requiring little education. Samburu recognize significant distinctions between different forms of employment, as became apparent in initial interviews concerning employment. The response of one Samburu elder is typical in this regard. Upon my asking him *"Itajinga lkasi?"* ("Have you been employed?" Literally "Have you entered work?") he cheerfully replied, *"Aa aa, lenkaina ake."* ("No, just manual labor.") Employment (*lkasi*, from the Kiswahili *kazi*) is seen by many Samburu as referring only to relatively good, steady employment—for instance, in the police or army. Local wage labor, particularly if it was short in duration, is typically not seen as *lkasi*. Long-term migratory wage labor in a nonprestigious job might also not be reported as *lkasi*. Although if specifically asked, people would universally agree that these were *lkasi*, many did not take it seriously enough to cite it as past employment. Hence, in order to get a full account of labor histories, it was necessary to include an extensive battery of questions aimed at eliciting all types of wage labor: "Have you worked?" "Have you done contracts?" "Have you ever been to Nairobi?" etc.

By far the most desirable job is in the military or police. Ten percent of adult men had been a soldier or policeman at some time, with 4.7 percent actively doing so at the time of research. There is a long history of Samburu in these professions, and many Samburu view being a soldier as their "natural" job. Although these typically do not require a great deal of education, they are relatively well-paying, offering steady work and a range of lucrative benefits. In recent years these benefits have been magnified for a small but notable minority of Samburu who have been sent on UN Peacekeeping Missions to Namibia and the former Yugoslavia, where they have earned wages on an international scale. There is also considerable prestige associated with admission into the army in particular, and the annual army recruitment in Maralal is a major spectator event, drawing both potential recruits and interested onlookers from around the district. Because of the prestige associated with the army, it was not uncommon for informants to spin fanciful stories concerning how they were almost taken at army recruitment or were taken but for some reason had to leave during training. There are negative connotations to these jobs, however, somewhat akin to the Luo notion of "bitter money" (Shipton 1989). There is a widespread belief that despite the lucrative nature of these jobs, soldiers and police never amount to anything—they are too pampered, never think of the future, and (in the case of police) are subject to the curses of those people who their jobs require them to harass. Ex-soldiers have the reputation of having short, drunken lives following retirement, though in actuality this is certainly far from universal. A smaller percentage of men (2.1 percent) are employed in professional work, both within and without the district—for instance as teachers or civil servants. For some, economic and social involvement in the home community remains high, but for the handful of Samburu who have positions that would rank them among the Kenyan social elite, involvement in the home community is relatively low.

By far the most common job, though somewhat less desirable, is being a watchman (*lashumeni*), usually in Nairobi. Of the total sample, 38.2 percent had been a watchman at some time, with 35.3 percent of the total sample having done so outside the district. Half of all current Samburu wage laborers (50.1 percent) were watchmen, such that 18.1 percent of the adult male population were watchmen at the time of the research. Although Sperling (1987) noted some negative connotations to this type of work, the only complaint I commonly heard regarding it was that the pay was generally quite low. Wages were typically on the order of 2,000 Kenya shillings per month ($30–$70)[1] though sometimes considerably lower, and occasionally higher. Work as a watchman has the advantage of being relatively easy to obtain. Although people occasionally have difficulty finding work, as a rule they get it in a relatively short period of time. Access to watchmen jobs is facilitated by the large number of Samburu already employed in them. They can assist newcomers in finding openings and can provide food and housing while they are looking for work. Frequently jobs may be found when a friend, relative, or age-mate decides to go home for a leave. In these cases a person will be called in to fill the job and will hold it until the other person returns. At times, these temporary jobs may turn into permanent ones.

This description holds generally for most other types of low-skill migratory work as well, such as herders and other farm/ranch work. These are, however, generally lower-paying and less sought after by most Samburu. The most common destination for labor migrants is Nairobi, though Mombasa and tourist areas on the Kenyan coast are also common. On the coast, however, the patterns are somewhat different. Many who go to the coast are not, in fact, formally employed but are "beach boys," whose means of livelihood is selling ornaments or spears. By and large, those who go to the coast are murran, though junior elders who have experience on the coast may continue to go for some time as elders. Similar to the young men of Gambia that Paula Ebron (1997) describes, the primary goal of these young Samburu men is not work per se, but rather to seek out a "*Mzungu* wife"—that is, a white girlfriend.

Some Samburu also work locally, though the dynamics are rather different and largely outside the scope of this chapter. Typically, local work is sporadic, low-paying, and of short duration—for instance, aiding in the construction of shops or fencing, or weeding agricultural plots. Exceptions to this are men employed as watchmen or with other duties at local shops, schools, or missions. Murran typically will not work locally, particularly in menial work, because it would be embarrassing to them. This is particularly the case if the work is performed in the open, and in full view of current or potential girlfriends in particular.[2] Some murran, however, might be seen as essentially locally self-employed as middlemen in the livestock trade.

In the total sample, 26.3 percent of adult males were living outside the district for the purposes of wage labor, with 51.8 percent having done so at some time, with rates of both being highly dependent on age. Labor histories were quite similar across the four communities, though current employment patterns differed somewhat. Rates of wage labor were essentially identical among the three communities where agriculture was not a central component of the local economy, ranging from 37 to 40 percent of adult males. In two of these, however, there were significant opportunities for local employment, such that migratory wage labor was at 28 percent of the local population in each. In the third (where only one man was employed locally), almost all wage labor was migratory, with 35 percent of adult males away for purposes of wage labor. Wage labor was much lower in the highland community, where agriculture was a central part of the local economy—24 percent were employed, and only 12 percent engaged in migratory wage labor. Among the total sample, migratory wage laborers averaged a lifetime duration of 71.3 months, with a median duration of 48 months.

Age, Masculinity, and the Cultural Construction of Wage Labor

Given the widespread practice of Samburu wage labor, it is important to in some way account for this process and its characteristics. Clearly, political economic factors are the central driving force behind Samburu labor migration in the historical and contemporary contexts. Widespread migratory wage labor developed in the context of the impoverishment of the Samburu pastoral economy, and some relationship continues to exist between wealth and participation in wage labor. This is, however, more of a threshold effect than a linear relationship. Members of the wealthiest families migrate at relatively low rates, as their labor is needed at home and resources are sufficient. Apart from this relatively small minority, migration rates actually vary little by wealth.

Samburu explanations for wage labor were examined through a series of semistructured interviews focusing primarily on men's experiences concerning marriage and employment, as well as general issues of social change. Interestingly, informants steadfastly maintained that the only really significant factor behind employment was problems experienced in getting food at home; that is, the person seeking employment (or in some cases, his family) was not getting enough to eat, and he was, therefore, forced to seek employment. Some informants would agree that migrants sometimes had other reasons—a desire for excitement, to join friends, or to escape a bad home situation.[3] Yet these other factors were cited as relatively unimportant reasons, and indeed characterized often as a kind of nonreason. When asked why migrants seek work, a typical response was "Some go because of (food) problems, others go out of recklessness." To go for some other cause was constructed, in essence, as going without cause.

Food issues are not a surprising reason for Samburu migration, given the widespread poverty that currently characterizes contemporary Samburu life. Yet, at the same time this only partially addresses key aspects of the migration process, both in its objective characteristics and Samburu subjective understandings of it. Food (or other economic) issues are not uncommon forces behind migration in many contexts, yet the migration patterns produced are not identical. Among WoDaaBe for instance, rural-urban migration is a common response to seasonal food deficits, yet migrants include both men and women of varying ages (White 1986). Among the Samburu, in contrast, wage labor is almost exclusively the domain of young men—murran, and to a lesser degree junior elders (approximately 20 percent of whom are unmarried, and hence still functionally are murran).[4] Why, then, do young men go to seek work? How is this related to constructions of their identity as men? What other practices may wage labor be related to? What are the meanings associated with wage labor and related practices?

A central argument that I will make is that wage labor must be understood in relation of these young men to their domestic groups. This is not to say that wage labor is an aspect of a household decision-making process. Migration is regarded as an individual rather than a group decision, and no quantitative or qualitative evidence suggests any type of coordinated family strategies concerning wage labor. No household characteristic—apart from exceptional wealth—affects migration patterns, and there are no household determinants concerning patterns of remittance. In short, wage labor must be understood as fundamentally an individual process but one constructed through the relationship of migrants to their domestic groups. Specifically, those who are most likely to migrate—junior males—are constructed as being largely outside of domestic economy—entitled to certain resources when these are adequate, but expected to look elsewhere when a household lacks the resources to support them.

Fundamental to an understanding of this process is a consideration of the cultural construction of the masculine identities of young Samburu men, particularly as these define their appropriate relationships to their domestic groups. Samburu masculine identity is fundamentally created in relation to the domestic sphere, particularly in regard to food. As Samburu males move from youth to murran and from murran to elder, a key aspect of their transformations is their shifting relationship to practices of food consumption, defined in relation to the house (*nkaji*), which is the domain of women. The rituals that serve as performative acts to induct a youth into murranhood are specifically concerned with eating practices, and they sever in fundamental ways his relationship to his mother and to her house as the source of his sustenance. The key ritual act that defines one's transition to full murranhood is a youth's dissolution of his relationship with his mother in her role as the provider of food, and his general acceptance of the *lminong* (prohibitions) that prescribe that he may eat no food seen by women.[5]

Although the most dramatic aspect of male initiation is the circumcision ceremony itself, upon completion of this a youth, though no longer truly a boy, is neither yet a true murran. Only at the end of this period of approximately a month is he inducted into full murranhood through a separate series of rituals. A full discussion of these rituals is beyond the scope of this chapter. However, these rituals culminate in the new initiate breaking an ox bone with his club. He takes half of this broken bone back to his mother, telling her that he is now returning what she has given him, and that he wants nothing more from her. From this point further the murran's eating behavior is governed by the *lminong* of murranhood, and he must no longer eat in his mother's house nor, more generally, eat any food that has been seen by women. These prohibitions typically continue throughout the seven to fourteen years of murranhood and several months into marriage, at which time *lminong* are reversed through the re-creation of the role of domestic food giver in the person of his wife (Holtzman 1996, 1999b).

The eating practices dictated by *lminong* are not simply a symbolic manifestation of the murranhood, but are in fact central to its constitution, and relatedly to the constitution of male identity more generally. No other offenses put a murran's social status to such deep questioning as those concerning food.[6] Being unusually rude or disrespectful, violent, or ill-tempered in inappropriate ways, being a notorious thief, or even possessing some degree of cowardice will certainly have a negative effect on a murran's status in the community but will not raise the question of whether he is a true murran. By being a *lanya ndaa*—someone who has eaten food seen by women, or who eats without his age-mates—the claim of being a murran is itself put into question.

Samburu explanations for the institution of murranhood frequently center around elements of domestic organization and eating practices. Generally this is framed around a need to reduce competition for food in the home. Because murran are stronger and have greater food needs than children, the presence of murran competing for food is seen to likely have deleterious effects on the children. Further, as murran are expected to be able to take care of themselves, they should leave children to feed comfortably in the home. The quintessential mode of eating for murran is to consume meat in the bush with other murran, either provided from the herds of the families of one or more murran or from livestock taken in a cattle raid. The frequency of this practice has, however, been significantly reduced by the contemporary decline of the livestock economy. A murran maintains some rights in the food of his mother's home—a portion of milk for him and his age-mates should be set aside—but if resources become inadequate in the home, he will be expected to find food elsewhere.

These aspects of the construction of Samburu masculine roles and identities are a crucial component of wage labor, both in its material aspects and its cultural interpretations. From this perspective, wage labor may be seen as a mechanism for removing young men from domestic economy, as is sanctioned by the construction of their masculine role. Seen in this light, wage labor might be readily compared with both traditional and newer practices. Clearly it bears similarities to the long-standing practice of murran fending for themselves in times of want—through cattle theft or other means. Interestingly, however, it also bears similarities to the recent practice of attending boarding school. Although both labor migration and boarding school attendance are complex processes for which no single explanation is wholly sufficient—and which differ in many ways—they share the characteristic of drawing young men out of household food allocation.

PATTERNS OF AGE, LOCATION, AND REMITTANCES

Quantitative data illustrate that wage labor is, indeed, practiced disproportionately by young men—murran, and to a lesser degree, junior elders. Overall participation in wage labor by murran in the total sample was 38.6

percent.[7] This is not significantly higher than participation by junior elders—33.5 percent. However, it is important to note that approximately 20 percent of these junior elders were still unmarried (hence, functionally murran). Moreover, much larger numbers of junior elders were in the army and police—jobs that one would not readily give up, and the social dynamics around which are considerably different. If one excludes from the sample those employed in these prestigious jobs, employment figures are reduced to 21.7 percent for junior elders compared to 35.2 percent of murran.

Analyzing age-based migration patterns by location also produces intriguing insights into the dynamics of wage labor. Moru, the most remote of the four communities, provides the fewest confounding variables. Approximately a four- to six-hour walk to any road, it is purely pastoral, with no opportunities for local employment and no education. Because it is the most traditional and the richest in terms of livestock, one might predict that migration rates here would be the lowest, but in fact, the inverse was the case. Rates of labor migration were highest, and there was the strongest tendency for migration to be the practice of the young. No one, in fact, older than a junior elder was living outside of the community. Moreover, rates of migration for murran were nearly three times that of junior elders (62.2 percent versus 23.3 percent) and are even more striking when one considers that, when high prestige jobs are excluded, the rate for junior elders falls to 14.6 percent but the rate for murran is unchanged.

The rates of murran employment are, in fact, far in excess of the other communities studied. Two of the other three communities, however, approach the rates found in Moru if one considers both school and employment—that is, if what one measures is being outside of domestic economy, rather than employment per se. Since those murran who are in school are in boarding school, they are eating elsewhere even if they are not employed. In Lodokejek, a highland community marginal for agriculture, 48.6 percent of murran were engaged in migratory wage labor. However, between school and labor migration, 62.6 percent of murran are outside of domestic food allocation. In Malasso, a highland community where agriculture is important, rates of migratory wage labor are overall considerably lower. Very few murran—only 12 percent—were migrants at the time of research. However, including those at school, 56 percent were outside of the domestic food allocation (see table 11.1).[8]

Remittance data also are indicative of wage labor by young men being an alternative to their participation in the household economy, rather than a component of it. A survey concerning patterns of remittances was administered in April–June, 1994 to households in Lodokejek and Lodungokwe, which included 117 members employed outside the district. This survey was undertaken within the context of the resurvey of these areas and was administered to all families who were found to have members employed. Data were

Table 11.1.   Migratory Wage Labor and Absence from Domestic Food Allocation
by Location

	Murran Engaged in Migratory Wage Labor	Murran Outside of Domestic Food Allocation (Wage Labor and Boarding School)
Moru (lowland, fairly remote; traditional; wealthy in livestock)	62.2	62.2
Lodokejek (highland; marginal for agriculture; relatively accessible)	48.6	62.5
Malasso (highland; high productivity for agriculture; relatively accessible; less traditional)	12	56
Lodungokwe (lowland; divided between pastoral areas and impoverished/ sedentarized pastoralists near small center)	34.7	38.4[1]

[1]This anomalously low figure may be due to overall underreporting of nonresident murran, which had presented itself in the context of the research in this community.

collected concerning the size and frequency of remittances, the method used
to remit wages to the home community, division of remittances within the
household, distribution of money when the wage laborer came home to visit,
and any livestock purchases made by the wage laborer in the past two years.
As this survey was conducted fairly late in the research period, it was possible
to check its accuracy with reference to significant quantities of less detailed
quantitative data on remittances, as well as understandings of wage labor derived from a range of qualitative data. Since it is not possible to measure actual remittances but only reported remittances, figures cannot be assumed to
be absolutely precise, but their consistency with other data do indicate a good
degree of accuracy. Remittances may be slightly overreported for wage laborers who "send money every month" but who do so through less reliable
means.[9] Inaccuracy in that quantitative data is, in a sense, itself a type of qualitative data concerning the type of relationship that the household asserts exists between them and the migrant. That is, whether money actually comes
every month, he is regarded as someone who sends the family money on a
consistent monthly basis.

Overall, reported remittance rates were fairly high. Annual remittances
ranged from between 0–30,000 Kenya shillings (approximately 70 KSh/dollar),
with an average of 5,926 and a median of 4,800. Among all wage laborers, 79.5
percent were reported to have remitted funds at some time during the year,

and 64 percent were reported to have remitted a monthly average of at least 200 shillings ($3–$4). Though this amount is not particularly substantial, even by local standards, it does indicate a commitment on the part of the wage laborer and can benefit a Samburu household, given its relatively low cash needs. Interestingly, purchase of livestock—an obvious use of wages by pastoralists—was very low; only 37.1 percent of wage laborers were reported to have purchased any livestock in the previous two years, and only 19.8 percent had purchased at least one cow or its equivalent.

As scholars frequently view migration as part of family strategies, consideration was made concerning the relationship of wage labor to household strategies, with the expectation of there being a relationship between wealth and remittances. Two scenarios were considered. In one, it was expected that because of greater household need, wage laborers from poorer households would be more likely to remit and to do so in greater quantity. Alternatively, members of wealthier households might remit more, as they had stronger material interests in maintaining the well-being of the household and in garnering good favor in the household in order to ensure their long-term stakes in its assets.

In fact, there was no correlation between wealth and rates or amounts of remittances. Additionally, no aspect of household composition, such as murran per household or wage laborers per household, was found to have any effect on rates or amounts of individual remittance. Nor did education have any effect on patterns of remittance. These findings are, in fact, not inconsistent with informants' statements, who generally characterize wage labor migration in individual, rather than collective, terms. The only variable that, in fact, was found to have a significant effect on remittances was marital status. Among married men, 87 percent were found to have remitted funds at some time during the year, with 72.5 percent remitting on average at least 200 shillings per month. In contrast, only 68.8 percent of unmarried men remitted funds at some time, with only 50 percent remitting an average of 200 shillings or more per month (see table 11.2).

The most significant factor, then, in structuring migratory wage labor concerns the relationship of migrants to their domestic groups. Those engaged in wage labor are disproportionately those who are expected culturally to be outside of domestic food consumption. In regard to remittances, whether a migrant sends home money, how often, and how much,

Table 11.2.   Patterns of Remittance by Marital Status

	Unmarried	Married
Percent remitting wages	68.8	87
Percent remitting at least 200 KSh/month ($3–$4)	50	72.5

are significantly affected by the relationship of that migrant to his domestic group—as an elder, responsible for overseeing the well-being of the family, or as a bachelor expected to distance himself from domestic life generally, and particularly in times of want.

CONCLUSION

Samburu explanations for migratory wage labor, with their emphasis on food shortages as a driving force behind wage labor, would seem to suggest a singularly economic explanation for contemporary widespread labor migration. While recognizing the centrality of contemporary poverty in driving migration, I have suggested that the specific forms of migration, and Samburu understandings of them, must be understood through a close reading of Samburu social processes, particularly the construction of the masculine identities of the young men who are the principal participants. The importance of food in shaping wage labor is an economic motivation constructed within a particular social context, with the principal participants coming from sectors of society whose identities are centrally constructed around the expectation that they will be distanced from domestic life and remove themselves entirely from domestic food allocation in times of want. There is the expectation that if there is nothing for them at home, murran should be able to take care of themselves and are indeed morally obligated to do so. In the past, herding with families with larger numbers of livestock, or eating livestock stolen on cattle raids, could play that role. Now, among these young men, whose masculine identity is intimately tied up with distance from the domestic sphere, going to eat in Nairobi may also fill this role.

ACKNOWLEDGMENTS

Research was funded by the National Science Foundation (Award # 9211892), the Population-Environmental Dynamics Project, the Center for African and Afro-American Studies of the University of Michigan, and the Rackham Graduate School. The Institute of African Studies of the University of Nairobi provided institutional affiliation in Kenya. Thanks go to Tom Fricke, Raymond Kelly, Conrad Kottak, Maxwell Owusu, Bilinda Straight, Pat West, and participants at the Society for Economic Annual Meetings, who have provided invaluable comments on earlier versions of this chapter.

NOTES

1. The research period was a time of wildly fluctuating exchange rates in Kenya, such that accurate conversion into dollars is problematic.

2. Murran-age youths who do not adhere to traditional practices will sometimes, however, work locally in all types of work.

3. For migrants with considerable education this was also cited as a factor. They went to school in order to get employed, and so they did.

4. Though these are beyond the scope of this chapter, there are many complexities in making demographic arguments for a society like the Samburu. Samburu demography is culturally constructed to an unusual degree at a number of levels. Social age is determined by the age set within which one has been initiated, and biological age is not considered notable (except if someone is very old or very young for his or her age set). There has always been a significant range of ages within any particular age set, and for various reasons this range has expanded in recent years. Among seminomadic pastoralists like the Samburu, the demography of particular areas is also constructed through choice—certain types of families are better suited for the opportunities presented by different areas. Consequently, there is significant demographic variation among the four communities, which may have effects on overall patterns of wage labor.

5. For comparative perspectives on transformations in male initiation of the relationship of youths to women, see, for instance Herdt 1982, Godelier 1986, Guttman 1997.

6. Perhaps the only worse offense might be (almost unimaginably) displaying pain during circumcision. Although a discussion of the parallels between these two domains is outside of the scope of this chapter, the extent to which each is based in a denial or control of negative bodily sensations might be fruitfully explored.

7. This figure excludes murran who were still in school, which would preclude them from seeking employment.

8. The fourth community, Lodungokwe—a lowland community encompassing both a small center of largely stockless pastoralists and more outlying pastoral areas—does not show a significant increase by including murran in school (who are very few). The overall figure for murran outside of domestic economy in Lodungokwe may be affected by the fact that in this community I experienced the greatest methodological difficulties in regard to the underreporting of nonresident murran.

9. For instance, 62.5 percent of respondents say that they receive their remittances through friends of the wage laborer who are returning from the place of work. Given the distances involved, difficulties in transport, and the possibility that a friend may not be going home every month, it seems unlikely that remittances could be that consistent. The effect of this on the amount of total annual remittances for any member of that group is unlikely to be greater than 25 percent—when people missed remittances on any type of regular basis, it was reported—and is probably lower, given that a missed remittance could be made up by a larger future remittance. Although the reported annual remittance for this group may be slightly high, it is grossly accurate.

REFERENCES

Amin, Samir. 1974. *Modern Migrations in Western Africa*. London: International African Institute: Oxford University Press.

Cliggett, Lisa. 2000. "Social Components of Migration: Experiences from Southern Province, Zambia." *Human Organization* 59(1): 125–35.

CPK (Colony and Protectorate of Kenya). 1934. *Samburu District Annual Report*. Nairobi: Kenya National Archives.

Du Toit, Brian. 1975. "A Decision-Making Model for the Study of Migration." In *Migration and Urbanization: Models and Adaptive Strategies*, ed. by Brian Du Toit and Helen Safa, 49–76. The Hague, Netherlands: Mouton Publishers.

Ebron, Paula. 1997. "Traffic in Men." In *Gendered Encounters*, ed. by Maria Grosz-Ngate and Omari H. Kokole, 223–44. New York and London: Routledge.

Glick Schiller, Nina, Linda Basch, and Cristina Blanc-Szanton. 1992. "Transnationalism: A New Analytic Framework for Understanding Migration." In *Towards a Transnational Perspective on Migration*, ed. by Nina Glick Schiller, Linda Basch, and Cristina Blanc-Szanton. *Annals of the New York Academy of Sciences*, vol. 645.

Godelier, Maurice. 1986. *The Making of Great Men: Male Domination and Power among the New Guinea Baruya*. Cambridge, U.K.: Cambridge University Press.

Guttman, Matthew. 1997. "Trafficking in Men: The Anthropology of Masculinity." *Annual Review of Anthropology* 26: 385–409.

Haenn, Nora. 1999. "Community Formation in Frontier Mexico: Accepting and Rejecting New Migrants." *Human Organization* 58: 36–43.

Herdt, Gilbert. 1982. *Rituals of Manhood: Male Initiation in Papua New Guinea*. Berkeley: University of California Press.

———. 1994. *Guardians of the Flutes: Idioms of Masculinity*. Chicago: University of Chicago Press.

Herzfeld, Michael. 1985. *The Poetics of Manhood: Contest and Identity in a Cretan Mountain Village*. Princeton, N.J.: Princeton University Press.

Holtzman, Jon D. 1996. *Transformations in Samburu Domestic Economy*. Ph.D. dissertation, Ann Arbor, Mich.: University of Michigan.

———. 1997. "Gender and the Market in the Organization of Agriculture among 'Pastoral' Samburu of Northern Kenya." *Research in Economic Anthropology* 18: 93–112.

———. 1999a. "Cultivar as Civilizer: Samburu and European Perspectives on Cultivar Diffusion." *Ethnology* (Monograph Series No. 17) 11–19.

———. 1999b. "Household, Gender, and Age Sets: Domestic Processes and Political Economic Organization among the Samburu of Northern Kenya." In *At the Interface: The Household and Beyond*, ed. by Nicole Tannenbaum and David Small, 41–54. Lanham, Md.: University Press of America

Hondagneu-Sotelo, Pierrette. 1994. *Gendered Transitions*. Berkeley: University of California Press.

———. 1999. "Introduction: Gender and Contemporary U.S. Immigration." *American Behavioral Scientist* 42: 565–76.

Hutchinson, Sharon. 1996. *Nuer Dilemmas: Coping with War, Money, and the State*. Berkeley: University of California Press

Mayer, Philip. 1961. *Townsmen or Tribesmen?* Oxford, England: Oxford University Press.

Meillassoux, Claude. 1981. *Maidens, Meals, and Money*. New York: Cambridge University Press.

Nolan, Riall. 1986. *Bassari Migration: The Quiet Revolution*. Boulder, Colo.: Westview Press.

Portes, Alejandro, and Robert Bach. 1985. *Labor Journey: Cuban and American Immigrants in the U.S.* New York: Academic Press.

Sassen, Saskia. 1988. *The Mobility of Labor and Capital*. Cambridge, England: Cambridge University Press.

Shipton, Parker. 1989. *Bitter Money*. Washington, D.C.: American Anthropological Association.

Spencer, Paul. 1965. *The Samburu: A Study of Gerontocracy in a Nomadic Tribe*. London: Routledge and Kegan Paul.

———. 1973. *Nomads in Alliance*. Oxford, England: Oxford University Press.

Sperling, Louise. 1987. "Wage Employment among Samburu Pastoralists of North Central Kenya." *Research in Economic Anthropology* 8: 167–90.

Stone, Glenn. 1997. "Predatory Sedentism: Intimidation and Intensification on the Nigerian Savannah." *Human Ecology* 25: 223–42.

Straight, Bilinda. 1997. *Altered Landscapes, Shifting Strategies*. Ph.D. dissertation, Ann Arbor, Mich.: University of Michigan.

White, Cynthia. 1986. "Food Shortages and Seasonality in WoDaaBe Communities in Niger." *Institute of Development Studies Bulletin* 17(3): 19–26.

12

Women and Work in a Brazilian Agricultural Frontier

Andréa D. Siqueira, Stephen D. McCracken, Eduardo S. Brondizio, and Emilio F. Moran

INTRODUCTION

A frontier area is not only a new biophysical environment but a new socioeconomic context for those arriving; every individual becomes part of new communities, social networks, associations, and conflicts. Agricultural frontiers also tend to be areas where there is an unbalanced demographic distribution, usually favoring men, and to be areas characterized by abundance of land and scarcity of labor. Migrating to a frontier area thus may bring new gender roles to women, as a variety of socioeconomic and cultural factors interact with one's household composition and previous experiences.

Studies of women in agricultural frontier areas in South America have demonstrated that women there may increase their participation in agricultural and household decision making in comparison to their previous situation in their places of origin (Meertens 1993). In other cases, women will experience a diminished access to resources and land security and an increased trend toward "housewifization" (Townsend 1993a), that is, the confinement of women to reproductive roles and house chores. Being confined to the household realm thus tends to decrease women's power within the household economic life and in the public arena (Townsend 1993a, 1993b). However, as diverse as other aspects of frontier life, gender roles vary within and across frontier settlements. Indeed, the few but important studies on women and frontier areas in South America confirm that inferences about women's work and role in frontier areas need to be grounded in empirical research.

In this chapter, we examine the role of gender in the patterns of family labor allocation and land use among household farmers on a frontier area in the Brazilian Amazon settled since 1970. Our discussion is based on data collected among 402 households in Eastern Amazon in 1998.[1] More specifically, we focus on the microlevel determinants of female household heads' participation in agricultural activities. In this chapter, "female household head" refers to the woman who is married to the male head. We examine the degree to which these women's participation in farm activities is affected by individual and household characteristics, household size and composition, patterns of land use (e.g., annual crops versus perennial crops versus pasture) and extrafamilial labor. Moreover, by taking into account variations in household characteristics, women's characteristics (e.g., age, education), and their economic role (e.g., off-farm activity) we examine the participation of female household heads in the household decision-making processes that relate to farm activities, household expenditures, and use of birth control methods. In presenting and discussing our results, we aim to contribute to the broader literature on women and agricultural work, especially to the still-sparse literature on women and frontiers and on joint household heads.

This chapter is organized in three parts. First, an overview of women and frontiers in South America and background information on Brazilian Amazon colonization are presented. The second part includes a description of the study area, data collection and processing, and results. The third part discusses the key topics of the chapter: household characteristics, land use and labor allocation, and women's participation in farm work and household decision making. Lastly, our conclusions are presented.

WOMEN AND FRONTIERS IN SOUTH AMERICA

As a family settles on a new farm lot, the initial work in a tropical frontier necessarily involves clearing of the forest, an activity requiring a large amount of labor. Subsequent land clearing will be affected by the households' consumption needs and production possibilities, in addition to macroeconomic opportunities (markets, credits, prices) and constraints (lack of roads, transport costs, market). As members of the household age and household composition changes over time, household farm strategies also change.

Migrating to a frontier may bring new roles to women but can confine them to old ones. Reviewing the sparse bibliography on women's agricultural participation in frontier areas in South America, Townsend (1993a, b) observes that overall there are at least four different processes changing gender roles in these areas. In her area of study (a Colombian frontier area), despite scarcity of labor, women are mainly confined to their reproductive roles when they migrate to the frontier. This pattern is further reinforced by the out-migration of daughters to cities, the unbalanced sex ratio favoring men, and a pattern of land distribution in which land is titled to men rather than to the couple. Out-migration of daughters to urban areas in search of off-farm jobs and/or schooling tends to increase the workload of female household heads in a sociocultural context in which domestic chores are considered women's work. Meertens studied another contrasting frontier area in Colombia, where women have increased their participation in agricultural activities and in household decision-making processes. Most of the women in this area claim that their reproductive roles are more valued there than they were in their place of origin (see Meertens 1993). In this second Colombian example, women also play an important role in cattle raising.

The differences between these two Colombian frontier areas are partially explained by cultural differences as well as by economic ones. Meertens's study area was mainly composed of Andean family households, which are reported to be much more egalitarian (see also Hamilton 1998; Weismantel 1988) than Latino ones. As well, livestock and trading are considered women's activities rather than men's among Andean groups. Moreover, the second site is also an area where profits generated by coca cultivation have supported the expansion of livestock activities, permitting women to remain in charge of several activities—agriculture, ranching, and trading. Yet most women in lowland Bolivia, despite also coming from an Andean culture, lose control over land resources and also the income generated by trading and care of small livestock when moving to a frontier area (Townsend 1993b). Finally, Townsend mentions the example of the eastern Brazilian Amazon, where "housewifization" of women is a consequence of capitalist penetration in the farming system, as exemplified by the work of Lisansky (1979; see also Hecht 1985b). In this case, the expansion of cattle ranching activities, greatly supported by government development programs, displaced smallholders, making both men and women landless. The few jobs available in the ranch enterprises are mainly for men, as cowboys. In this context, women mainly work as housewives, maids, and, in many cases, prostitutes (see Lisansky 1979; Hecht 1985b).

Our study case differs from the ones described by Lisansky and Hecht. It is a settlement of smallholders who have secure land rights. Although there has been an increase in pasture area during the past fifteen years, this activity is undertaken mainly by small and medium farmers. Thapa, Bilsborrow, and Murphy (1996) present a similar case on the Ecuadorian Amazon frontier, also in a settlement of small farmers. Drawing on data collected from 367 households in 1990, they discuss the determinants of women's agricultural participation. The authors show that women's participation in farm activities is strongly affected by the type of land use. Greater areas in perennial crops (coffee) rather than pasture increase the odds of women's labor. Perennial crops require a greater amount of household labor, including women's. Women with previous experience in agriculture are more likely to work on the farm, as well as those who have more children, even young ones. As pointed out by the authors, women here are doubly burdened by their reproductive and agricultural roles. Off-farm income has a strong effect of reducing women's participation in agricultural work, and higher educational level and an older age of the women have only a slight effect on their work loads (ibid., 1327). In summary, "housewifization" of women in this context is a function of land use (pasture versus coffee), higher income, and age. In the one side, pasture expansion, although leading to higher deforestation, lessens women's farm workload; conversely, it may undermine their decision-making status within the household. Less participation in agricultural activities can indeed represent less workload and higher economic and social status for women; however, the consequences of "housewifization" for the internal dynamics of the households' decision making are still not well understood.

GOVERNMENT COLONIZATION PROGRAMS IN THE BRAZILIAN AMAZON

In 1970, with financial loans from international banks and multinationals, the Brazilian government started a new "modernization" program for the country as a whole, and especially for the Amazonian region (see figure 12.1). The *Plano de Integração Nacional* (PIN—The National Integration Plan) was created and was aimed at interconnecting the various parts of the Amazon region internally and with the rest of the country while promoting human occupation

FIGURE 12.1
Study area.

of the region through government colonization programs. These colonization plans were a conservative political alternative to calls for land reform by landless people from several parts of the country. They were also a strategy to guarantee national security, as it was believed that Brazil could lose this part of its national territory and its natural resources to foreign countries if it was not fully occupied and developed. A major feature of the national integration plan was the construction of a road network to integrate Amazonia from east to west by means of the Transamazon Highway, and from north to south by means of the Cuiabá-Santarém Highway (in parallel to the Belém-Brasília connection). Once completed, these roads would then connect most of the region, previously accessible only by boat or airplane. The first part of the plan proposed colonization by small farmers and livestock investment, each one fulfilling a role in a larger scheme that involved roads, urbanization, and multipurpose infrastructure without any precedent in Brazilian history.

The colonization plan aimed to settle 100,000 families (over five years) in 100-hectare lots along the Transamazon Highway. According to the plan, small farmers would specialize in food crops for the first three years, and each year colonists would plant more of their land in permanent and cash crops, such as coffee, sugar, black pepper, and *guaraná*. Each colonist was to also leave 50 percent of his total area as a reserve of untouched forest. The bulk of candidates for colonists were landless people from the Northeast region and other parts of the country. Candidates from the South and Southeast regions, the most economically developed regions of Brazil, were considered essential as "cultural brokers," as governmental planners believed colonists from these regions could bring innovative technologies to the area and would help "modernize" colonists from other parts of the country. A large family, literacy, and extensive agricultural experience were also considered essential characteristics of the preferred candidates. They were also supposed to be no younger than twenty-five or older than forty-five years old (Moran 1981). Land titles were given to men and rarely to women.[2]

In order to attract settlers, the government promised a variety of benefits, such as bank credits for subsistence crops, six months of minimum wage at the time of arrival, food subsidies, school, medical and health services, and transportation, storage, and commercialization of the colonists' production (ibid.). However, the first three years of colonization were considered unsuccessful, and they were interpreted as a failure of the plan (Browder 1988; Hecht 1985a; Ianni 1979; Mahar 1979; Velho 1972; Schmink and Wood 1992; and others). "Blaming the victim" (Wood and Schmink 1979) is probably the best expression to describe the end of the government-directed small farmer colonization projects in the Amazon. After 1974, the government changed its focus away from small farm colonization and started financing large enterprises, such as cattle ranches, mining, lumber, and large-scale agriculture for export. Fewer and fewer resources were devoted to colonization projects. By

1980, INCRA (*Instituto Nacional de Colonização e Reforma Agrária*)—the governmental institution responsible for the colonization project—recognized that fewer than 8,500 families had been settled in the Amazon through their program (Miranda 1990: 41).[3]

THE STUDY AREA

The Altamira region was one of the most important foci of the governmental colonization program briefly described above. The majority of farm properties were initially settled between 1970 and 1978, but farm plot occupation continues up to this date. The first colonists were located in plots of about 100 ha (500 m × 2,000 m) along the highway or along its feeder roads, and close to Altamira town. New waves of migrants moved further down the highway or further along the feeder roads. The pattern of colonization exhibits the "fish-bone" pattern of many land-distribution colonization projects in the Brazilian Amazon (Moran, Brondizio, Mausel, and Wu 1994).

In Altamira, which is among the oldest agricultural frontiers in the Amazon, about 30 percent of the original colonists remain on their plots. These farmers have settled permanently, breaking the pattern of continued migration. In many ways, the region of Altamira is no longer a frontier but a settled group of people, although new plots continue to be opened at the ends of feeder roads by farmers driven by their own needs and efforts as well as by farmers settled by governmental agencies.[4]

Our study area was defined by a group of approximately 3,800 farm lots arranged according to different adjacent projects implemented by INCRA during the past thirty years. It cuts across the municipalities of Altamira, Brasil Novo, and Medicilândia, in the state of Pará (see figure 12.1) and encompasses an area of about 355,000 ha stretching from about 18 km to 140 km of the Transamazon Highway west of Altamira town.

In terms of economic and land use/agriculture phases, the history of the study area can be divided into three main periods: 1972–1978: subsistence crops such as rice and beans were dominant in the region; 1978–1988: highest production of perennial crops such as cocoa and black pepper; 1988–present: cattle ranching expansion and coexistence with other farming activities (Castellanet, Simões, Celestino Filho 1994).

DATA COLLECTION AND DATA PROCESSING

In 1998, two survey instruments were used to collect information from a sampled 402 farmers, about 1,986 individuals, along the Transamazon Highway and its feeder roads. One was related to household social and demographic characteristics, and the other was related to environmental characteristics and land use history of the property. The fieldwork team consisted of a pair of interviewers. The former survey was usually carried out with the female household head, and the latter with the male household head. The interviews lasted about 1.5 to 2.5 hours each, with additional time taken to visit the lot and for conversations addressing issues raised during interviews.[5]

We used a stratified sampling frame for selecting properties and households according to the time of settlement. Farm plots were selected according to exploratory data analysis of five land use/cover maps from aerial photomaps (1970 and 1978) and from Thematic Mapper satellite images (1985, 1988, 1991, 1996), on which a property grid layer was overlaid (see also McCracken et al. 1999; Brondizio et al. 2002). The descriptive and statistical analysis presented here was carried out using the Access database program and Stata 5.0 statistical software.

For this chapter, several models were developed to analyze the microlevel determinants of female household heads' participation in domestic tasks and childcare, gardening and yard animals, cattle care, agricultural tasks, and off-farm activities.[6] We coded each activity with a 1 if the woman was involved in the activity and a 0 otherwise. We then carried out a multivariate logistic regression analysis on individual characteristics of these women, their households, household composition, agricultural emphasis, and the use of extrafamilial labor. We present our results in the form of odd ratios in table 12.1. Values above 1 imply a greater probability of women's participation in any of the listed activities, and values below 1 represent less probability associated with the variable category. We aggregated the agricultural activities into two groups, "moderate" and "heavy." The former includes harvesting, planting, weeding, and product processing (making manioc flour, drying cocoa and/or pepper). The latter includes felling trees and burning. Our category of "cattle care" also includes milking.

We ran six models, one for each of the activities, each considering four sets of independent variables.[7] Our first set of independent variables included women's demographic characteristics, such as age, age squared, and years of schooling. As discussed above, among the study population, domestic and agricultural activities are associated with gender and age. We predicted that years of schooling would affect women's participation on agricultural work and off-farm activities; that is, that more years of schooling would lower a woman's probability of working in agricultural activities and raise her probability of having off-farm activities. The second set of variables included some characteristics of the women's husbands and of their household, such as whether her husband worked off-farm, the regional origin of the household, and religion. Our third set of variables included those related to household composition. We predicted that a higher number of children under age five in the household would reduce women's participation in farm and off-farm activities. Overall, we also predicted that a higher number of females age fifteen to nineteen in the household would decrease female head participation in domestic tasks, and the number of males age twenty to fifty-nine would decrease her probability of working in agricultural activities. Our last set of variables included characteristics of the farm and extrafamilial labor. We predicted that a greater percentage area of the farm in crops (annuals and perennials) would increase women's probability of work, and a greater percentage area in pasture would decrease women's demand to work in the farm. We predicted that extrafamilial labor would decrease women's workload in farm activities but would increase their domestic tasks.

RESULTS

Household Characteristics

Out of our sample, about 34 percent of the farmers obtained their land directly from INCRA. Those arriving after 1975 usually bought their farms from earlier colonists or farmer owners, and a small number obtained their properties through inheritance. The time of occupation of the farm plots varied between one and thirty years, including a few (thirty-two farmers) who were in the area before the colonization program (i.e., before 1970). The mean area occupied by our informants is 95.5 ha lots, but there are a few larger landholders (*glebistas*) who have areas of 300–500 ha.

The observed pattern in family size and organization is much closer to the current Brazilian urban pattern than the one expected for a rural area; that is, it is nuclear and relatively small. The current household size is about 4.6 individuals, with a minimum of one individual and a maximum of thirteen. The mean size of household families is similar across all households; that is, there is no significant difference in household size among new and older settlers. Longer-residing settlers tend to have a slightly larger household (<1975 = 5.9) than new ones (>1990 = 4.5). About 80 percent of households are nuclear, formed by a couple or widow and their/her children. In a few cases, we found couples without children, and we found only three cases of single individuals. Couples without children typically were older, and their children had already left the household. In the few cases observed of multiple families living under the same roof, it is usually a son who brings his wife to live in his parent's house, and rarely a daughter who brings her husband to her parents' house. Fewer still are the cases of extended household families, and most of them are formed by an old couple or widow and their/her grandchildren. Marriage is the most common reason (about 68 percent) to leave a parents' household, for both sexes, followed by search for jobs (about 11 percent), schooling (about 10 percent), and other reasons (11 percent). On the other hand, most of the incorporation into the household is through birth (about 72 percent), with marriage representing only about 10 percent.

Figure 12.2 shows the current age and sex distribution of the study population. Overall, this figure illustrates two main processes taking place in the

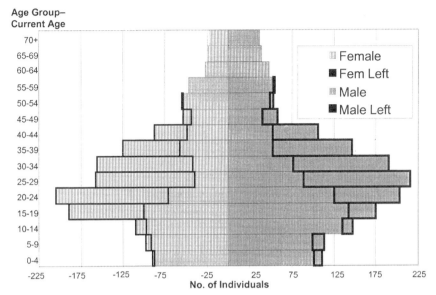

FIGURE 12.2
Current age/sex of household members (original and joining) and children who left home.

area: the general aging process of households on this by-now thirty-year-old frontier, and the overall loss of labor from children as these become young adults and leave their natal households, especially women. In all five-year age intervals there are more males than females, which seems to be a common pattern observed in frontier areas. The sex ratios of children remaining on the farm by age group indicate a differential gender pattern associated with staying in or leaving the domestic unit. Within the age group of fifteen to nineteen, more than half of all daughters no longer live on the farm lot, compared to only 16 percent of their brothers. By age twenty to twenty-four, 81 percent of daughters have left, but 41 percent of sons remain (see also McCracken, Siqueira, Moran, and Brondizio 2002).

   The current sex ratio is much more balanced than the initial migration flows to the region. Figure 12.3 illustrates what could be called the "gender selectivity process" on arrival. When arriving on the frontier, households are composed of predominantly young members, with slightly more males than females. This pattern of male-dominated sex ratios, even among infants and children and continuing through the early twenties, suggests selectivity in favor of male labor as families migrate to the frontier. Among children who were age fifteen to nineteen when their parents arrived on the farm lot, only 80 percent of daughters, compared to 94 percent of sons, came as part of the household. Among the age group twenty to twenty-four, 73 percent of sons

**Age Group–
Arrival Age**

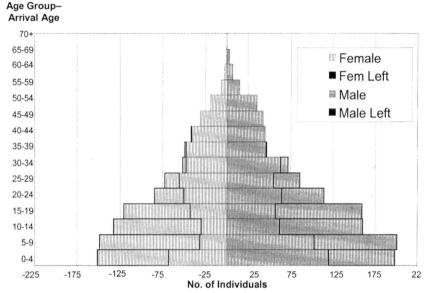

FIGURE 12.3
Age/sex of household members at time of arrival.

came with their parents to the farm, but only 45 percent of daughters did the same.

As discussed elsewhere (see McCracken and Siqueira n.d.), perhaps the most important change taking place at the level of household is related to reproductive behavior, that is, the number of children and women in their reproductive years (age fifteen to forty-nine) are bearing. For the past twenty years, we observed a rapid fertility decline among the women in this frontier area. For the late 1960s and early 1970s, fertility for women in the study was very high, on the order of ten to eleven children per woman. However, these higher levels of fertility observed were probably inflated by the fact that government programs favored large families in the initial years of colonization. By the 1980s, fertility declined to about 4.3 children, and we observed that by age twenty-nine, more than 40 percent of women had been sterilized by tying their tubes. Sterilization is a common procedure elsewhere in Brazil, but it was unexpected on a frontier area due to the reported scarcity of labor. The current fertility rate is still between 0.5 and 0.8 children above the rest of rural Brazil, but the decline in fertility observed here is as important as the rapid fertility decline observed in the country as a whole.

Land Use, Labor Allocation, and Women's Participation in Farm Work

Cattle ranching activities are nowadays considered the most profitable and economically secure activity by local farmers. As in other parts of the Amazon

Basin (and not only in Brazil), small farmers regard cattle ranching as the primary avenue to a higher economic and social status (Pichon, Marquette, and Murphy 2002). Independent of their time of arrival in the region, the majority of our informants (about 95 percent) have some area in pasture, whose extent varies between 1 and 370 ha. The mean area in pasture is about 41 ha, and the mean size of the cattle herd is sixty-eight head. However, the variation among farmers is also great, with a minimum of 1 and maximum of 2,000 animals. Most of the cattle production is for beef, and only about 20 percent of our informants sell fresh milk or cheese to local urban markets. Compared to agricultural activities, cattle demand a smaller amount of labor once the pasture is established. Care of cattle is usually a men's activity that starts at an early age. For the ten- to fourteen-year-old age group, about 61 percent of male household members are already involved with cattle care, but only 18 percent of females in this age interval are. The highest percentage of male participation in this activity is in the fifty to fifty-four age group, with about 79 percent of all males carrying out this activity. The highest female participation rate in caring for cattle is in the age group of thirty-five to thirty-nine years old (about 29 percent) (see figure 12.4). Milking cows is also a men's activity, but women are usually involved in the process of making cheese. The overall women's participation in milking/caring for cattle is 22 percent.

Our data suggest that on farms that have an emphasis on cattle ranching, female household heads tend to work less in agricultural activities and more in domestic tasks (table 12.1). This sign of "housewifization," however, is not statistically significant. The number of men between twenty and fifty-nine years old in the household does affect women's participation in cattle care. For each man between twenty and fifty-nine years old in the household, the probability of the female household head working in this activity decreases by about 35 percent. We clearly observe a "work substitution" effect; that is, those men are doing work that otherwise the female household head would probably do. Presence of temporary labor also suggests a reduction in women's cattle work, but it is not statistically significant. If her husband has an off-farm activity, a woman's probability of cattle work decreases enormously (82 percent according to our analysis).

Felling forest and/or cleaning off secondary succession vegetation from a pasture area are mainly done by men and involve heavy physical labor, given the fact that most of these activities are done manually. Pasture maintenance is done all year long and also often with the help of hired labor. Fifty percent of our sample households reported hiring temporary labor to carry out this job and/or to help them do it. The overall women's participation in these "heavy" agricultural tasks is 32 percent. The number of children in the household under five years old and the number of men between twenty and fifty-nine years old reduce a female's probability of working on this activity by 40 percent and 30 percent, respectively (table 12.1). It seems that care of children

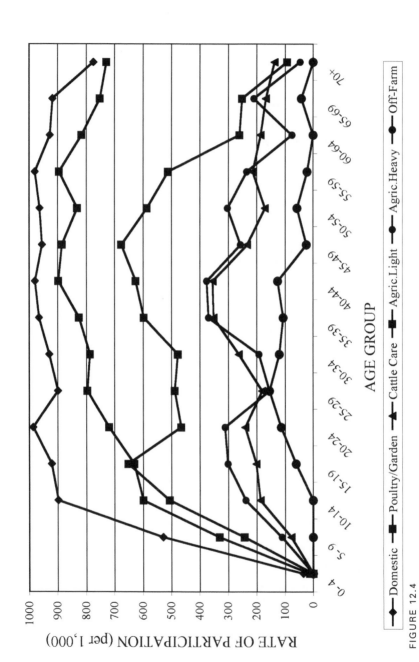

FIGURE 12.4

Age-specific rates of participation, females, Transamazon Highway.

Legend: ◆ Domestic — ■ Poultry/Garden — ▲ Cattle Care — ▶ Agric.Light — ● Agric.Heavy — ● Off-Farm

RATE OF PARTICIPATION (per 1,000)

AGE GROUP

Table 12.1.   Predictors of Female Household Head Work in Domestic, Farm, and Off-Farm Activities

	Odds Ratios					
Dependent Variables Independent Variables	Domestic Task	Gardening Poultry	Cattle Care	Agric. Tasks "Moderate"	Agric. Tasks "Heavy"	Off-Farm Activity
Individual						
Age	1.1112	1.1043	1.1768**	1.2534**	1.1574*	1.4265*
Age-squared	0.9984	0.9987*	0.9980**	0.9971**	0.9979**	0.9954**
Yrs. 0f Schooling	1.1276	0.8685**	1.0130	0.9430	0.8870	1.5069**
Household/Husband						
Husband Works Off-Farm	0.0892**	0.3065*	0.1806**	P0.4882	0.9258	2.7811
Regional Origin of HH: NE	0.6290	0.8692	0.6236*	1.0155	0.9801	1.2512
Religion of HH: Protestant	0.5023	0.7962	1.0249	0.8384	0.9021	4.9140**
Household Composition						
No. of Children <5	0.8180	0.9404	1.2261	0.8865	0.6183**	0.8594
No. of Children 5–9	0.9436	1.2801	0.7777	0.9359	0.9651	0.7523
No. Females Age 10–14	0.7236	0.8197	1.1480	1.4305	1.4355	0.5127
No. Males Age 10–14	(Not Incl.)	1.1569	1.0670	1.0943	1.2713	0.7008
No. Females Age 15–19	0.4178	0.8816	1.0398	1.0124	1.1757	2.2788*
No. Males Age 15–19	1.3335	0.9146	0.9539	0.9661	0.7204	0.6624
No. Females Age 20–59	1.5971	1.0859	0.8810	1.1539	1.7984*	3.3424**
No. Males Age 20–59	0.8783	0.9331	0.6669**	0.8172	0.6778**	0.7816
Farm Activities/Extrafamilial Labor						
Agricultural Emphasis: Pasture	1.6963	0.9369	1.5091	0.7216	0.7510	2.4467
HH Hires Temporary Labor	0.3768*	0.6586*	0.6736	0.3977**	0.3073**	0.1490**
HH has Sharecroppers/Perm. Workers	0.3295	1.0570	0.8251	0.7208	0.3350**	0.1545*
Number of Observations	274	372	372	372	372	372
Chi-sq.	25.07	27.93	33.68	79.05	72.12	55.53
Prob > chi-sq.	0.0686	0.0458	0.0092	0.0000	0.0000	0.0000
Pseudo R2	0.2056	0.0896	0.0818	0.1535	0.1698	0.3217
Log Likelihood	−48.4366	−141.8898	−180.9884	−217.9833	−170.3585	−58.5289

Note: ninety-eight cases not used in model 1 as var. m10-14 explains activity completely.
*0.05 level; **0.10 level.

under five is less compatible with heavy agriculture work than with other domestic and farm activities, and men between twenty and fifty-nine years old in the house substitute for the female household head in this work. On the other hand, a higher number of women between twenty and fifty-nine increases the probability of a female household head working in this activity by 80 percent. As expected, the presence of temporary and permanent/sharecropper labor reduces her probability of work to about 70 percent. Education also has a significant negative effect on this work, reducing it by about 12 percent for each year of schooling.

Groves of cocoa, a perennial crop, exist on 35 percent of the farms. On average the groves have about 14.2 ha or about 14,200 trees, with a minimum of 0.10 ha and maximum of 50 ha. Unlike pasture, cocoa cultivation requires better soils (alfisols—*terra roxa*). A cocoa tree takes about three to five years to produce fruit, and it can continue for several decades. The maintenance of the grove requires continuous pruning of the trees. Once fruit production is established, the annual harvesting and breaking of the cocoa shell to extract its seeds are the activities that require the greatest amount of labor. At this time, all members of the household, including children, take part in this activity. The seeds are then dried in the sun in order to take off the fruit pulp. Once dried, the seed is sold to local brokers. The overall women's participation in cocoa production is about 65 percent. Among those cultivating the fruit, the use of sharecroppers is becoming a common arrangement—16 percent of all sample farmers had sharecropper arrangements at the time of the interview.

Currently, black pepper is only cultivated by 13.4 percent of all informants, on an average area of about 1.6 ha, with a minimum of less than 1 ha and a maximum area of 6 ha. Pepper does not require fertile soil, but the cost of inputs is high. It starts to produce after about two years. Prices in the market are increasing recently, but the farmers' response to this stimulus may be slower due to higher investments and recent experience with a fungus disease (*Fusarium s. piperi*). Like cocoa, the harvesting and drying of pepper involve all household members, regardless of gender (figures 12.4 and 12.5).

Annual crops, such as rice, beans, corn, and manioc, are cultivated by 50 percent of the farmers, and most of this production is currently for household consumption. The reported mean area in annuals was about 2.5 ha, with a minimum of less than 1 ha and a maximum of 40 ha. Slash and burn is the method used and usually is carried out by men, but the weeding and harvesting involve women of different age groups.

Besides age, the only other variable that has a significant effect on a female household head's participation in "moderate" agriculture is the presence of hired labor in the farm. This reduces the female head's probability of work in this activity by about 60 percent. Our data suggest that the presence of sharecroppers reduces women's participation as well, but these results are not statistically significant (table 12.1).

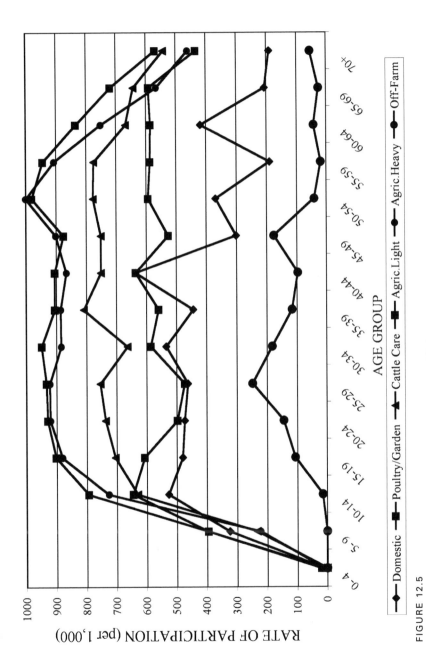

FIGURE 12.5

Age-specific rates of participation, males, Transamazon Highway.

A combination of several agricultural activities, such as slashing, burning, planting, weeding, harvesting, drying cocoa and pepper, and processing manioc flour involves about 60 percent of all members of the study households. Usually household members are involved in more than one activity. This participation in the farm's activities starts at an early age, about ten years old for both sexes. For the age group ten to fourteen, between 20 percent and 70 percent of male children and between 5 percent and 40 percent of female children are helping their parents and/or siblings in one of these activities. In all age groups, men's participation is higher than women's (figures 12.4 and 12.5).

About 40 percent of the study households have home gardens, and 97 percent of them raise yard animals, both mainly for household consumption. Women tend to be responsible for caring for small animals more often than their male counterparts (see figures 12.4 and 12.5), but there are no clear gender differences in gardening activities, and they tend to increase for both men and women with age. The overall women's participation in these activities is 62 percent.

Increased age and years of schooling affect women's participation in gardening and care of yard animals; in both cases they tend to work less in these activities (table 12.1). The husband's off-farm activity reduces the wife's probability of working by 70 percent in gardening and with poultry, and the presence of temporary labor reduces her probability by about 35 percent of working in these activities. Household sex and age composition do not have any effect on female head's participation in these activities.

Domestic chores (including house cleaning, preparing food, and childcare) are carried out predominantly by women, although at young ages both boys and girls are involved in these household-related activities. The overall women's participation is 92 percent. The gender gap tends to increase with age. More than 90 percent of young teenage girls are engaged in domestic tasks, and approximately 90 percent of boys are involved in agricultural activities. These participation rates also illustrate the importance of children's labor to the overall economy of colonists' households (figures 12.4 and 12.5).

Last but not least, years of education, household composition, and presence of extrafamilial labor do have strong effects on the probability that a female household head has an off-farm activity (table 12.1). For each year of schooling, a female head's probability of having an off-farm activity increases about 50 percent. The number of other women between ages fifteen and nineteen and twenty to fifty-nine years old in the household increases her odds of taking up an off-farm activity about two and three times, respectively, so these women in the household are probably substituting for the female household head in other farm and domestic activities. On the other hand, the presence of temporary and permanent labor on the farm decreases the female head's probability of having an off-farm activity by about 85 percent in both cases.

Being a Protestant also increases her probability almost five times, but its significance needs further investigation to be understood.

Household Decision Making

Based on information provided by the female household heads related to decision making in the household, we now examine which individual and household characteristics may affect household dynamics. We focus on three subjects: what to cultivate in the farm, household expenditures, and use of birth control; and how these decisions are affected by women's participation in agriculture work, women's participation in off-farm activities, schooling, husbands' age, and the current capital index of the household.[8]

What to plant and how are decisions that farmers have to face periodically. About 50 percent of the husbands make these decisions by themselves, in comparison to only 6 percent of wives. However, about 26 percent of women reported making these decisions as a couple, and 18 percent as a family (table 12.2). Do women who take part in agricultural activities tend to have higher participation rates in deciding what to plant and how? The percentage of women who decide by themselves is almost two times higher for those who work in agricultural activities than for those who do not work, but even so the percentage is low (about 7.5 percent and 4 percent, respectively). Joint decisions increase slightly for women who work in comparison to those who do not work, from about 22 percent to 29 percent. However, for both groups of women, decisions made by husbands by themselves are still high, about 50 percent.

More than on farming, about 60 percent of households make joint decisions on how to allocate household resources. About 27 percent and 3.5 percent of husbands and wives, respectively, decide by themselves about household expenditures. Women who work on off-farm activities make more decisions about this subject than those who do not work (8.7 percent and 3 percent, respectively) (table 12.2).

The age of the male household head affects the percentage of their joint decisions. The older the husband is, the lower the percentage of couples making joint decisions. Younger husbands seem to be more democratic than older ones. However, for older husbands, family participation in decisions related to the farm activities increases, to almost three times greater than for younger ones. This is probably related to the household developmental cycle, in which farm activities also include grown children (usually male children). In relation to birth control, the situation is reversed. Wives with young husbands have a higher percentage of joint decisions, and wives of older ones (age fifty or older) tend to make this decision as individuals, and less often as a couple (table 12.2).

Current household capital index (see note 8) also has a positive effect on the percentage of joint decisions. The higher the capital index, the higher

Table 12.2. Percent Participation on Decision Making in the Households, Altamira Region, Brazil, 1998

What to Plant	Agriculture		Age of the Household Head			Years of Schooling				Capital Index		
	Yes	No	<30	35–49	50+	None	1–3	4	5+	High	Medium	Low
Wife	7.34	3.97	7.41	2.7	7.25	7.14	3.14	11.27	5.17	0	11.43	5.13
Husband	49.32	50.33	51.85	54.95	46.38	47.62	49.06	47.89	56.9	41.38	47.14	51.28
Couple	28.96	21.19	33.33	35.14	18.84	25	22.01	30.99	31.03	55.17	25.71	22.71
Family	13.57	23.18	7.41	7.21	25.6	17.86	25.16	8.45	6.9	3.45	12.86	20.15
Others	0.81	0.66	0	0	1.45	2.38	0	1.4	0	0	1.43	0.73
DK	0	0.67	0	0	0.48	0	0.63	0	0	0	1.43	0
Total (%)	100	100	100	100	100	100	100	100	100	100	100	100

Spend Money	Off-Farm		Age of the Household Head			Years of Schooling				Capital Index		
	Yes	No	<30	35–49	50+	None	1–3	4	5+	High	Medium	Low
Wife	8.7	3.15	1.85	2.7	4.35	4.76	3.77	1.41	3.45	3.45	5.71	2.93
Husband	17.39	27.79	27.78	21.62	29.95	29.76	27.67	28.17	20.69	20.69	27.14	27.84
Couple	73.91	59.89	70.37	71.17	52.66	52.38	59.12	61.97	75.86	72.41	55.71	60.81
Family	0	8.6	0	4.5	12.08	11.9	8.81	8.45	0	3.45	11.43	7.69
Others	0	0	0	0	0.97	1.19	0.63	0	0	0	0	0.73
DK	0	0.57	0	0	0	0	0	0	0	0	0	0
Total (%)	100	100	100	100	100.01	100	100	100	100	100	100	100

Birth Control			Age of the Household Head			Years of Schooling				Capital Index		
			<30	35–49	50+	None	1–3	4	5+	High	Medium	Low
Wife	—	—	14.81	19.82	22.22	30.51	24.46	17.46	27.66	16.67	22.64	25.97
Husband	—	—	3.7	6.31	3.86	5.08	5.76	7.94	2.13	8.33	5.66	5.19
Couple	—	—	68.52	60.36	43.48	57.63	60.43	68.25	70.21	70.83	60.04	61.47
Family	—	—	0	0.9	0.48	0	0.72	1.59	0	0	6	0.87
Others	—	—	0	1.8	8.21	6.78	8.63	4.76	0	4.17	5.66	6.49
DK	—	—	12.96	10.81	21.14	0	0	0	0	0	0	0
Total (%)	—	—	100	100	100	100	100	100	100	100	100	100

the percentage of couples taking joint decisions on all three subjects. Women in households with a low capital index tend to decide alone more often about their contraceptive methods than those with a higher capital index (table 12.2). However, the higher the capital index, the lower is the percentage of family participation in decisions on farm crops and household expenditures.

DISCUSSION

We still observe a demographic imbalance in this thirty-year-old frontier area in favor of men. Women are more likely to leave their family households at earlier ages than men, usually for marriage and schooling. Young men are more likely to stay on the farm longer, which seems to be a household "labor retention" strategy in an environment with a reported scarcity of labor. Women's reported access to land rights through inheritance is also inferior to that reported for their male siblings. On the other hand, families tend to invest in girls' schooling more often than boys'; and education increases women's off-farm activities and income. Investing in women's education seems to also be a household strategy of spreading risks while broadening the household's social and economic network and/or a way of compensating women for their decreased access to land.

The rapid fertility decline observed among women in the frontier and decisions regarding use of contraceptives are also positively correlated with women's level of education and reported better access to health care. These young generations are breaking a pattern of large rural families, even in the face of a scarcity of labor. Patterns of household size, composition, and fertility rates are close to urban ones. Most families are nuclear and relatively small. The rapid fertility decline observed among women in this frontier area is similar to the rates observed in Brazil as a whole, illustrating a narrowing of rural-urban patterns. The overall point to be made is that the Brazilian fertility decline was marked during a relatively short period of time and has been unexpectedly no less important on the frontier area than in the rest of the country. Women's perspectives on their reproductive behavior often included considerations related to children's education costs. Fewer children mean more chances that the family may be able to afford paying for their educations. Despite recognizing the importance of children's participation in farming activities, education is perceived as a key factor for the children and also for the family's economic success in the future. Most of the women interviewed expect their children to study, and ideally, to succeed in a paid job occupation in the city. Urban life, usually perceived as the possibility of having a permanent job, is considered far easier than making a living on the farm. Women also mentioned a reduced number of children as a way to improve their well-being. For them, fewer children mean less workload. It also means better health, as bearing many children was mentioned as a way to decrease women's vitality (field notes 1998, 2001).

Family labor is still essential for colonists' farming activities. Women from different age groups participate in all household economic domains, including domestic chores, farm labor, and off-farm activities. Their participation in different activities varies according to the developmental cycle of their household, their years of education, the presence of extrafamilial labor, and also the farming system.

Age is a consistently important predictor of women's pattern of participation in farm work, except in the case of domestic tasks. That is, women of all ages are involved in domestic activities. What we observe is a curvilinear relationship between age and these activities. It is lower below twenty years, increases in the twenties and thirties, and decreases again after the forties.

A few variables explain most variations in the amount of domestic tasks performed by female household heads. When the husband has some off-farm activity and the household hires temporary labor, women work significantly less in the house. Off-farm activities usually indicate a higher cash flow in the household, and thus greater probability of hiring outside labor. However, in our model we predicted increased demand for domestic services in the presence of hired farm labor, as women tend to cook for hired workers, but not the reduction of work that we observed. Our data suggest that young women between ages fifteen and nineteen are the ones taking the responsibility for domestic tasks instead of the female household head.

Our data also suggest that on farms with emphasis on cattle ranching, female household heads tend to work less on farm activities and more on domestic tasks. When we control for the current household composition, we observe that female household participation in agricultural activities is not statistically significantly affected by the type of land use. The number of male household members twenty to fifty-nine years old has an important correlation with the probability of women's participation in agricultural activities, independently of whether there is an emphasis on perennial crops, annual crops, or pasture. The presence of hired labor is also an important factor in reducing the number of agricultural activities women carry on.

Women's participation in "heavy" agricultural tasks is affected by household composition, the presence of temporary and permanent extrafamilial labor, and women's education, but in different directions. Extrafamilial labor, the presence of male adult household members, women's education, and having children under five years old in the household all decrease women's participation in heavy agricultural tasks. It seems that only in this case is women's participation in farm activities affected by the presence of young children in the household. On the other hand, the presence of other female household members increases the female household head's participation in heavy agricultural work. We observe a "work substitution" effect in which these women are "filling in" for the female household head in her domestic duties.

Female household head participation in "moderate" agricultural activities is more predictable. Besides women's age, the only other variable that has a negative effect on female household head participation on "moderate" agriculture is the presence of hired labor. A woman's participation in off-farm activities is clearly related to her educational level, but also is related to the availability of other women in the household able to "substitute" or "fill in" with expected gender roles. This includes the presence of family members or extrafamilial labor. Off-farm activities for women often include teaching and health care positions, as well as trading.

On decisions related to the management of the farm, such as what to plant and how, women's participation tends to be limited. On the other hand, women are more actively involved in the allocation of household resources. In both cases, however, a woman's decision-making power reflects her level of involvement in direct agricultural labor, her contribution to household income, her level of education, and her proximity to her kinship network, providing a safety net of social and economic support in the frontier area.

CONCLUSION

Overall participation rates in farm and domestic activities suggest strong patterns associated with age, gender, and years of education, but they also vary according to household composition and/or socioeconomic conditions, and they vary over the course of farm development. In general, young adolescent girls take on domestic duties early on, and are involved with caring for younger children and tending to animals. Teenage boys are incorporated into caring for cattle and milking, areas in which they are twice as likely to be involved as their female counterparts. Gender differences are most pronounced throughout adulthood in activities such as felling trees, burning, and weeding, in which men are three to four times more likely to be involved. The gender differences are less in harvesting and processing agricultural products, in which a larger share of women is involved. The pattern of participation in these agricultural activities typically declines for women in their early twenties as they begin childbearing, increases again, and then declines after age forty-five. For men, participation in these activities reaches a high level by their early twenties, remains high through their early fifties, and then steadily declines. However, in the making of manioc flour or in gardening near the house, there are no clear gender differences.

Regarding women's activities and household labor arrangements, we observe at least three different processes taking place in households in the frontier area. First, women are still fewer in number by comparison to men, even in this already thirty-year-old frontier. They tend to leave their parents' household at earlier ages than their brothers. They leave to marry or go in search of higher education. For those who stay, we observe that types of land use and family composition affect women's overall participation in farm activities. Second, both cattle ranching and annual crop production are significantly associated with reduced farm work among women, compared to women living on farms with a predominant emphasis on perennial crops such as cocoa. We may say that an emphasis on cattle raising leads to "housewifization" of women, a pattern similar to that described by Thapa, Bilsborrow, and Murphy (1996) in a frontier area in the Ecuadorian Amazon. Third, we also observe a "work substitution" effect, freeing female heads from the farm and domestic workload. On the one hand, availability of younger male household members as well as hired labor significantly reduces the agricultural workload of women, leading them toward "housewifization," off-farm employment, or on-farm entrepreneurship. On the other hand, a high number of other adult women in the household increases the head's probability of work in heavy agriculture and off-farm activities. Again, we observe a "work substitution" effect. In this case we observe an inverse of "housewifization" for the female household head, as her participation in farm activities increases as younger women in the household are taking up the slack in domestic activities. In summary, domestic chores are predominantly carried out by women (wives, daughters-in-law), but who is taking the greatest share of them varies according the household's composition and its developmental cycle.

Women's participation in agricultural and off-farm activities does have an effect on the decision-making processes taking place inside the households. Women who work in agricultural and off-farm activities tend to have a higher percentage of joint decisions related to farm activities and household expenditures. We may say that a woman increases her bargaining power in the household realm when she undertakes any economic activity. However, more years of schooling, younger husbands, and higher capital index seem to have an independent effect of increasing women's joint participation in all decisions.

Perhaps the explanation for the observed rapid fertility decline among frontier women rests on the broader institutional, economic, and cultural changes taking place in the country as a whole since the late 1950s. Rapid urbanization, the expansion of the consumer society, the extension of social security coverage, the increase in mass communication, and better access to health care are possible causes or incentives for the changes observed in household decisions and women's reproductive behavior of these frontier women. Despite being in a rural environment, people in our study area have been affected by those broad national changes. Reported access to health care in the frontier is usually better than in the woman's place of origin. Exposure to TV is widespread. Most of the people have continual ties with regional urban centers, such as Altamira. Children and teens attend schools in towns; wives and husbands go shopping and market farm produce. Rather than being isolated, these frontier women and men are engaged in urban life in many ways. Rather than being separate worlds, rural and urban areas form a continuum. Women's increased access to education, information, and birth control may be building up a new role for women and reinforcing an ideal of joint households, where men's and women's work alike are considered essential to farm maintenance.

NOTES

1. The data presented in this chapter are part of a broader study that addresses the relationships between household demography and socioeconomic characteristics and the patterns of land use observed at the level of the farmer's individual plot. This was funded by the National Institutes of Health as "Amazonian Deforestation and the Structure of Households: A Georeferenced Approach," with coprincipal investigators E. Moran and S. McCracken, Anthropological Center for Training, Department of Anthropology, Indiana University, 1997–2001, NICHD #9701386A. (See also McCracken et al. 1999; McCracken et al. 2002; Moran et al. 2002; and Brondizio et al. 2002.)

2. Only after the new National Constitution in 1988 were women entitled to receive land tenure rights in government programs of colonization and/or land reforms in Brazil (see Deere and Leon 1999 for further discussion on gender and agrarian reform in Brazil).

3. Yet in 1980 the number of colonists along the Transamazon Highway was estimated as much higher than the official figure, due to "spontaneous" migration to the region that occurred mainly after 1974, when the government interrupted most of its colonization plans (Miranda 1990).

4. At the time of our fieldwork research a new settlement of colonists was underway in our study area. The municipal government of Medicilândia was distributing land at the ends of feeder roads with the technical assistance of INCRA (*Gleba Surubim*) (field notes 1998).

5. In the summer of 2001, about one-third of the households sampled in 1998 were interviewed again, and the first author carried out several in-depth interviews with women regarding their reproductive choices.

6. For the discussions on the predictors of women's participation in domestic, farm, and off-farm activities, we included only the female household heads (n=372), excluding widows, divorced women, and those who did not live on the farms. However, they are included in our original sample and analysis of labor allocation.

7. Previously, we had included in our models variables indicating the socioeconomic status of the household. Those were tossed out because they did not explain any of the differences observed.

8. Current capital indexes were calculated based on the assets (rural property, rural house, urban house, business) the farmer family reported having at the time of the interview. The index ranges from 1 to 3. Higher scores mean a greater number of assets.

REFERENCES

Brondizio, E., S. D. McCracken, E. F. Moran, A. Siqueira, D. Nelson, and C. Rodriguez-Pedraza. 2002. "The Colonist Footprint: Towards a Conceptual Framework of Deforestation Trajectories among Small Farmers in Frontier Amazônia." In *Patterns and Processes of Land Use and Forest Change in the Amazon*, ed. by Charles Wood and Roberto Pooro, 133–61. Gainesville: University of Florida Press.

Browder, J. 1988. "Public Policy and Deforestation in the Brazilian Amazon." In *Public Forest and the Misuse of Forest Resources*, ed. by R. Rapetto and M. Gillis. New York: Cambridge University Press.

Castellanet, C., A. Simões, and P. Celestino Filho. 1994. *Diagnóstico Preliminar da Agricultura Familiar na Transamazônica: Indicações para Pesquisa-Desenvolvimento.* Belém, Brazil: EMBRAPA/CPATU.

Deere, C. D., and M. León. 1999. "Towards a Gendered Analysis of the Brazilian Agrarian Reform." Occasional Papers, Latin American Studies and Caribbean Studies, Storrs, Conn.: University of Connecticut.

Hamilton, S. 1998. *The Two-Headed Household, Gender, and Rural Development in the Ecuadorian Andes.* Pittsburgh: University of Pittsburgh Press.

Hecht, S. 1985a. "Environment, Development, and Politics: Capital Accumulation and the Livestock Sector in Eastern Amazonia." *World Development* 13(6): 663–84.

———. 1985b. "Women and the Latin American Livestock Sector." In *Women as Food Producers in Developing Countries*, ed. by Jamie Monson and Marion Kalb, 51–69. Los Angeles: UCLA African Studies Center and African Studies Association OEF International.

Ianni, O. 1979. *A Luta pela Terra.* Petrópolis, Brazil: Editora Vozes.

Lisansky, J. 1979. "Women in the Brazilian Frontier." *Latinamericanist* 15(1): 1–3.

Mahar, D. 1979. *Frontier Development in the Brazilian Amazon: A Study of Amazonia.* New York: Praeger.

McCracken, S. D., E. Brondizio, D. Nelson, E. F. Moran, A. Siqueira, and C. Rodriguez-Pedraza. 1999. "Remote Sensing and GIS at Farm Property Level: Demography and Deforestation in the Brazilian Amazon." *Photogrammetric Engineering and Remote Sensing* 65(11): 1311–20.

McCracken, S. D., and A. Siqueira. n.d. *Fertility Decline in an Amazonian Agricultural Frontier of Brazil: New Evidence for Old Debates, Population and Development.* Paper presented at the Annual Meeting of the Population Association of America, Los Angeles, California, March 23–25, 2000.

McCracken, S. D., A. Siqueira, E. F. Moran, and E. Brondizio. 2002. "Land-Use Patterns on an Agricultural Frontier in Brazil: Insights and Examples from a Demographic Perspective." In *Patterns and Processes of Land Use and Forest Change in the Amazon*, ed. by Charles Wood and Roberto Porro, 162–92. Gainesville: University of Florida Press.

Meertens, D. 1993. "Women's Roles in Colonisation: A Colombian Case Study." In *Different Places, Different Voices: Gender and Development in Africa, Asia, and Latin America*, ed. by Janet H. Monsen and Vivian Kinnaird, 256–69. New York: Routledge.

Miranda, M. 1990. "Colonização Oficial na Amazônia: O Caso de Altamira." In *Questões sobre a Gestão do Território*, ed. by B. Becker, M. Miranda, and L. Machado, 35–46. Brasilià, Brazil: UNB and UFRJ.

Moran, E. F. 1981. *Developing the Amazon*. Bloomington: Indiana University Press.

Moran, E. F., E. Brondizio, P. Mausel, and Y. Wu. 1994. "Integrating Amazonian Vegetation, Land Use, and Satellite Data." *Bioscience* 44(5): 329–38.

Moran, E. F., E. Brondizio, and S. D. McCracken. 2002. "Trajectories of Land Use: Soils, Succession, and Crop Choice." In *Patterns and Processes of Land Use and Forest Change in the Amazon*, ed. by Charles Wood and Roberto Porro, 193–217. Gainesville: University of Florida Press.

Pichon, F. C. 1996. "Settler Agriculture and the Dynamics of Resource Allocation in Frontier Environments." *Human Ecology* 24(3): 341–71.

Pichon, F., C. Marquette, and L. Murphy. 2002. "Choice and Constraint in the Making of the Amazon Frontier: Settler Land Use Decisions and Environmental Change in Ecuador." In *Patterns and Processes of Land Use and Forest Change in the Amazon*, ed. by Charles Wood and Roberto Porro. Gainesville: University of Florida Press.

Schmink, M., and C. Wood. 1992. *Contested Frontier in Amazon*. New York: Columbia University Press.

Siqueira, A., and S. D. McCracken. 2001. *Frontier Women and the Rural-Urban Continuum: Fertility Decline, Household Labor Strategies, and Schooling along the Transamazon Highway*. Paper presented at the XXIII Annual Meeting of the Latin American Studies Association (LASA), Washington, D.C., September 6–10, 2001.

Thapa, K. K., R. E. Bilsborrow, and L. Murphy. 1996. "Deforestation, Land Use, and Women's Agricultural Activities in the Ecuadorian Amazon." *World Development* 24(8): 1317–32.

Townsend, Janet. 1993a. "Housewifisation and Colonisation in the Colombian Rainforest." In *Different Places, Different Voices: Gender and Development in Africa, Asia, and Latin America*, ed. by Janet H. Momsen and Vivian Kinnaird, 270–77. New York: Routledge.

———. 1993b. "Gender and the Life Course on the Frontiers of Settlement in Colombia." In *Full Cycles: Geography of Women over the Life Course*, ed. by Cindi Katz and Janice Monk. New York: Routledge.

Velho, O. 1972. *Frentes de Expansão e Estrutura Agrária*. Rio de Janeiro, Brazil: Zahar.

Weismantel, M. 1988. *Food, Gender, and Poverty in the Ecuadorian Andes*. Philadelphia: University of Pennsylvania Press.

Wood, C., and M. Schmink. 1979. "Blaming the Victim: Small Farmer Production and Amazon Colonization Project." *Studies in Third World Societies* 7: 77–93.

Index

About the Contributors

Srimati Basu teaches in the Departments of Women's Studies, Sociology/ Anthropology and Asian Studies at DePauw University. Her work has been published in *She Comes to Take Her Rights: Indian Women, Property and Propriety* (SUNY Press, 1999), in the anthologies *Signposts: Gender in Post-Independence India* (Rutgers University Press, 2001), *Religion and Personal Law in Secular India* (Indiana University Press, 2001), *Confronting the Body: The Politics of Physicality in Colonial and Postcolonial India* (2002), and in the journals *Feminist Media Studies, Trouble and Strife,* and *Indian Journal of Gender Studies.*

Aurora Bautista-Vistro is an assistant professor at the Department of Anthropology of the University of the Philippines–Diliman. She received a Fulbright-Hayes doctoral enrichment in 1997–1998 which allowed her to do a specialization in economic anthropology. Her research areas are in Northern and Southern Luzon Philippine communities.

Evelyn Blackwood is an associate professor in the Department of Sociology and Anthropology, Purdue University. She has written several articles on the Minangkabau of West Sumatra. Her most recent book on the subject is entitled *Webs of Power: Women, Kin, and Community in a Sumatran Village* (Rowman & Littlefield, 2000).

Eduardo S. Brondizio is an assistant professor with the Department of Anthropology, assistant director of the Anthropological Center for Training and Research on Global Environmental Change (ACT), and a research associate at the Center for the Study of Institution, Population, and Environmental Change (CIPEC), at Indiana University. His work concentrates on land use change, ethnobotany, commodity markets for forest products, and rural development in

Brazil, particularly in the Amazon region; long-term ethnographic work concentrates on riverine Caboclo communities of the Amazon estuary and colonist farmers of the TransAmazon. His work has contributed to the development of integrative methodologies, such as combining ethnographic and survey research and remote sensing tools. Additionally, his work has been published across anthropological and environmental sources. For more detail, please see his website at php.indiana.edu/~ebrondiz.

Katherine E. Browne is an associate professor in the Department of Anthropology at Colorado State University. Browne's research in the French Caribbean involves the intersection of postcolonial economies, hybrid identities, gendered ideologies, and local engagements with modernity. She is presently heading—with research partner Carla Freeman (Emory University)—a three-year, comparative project in the French, Spanish, and British Caribbean. Data from the pilot phase of this project is the subject of the author's chapter in this volume. Browne has also been awarded funding by NSF to produce a video documentary of Caribbean women entrepreneurs. Browne's work is published in *Human Organization, Gender & Society, Ethnohistory, Research in Economic Anthropology,* and other journals. She is completing a book manuscript for The University of Texas Press about the role of creole identities as well as the French welfare economy in fueling the widespread, cross-class informal economy in Martinique.

Lisa Cliggett (Ph.D., Indiana University, Bloomington, 1997) is an assistant professor of Anthropology at the University of Kentucky, Lexington. Her research and teaching interests include ecological and economic anthropology, social organization, migration and frontier settlement, aging, and anthropological demography, with a regional emphasis on sub-Saharan Africa and the Caribbean. She recieved a Fulbright grant for her doctoral research in Zambia, and held a Mellon postdoctoral fellowship in Anthropological Demography at the University of Pennsylvania before joining the University of Kentucky. Her current research program focuses on migration and environmental change in a buffer zone to one of Zambia's national parks.

N. Thomas Håkansson is a social anthropologist, and specializes in the political-economy of noncapitalist societies. He has done extensive fieldwork in Kenya and Tanzania, and is the author of the book *Bridewealth, Women, and Land: Social Change among the Gusii of Kenya* (Almqvist & Wiksell International, 1988) as well as numerous articles on social organization and regional/global economies in East Africa. He is an adjunct associate professor of Cultural Anthropology, and a research associate at the Division of Human Ecology, Lund University, and the Appalachian Center, University of Kentucky.

Jon D. Holtzman is a cultural anthropologist whose work centers on Samburu pastoralists in northern Kenya, and Nuer refugees in the United States. His research focuses on issues of gender and social change, with particular emphasis on the domestic politics of food. He is also interested in contemporary and historical processes of globalization and transnationalism, and his work grapples with the issues of situating anthropological subjects within broader cultural flows without subjugating their agency and their meanings in the process. His work has appeared in such journals as *American Anthropologist*, *American Ethnologist*, and the *Journal of the Royal Anthropological Institute*. He is the author of *Nuer Journeys, Nuer Lives: Sudanese Refugees in Minnesota* (Allyn and Bacon, 2000). He is currently a visiting assistant professor in the Department of Sociology and Anthropology of Kalamazoo College.

Stephen D. McCracken is a social demographer with interest in health, environment, and population dynamics in Latin America. He received his M.A. in Latin American Studies from the University of Florida and a Ph.D. in Sociology from the University of Texas at Austin. Between 1989 and 1995 he was a professor in the graduate program in Demography at the Center for Regional Planning and Development at the Federal University of Minas Gerais, Brazil. In 1995 he began collaborations with colleagues at the Anthropological Center for Training and Research on Global Environmental Change (ACT), Indiana University, on projects in the Brazilian Amazon. His work has focused on integrating survey data, demographic analysis, and remote sensing through the use of geographic information systems. He currently works on international reproductive health surveys in the Demographic Research and Program Evaluation Team at the Division of Reproductive Health, Centers for Disease Control and Prevention.

B. Lynne Milgram is an associate professor in the Faculty of Liberal Studies at the Ontario College of Art and Design, Toronto, Canada, and adjunct faculty, Faculty of Graduate Studies (Anthropology), York University, Toronto. Her research on gender and development in the Philippines analyzes the political economy of social and cultural change with regard to "fair" trade, women's work in crafts and agriculture, and microfinance initiatives. Her new research explores women's engagement in the secondhand clothing industry and related issues in migration in the northern Philippines. Her recent articles include: "Banking on Bananas, Crediting Crafts: Financing Women's Work in the Philippine Cordillera" (*Atlantis Journal*, 2002) and "Situating Handicraft Market Women in Ifugao, Upland Philippines: A Case for Multiplicity" (2001).

Emilio F. Moran is the James H. Rudy Professor of Anthropology at Indiana University, a professor of Environmental Sciences, an adjunct professor of Geography, director of the Anthropological Center for Training and Research on

Global Environmental Change (ACT), and codirector of the Center for the Study of Institutions, Population and Environmental Change (CIPEC). He is also the lead scientist of the Land Use Cover Change (LUCC) Focus 1-Land Use Dynamics Office. Dr. Moran is the author of six books, nine edited volumes, and more than 100 journal articles and book chapters. He is trained in anthropology, tropical ecology, tropical soil science, and remote sensing. His research has focused on the Amazon for the past thirty years.

K. Anne Pyburn is the director of the Chau Hiix Project investigating the political economy of an ancient Maya community, research that the government of Belize and the residents of Crooked Tree have allowed and facilitated. The Chau Hiix Project promotes education, public outreach, and economic development. Pyburn is also the director of the MATRIX Project (Making Archaeology Teaching Relevant in the XXI Century; www.indiana.edu/~swasey/matrix/), and an associate professor of Anthropology at Indiana University. She writes about ethics, gender, education, community involvement, and the archaeology of the ancient Maya.

Katharine N. Rankin is an assistant professor of Geography and Planning at the University of Toronto. She is currently conducting comparative research on the gender politics of development institutions in Nepal and Vietnam with funding from the Social Sciences and Humanities Research Council [Canada]. Prior research focuses on economic liberalization policies in Nepal and their articulation with gender and caste ideologies, and draws implications for planning and development. This research has been published as scholarly articles in *Economy and Society* (2001), *International Planning Studies* (2001), *Journal of Feminist Economics* (2002), and *Gender, Place and Culture* (2003). It will also appear in the forthcoming *The Cultural Politics of Markets: Economic Liberalization and Social Change in Nepal,* under contract with Pluto Press.

Andréa D. Siqueira is a research associate in anthropology at Indiana University. Her research interests include the human and physical dimensions of land use in Amazonia, forest regeneration, and landscape studies.

Cynthia Werner is an assistant professor of anthropology at Texas A & M University. She has been doing fieldwork in post-Soviet Central Asia, especially Kazakhstan, since 1992. Her research interests in economic anthropology include gift exchange, household networking, market women, and international tourism development. Her current research project examines the social, psychological, and economic impacts of nuclear testing in northern Kazakhstan. Werner is also the coeditor (with Norbert Dannhaeuser) of *Research in Economic Anthropology* published by JAI Press.

About the Editor

Gracia Clark (Ph.D., Cambridge) is an associate professor of anthropology at Indiana University, Bloomington. Her research with market traders in Kumasi, Ghana, began in 1978, and she consulted for United Nations agencies and the U.S. Agency for International Development before and after her doctorate. She has written on the informal sector, food security, structural adjustment, and alternative development, in addition to classic ethnographic topics such as kinship, marriage, and households. Her edited volume *Traders Versus the State* (Westview, 1988) was followed by an ethnography, *Onions Are My Husband* (Chicago, 1994), based on her continuing fieldwork in Kumasi Central Market. She is presently analyzing life stories narrated by Kumasi market women, including market leaders, to formulate traders' models of family, commercial, and community prosperity and leadership. Her current interests include research methodology, international feminisms, and local ideas of gender and development.